PLAYS FROM ACTORS THEATRE OF LOUISVILLE

BROADWAY PLAY PUBLISHING INC.

357 W 20th St., NY NY 10011
212 627-1055

PLAYS FROM ACTORS THEATRE OF LOUISVILLE
© 1989 Broadway Play Publishing Inc

All rights reserved. This work is fully protected under the copyright laws of the United States of America. No part of this publication may be photocopied, reproduced, stored in a retrieval system, or transmitted, in any form or by any means, electronic, mechanical, recording, or otherwise, without the prior permission of the publisher. Additional copies of this play are available from the publisher.

Written permission is required for live performance of any sort. This includes readings, cuttings, scenes, and excerpts. Please consult the opening pages of the individual plays herein to see who represents the stage production or other rights.

Cover art may be reproduced only by permission of Broadway Play Publishing Inc.

First printing: March 1989
ISBN: 0-88145-072-3

Design by Marie Donovan
Word processing done in WordMarc Composer Plus. Set in Palatino using Xerox Ventura Publisher.
Printed on acid-free paper and bound by BookCrafters, Inc., Chelsea, MI.

CONTENTS

Actors Theatre of Louisville: An overview v
Introduction — Jon Jory vii
Publisher's Note — Christopher Gould ix
COUP/CLUCKS — Jane Martin 1
CRIMES OF THE HEART — Beth Henley 71
FOOD FROM TRASH — Gary Leon Hill 141
GETTING OUT — Marsha Norman 213
TALES OF THE LOST FORMICANS — Constance Congdon 279
THE UNDOING — William Mastrosimone 343
Chronology of New Plays Presented at Actors Theatre of Louisville 395

This volume was edited by Actors Theatre of Louisville Literary Manager Michael Bigelow Dixon, with special assistance from ATL Literary Associate Kathleen Chopin.

The Publisher would also like to acknowledge the cooperation of ATL Producing Director Jon Jory and contributions from the following members of the ATL staff: Marilee Hebert-Slater, Julie Beckett Crutcher, Marcia Dixcy, Sonja Kuftinec, Nancy Klementowski, Jimmy Seacat, and Thomas Augst.

ACTORS THEATRE OF LOUISVILLE:
AN OVERVIEW

Actors Theatre of Louisville, under the direction of Jon Jory, is best known for its devotion to the production of new plays. Its annual Humana Festival of New American Plays, now in its second decade, continues to celebrate the contemporary American playwright. By addressing the evolving needs of playwrights in the ever-changing environs of new play development, the Humana Festival has been able to incorporate a wide spectrum of thematic concerns, theatrical forms, and styles of dramatic literature.

Historically, the Humana Festival has introduced numerous plays into the American theater's general repertoire and many have also been performed abroad. Among some of the better known are THE GIN GAME by D.L. Coburn, CRIMES OF THE HEART by Beth Henley, GETTING OUT by Marsha Norman, Wendy Kesselman's MY SISTER IN THIS HOUSE, LONE STAR by James McLure, AGNES OF GOD by John Pielmeier, EXTREMITIES by William Mastrosimone, TALKING WITH by Jane Martin, DANNY AND THE DEEP BLUE SEA by John Patrick Shanley, EXECUTION OF JUSTICE by Emily Mann, TENT MEETING by Larry Larson, Levi Lee, and Rebecca Wackler, ALONE AT THE BEACH by Richard Dresser, and LLOYD'S PRAYER by Kevin Kling.

Actors Theatre's New Play Program encompasses the Humana Festival, the National One-Act Play Contest, writer-in-residence programs, and ongoing contact with over one hundred writers. From 1980 through 1985 Actors Theatre also produced a festival called SHORTS dedicated entirely to one-act plays. During those six years of developmental work more than 150 one-act and mini-plays were produced. Currently, of the 2,500 scripts submitted each season, the majority are entries in the National One-Act Play Contest for the Heideman Award.

In addition to work with new plays, Actors Theatre produces an additional twenty plays each season in its varied repertory. An important focus is the yearly Classics in Context festival which allows the theatre to join with Louisville's other arts institutions in examining a cultural period through literature and art. In 1990 Actors Theatre will begin a ten-year project to celebrate and reconsider the dramatic literature of the 20th century in America. Each year from 1990 to 1999, ATL will produce one or more plays from successive decades along with discussions, exhibits, and other educational support. The 20th Century Project will culminate in the year 2000 with a Futurist Festival — focusing on trends in the theatre as well as dreams and visions of artists at the brink of the 21st century.

Founded in 1964, Actors Theatre operates in a two-auditoria complex performing its regular season from September through June, with special production projects and tours during the summer, including an extensive international touring program. Annually, audiences number over 240,000. Actors Theatre has received the following major awards for its work: a special Tony Award for Distinguished Achievement in Theatre; the James N. Vaughan Memorial Award for Exceptional Achievement and Contribution to the Development of Professional Theatre; and the Margo Jones Award for the production of new plays.

INTRODUCTION

The fact that you can now publish a series of books from individual American theaters filled with the best new plays they have produced demands celebration. Twenty years ago it would have been difficult to create a single volume of substantial new work from the entire nation outside New York City! I take this to signify a wave of good work, a real generation of writers, and high old times indeed for America's theaters, creators, and audiences.

It is, of course, impossible to tell from our perspective who the leaders of this generation might be. Is there a Miller, a Williams, an Odets, a Shepard (yes, he's an earlier generation now!), or a Wilson? But while we wait for time and the critical community to make their selections, it's a pleasure for the American theater to be back in the position of having no end of nominees!

Is this new generation definable as a whole? I think so. They are moving, sometimes tentatively, sometimes explosively, away from the realism that has dominated our stages. When asked to typify the American play, the English critic Michael Billington said it was "six people seated around a dining room table, drinking whiskey and excoriating their family." Well, we've definitely gotten as far as removing the table.

Now there are odd sorts of poetry and a delight in language that feel distinctive. There's a sense of social outrage and a commitment to national change resulting in a more political theater. There is more refreshing irony and cynicism and satire than we saw even a decade ago. It's not a theater of rich people having fun, or a solipsistic theater of personal symbol and metaphor, or a wilderness of personal neurosis or tragic alienation; it is a working theater of insight and longing for change.

What do the works in this volume have in common? They are richly theatrical; each writer's "voice" is unique; they are actually about something; and they are generous to their audience in terms of language, effects, jokes, characters, and story. They are linear without making a fetish of it and embody an informed optimism based on pointing out what needs fixing. Every single one of them is about getting out of something that confines. While the circumstances close in, they pack their bags, saw through their bars, and sing.

These writers have become known or remained a secret as the casino rules of the American theater have dictated. But because they live and work in a period when it's practically impossible to know when you're a success, they've had to stop worrying about it. There is no Broadway of any consequence for the serious new American play, and no matter how you frame it, the national press can't keep track of what happens outside of New York City. Thus the American writer often blooms unseen, which at worst keeps bread off his/her table or at best allows everyone to simply get on with the work without preening or despair. The writers represented in this volume and perhaps a hundred others make this a rich, contentious, rewarding theatrical era unlike any other.

Why are these plays in this book? Because they entertain richly and bear witness with skill. God knows that's reason enough.

Jon Jory
Producing Director
Actors Theatre of Louisville

PUBLISHER'S NOTE

This collection of six full-length plays is the fourth in a series that I call "The Great Theaters of America". As a New York City publisher, the influential theaters here were the logical places to start, so the first three collections were from the New York Shakespeare Festival, Circle Rep, and Playwrights Horizons. With this solid base, the next step was to really represent the theaters of America, and what better place to start than Actors Theatre of Louisville?

There have always been two overlapping motivations behind these collections. The first was to put in print our foremost contemporary playwrights in the context of the theater with which they were most often associated: Lanford Wilson at Circle Rep, Christopher Durang at Playwrights Horizons, David Rabe at the Shakespeare Festival, and now Marsha Norman and Beth Henley at Actors Theatre.

The second motivation was to put into print plays that had been produced by these theaters but were still unpublished. A surprising number of wonderful plays by well-known playwrights were languishing: TIME TRIAL by Jack Gilhooley, SNOW ORCHID by Joe Pintauro, JUNGLE COUP by Richard Nelson, and at Actors Theatre THE UNDOING by William Mastrosimone, to cite a few.

My dream is that these anthologies will be used around the country by professors who are teaching contemporary drama. These collections, I feel, offer a unique combination of great plays and great, active playwrights. Also, these anthologies give a strong sense of how these theaters define and realize their commitment to new plays.

Christopher Gould

COUP/CLUCKS
Jane Martin

COUP/CLUCKS
© Copyright 1982, 1984 by Alexander Speer as trustee for Jane Martin

The stage production rights to this play are represented by Dramatists Play Service, 440 Park Ave South, NY NY 10016, 212 683-8960.

All other rights are represented by Alexander Speer, Actors Theatre of Louisville, 316 W Main St, Louisville KY 40202, 502 584-1265.

ABOUT THE AUTHOR

Jane Martin is a Kentuckian and has served as Playwright-in-Residence with Actors Theatre of Louisville. She first came to national attention for TALKING WITH, a collection of monologues that premiered at Actors Theatre in 1981. The Manhattan Theatre Club had the first New York production of the play in 1982. Since that time the play has been performed around the world. *Theater Heute* magazine of West Germany designated TALKING WITH the Best Foreign Play of the year. Actors Theatre has presented monologues from TALKING WITH at international engagements in Athens, Belgrade, Sofia, Bucharest, Warsaw, Krakow, Budapest, and Brno as well as at the Festivals of Sydney and Perth and the Dublin Theatre Festival.

Other Martin plays include THE BOY WHO ATE THE MOON (1981), COUP/CLUCKS (1982 SHORTS Festival at Actors Theatre of Louisville), SUMMER (1984 SHORTS), and TRAVELIN' SHOW (1987 tour to Warsaw). TALKING WITH is published by Samuel French, as are SUMMER, THE BOY WHO ATE THE MOON, TRAVELIN' SHOW, and CUL-DE-SAC, in a collection entitled WHAT MAMA DON'T KNOW.

COUP/CLUCKS was first presented by Actors Theatre of Louisville on 4 November 1982. The cast, in order of appearance, was as follows:

COUP

MIZ ZIFTY	Jen Jones
DON SAVANAH	William Mesnick
BEULAH	Beatrice Winde
BRENDA LEE	Dawn Didawick
TOOTH	Dierk Torsek
ESSIE	Jessie K. Jones
BOBBY JOE	Daniel Jenkins
DR. KENNEDY	Reuben Green

CLUCKS

TRAVIS	Murphy Guyer
TOOTH	Dierk Torsek
BOBBY JOE	Daniel Jenkins
PRITCHARD	Ray Fry
RYMAN	William Mesnick
ZITS	John Short
DR. KENNEDY	Reuben Green
ESSIE	Jessie K. Jones
Director	Jon Jory
Set Design	Paul Owen
Costume Design	Karen Gerson
Lighting Design	Jeff Hill
Sound Design	Mollysue Wedding.

COUP

(The play takes place in the living room of MIZ ZIFTY's *home, on the morning of July Fourth, in the small town of Brine, Alabama. The set is realistic in that it represents accurately, if sparely, a Victorian room in a home built at the end of the last century. It is expressionistic in the sense that architectural detail is selective and all of it—floor, ceiling, and walls—is white. The furniture, a melange of French and English antiques, is white as well. The properties, even the flowers, share this absence of color. The costumes, however, provide bright accents and are, when demanded, exact copies of their counterparts in the film version of "Gone With the Wind.")*

(The lights reveal MIZ ZIFTY, *a woman in her mid-to-late- sixties, dressed in Scarlett O'Hara's green-flowered, white muslin party dress.* MIZ ZIFTY *is the social lion of this small world and is preparing for her annual appearance in the Tara Parade and Ball. Behind her,* DON SAVANAH, *a man in his early thirties, arranges her hair. Born in Brine, he fled to New York only to be drawn back to the South when his mother died. He is nattily dressed with considerably more flair than is considered correct locally. His manner is an odd combination of simple straight-forwardness and an extroverted flamboyance. He is no fool.)*

DON: *(Working on* MIZ ZIFTY's *hair)* Why did I come back to Brine, Alabama? Leave the bright lights of New York City? Cowardice, I suppose. I swear, wherever I go I feel like a fly in a frogpond. Victim-in-residence. They ever made a movie about me they'd call it "Born to Shake." Makes me just furious I can't change my nature. Know who I'm comin' back as in my next life? John Wayne. *(Handing her a mirror)* Here, peek.

MIZ ZIFTY: *(Doubtfully)* Well...

DON: Darlin', you're the personification, that's what you are.

MIZ ZIFTY: You'd think the very least the Good Lord could have done would have been to make old age pretty.

DON: Oh, poo. If Ashley Wilkes doesn't nibble you like a praline, the man's a stone. So, anyway, I'd quit my hair stylin' job 'cause I was petrified to take the subway, and there I was, catatonic in Times Square, appalled by the sheer unendurable ugliness, transfixed by the lack, the absence of any beauty, anything soothing to the soul, when suddenly I was struck from behind...hard enough to see stars. I turn, and there is a wild man, a Martian savage dressed entirely in debris. Had on plastic Clorox bottles for shoes, white garbage bags wrapped for leggins, cardboard mailing tubes on his arms, face caked with filth, plus he had on, so help me Hannah, an actual medieval breastplate. Like out of a museum, darlin'. And this staff he struck me with is covered with "Nixon's the One" buttons. Well his wild blue eyes lock with mine, he grabs my Pierre Cardin tie, shakes me like a rag doll and shrieks in my face, "Why don't you weirdos get the hell out of New York City!"

MIZ ZIFTY: That doesn't surprise you I hope. That's normal Yankee behavior.

(BEULAH, MIZ ZIFTY's *sixty-year-old black maid, enters, carrying a tray which holds several bowls of finger-foods. She places them about the room.*)

DON: Well, I fled, darlin', fled home to Brine. Our rednecks may be mean, dumb, and violent, but at least they are not dressed in medieval breastplates. You seen 'em out on the square this mornin'? Waiting t'laugh y'all to shame?

MIZ ZIFTY: Primitive barbarians, ought to be moved on with a cattle prod.

BEULAH: Here, here!

DON: *(Stands back to look at* MIZ ZIFTY*)* Well, I guess that just about dots the 'i'.

MIZ ZIFTY: I was not raised to be intimidated by white trash.

DON: There.

MIZ ZIFTY: My twenty-third annual and consecutive year as Scarlett O'Hara.

BEULAH: Huh! *(She exits into the kitchen.)*

MIZ ZIFTY: Heroine of the South. Flower of a lost civilization. You know that Coretta whatever, the one who wears purple paisley dresses with pink cowboy boots?

DON: You mean Coretta's Beauty Nook, last bastion of the concrete beehive hairdo? Miss Hands-of-Stone?

MIZ ZIFTY: Yes, *that* one. Came to a D.A.C. meetin' uninvited and suggested we replace the Tara Parade and Ball with a greased pig mud-grab and a donkey baseball celebrity night game. Said that would really get the community *involved*.

DON: Well she's just perfect for donkey baseball. 'Course when you were ridin' her your hands would get stuck in her hairspray.

MIZ ZIFTY: The Tara Parade is Brine, Alabama's cultural Alamo and it will become a donkey baseball game over my shot-dead body.

DON: Well, I admire your raw nerve but those Cro-Magnons out there.... Lord have mercy!

MIZ ZIFTY: Just the whiff of fear and they sting like honeybees.

DON: *(He shivers.)* Pick-ups, crossed eyes, shotguns, an' buck-knives.

MIZ ZIFTY: All you boys of good family gone soft as fudge candy. Where is the Southern elite with the barbarians at the gate? All gone to Hilton Head, that's where. Scaredy-cats. In ancient Sparta young boys would allow the foxes held under their tunics to eat away their vitals rather than show a shred of pain. Courage is a made quality, not a born one. See here? *(She lifts her sleeve to show a safety pin pinned through the flesh of her upper arm. BEULAH enters, carrying a feather-duster, with which she proceeds to dust various objects.)*

DON: My God, there's a safety pin clipped through your flesh!

BEULAH: Ain't the only one either. Some nights she looks like a tailor mark her for alterations.

MIZ ZIFTY: Pain doesn't bother me. I like it. I'm vaccinated against it. When called upon to suffer I'll be prepared.

DON: You may be a small-town girl, darlin', but you've got a real future in a New Wave band.

MIZ ZIFTY: Scarlett O'Hara suffered, and I am Scarlett O'Hara. *(Turning in dress)* Well, do I pass muster?

DON: Darlin', you got her down in spades.

BEULAH: Who you callin' a spade?

DON: Oh shush.

MIZ ZIFTY: That is a piquant homily, Beulah, and not a racial slur.

BEULAH: Well, I got a pecan homily says you're too damn old t'go gettin' doxied up like a Southern belle.

MIZ ZIFTY: Great ballerinas play young girls well into their maturity.

BEULAH: You mean thirty-five maturity or sixty-five maturity?

DON: Well aren't we a prickly little pear today?

BEULAH: And you're still a big old fruit. *(She exits into the kitchen.)*

MIZ ZIFTY: I will not have squibble-squabblin', y'all hear me? After the parade I don't care a hat if the two of you beat each other to doll rags, but right now I want...no, I insist...on harmony. *(Looking at the back of her dress)* Am I ridin' too low?

DON: Just billows right over your hoops.

BEULAH: *(Entering, still puttering and muttering)* Fourth of July in the wax museum.

MIZ ZIFTY: Now remember, best port glasses when we come back for refreshments after the parade, and most important, the place cards must correspond to the flower-favors handed out as the guests arrive.

BEULAH: *(Heading for the kitchen and exiting)* Whole lot of damn trouble for one damn glass of wine.

DON: *(To* MIZ ZIFTY*)* Here, slip on these green, flat-heeled morocco slippers. *(He kneels down to help her.)*

MIZ ZIFTY: I just love your new touches.

DON: Why you keep such ill-tempered help I'll never know.

MIZ ZIFTY: She was given to me as a personal maid by Mother on my wedding day and she's been with me ever since. It is only irresponsible Yankees who change their servants on a whim.

DON: They're so rude up there they don't even smile when you're makin' love to 'em.

MIZ ZIFTY: My great-Uncle, Attila Zifty, contended that all Yankees suffer a derangement of the blood brought on by drinkin' inferior bourbon, ridin' lop-gaited horses, and listenin' to German-born opera singers until they became mad as hatters. Well I do hope Melda is sending over Bobby Joe with my cinch and sashed-straw.

DON: Thank God Southern girls are still taught to sew. Well, it's just a cryin' shame you don't have a Rhett Butler with real panache.

MIZ ZIFTY: I inquired after your availability.

DON: No, I don't think those "Hee Haw" regulars out there are ready for me.

MIZ ZIFTY: In any case, Travis Scroggins, however unwillingly, has escorted me at both the Tara Parade and Ball for five years, and there is no disputing he's a ringer for Mr. Gable.

DON: Oh, he was my idol in high school. Only boy could crush beer cans with his teeth. If I'd been more sure of myself, I would have invited him to the prom.

MIZ ZIFTY: With so many leaving town for Houston, we are fortunate to have any Rhett Butler at all. *(*BEULAH *returns with a rubber plant. She crosses to the front door and places the plant outside.)* You have the oleanders out Beulah?

BEULAH: *(Returning)* Uh-huh, and the hydrangeas, geraniums, coleus, magnolias, pink-crepe myrtle, and those four damn rubber plants you had sent over from the florist.

MIZ ZIFTY: All flowers they had at antebellum balls. Now, you remember to remind any young ladies who do not realize that married women sit separately, to go round to the screen porch.

BEULAH: These cats round here always find the right wall. *(She goes out to the kitchen.)*

MIZ ZIFTY: Honestly. Will you be goin' as Rene Picard again, Don?

DON: I don't dare the parade, but I wouldn't miss the ball. It's a teensie part in the movie, but it's worth it to dress as a Louisiana Zouave. *(The doorbell rings.)* Good heavens, I'm not even dressed.

MIZ ZIFTY: Well, I'm dyin' to see, so you go on.

DON: You're sure?

MIZ ZIFTY: I believe my mother trained me to deal with early arrivals. You perfectly positive you won't parade? *(BEULAH enters to answer the doorbell.)*

DON: Maybe when I put it on I'll find my courage like the Cowardly Lion. *(He exits.)*

BEULAH: *(Ushers in BRENDA LEE and TOOTH. BRENDA LEE is an odd combination of Belle and tough cookie. He is a redneck once-removed. She is dressed as Melanie in grey organdy, and he is resplendent as Ashley Wilkes.)* Here's some more nuts for your nut mix. *(BEULAH exits back to the kitchen.)*

BRENDA LEE: Lord, it's so hot out there I'm gettin' mascara down my cleavage! Ooooo, I just hate walkin' by those boys in the square.

TOOTH: Ol' Dim Danny dropped a quarter down her boobies.

BRENDA LEE: *(Hitting him)* You be quiet. *(Goes to MIZ ZIFTY)* Golly gee, you just look good enough to eat! Will you look at this? Just scrumptious, I swear. *(To TOOTH)* Don't she just put Vivien Leigh to shame!

TOOTH: *(Tipping his hat)* How you doin' Miz Zifty?

MIZ ZIFTY: *(Curtsying)* Mr. Ashley Wilkes, I do believe.

BRENDA LEE: Said he wasn't goin' to parade today but I just told him if that was the case he could kiss his nighttime privileges goodbye. Buy him a duck or a Barbie Doll, the ol' poop. *(Hits him, goes to MIZ ZIFTY.)* I'm just lovin' that flowered muslin. Jes' how many yards did that take?

MIZ ZIFTY: Scarlett's original took twelve yards, but this took somewhat more.

BRENDA LEE: No such thing. Looks like she got a seventeen-inch waist, don't it Tooth?

TOOTH: You bet. Where's Travis?

MIZ ZIFTY: Mr. Scroggins has not as yet made his annual appearance.

BRENDA LEE: Just scared to death he'll hafta go out there alone.

TOOTH: What he was drinkin' last night I sure hope he makes it. Went through four cases of beer.

BRENDA LEE: Shush up y'ol' redneck! *(Hits him)* I honestly don't know how a nice Southern deb like myself ended up with a dirt farmer like you.

TOOTH: Probably 'cause you stuck yer hands in my pants.

BRENDA LEE: Now you just hush! These men have already been out playin' softball, hog callin', drinkin' beer, an' heaven knows what else, an' it's not even twelve noon.

TOOTH: Man don't get drunk on July Fourth ain't patriotic. Tell you one thing. Way it is out there now, Miz Zifty, come the parade yer gonna sweat fierce.

BRENDA LEE: Southern gentlemen don't say sweat.

TOOTH: What they say?

BRENDA LEE: Dew or dewey.

TOOTH: *(To* MIZ ZIFTY*)* Well, then, you two'll git dewey and I'll jes sweat my butt off.

BRENDA LEE: *(To* MIZ ZIFTY*)* Essie says y'all are goin' to say lines this year.

MIZ ZIFTY: Well, it was Mr. Savanah's idea really.

TOOTH: *(Snorting)* Mr. Savanah!

BRENDA LEE: At the band shell?

MIZ ZIFTY: That is correct. The parade will pause briefly in the park and Mr. Scroggins and myself will represent the passage where Rhett Butler wagers Scarlett a box of bon-bons against a kiss that the Yankees will take Atlanta.

BRENDA LEE: Excitin'! You know Essie's been drillin' Travis on those lines since Christmas but I don't know....

MIZ ZIFTY: In case of a lapse of memory, I will prevail on Mr. Savanah to prompt.

TOOTH: He ain't Mr. Savanah. He is plain ol' Don Snots.

BRENDA LEE: You were just little boys then.

TOOTH: Yeah, an' some of us grew up to be big boys, an' some of us went to New Yawk an' turned into somethin' else entirely.

BRENDA LEE: Don Savanah is a marvelous name for a hairdresser.

TOOTH: Guess you ladies just didn't want somebody named Snot gittin' his hands in your hair.

BRENDA LEE: I swear sometimes you just have the raisin' of a hog.

TOOTH: You know what downhill is? All the good ol' boys leave for Texas, an' the only folks movin' in is a colored dentist and a hairdressin' fairy.

MIZ ZIFTY: We do not use that word in the South, young man, ever. Mr. Savanah is simply a perennial bachelor.

TOOTH: Well it gives me the willies, shakin' his hand. Feels like Teflon.

MIZ ZIFTY: I prefer that a man not have the skin of a rhinoceros.

TOOTH: No matter what I got on, he says it oughta be took-in in the back.

MIZ ZIFTY: Mr. Savanah is sensitive to apparel. He is the official costumiere for the Tara Ball.

TOOTH: Well, he's just a tad too interested in my back-seam.

BRENDA LEE: Honey, he flies down to Birmingham on the weekends for his social needs. Now I don't want to hear any more rough talk.

(DON *reappears as a Louisiana Zouave, wearing a red jacket and baggy, blue-and-white striped pants.*)

DON: Voila!

BRENDA LEE: Now that's cute!

DON: "Respectable? All my days I was respectable until ze war set me free lak ze darkies...."

BRENDA LEE: So cute!

DON: "Never again must I be deegnified and full of ennui. Lak Napoleon I follow my star!" (BRENDA LEE *applauds.*) God, don't you just love "Gone With the Wind"!

BRENDA LEE: Love it!

DON: Lord, I've seen that movie nine times in a week.

BRENDA LEE: Ain't he just slick as a baby's bottom?

MIZ ZIFTY: Absolutely perfect.

DON: *(Looking briefly at* TOOTH*)* Those trousers look like they need to be taken up in the back.

TOOTH: I like to wear 'em loose, Horse.

DON: *(Turning to* BRENDA LEE*)* Well don't we just look like peaches and cream!

BRENDA LEE: Don't think I don't know why y'all picked me for this part.

MIZ ZIFTY: Because the sweet grey satin and accordian petal pleating set off your coloring, dear.

BRENDA LEE: 'Cause in the book Melanie is jes' plain as ol' dish water.

MIZ ZIFTY: It also speaks of creamy skin, and brown eyes that have the still gleam of a forest pool in winter, when brown leaves shine up through quiet water.

BRENDA LEE: Honey, rotten leaves don't constitute no compliment to me. What's happenin' to me is the worst thing can happen to a corn-fed, all-American, cheerleader-type like me. I'm losin' the cutes. Cain't bounce up and down and squeal no more, cain't risk a giggle, an' a pony tail makes me look like Trigger. Tooth Gannet, can you honestly stare me right in my brown eyes an' tell me I'm cute?

TOOTH: Well, no.

BRENDA LEE: See?

TOOTH: But yer lookin' a whole lot more like Joanne Woodward.

BRENDA LEE: Joanne Woodward is fifty years old! I can't go out in the Tara parade lookin' like Joanne Woodward!

DON: Now, honey, Joanne Woodward smoulders.

BRENDA LEE: I ain't your honey, I don't care to smoulder, an' I wanna be cute!

(BEULAH *enters, bringing a coffee service.*)

DON: Missy, when the fire bank's low is when the coals git hot.

BRENDA LEE: *(Suspicious)* Really?

DON: You on a direct flight from cute to sexy.

BRENDA LEE: You mean it?

DON: Cross my heart.

BRENDA LEE: You ain't jes' sweet-teasin'?

DON: Wanna go out to the drive-in an' go all the way?

BRENDA LEE: *(Punching his arm)* Y'ol' cute thing! Well thank goodness, thank-double-goodness! Sexy is more eighties anyway. Don't you think? I think so. Maybe I'll have this cut lower next year. Lordy, don't you love dressin' up? Three cheers for the Tara Parade. Rescues at least one day from the ugly present. *(Gunshots outside)* What on Earth is that?

TOOTH: Boys is gittin' restless.

BRENDA LEE: Those boys loved cute. I hope "sexy" don't git 'em too riled up.

MIZ ZIFTY: My father trained me to face that rabble down.

BRENDA LEE: Such a tiresome, ugly ol' world out there. I swear there's nothing left but make-believe. Scarlett O'Hara, dancin', twinkle-lights, all of us singin' "Bonnie Blue Flag." There can't have been anything as beautiful in all history as the Ol' South before the Yankees came an' broke it.

MIZ ZIFTY: There are a few precious moments in history when culture, breedin', an' imagination combine to create, for split seconds, an earthly paradise, an' our Cotton Kingdom was one.

(BEULAH *applauds. They turn to look at her.*)

BEULAH: How about the slaves?

DON: Oh, hush up!

BEULAH: They git in on this-here paradise?

MIZ ZIFTY: We do not wish, once again, to hear about the slaves at this time.

BEULAH: Yo' Grandaddy had him three hundred in his earthly paradise.

MIZ ZIFTY: Slavery was simply the system of welfare benefits of that time.

BEULAH: An' what was floggin'?

MIZ ZIFTY: We never flogged, we spanked.

BEULAH: An' your Grandaddy shootin' my Grandaddy?

MIZ ZIFTY: A dreadful mistake for which my family has for always and ever been tryin' to make up to your family, which is precisely, as you very well know, the reason I bought you in the first place...I mean hired you.

BEULAH: You know what I do with you in my dreams? I eat you with barbecue sauce. (*She exits back to the kitchen.*)

TOOTH: How come you let that old woman talk to you like that in your own house?

MIZ ZIFTY: Because she is the single, last black domestic in this town and must be treated with all the rights and privileges of an endangered species.

BRENDA LEE: Well I swear, I'd rather do for myself! Shoot, I'd fix my own dinner if somebody'd teach me.

MIZ ZIFTY: Now that is precisely the mistake your generation makes, if I must say so. Doin' for yourself causes the terrible frustration, loneliness, and agitation of spirit that leads you straight down the primrose path to Yankee feminism. I guarantee you that ninety percent of the problems in any marriage could be solved by a live-in maid.

BRENDA LEE: (*To* TOOTH) You listenin' to this, Tooth?

TOOTH: Where the hell am I going to get a live-in maid?

DON: Name a price.

TOOTH: Over my dead body.

DON: Oooooooo, kinky.

TOOTH: Now you knock that off!

ESSIE: *(Offstage voice)* Miz Zifty?

MIZ ZIFTY: In here dear.

(ESSIE *enters. She is the wife of Travis, who was to play Rhett Butler. She is* BRENDA LEE's *best friend. Currently she is dressed as Mammy, Scarlett's servant in* "Gone With the Wind," *bandanna, black-face, and all.*)

ESSIE: Well I'm afraid we have just a peck of trouble.

MIZ ZIFTY: God's nightgown! Who are you?

BRENDA LEE: Jiminy Cricket!

ESSIE: I'm Essie.

BRENDA LEE: Essie!

ESSIE: Well goodness, surely you can recognize my voice?

BRENDA LEE: That's not Essie.

ESSIE: Lord's sake, Brenda Lee!

BRENDA LEE: How old was I when I lost my virginity?

ESSIE: Eighth grade on the class hayride.

BRENDA LEE: Lord, it is Essie!

TOOTH: Travis see you got up like that?

ESSIE: Mr. Travis Scroggins does not dictate the way I dress.

TOOTH: May not care how you dress, but he's pretty picky about your race.

BRENDA LEE: He musta been mad as a mud-dauber!

ESSIE: Smoke comin' out of both ears.

BRENDA LEE: Did he hit himself like he does sometimes?

ESSIE: Blacked his own eye an' knocked the princess phone through the kitchen window.

BRENDA LEE: Well it's...

MIZ ZIFTY: *(Taking charge)* Get yourself home and scrub your face!

ESSIE: It is time for a change and I won't.

MIZ ZIFTY: This is no change, young woman, it is a calamity!

ESSIE: Well, it's hateful injustice that there are no black characters represented at the Tara Parade and Ball.

MIZ ZIFTY: They are are minor characters.

BRENDA LEE: Plus colored people don't waltz.

ESSIE: Great heavens, they are not invisible. They are there. They are in the book. They are black and they are in the book.

MIZ ZIFTY: I never notice them when I read it.

ESSIE: Well you are gonna to notice them today!

DON: Why don't you let me get you a Coke?

MIZ ZIFTY: I forbid you to parade in that outfit.

ESSIE: Mammy, Prissy, Park, and Big Sam are just as important a part of "Gone With the Wind" as any white person.

MIZ ZIFTY: The Tara Ball, young woman, is not an issue. It is a charitable event.

ESSIE: To benefit the Daughters of the Confederacy, which has no black members.

MIZ ZIFTY: No colored person has ever made application.

ESSIE: And no lamb hands the lion a knife an' fork either!

MIZ ZIFTY: And in that inflammatory get-up you intend to dance the night away?

ESSIE: I can do the Virginia Reel just as well black as white.

MIZ ZIFTY: And just who, pray tell, do you assume will partner you?

ESSIE: Some liberated gentleman who does not assume that race can be contracted like influenza.

MIZ ZIFTY: There is, thank heaven, no such person in Brine, Alabama!

DON: I'll dance with her.

ESSIE: Thank you! Thank you very much.

TOOTH: Sure. You two'll just be the couple of the year.

MIZ ZIFTY: I will not have twenty-three years of herculean labor against incalculable odds and philistine indifference flushed down the drain by a Northern-educated twit whose total misunderstanding of "Gone With the Wind" has parboiled her brain!

TOOTH: You sure your dental bills ain't gittin' too high?

BRENDA LEE: Oh my, oh my.

ESSIE: And just what exactly does that mean?

TOOTH: Nothin'. Jes' seen your car over to the dentist's.

ESSIE: It just so happens I am having my teeth capped. (BEULAH *enters from the kitchen.*)

TOOTH: Sure you are.

ESSIE: I am!

TOOTH: Well, I just hope Travis leaves 'em in yer mouth.

ESSIE: *(Irate)* You are awful, horrible, small-minded, bigoted people!

BEULAH: *(Loudly)* What in hell you think you doin', white girl?

ESSIE: *(Caught off balance)* Doin'?

BEULAH: You got about four seconds to git that impertinence off you 'fore I come down on you like a duck on a June bug.

ESSIE: Oh Beulah....

BEULAH: What you think you're doin' get up like some plantation nigger?

ESSIE: This is Mammy, Beulah. She's the most beautiful character in "Gone With the Wind."

BEULAH: Beautiful. There ain't no slave that's beautiful, Missy, an' there ain't no white woman alive on this planet gonna mock the pain of slavery long as I'm around.

ESSIE: I'm not mockin'. Oh, Beulah, really, really I'm not.

BEULAH: I don't care if you make jack-ass fools out of yoselves, paradin' aroun' in your Johnny Reb, hand-me-down, slave-tradin', black-floggin', antebellum outfits, but there ain't gonna be no black-face minstrel show carryin' on in my town, an' you can count on that.

ESSIE: But I didn't mean....

BEULAH: Ain't nobody in the South meant nothin' 'bout nothin' in two hundred years, but we still keep gettin' it in the neck. Now you git that black shoe polish offa your face or I'll damn well scrub it with a cheese grater an' whitewash it like a damn picket fence! (ESSIE *bursts into tears as* BEULAH *exits to the kitchen.*)

BRENDA LEE: Now look what you've done.

ESSIE: Everything I touch turns to cow pies.

DON: *(Handing her a handkerchief)* Here, use this.

ESSIE: I could just cry myself to sleep.

DON: Poor baby.

BRENDA LEE: Will someone explain to me why colored people will not let us do one solitary thing for them? I mean for years they've wanted to be in the Tara Parade and now...(*Pointing to* ESSIE) we let one in and look what happens.

(ESSIE *breaks out sobbing again.*)

DON: (*Sitting* ESSIE *down*) What you need is one of Don Savannah's imported-from-Paris lemon pastilles.

ESSIE: I hate lemon pastilles.

MIZ ZIFTY: Now, what we have to do is get you dressed as India Wilkes as you were meant to be.

ESSIE: I can't.

BRENDA LEE: It's a scrumptious dress.

ESSIE: I just can't.

MIZ ZIFTY: Never say can't.

BRENDA LEE: Remember Little Toot?

ESSIE: Little Toot?

(BRENDA LEE *makes a train whistle sound.*)

BRENDA LEE: I *think* I can, I think I can, I think I can...toot, toot...I know I can, I know I can, I know I can, I *will!*

(ESSIE *breaks out crying again.*)

TOOTH: I'm in a damn nut hutch!

BRENDA LEE: Great gollywhompers, it's eleven forty-five!

MIZ ZIFTY: Quarter-of?

BRENDA LEE: That's right.

MIZ ZIFTY: Lord have mercy! We're supposed to be formed up behind the band at twelve. (*To* TOOTH) Go into the kitchen and bring me some dish rags and Crisco. (*To* DON) Run for your life and bring this child the mustard silk India Wilkes dress. In a twinklin', you hear? Shoo! (*To* ESSIE) You're sure to look so glamorous in that silk dress you won't care what happens to colored people. Now where's your handsome husband, our esteemed Rhett Butler?

ESSIE: He won't.

MIZ ZIFTY: Won't what?

ESSIE: Won't be Rhett Butler.

MIZ ZIFTY: He is Rhett Butler.

ESSIE: Says he won't say no dumb lines, tired of his cronies laughin' at him, says he won't go out there with his wife playin' Aunt Jemima, and Rhett Butler is an asshole just like everybody else from Charleston.

MIZ ZIFTY: I happen to be from Charleston.

ESSIE: He says you're included. He also happens to be too dead drunk to walk.

TOOTH: *(Reappears from kitchen)* Ol' Beulah won't give me the Crisco. Says it's for cookies, not nitwits.

DON: *(Returning with the dress)* You're gonna look sensational, and I know cause I tried it on.

MIZ ZIFTY: *(To ESSIE)* You march right on home and drag that ruffian back here by his ear.

ESSIE: It won't matter.

MIZ ZIFTY: Won't matter?

ESSIE: I already got someone else.

BRENDA LEE: For Rhett Butler?

ESSIE: Yes, I did.

MIZ ZIFTY: For the Parade and the Ball?

ESSIE: I just said that. Didn't I just say that?

DON: *(Undressing ESSIE)* We'll just get you out of these rags.... Where's the Crisco?

TOOTH: I jes' told you she won't hand it over.

DON: *(Going to the kitchen)* She will hand it over to me or I will expose myself.

MIZ ZIFTY: *(To ESSIE)* The Daughters of the Confederacy offer these roles by majority vote.

ESSIE: Well, we only had an hour.

MIZ ZIFTY: I would have tendered the role to Judge Parseghian.

BRENDA LEE: Lord, he's three-sheets-gone in the nursin' home! Step out of this.... *(To ESSIE)* There isn't another single soul in this town could pass for Clark Gable at dusk with the light behind 'em. Jimmy John McLean?

ESSIE: Yuk.

MIZ ZIFTY: Colonel Carter?

ESSIE: Are you jokin'?

BRENDA LEE: Have you seen that man's teeth? I wouldn't touch him with a surgical sponge.

MIZ ZIFTY: Well who for heaven's sake? Who?

DON: *(Enters with the Crisco and rags)* Voila, the Count of Monte Crisco!

BRENDA LEE: Oh, you got it. Good.

DON: I have shown our Beulah things no white woman has ever seen before.

BRENDA LEE: She's not white, sillykins.

DON: Well she is now. *(To* TOOTH*)* Fetch me a towel, will you Horse?

TOOTH: *(Going)* I just can't picture this happenin' in Brine, Alabama.

DON: Is there a single soul here who gives two hoots for the Tara Parade?

MIZ ZIFTY: I am tryin' to find out....

DON: Because you are all standin' stock still like shock victims and time is passin'.

MIZ ZIFTY: ...who my Rhett Butler....

DON: At ten minutes to twelve it doesn't matter if it's Rin Tin Tin in a top hat! We have to hurry! Now there is just no time for your hair, Brenda Lee....

BRENDA LEE: But I want it cute....

DON: You will just have to...

BRENDA LEE: Fluffy. Fluffy and cute!

DON: ...give it a lick and a spit curl....

BRENDA LEE: Oooooo, you make me so crazy....

DON: *(Bringing* MIZ ZIFTY *over to her)* And take the former Miss Magnolia of some undetermined pre-war year with you....

BRENDA LEE: *(Gathering her things)* I could just throw a hissy....

DON: *(Pushing them out)* And cinch her waist till her eyes pop an' she whistles "Dixie" out her ears....

MIZ ZIFTY: But Don darlin'....

BRENDA LEE: Cute, make it cute....

MIZ ZIFTY: Don....

DON: *(Closing the door on them)* Out! *(Leaning on it)* Lord have mercy.

ESSIE: I don't see how you could ever, ever come back here from New York.

DON: *(Starting to clean her face with the Crisco)* Home, darlin', is where, when you have to go there, they have to take you in.

ESSIE: Who said that?

DON: Every poor faggot who ever left Dixie.

ESSIE: You're so hard on yourself.

DON: Just old enough to eat the pancake plain, darlin'. Know what I was in New York? Wallpaper. Chopped liver. Nuthin' at all! When Momma died and left me the beauty shop, I just packed up my troubles in my ol' kit bag an' caught the Continental Trailways home.

ESSIE: But isn't it hard to be different?

DON: *(Smiling)* Different? *(Gunshots outside)*

ESSIE: *(Indicating outside)* Don't they scare you?

DON: Honey, I'm panicky wherever I am, so I might as well be petrified where I can do the accent.

ESSIE: Well it beats me down...I just want to show 'em...just once....

DON: *(Working on her face)* Look over there.

ESSIE: It's like they build the ceilings so low here, it won't let you grow up. It's a physical pain to stop growing and know it. Don't you think so?

DON: I wouldn't know darlin'. I'm like Peter Pan. I don't want to grow up. *(Looking at her face)* My God, you're white! I want you to have my babies!

ESSIE: *(Giggling)* You stop it!

DON: Now, just a lick and a promise.

ESSIE: These people are starvin' to death on short rations of the mind. You know how when you put a nice plump sausage patty in the pan an' it sizzles a little while, and comes out three times smaller? Well, Brine, Alabama is the pan.

DON: An' ol' Travis, the ex-Rhett?

ESSIE: Bein' fried away at an even faster rate. Such a King Moose when we were growin' up. Sexy as sin. You could lose your virginity just lookin' at him. First time he touched me it raised welts. You could see the shape of his hands in perfect red marks on my body. First Momma fainted an' then she sent me North for a year with Aunt Bettina. He had a mind, too, but where, oh where, has it gone? Gone like the water in the sausage.

DON: Well, if it's any consolation there is damn few of us gettin' better. There. You're so clean the hogs wouldn't know you. *(TOOTH enters with the towel.)*

TOOTH: Sorry. Had to make a pit stop.

DON: *(Taking the towel)* Will you do one more thing for me?

TOOTH: Yeah, what?

DON: Take off all your clothes and pretend you're a gorilla?

TOOTH: You gonna get it, Horse.

(BRENDA LEE *re-enters with a comb and mirror.*)

DON: *(Hands* ESSIE *dress)* Now you put this on and pack up your troubles in a ol' kit bag.

BRENDA LEE: Will somebody do somethin' with this unmanageable mop on my head? I swear it looks like garden mulch in a high wind.

DON: *(Turning to* BRENDA LEE*)* Melanie honey, I told you you're too old for cheap wigs. *(He fusses with her hair.* ESSIE *dresses.)*

BRENDA LEE: I got Miz Zifty laced an' cinched an' now she's decided on a two-minute cucumber facial.

DON: Over the rouge?

BRENDA LEE: Just around the eyes, to tighten up the laugh lines.

DON: *(Still working on her hair)* Honey, if those are laugh lines, that woman's spent her whole life in hysterics.

ESSIE: Will you zip me up, Tooth?

TOOTH: *(Doubtfully)* Well....

ESSIE: Good Lord, Travis isn't here to eat you! *(He catches flesh in the zipper.)* OW.

BRENDA LEE: Here, let me. *(To* TOOTH*)* Butterfingers!

DON: *(Looking at* TOOTH, *appalled)* Ashley Wilkes, do you call that a bow tie?

TOOTH: *(Backing away)* Nosiree.

DON: *(Exasperated)* Look. I am a human being, not the Creature of the Black Lagoon. I am trying to improve your appearance, not your sex life. Now stand still, or I'll whip your ass. (DON *slaps him on the behind and* TOOTH *is astounded enough to stand still as* DON *fixes his tie.)*

BRENDA LEE: *(Whispers to* ESSIE*)* You jes' nervous as a pig on ice.

ESSIE: *(Guiltily)* I am?

BRENDA LEE: Your Rhett Butler isn't who I think it is, is it? *(*ESSIE *nods yes.)*

ESSIE: Well, maybe...

BRENDA LEE: My God, you're a lunatic.

ESSIE: Well, why not?

BRENDA LEE: Travis is gonna have a conniption.

ESSIE: Well, maybe it will wake him up.

BRENDA LEE: It'll turn his blood to Dr. Pepper.

DON: *(Finishing with* TOOTH*)* Much better.

ESSIE: He jes' drills on my teeth an' talks.

TOOTH: *(Grudgingly)* Thanks.

DON: Don't mention it.

ESSIE: He has an actual brain. *(The doorbell rings.* ESSIE *clutches her heart.)* Oh God.

BRENDA LEE: I can't staaaaaand it! I can't. I'll throw up.

MIZ ZIFTY: *(Offstage)* Would one of you girls get that?

*(*BEULAH *enters.)*

DON: I will.

BEULAH: You touch that door you're a dead pale.

BRENDA LEE: I just can't staaaaaand it!

BEULAH: Don't want nobody sayin' I'm not doin' my job. *(Goes to the door)*

DON: *(A presentation)* And now, from Charleston, the notorious blockade runner, the ironic, disreputable, Rhett Butler! *(*BEULAH *opens the door.* BOBBY JOE BIGUN, *a boy of seventeen, dressed in old jeans, a t-shirt, and an Atlanta Braves baseball cap plus clod hoppers is revealed.)* Taa-daa!

BOBBY JOE: How y'all doin'?

BRENDA LEE: *(Relieved it wasn't who she thought)* Thank God.

BEULAH: Bobby Joe Bigun, what you want?

BOBBY JOE: Melda sent me over with some stuff she sewed up for Miz Zifty.

DON: *(Struck)* My God, you're like a Botticelli angel. Who are you?

BOBBY JOE: Bobby Joe Bigun, come on a delivery.

DON: Well you come right in here and take off your cap. *(Leads him in, and removes the cap)* My dear, you're translucent!

ESSIE: Now Don...

BRENDA LEE: Bobby Joe? *(He doesn't answer, stares open-mouthed at* DON.*)* Bobby Joe?

BOBBY JOE: Huh?

BRENDA LEE: You don't close that mouth you're gonna catch flies. *(Hits him)* Whatcha got?

BOBBY JOE: Big straw hat an' a waist-cincher.

BRENDA LEE: Good

DON: *(Almost moved to tears by the boy's voice)* Big straw hat an' a waist-cincher!

ESSIE: Don...

BEULAH: Hand that stuff over. *(BOBBY JOE does. A small band is heard striking up.)* Ol' Pritchard finally got there with his tuba, so y'all better get a move on. *(She takes hat and cincher to MIZ ZIFTY.)*

DON: Do you think any of us were ever that young once?

ESSIE: *(Putting a hand on DON's shoulder)* You hush now.

DON: God, how I hate mortality!

BOBBY JOE: What's the matter with him?

ESSIE: I think you must remind him of somebody. Let me just try to rustle you up a Coke. *(She starts for the kitchen.)*

BOBBY JOE: If it ain't no trouble.

ESSIE: No trouble at all. *(She exits.)*

DON: *(Shaking his head)* Lord, every time I think I'm cured.

BOBBY JOE: Huh?

BRENDA LEE: *(Changing the subject)* Well now, how's your sweet Momma?

BOBBY JOE: Dead.

BRENDA LEE: Honey, I didn't know!

BOBBY JOE: When I got married she moved down to Palmetto Sands, Florida an' got herself into the sauce pretty hard, an' one night a while back she took off all her clothes, 'cept her panty hose, an' was dancin' on the Interstate at two-thirty a.m. when a sixteen-wheel Bekins movin' van blew her apart at seventy-five miles an hour.

BRENDA LEE: That's just horrible!

BOBBY JOE: Well, she always did like to dance.

DON: Is there any chance you just fell from the sky?

BOBBY JOE: No sir, I rode my bike over.

BRENDA LEE: Well how's your hard-workin', adorable Daddy?

BOBBY JOE: Dead.

BRENDA LEE: Oh for heaven's sake, never mind! *(She moves away from him.)*

BOBBY JOE: *(Oblivious)* Felt bad about Momma an' got hisself scarfed up by a threshin' machine.

TOOTH: *(Imitating machine)* Chomp, chomp! *(BRENDA LEE whacks him.)*

BOBBY JOE: I still got one of his shoes.

BRENDA LEE: Yuck!

ESSIE: *(Entering with a drink)* Onliest thing she's got is iced tea.

BOBBY JOE: It's okeydokey.

(MIZ ZIFTY enters, ready for the parade.)

MIZ ZIFTY: Here I come. *(Sees BOBBY JOE)* Oh good, they got you a cool drink. You tell Melda she's a heavenly angel.

BOBBY JOE: Yes ma'am.

BRENDA LEE: My zipper jes' won't stay shut.

MIZ ZIFTY: Here, use the safety pin from my arm. *(BRENDA LEE removes it from her.)*

BRENDA LEE: You're a real life saver.

(Doorbell rings.)

BOBBY JOE: *(Astounded, to DON)* She got a safety pin in her arm.

DON: *(Deadpan)* I know. Want one?

(Doorbell again)

MIZ ZIFTY: Perhaps this is our mysterious Rhett.

BRENDA LEE: *(Stricken, to ESSIE)* Oh my Gawd!

MIZ ZIFTY: *(Suspicious)* Why don't you let in your guest, Essie? *(ESSIE, rooted, can only shake her head no.)* Brenda Lee?

BRENDA LEE: Oh my Gawd, oh my Gawd. *(She doesn't move. Doorbell again.)*

BEULAH: *(Entering)* I'm comin'.

MIZ ZIFTY: *(Stopping her)* I believe I will see to this visitor myself. *(She goes to the door and opens it. DR. KENNEDY, the black dentist, stands there dressed as Rhett Butler.)*

DR. KENNEDY: Surprise.

MIZ ZIFTY: Jesus wept!

DR. KENNEDY: "Scarlett, never at any crisis of your life have I ever known you to have a handkerchief."

(MIZ ZIFTY tumbles to the ground in a dead faint.)

Jane Martin

BOBBY JOE: Holy Tamoley!

(BRENDA LEE *begins emitting a high-pitched shriek.*)

BEULAH: *(An order)* Y'all stop screamin', you dumb twit. (BRENDA LEE *does.*)

DR. KENNEDY: Good morning, Miz Scroggins.

ESSIE: Good morning, Dr. Kennedy.

DR. KENNEDY: If you'll excuse me for a minute. (*He kneels by* MIZ ZIFTY.)

TOOTH: *(A low whistle)* Well now, you're jes' full of suprises.

DR. KENNEDY: *(Smiling down at* MIZ ZIFTY*)* I see you peeking at me.

MIZ ZIFTY: I am not peekin' at you!

DR. KENNEDY: Out cold, huh?

MIZ ZIFTY: You will leave my house at once.

DR. KENNEDY: We couldn't talk this over?

MIZ ZIFTY: I will scream the house down.

DR. KENNEDY: Well, I'd enjoy that.

MIZ ZIFTY: *(Rising as she carries on)* Help! Murder!

ESSIE: Miz Zifty....

MIZ ZIFTY: Rape! Terrorists! Help! Black Muslins!

DR. KENNEDY: Muslims.

MIZ ZIFTY: What?

DR. KENNEDY: You said muslin, you meant Muslim.

MIZ ZIFTY: Are you sure it's not muslin?

DR. KENNEDY: Muslin is cloth, Muslims eat white children.

ESSIE: Harold....

MIZ ZIFTY: Help! Help! Out this minute! Bombin' airports, killin' women an' children, highjackin' planes. Where's my pistol?

BEULAH: *(Unmoved)* In the drawer.

MIZ ZIFTY: Thank you. Sabotagin' everythin'. Outside agitators. Murderin'-liberal-humanist-trash! *(Rummaging for the pistol)*

BRENDA LEE: Ummmm, Miz Zifty.... (MIZ ZIFTY *finds the pistol.*)

TOOTH: Hell, look out!

MIZ ZIFTY: *Go*-rilla!

TOOTH: Look out!

MIZ ZIFTY: *(Fires pistol, which simply clicks)* What's the matter with this thing?

BEULAH: Ain't loaded.

MIZ ZIFTY: Well, gimme a knife. I'll skin him. I'll sell his hide.

BEULAH: Sure, why not. *(She exits to the kitchen.)*

MIZ ZIFTY: Go back to Africa!

DR. KENNEDY: I'm from Detroit.

MIZ ZIFTY: Y'already got the North, overrun the East, ruint our nation's capitol. Why can't you leave us Brine, Alabama?

DR. KENNEDY: I needed a job and you needed a dentist.

MIZ ZIFTY: A white dentist. White like my teeth.

DR. KENNEDY: In that case I think you're lookin' for an oriental dentist.

MIZ ZIFTY: A big, tall, blond, Swedish-lookin' dentist outa Minnesota!

BEULAH: *(Reenters)* Here's your knife.

MIZ ZIFTY: That's a cake knife! I can't kill him with a cake knife. Go get me a cleaver.

BEULAH: Sent it out to be sharpened.

MIZ ZIFTY: Well go next door an' borrow one!

BEULAH: Sure, why not. *(She exits.)*

MIZ ZIFTY: For the last time, sir, flee for your life.

DR. KENNEDY: I can't actually.

MIZ ZIFTY: I warn you, Sir. I have sent for a cleaver.

DR. KENNEDY: I just love "Gone With the Wind." My daddy took us everytime it came out. Funniest damn white people I ever saw.

MIZ ZIFTY: Get out!

DR. KENNEDY: Loved that Clark Gable though. Loved him! Shoulda seen my imitation. Used to get me laid regular as clockwork.

TOOTH: Mine was Humphrey Bogart. *(He is stripping off his Ashley Wilkes costume.)*

MIZ ZIFTY: *(To* TOOTH*)* Animal! *(To* DR. KENNEDY*)* Jungle bunny!

BRENDA LEE: *(Seeing what* TOOTH *is doing)* Darlin', what are you doin'?

TOOTH: You think I'm goin' into the town square in Brine, Alabama, in front of half the Ku Klux Klan in the state, playin' Ashley Wilkes to his Rhett Butler yer jes' crazier than a whore in a monastery.

(BEULAH *enters and hands* MIZ ZIFTY *a meat tenderizer.*)

BEULAH: Here.

MIZ ZIFTY: This is not a cleaver.

BEULAH: They didn't have one so I brought you a meat tenderizer.

DR. KENNEDY: *(Smiling)* It is your intention to murder me at high noon with a meat tenderizer?

BRENDA LEE: *(To* TOOTH*)* You can't go out there stark nekked.

MIZ ZIFTY: *(To* DR. KENNEDY.*)* I would not soil my implement. *(She throws it at his feet.)*

TOOTH: *(Still undressing, to* BRENDA LEE*)* Helluva lot rather be a fool than a target.

ESSIE: *(To* MIZ ZIFTY*)* Please don't be angry.

MIZ ZIFTY: Angry? I am far beyond angry.

ESSIE: If you marched with him, you'd be a legend in Brine.

TOOTH: Most likely a real dead legend.

ESSIE: *(To* TOOTH*)* You white boys are all as yellow as canaries!

TOOTH: Tweet, tweet.

MIZ ZIFTY: And you are obviously a deranged person in need of electric shock therapy.

BOBBY JOE: I ain't yellow.

ESSIE: You are yellow.

BOBBY JOE: I ain't yellow.

ESSIE: You are yellow.

DON: *(Sitting)* I can't pay the rent. You must pay the rent. I can't pay the rent. You must pay the rent.

ESSIE: *(Pointing to Ashley's clothes* TOOTH *is dropping on the floor)* Then put those on.

BOBBY JOE: That there Gone-With-the-Window suit?

ESSIE: I dare you.

MIZ ZIFTY: I want that Uncle Remus out of here!

ESSIE: If you'd just walk with him, you'd have the biggest crowd your parade ever saw.

MIZ ZIFTY: Scarlett O'Hara would dig turnips out of granite cliffs with her bare bleeding hands before she would be seen, arm in arm in public, with a gentleman of color.

DR. KENNEDY: "Gentleman of color" is nice.

BOBBY JOE: *(Having mulled over the one challenge no Southern teenager can bear)* You say you dare me?

ESSIE: Double dare you. Triple dare you. Dare you on your dead momma's soul.

BOBBY JOE: Golly!

MIZ ZIFTY: *(To BEULAH)* Get me out of this dress! *(BEULAH goes to her, undoes the cinch, and begins to help her out of her dress.)*

ESSIE: *(To BOBBY JOE)* Plus, I bet you twenty dollars and my ten-speed racin' bike.

BOBBY JOE: The one with the foot stirrups? *(A cry of triumph, a fist raised in the air.)* Hell, I'll do 'er! *(At top speed, he starts putting on the clothes TOOTH has taken off.)*

BRENDA LEE: *(To TOOTH)* I thought I threw out that damn undershirt!

DON: *(Watching)* I think I'm in love.

MIZ ZIFTY: I am retiring to my room, having removed this gown as I will officially remove the patronage of the Daughters of the Confederacy from this year's Tara Parade and Ball. And when I return, I assume you will return the favor by removing yourself, and your uninvited escort, from these premises.

ESSIE: But he is an educated man! A dentist! He went to Rutgers University!

MIZ ZIFTY: *(Stepping out of the dress in her slip)* That is, if I may say so my dear young lady, no skin off my butt! *(She exits.)*

BEULAH: My! Ain't that ol' woman got style? *(She exits after her, carrying the dress.)*

TOOTH: *(To BOBBY JOE, who is still dressing)* You wrong about not being a canary, Horse. They gonna tar you, feather you, an' toss you in the drunk tank 'til you beg fer birdseed.

BOBBY JOE: Yeah, but she dared me.

ESSIE: *(To DR. KENNEDY)* What in hell have I gotten you into?

DR. KENNEDY: This is Brine, Alabama, Mrs. Scroggins. Whatever it is, it beats watchin' the slugs drown in beer.

(BEULAH re-enters.)

ESSIE: What's she doin', Beulah?

BEULAH: Sittin' at her vanity, stark naked, eatin' peanut brittle and watchin' "The Dukes of Hazzard."

TOOTH: *(Now completely undressed, he wears a t-shirt that says "No Sheet" and under that "United Klans of Alabama" and shorts with Playboy nudes printed on them.)* Those boys out there may be small-town, red-neck, dumb-ass, swamp-ramuses, but they ain't crazy. Y'all in here have got hamster-spit for brains, an' when you go out that front door they gonna skin ya, an' quilt ya!

DR. KENNEDY: *(To BEULAH)* You wouldn't have a cup of coffee would you?

BEULAH: A fresh pot with cream from the dairy, an' home-made pralines.

BOBBY JOE: *(Wrestling with his cravat)* Cain't do these dang watchamacallit, thingmabob, gew-gaw, doo-dads.

DON: Here you clumsy thing, let me do that. *(Goes to BOBBY JOE)*

BEULAH: Anybody else want a cup?

BRENDA LEE: I don't believe my shattered system can bear caffeine.

TOOTH: *(At the door)* Brenda Lee, you comin' with me?

BRENDA LEE: I can't.

TOOTH: You ain't scared?

BRENDA LEE: Scared? Scared!? I am pee-pee petrified! But I can't just leave Essie alone.

TOOTH: You don't know who's out there on that square, spittin' tobacco and waitin' for the parade?

BEULAH: *(Going for the coffee)* Bunch a toothless, one-eyed, peanut farmer honkies, who got pork barbecue for brains. *(She exits.)*

DON: *(Finishing with BOBBY JOE)* Boy, I never saw anyone look so tacky, but with your eyes it just doesn't matter.

TOOTH: Jackson "Nut Cutter" Cartwright is out there with his maniac brother Ferd; Ryman Stoner, local National Socialist Nazi; Dim Danny Bone, scalped his wife with a baling knife; an' Big Beaver Wansettler, severed his uncle's arm in a fight with his bare teeth! And hell, those are the moderates.

BOBBY JOE: Guess I'll get in a lot of trouble, huh?

TOOTH: Bobby Joe, trouble don't quite describe it.

BOBBY JOE: Shoot, I'm always gettin' in trouble. Called me "Catastrophe" in high school. Set off a six-car accident. Broke my arm fallin' down one step. Ate a cheeseburger with a bottlecap in it. Got rabies from my own dog. I guess I'm the right fella for this deal.

DR. KENNEDY: You really man enough to go out there with me, Boy?

BOBBY JOE: Shoot, I ain't doin' this for you, Mister. I'm doin' this for a ten-speed bike.

DON: My dear young man, I would walk through fire for you. *(He exits to* MIZ ZIFTY's *room.)*

TOOTH: *(To* DR. KENNEDY; *gunshots)* You gonna do it, huh?

DR. KENNEDY: *(Grinning at* ESSIE*)* I guess so.

TOOTH: *(To* ESSIE*)* You goin' out there with him?

ESSIE: I guess so.

TOOTH: Brenda Lee?

BRENDA LEE: I guess so.

TOOTH: Brenda Lee, I am your devoted husband, but I am too old to die in a remake of "Gone With the Wind." Y'all must be on hard drugs, you know that? Nutcutter Cartwright has got hair on the palms of his hands. Ain't nobody gives a crap about this parade. It's a damn laughin' stock to begin with. Everybody in town thinks that ol' lady belongs in the dribble shop. Hell, the movie hasn't even played here in fifteen years, there's only three of you got costumes on, an' you Woody Woodpeckers is out on parade without the damn character the whole damn book's about anyway! Hell, you don't even have a Scarlett O'Hara!

DON: *(Enters in drag in the Scarlett gown, with hat and lipstick in place)* "As God is my witness, I will never be hungry again!"

BOBBY JOE: Howdy-doody-diddley-damn!

BRENDA LEE: Don Savanah, you look just beautiful! *(To* TOOTH*)* Ain't he wonderful?

TOOTH: It's a walkin' nightmare.

DON: *(Crossing to* TOOTH, *as Scarlett)* "Why Charles Hamilton, you handsome old thing you! I'll bet you came all the way down here from Atlanta just to break my poor heart!"

TOOTH: *(Fleeing)* Git off me. Stay the hell over there. *(*DON *makes a feint toward him.)* I swear, I'll burn 'em off an' you'll be Scarlett O'Hara!

DON: "Well, you stay right here 'cause I want to eat barbecue with you. And don't go philandering with those other girls 'cause I'm just as jealous as a Yankee at a Charleston Ball." *(Dropping down to a real "butch" voice)* Don't worry, Horse, I ain't gonna mess with ya.

BRENDA LEE: I swear you could be in the movie. Hell, you're better than the movie.

DON: Well, what do you think, Dr. Kennedy? Want to get out there an' raise a little hell?

DR. KENNEDY: *(Smiling)* I'm not sure you are exactly what we are trying to say.

DON: Now Dr. Kennedy, we're not prejudiced are we?

DR. KENNEDY: Well, maybe we are...just a little.

DON: Isn't life just full of surprises?

DR. KENNEDY: On the other hand, I'm sure you'll admit it's maybe the best idea to tell those boys outside one simple thing at a time.

DON: Yes, I'll admit that's a point. Be a fabulous sequel though.... *(Links his arm through* DR. KENNEDY's*)* Guess who's coming to dinner! *(*DR. KENNEDY *laughs and disengages himself.)*

ESSIE: *(Going over to him)* I do know one thing...

DON: What you know, Aunt Jemima?

ESSIE: *(Kissing him on the cheek)* You are braver than the "King of the Beasts."

DON: Surprised the hell out of me. *(To* BOBBY JOE*)* Well Ashley, it's all for you, darlin'? What do you say?

BOBBY JOE: *(Who has been standing, stunned)* Huh-uh.

DON: Huh-uh?

BOBBY JOE: Huh-uh! No sir. Nosireebob. No way. Huh-uh! *(Starts taking off the costume)*

DON: I'd be twice as scared as you.

BOBBY JOE: No sir. Huh-uh.

DON: I dare you.

BOBBY JOE: You dare me? *(Stops for a beat and looks at him)* No way, Jose. Y'all just too rich fer my blood. Meanin' no disrespect. *(To* ESSIE*)* Guess I owe you twenty dollars.

*(*BEULAH *enters with the coffee.)*

ESSIE: Never you mind, Bobby Joe.

BEULAH: *(Handing out the coffee)* Dr. Kennedy?

DR. KENNEDY: Hey, thanks.

BEULAH: *(To* DON*)* You care for a cup of coffee, Miss Scarlett?

DON: Just give me the caffeine intravenously.

BEULAH: One lump or two?

DON: *(Helping himself)* Six. *(Watching as* BOBBY JOE *finishes)* It's always been my dream to watch this many men undress in Brine, Alabama. Unzip me? *(Starting to take off the hat and then the dress)* Oh well. There's nothing sadder than a drag queen on the Fourth of July. *(A loudspeaker outside: "You hear me? One, Two, Three, One, Two, Three. O.K., listen up now....This here is the 23rd Annual Independence Day Tara Parade, an' I wanna hear you boys give 'er a send off." Rebel yells are heard. To* BEULAH:*)* Would you take this rag out of here, before I cry on it?

BEULAH: *(Taking dress and exiting)* Oh, the sights I've seen.

TOOTH: You comin' on, Bobby Joe?

(Small marching band strikes up.)

BOBBY JOE: Soon as I gits my sneaks on.

BRENDA LEE: *(To* ESSIE, *scared)* Band struck up.

ESSIE: *(Equally scared)* Don't I know it.

BRENDA LEE: *(Sees* DON *holding the dress he took off)* You all right, darlin'?

DON: Oh, I may live.

BRENDA LEE: Now jes' don' dwell on it.

DON: Dwell on it?

BRENDA LEE: Jes' forget it, don' think about it.

DON: Jes' not meant to be.

BRENDA LEE: *(An idea)* Hey, you remember, "I'll think of it all tomorrow at Tara. I can stand it then."

DON: *(Picking it up)* "Tomorrow, I'll think of some way to get him back."

BRENDA LEE: Yes. Yes. *(Both speaking together)* "After all... *(*ESSIE *joins the other two.)*...tomorrow is another day!" *(They hug and laugh.)*

BOBBY JOE: *(Moving over to* TOOTH*)* All set.

TOOTH: Brenda Lee Gannet?

BRENDA LEE: Huh-uh. No sir. No way. Huh-uh.

TOOTH: Let's go, Bobby Joe.

ESSIE: Y'all take care now.

BOBBY JOE: Yes Ma'am.

DON: *(To* BOBBY JOE*)* Better zip up your fly, Horse.

BOBBY JOE: *(Embarrassed)* Yes Ma'am.

TOOTH: So long, Doc.

DR. KENNEDY: *(Putting on the accent)* See y'all at da' lynchin', Massa Wilkes.

TOOTH: *(Resigned, rather than mean)* Probably ain't too far wrong, Doc. *(*TOOTH *and* BOBBY JOE *exit.)*

DON: Well, at least I know where she keeps the gin. *(Goes to get it)*

BRENDA LEE: Oh dear.

DR. KENNEDY: *(Energized)* Tell you what, this is going to be a bona fide hoot!

BRENDA LEE: How can you say that?

DR. KENNEDY: I'm a contrary person, Mrs. Gannet.

ESSIE: *(To* BRENDA LEE*)* Give me a hand with this snood?

BRENDA LEE: If I can control the shakes. *(*DON *sits drinking.* BRENDA LEE *goes to* ESSIE. *Speaks low)* You two better be so careful a fly couldn't light on you.

DON: Care for a hit, Reverend?

DR. KENNEDY: *(Rubbing his hands)* No thanks. Feeling rowdy already.

BRENDA LEE: There, I believe that's it. *(Steps back from* ESSIE*)*

ESSIE: My, the three of us make a pretty poor excuse of a Tara Parade.

BRENDA LEE: Serried ranks, just like the Confederate boys at Gettysburg.

ESSIE: Not even an Ashley Wilkes or a Scarlett O'Hara.

BRENDA LEE: We seem to have run through 'em like a bag of salt-water taffy.

DR. KENNEDY: Mr. Don Savanah?

DON: *(Looking up)* Say what?

DR. KENNEDY: You care to forfeit your life for the Confederacy as Mr. Ashley Wilkes?

DON: Ashley Wilkes?

BRENDA LEE: That is...

ESSIE: What?

BRENDA LEE: ...it!

DON: I can't do that.

DR. KENNEDY: Yeah you could.

BRENDA LEE: Yes, you can!

DON: But Leslie Howard is such a wimp.

BRENDA LEE: Wimp? He made ten thousand Southern girls jes' throw their skirts right over their heads!

DON: But I'm shakin'!

ESSIE: Please?

DON: Well...

BRENDA LEE: We need the company!

DON: *(Rising)* Oh God, why not.

BRENDA LEE: *(Clapping her hands in delight)* Wake up the snakes, days-a-breaking!

DR. KENNEDY: *(Offering his hand)* Put 'er there, my man.

ESSIE: *(Laughing)* Gawd, don't you wish Travis was here?

BRENDA LEE: He'd just beat himself to a pulp.

DON: *(Starting to dress)* The epitome of Southern manhood. Now this is really drag.

DR. KENNEDY: You know, I don't plan to spend my life in Brine, Alabama, folks. I mean, this has been an interesting gig, but I currently have a wife claiming political asylum in Michigan, and a dead cat nailed to my door. An' after today...after today, I might just need to get real serious about selling this practice. So, uh, what I'm trying to say is, anybody who has to live here just might want to get off the bus at this stop. See what I mean? *(Nobody answers.)* Don't be shy. *(Nobody answers.)* O.K., Christians. It's an honor to be dinner with you.

BRENDA LEE: I'm so nervous I keep eating my lipstick.

ESSIE: We really do have to scoot.

BRENDA LEE: You better tell Beulah we're on our way.

ESSIE: *(At foot of the stairs)* Beulah!

BEULAH: *(Offstage)* I hear you.

ESSIE: Parade's startin'. You tell Miz Zifty I'll be back bearin' gifts and apologies.

BEULAH: Jes' fainted again.

ESSIE: Miz Zifty did?

BEULAH: Don't worry, I got 'er.

BRENDA LEE: *(At the window)* Lord, that poor scraggly band's jes' down the block.

ESSIE: Are we really doin' this?

BRENDA LEE: We're really doin' it, darlin'. "Now I lay me down to sleep, I pray the Lord my soul to keep. If I should die before I wake, I pray the Lord my soul to take." There!

ESSIE: O.K., here we go.

BRENDA LEE: Here we go!

BEULAH: *(Appearing dressed as Scarlett O'Hara)* Y'all ain't goin' nowhere without me, honey!

BRENDA LEE: Jesus-eats-popsicles!

DON: Margaret Mitchell just banged her head on the coffin lid!

BEULAH: *(Turning about)* How I look?

DR. KENNEDY: I'm not sure, honey, but six Southern states just levitated.

BRENDA LEE: Oh my, oh my, oh my.

ESSIE: Brenda?

BRENDA LEE: *(Grabbing the glass from DON)* For Gawd's sake, gimme that gin! *(She takes a big swig.)*

BEULAH: If only my momma could see me now.

DR. KENNEDY: Well, I hope she'd have a sense of humor.

ESSIE: *(At the window)* Here they come!

DR. KENNEDY: *(Gesturing for them)* O.K. troopers, let's form it up. *(They arrange themselves by the door with ESSIE and BRENDA LEE first, then DON, then DR. KENNEDY and BEULAH.)*

BRENDA LEE: I'm as nervous as a long-tailed cat on a porch full of rockin' chairs.

ESSIE: Well, let's just hold hands and squeeze.

DON: I'm doin' it.

DR. KENNEDY: On three.

BRENDA LEE: I just hope there is life after death.

DON: Stick your chests out, girls. We're gonna show those crackers something they have never seen before!

ESSIE: *(Crossing herself)* Jesus and Mary take care of your own.

DR. KENNEDY: One, two, three, hit it!

(They open the door. The band is directly opposite and "Dixie" is being played loudly. DON grabs BRENDA LEE's and ESSIE's hands for a split second.)

BRENDA LEE: How do I look?

DON: Cute and desperate.

BRENDA LEE: Well, as long as I look cute. Oh my, oh my, oh my.

DON: All right Tara, let's kick ass. *(ESSIE and BRENDA LEE go out, heads high. DON starts to follow, pauses, looks out, and then turns back.)* Oh my, oh my, oh my. *(He exits with arms extended like a rock star greeting his fans.)*

DR. KENNEDY: Dr. Harold Kennedy.

BEULAH: Mrs. Beulah Comstock Ariadne Brown.

DR. KENNEDY: I just have this feeling we aren't going to forget each other.

BEULAH: Those two-bit peckerwoods out there are goin' to choke on a chaw and pee fifteen feet in the air!

DR. KENNEDY: *(Offering his arm, which she takes)* Frankly my dear, I don't give a damn.

(They exit, leaving the door open, as "Dixie" becomes a crescendo. Lights out.)

END OF PLAY

CLUCKS

(The action of the play takes place on the lawn, sidewalk, and street fronting of the home of Dr. Harold Kennedy *in the small Southern town of Brine, Alabama. It is approximately midnight on the Fourth of July. Night sounds. A train passes. Firecrackers in the distance.* Travis Scroggins, *a powerfully built but worn man of about forty, enters stealthily, carrying an airline flight bag. He is dressed in jeans and a plaid shirt with the sleeves rolled up. He hunkers down, watching the house for a minute. We can see that the lights are on, though the Venetian blinds are drawn. He looks away toward us, seemingly searching for something. He whistles a bird call. Waits. Tries to find enough light to look at his watch. Whistles again. Nothing.)*

Travis: Double-eyed-damn! *(Making sure he is unobserved, he takes a sparkler out of his shirt pocket. Searches for and finds a matchbook. There is one left. Looks around once more. He lights the sparkler, throws away the empty matchbook, and sings "Bonnie Blue Flag" in something of a stage whisper.)*
"We are a band of brothers,
And native to the soil,
Fighting for the property
We gained by honest toil.
And when our rights are threatened,
The cry rose near and far
Hurrah for the Bonnie Blue Flag
That bears a single star.
Hurrah! Hurrah! For Southern rights, hurrah!
Hurrah for the Bonnie Blue Flag
That bears a single star." *(The sparkler sputters out. He looks quickly around. There is the applause of a single listener from off stage. He hits the dirt. Silence. He whistles. Nothing. He speaks guardedly.)* Yo Ryman? Pssssst? That you, Ryman?

Tooth: Nope, it's the Avon Lady.

Travis: Tooth? What the hell...

Tooth: *(Enters wearing his Shell station coveralls)* Man, Travis, your bird calls are piss-poor. Sounds like a grackle in the missionary position.

Travis: Sure as hell wasn't whistlin' for you.

TOOTH: Liked your dog-an'-pony show though. Singin' away. You got another sparkler, I'd like to hear "Jesus Wants Me For a Sunbeam." (*Frustrated,* TRAVIS *growls and hits himself several times on the chest.*) Lord, Travis, don' start in. Thought you wasn't gonna beat yourself up no more.

TRAVIS: You see Ryman?

TOOTH: That boy's crazy as a goggle-eyed perch.

TRAVIS: Never you mind.

TOOTH: Shot off a toe doin' Western fast-draw, an' blew up his own garage messin' 'roun' with explosives.

TRAVIS: You see him or not?

TOOTH: He's down to the station, playin' Pac-Man.

TRAVIS: Crap!

TOOTH: Boys say you got a ride on.

TRAVIS: You blind, deaf, an' dumb, turkey? What you think went on here this afternoon? Hell yes, we got a ride on. You in?

TOOTH: Nosirree, Horse. Hung up m'sheet.

TRAVIS: Yer pussy-whipped, an' Ryman's playin' Pac-Man. Jes' what is it you want, buddy?

TOOTH: Played me some soft ball, dropped by the pie sale, saw me the parade an' took in the fireworks. Thought I'd just come on down here an' see you git shot.

TRAVIS: Saw the parade, huh?

TOOTH: Never saw so many good ol' boys go apeshit at the same time. Colonel Carter got so pissed-off he passed out, an' "Nutcutter" was pickin' his teeth and damn near bit clean through his index finger.

TRAVIS: Didn't nobody stop 'em, though, did they?

TOOTH: Too many smokies.

TRAVIS: So damn what? Man, it gits me hot! You see them coloreds?

TOOTH: Scarlett O'Hara, Rhett Butler? Paradin' right down the street with our wives! Took six guys t'hol' me down an' a smokie t'sit on m'face.

TOOTH: Yeah, you seemed a little peeved.

TRAVIS: How come you didn't have no clothes on?

TOOTH: Dead drunk. Wasn't marchin' in no African parade.

TRAVIS: Buddy, we better build ourselves an ark 'cause it's the damn end of the world, tha's all I know! Colored in the Tara Parade! Desecratin' the only damn book that's got more literature to it than the damn Bible for Gawd's sake! Miz Zifty's damn maid got up like Scarlett O'Hara for hell's sake. What the hell kind of South are we livin' in, that's what I want to know? Takin' our jobs, takin' our land, takin' our wives, an' now, ding-dang it, they've gone an' takin' our only damn book! Shoot! Essie an' Brenda Lee jes' smilin' an' wavin', big as life an' twice as sassy, sellin' you, me, an' Alabama right down the river, right out in front of Gawd an' damn-all everybody! *(He pounds on his body a couple of times and gives himself a good one to the jaw.)*

TOOTH: Care for an almond?

TRAVIS: You know them almonds is shelled by colored, don't ya?

TOOTH: Ain't even shelled by humans. Shelled by machine now.

TRAVIS: Well, I don' like machines, and I sure as hell don' like colored.

TOOTH: How are ya on almonds?

TRAVIS: Gotta sit here an' suck m'thumb 'cause Ryman's got the damn sawed-offs.

TOOTH: Yeah, I seen he had yer twelve-gauge pump.

TRAVIS: Crazy bastard saws his off too close to the guard-mount. Gonna blow his damn hand off an' hafta play the Pac-Man with his teeth.

TOOTH: You ain't plannin' t'shoot nobody, are ya, Horse?

TRAVIS: Gonna make things hot enough so Rastus over there catches him the next flight outta here back to Sodom an' Gomorrah.

TOOTH: Shoot, his wife left soon as you started nailin' those dead cats to his door. He'll be gone anyway, soon as he can sell the practice.

TRAVIS: What the hell he doin' here, anyroad? Let him pull those chimpanzees' teeth up North.

TOOTH: Hell, it's lucrative, Trav. Ain't a good ol' boy south of Nashville that don't have rotten teeth.

TRAVIS: There ain't a coon born good enough to touch a white man's teeth. Hell, I guess I gotta go git Ryman.

TOOTH: Tell you what, sport. I wouldn't git within five miles of Mr. Ryman "White Power" Stoner when that crackpot's holdin' a loaded shotgun.

TRAVIS: He'll do what I damn-well tell him, or I'll twist that little make-believe Nazi up till he comes out lookin' like a damn swastika.

TOOTH: Got you a solitaire ride, huh?

TRAVIS: Ain't a white man with two balls left in Brine, Alabama.

TOOTH: Thought y'all still had Billy Q.

TRAVIS: Said he hadda babysit his kids.

TOOTH: Moon?

TRAVIS: Wife wouldn't let him. Dim Danny Bone an' Nutcutter chugged them a gallon Cherry Bounce, an' somebody jes' propped 'em up against the goal-posts out to the high school. Colonel Carter say his 'lectric wheelchair's broke, an' Mac Bob claims he's got a calf comin'.

TOOTH: Yeah, an' he's most likely its Daddy.

TRAVIS: Big damn talkers.

TOOTH: Hell, Horse. Who cares about some hickville parade where they decorate tricycles with red crepe paper an' pull a pet skunk in a Speedo wagon, anyway? Le's you an' me drop by my trailer, eat us a box of vanilla wafers, an' kill a fifth a' Rebel Yell.

TRAVIS: I'm on the business of the Invisible Empire here, man.

TOOTH: Don't gimme no Invisible Empire. Hell, that stuff's gotten to jes' be one big ol' panty-raid. Let the air outta a few tires, burn a few crosses, gift-wrap some dog doody an' leave it on the porches. Ol' Beulah caught me hidin' in her zinnias an' called up my mama at the nursin' home an' told on me. That was it for me, buddy! Shoot, Travis, when they shut down the egg picklin' plant, all the coloreds moved to Houston, lef' the rest of us here like flies stuck t'fly paper. Hell, I wish them colored's come back jes' fer company. If we had us a skyscraper, an' we pissed off the top in all four directions, there wouldn't be a thousand people get wet.

TRAVIS: Can't jes' lay down an' play dead.

TOOTH: Can't jes' sheet up an' play Klan.

TRAVIS: You can kick yer manhood in the nuts if y'all want, but I'm standin' up fer America, buddy. I don' want m'boys seein' Red Chinese playin' fer the Dallas Cowboys.

TOOTH: Red Chinese ain't never gonna play fer the Cowboys 'cause they don't use drugs. All that Klan talk about a white-caucasian-righteous-Christian-culture is just pissin' in the wind. Way back when we shoulda put the coloreds on the boat back t'Africa, nuked them Ruskies down to a low-rise parkin' lot, turned Japan into a miniature umbrella factory, and then seceded an' give them knee-jerk liberals an' Jews the state of New Yawk an' let 'em talk each other to death. But, oh no! Ever' time we got anybody down we jes' let 'em right back up. White man's the victim of moderation, Travis. Hell, we always gave a sucker an even break. Thought we done them damn Indians in, an' now they're right back buyin' Maine and drivin' Cadillacs. Want to know where we're at, Travis? Russians got our know-how, Japs got our money, coloreds got our jobs, Arabs got our women, Jews got our education, liberals got our government, an' all we got left is Dolly Parton and these sad-ass panty-raids...an' I ain't too damn sure about Dolly Parton. Hey, Horse, they got us so screwed up you gonna git yerself shot by a stone-Baptist-Nazi while yer tryin' to make Brine, Alabama safe fer Rhett Butler.

TRAVIS: Well, I'm damn sorry fer a man talks like that on the Fourth of July. Damn sorry.

TOOTH: Listen, buddy. I got this funny feelin' that you take yer one-man Klan to that Nigra dentist's tonight, yer gonna end up showin' yer circumcised to the coroner.

TRAVIS: Looky here, fat man. When the Klavern got down to six, seven members an' y'all wanted me to move up from Klallif to Grand Kludd, I give up Kiwanis and my Wednesday bowlin' league t'try to git you boys back some pride and self-respect.

TOOTH: Quit yer bowlin' league, hell. They threw you out the night you ran three straight gutters an' 'en shotput yer ball right through that fifteen thousand dollar pin-setter.

TRAVIS: *(Grinning)* Now that was a good night. (TOOTH *laughs. A pause; they stand looking out.)*

TOOTH: This ol' Alabama's a pretty place.

TRAVIS: Yeah, it's a nice place fer poor people.

TOOTH: Hey, I got 'er. Le's see if ol' Eulanie J. wants t'git laid hangin' upside down on the park jungle-gym like she did that one time.

TRAVIS: That was fifteen years ago, Tooth.

TOOTH: Bet she's still practicin'.

TRAVIS: You got some reason you wanta warn me off this ride?

TOOTH: Reason?

TRAVIS: *(Measuring him)* Reason.

TOOTH: Naw. *(Pause)* How's Essie?

TRAVIS: 'Bout half crazy. Hell, you seen her paradin' with Rhett Butler.

TOOTH: You was s'posed t'be Rhett Butler.

TRAVIS: *(Hot)* You gonna walk around with yer wife done up like Lil' Black Sambo?

TOOTH: You piss her off, Horse. Thinks you jes' took on Grand Kludd t'git outta the house.

TRAVIS: How'm I gonna stay in the house with a woman wants me to learn French off a cassette tape? That damn woman don't never let up. Cuts stuff outta the paper an' pastes it on my plate. Finish my grits an' there's "E.R.A." starin' me in the face. Got in some record club. "Couldn't we stay home one night, listen t'Ludwig damn Beethoven?" Shoot! 'At ain't no way fer a man.

TOOTH: Man should be out puttin' cottonmouths in mailboxes an' shakin' itchin' powder onto people's hung-out clothes by moonlight.

TRAVIS: Them coloreds moved out two weeks later.

TOOTH: Moved out 'cause he got him a job off-shore drillin' down t'Texas. Hell, you wanted that job.

TRAVIS: No way, buddy. That foreman was dumb, black, an' a Pope-kissin' Catholic.

TOOTH: *(Irritated)* Hell, yer wife's a Catholic.

TRAVIS: You callin' my wife a Catholic?

TOOTH: She is a Catholic.

TRAVIS: *(Furious)* I know she's a Catholic, but you sure as hell better not call 'er one! Now you callin' her a Catholic or not?

TOOTH: Travis, I been beating you up every Fourth of July since fifth grade, an' the plain fact is I'm wore out with it. Same every time...drink us some Buds, drive aroun' litterin', do a little Klanprankin', then you pick a fight an' I ream yer butt up one side an' down the other an' deliver yer bleedin', unconscious body back to Essie. Then she calls the cops on me an' we call it a night. Jes' fer variety, le's go on out t'the auto dump an' I'll sit n' watch while you slam yer head in the car doors.

TRAVIS: I ain't cleanin' yer plow, or goin' t'the auto dump or playin' pineapple-upside-down cake with Eulanie J....I got some white man's business to attend to. *(A hooded figure has appeared out of the darkness on the other side of the stage.)*

BOBBY JOE: Y'all freeze! *(TRAVIS hits the dirt with a flying leap. TOOTH crouches.)*

TOOTH: Who's that?

BOBBY JOE: Jes' me.

TOOTH: Bobby Joe?

BOBBY JOE: How y'all doin'?

TRAVIS: *(Mortified and furious)* Goddamnit Bobby Joe! Ow!

BOBBY JOE: Jiminy Cricket, I was jes' kiddin'. *(He is completely robed as a Klansman, marred only by the fact that his robe has been made with a flowered, cotton sheet.)*

TOOTH: *(To TRAVIS)* Yer nose is bleedin'.

TRAVIS: Prolly broke the damn thing again.

BOBBY JOE: *(Serious; interested)* Y'all hit the dirt, huh? That how you did it in Vit Nam?

TRAVIS: Never min' what I did in Vit Nam. I tol' you t'stay offa us.

BOBBY JOE: I wish I'd been in Vit Nam.

TRAVIS: Din't I see you come out of Miz Zifty's house where them Nigras was gittin' up fer the parade?

BOBBY JOE: Jes' spyin' on 'em. Melda sent me on a delivery.

TOOTH: What the hell you got on?

BOBBY JOE: Melda run it up for me on her Singer.

TRAVIS: Love-a-duck, boy! Might as well jump up at a N. double A.C.P. meetin' an' jes' tell those yard apes we be ridin' t'night.

BOBBY JOE: *(Astounded)* You been to a N. double A. C. P. meetin'?

TRAVIS: Ain't no Martin Lucifer coon-show in Brine, Alabama, boy. I'm talkin' about the Klan ridin'.

BOBBY JOE: S'posed t'come on a horse? Where'd you git a horse?

TRAVIS: Din't come on no horse, I come in my Toyota.

BOBBY JOE: You said I oughta jump up at the N.A.A.C.P. an' tell 'em you was ridin'.

TRAVIS: Klan mission's a "ride." Called "a ride." Been that way fer a hundred years.

BOBBY JOE: They ain't had Toyotas fer a hundred years.

TRAVIS: You need a air-controller fer the space between yer ears.

BOBBY JOE: Yer nose is bleedin'.

TRAVIS: Git on home.

BOBBY JOE: Aw, come on Uncle Travis. When I's sixteen y'said I could join up at seventeen, and when I's seventeen y'said eighteen. Well I'm nineteen an' I wanna git in on the fun an' make Alabama safe fer white women.

TOOTH: Horny as you are, Bobby Joe, this state ain't never goin' t'be safe fer white women.

TRAVIS: *(Peering)* What you got on that sheet, boy?

BOBBY JOE: Only one I got.

TRAVIS: You got flowers on that sheet?

BOBBY JOE: Weddin' present.

TRAVIS: *(Astounded)* You got little bitty violets on yer sheet? You makin' fun on me, Bobby Joe?

BOBBY JOE: Shoot no, Uncle Travis.

TRAVIS: There's a door in yer heart that "funny" don't go through. Place where a man keeps what's sacred. Man don't have a place where there's no laughin' ain't no man, Bobby Joe.

BOBBY JOE: I got a place in my heart.

TRAVIS: There been three American presidents wore these robes...

BOBBY JOE: Harding, Coolidge, an' McKinley...

TRAVIS: That's right!

BOBBY JOE: ...I 'member 'em 'cause they all sound like air conditionin' companies.

TRAVIS: You got a picture of Jesus in yer house, boy?

BOBBY JOE: Yes, sir.

TRAVIS: What kinda robe he got on?

BOBBY JOE: White robe.

TRAVIS: You damn betcha. Ain't no little bitty violets on that man's robe. *(Takes something out of his pocket)* You know what this is? *(Holds it out)*

TOOTH: Lord, don't take that thing out!

BOBBY JOE: It's an eyeball.

TOOTH: Makes me sick to my stomach.

TRAVIS: Glass eyeball. Used to be in Willy Creel's head. Willy had him the Robert E. Lee Diner out to the Trimble Bypass an' he was servin' the colored. Now, I went out there to reason with him. He said he'd serve who he damn-well pleased an' the Klan could go diddle itself on a Roto-rooter. Started to walk off an' I hit him so hard with a napkin dispenser his glass eye popped right out.

BOBBY JOE: Popped out?

TRAVIS: *(Makes the sound)* Pop. Jes' like a champagne cork. Landed in ol' Lady Gannet's oatmeal. She's watchin us, see, an' next bite she swallows the damn thing whole. When I'd cleaned Willy's plow, I tol' Gannet that eye ever turned up, I wanted it. She's a good ol' girl, said she'd work on it. Few days later, when she delivered my eggs, there was eleven Plymouth browns an' Willy Creel's eye in the egg carton. Had it ever since. Now you take it, to remember a man fights for what's sacred.

BOBBY JOE: Golly, thanks Uncle Travis. Hope I don't throw up.

TOOTH: *(Claps* BOBBY JOE *on back)* Pretty nice, huh? Y'all come by my trailer, we'll have a drink on 'er.

(A man is heard singing.)

PRITCHARD: *(Offstage)* "Ridin' the night
Come the forces a'light
In the service of bold liberty...."

TOOTH: *(Recognizing the sound)* Pritchard. *(*TRAVIS *slaps his forehead in dismay.)*

PRITCHARD: *(Enters; seventy years old; been drinking; completely robed, with a Klansman on horseback appliqued on the back; finishes the song)*
"Though the tempest may toss
We hold firm to the cross
In the land of the brave and the free." *(Finishes with a flourish)*
Howdy boys. Howdy Doody! Wheeeeeee-oooooo! Let's ride!

TRAVIS: You mind keepin' it down to a mild roar, Pritch?

PRITCHARD: S'posed t'sing when y'ride, Sonny.

BOBBY JOE: You got a Toyota too?

PRITCHARD: Dead quiet. Moon, crickets, coon dogs, nothin' moves...then, BANG, we sweep down outta the hills, thunderin' hoofbeats, singin'. Y'look up. There we are, hundreds of us drawn up in a line on the ridge. Silent sentinels.

BOBBY JOE: What ridge?

PRITCHARD: Any ridge.

BOBBY JOE: We ain't got a ridge.

PRITCHARD: On the hill then.

BOBBY JOE: We ain't got a hill.

PRITCHARD: On toppa the damned Burger King then. What difference does it make?

BOBBY JOE: How you gonna git the horses up on the Burger King?

TRAVIS: Shut the hell up, Bobby Joe! *(Goes to* PRITCHARD*)* Pritch, this here's a pretty serious ride fer a man yer age.

PRITCHARD: Listen here, boy. When I was Gran' Kludd, I usta donate my ol' silks t'yer momma so she could cut 'em up fer diapers for yer extra-sensitive butt.

TRAVIS: Gonna fire a cross on the Nigra dentist's lawn, an' they say that boy's got him a gun collection.

BOBBY JOE: Dr. Kennedy? You gonna flame Dr. Kennedy's?

PRITCHARD: What in Peter, John, Paul er Judas you wearin', boy?

BOBBY JOE: Onliest one she had.

PRITCHARD: You cain't go Klannin' around like that.

TRAVIS: Hell, I already tol' him...

PRITCHARD: Cain't go ridin' done-up like a giant pair a' whore's panties.

TRAVIS: You git it off now, boy.

BOBBY JOE: No disrespect, Uncle Travis, but I jes' cain't do 'er.

TRAVIS: Well, I'm gonna peel ya like a damn onion an' stuff Melda's sheet up yer butt till yer hair turns red an' y'feel like Raggedy Andy.

BOBBY JOE: Ain't got me nothin' on underneath, Uncle Travis.

TOOTH: You bare-nekked under there?

BOBBY JOE: First time I wore one, an' I didn't know. Thought she was maybe like a kilt.

TRAVIS: That's yer Scottish clan, not yer Ku Klux Klan, ya damn fool.

PRITCHARD: Man desecrates the Invisible Empire we're s'posed t'give him a tar bath.

TRAVIS: He cain't desecrate it. He ain't in it.

BOBBY JOE: Y'all said I was a trainee.

TRAVIS: A trainee don't go on missions. Trainee don't wear no sacred garb. A trainee jes' buys the beer an' chile-spice Fritos fer the victory celebration.

BOBBY JOE: Hell yes, I got the beer an' the Fritos!

TRAVIS: You git two cases a' Bud like I tol' you?

BOBBY JOE: Din't have no Bud...sold out.

TRAVIS: *(Suspicious)* What kind you git?

BOBBY JOE: Miz Trable said it was a good kind.

TRAVIS: What kind did you git?

BOBBY JOE: Lowenbrau.

TRAVIS: *(Completely appalled)* Lowenbrau!

BOBBY JOE: Light.

TRAVIS: *(Crazed)* Light!

TOOTH: Easy, big fella.

TRAVIS: Ku Klux Klan can't go 'round suckin' on some dumb-butt, foreign, diet-beer.

PRITCHARD: Cain't even get drunk on 'at stuff, ya jes' bloat.

BOBBY JOE: I kin go back. They got Miller's.

PRITCHARD and TRAVIS: *Miller's?*

PRITCHARD: That ain't beer. They make rat's piss outta ol' fermented oranges.

TRAVIS: Tastes like some kinda cardboard, carbonated...

PRITCHARD: Reconstituted, by-God frozen...

TRAVIS: Cough-medicine-type, aluminum-tastin' fruit juice!

PRITCHARD: Make ya toss yer cookies.

TRAVIS: Hey boy, I'm out there lawbreakin' an' killin' an' rapin' an' terrorizin' an' I damn well want me a man's beer!

(A church bell sounds the half hour.)

TOOTH: Say compadres, it's 'leven thirty an' the state cops is gonna be makin' their drunk an' disorderly run, so 'less you're lookin' to do tank time in Hueytown I'd jes' pack this one in.

TRAVIS: Smokies ain't gonna go garbage collectin' till midnight. We'll be here an' gone. Missin' some hands, Pritch. You wanna ride?

PRITCHARD: Does the Pope smoke dope? Hell, yes.

TRAVIS: Tooth?

TOOTH: I jes' cain't help y'out, Horse.

BOBBY JOE: I'll do 'er.

TRAVIS: *(Shaking his head)* Hell, why not?

PRITCHARD: *(To* BOBBY JOE*)* Stick yer hand up. Other hand. Now say after me...I, Bobby Joe Bigun...do before God an' Man...most solemnly swear...that I dedicate...my life...my fortune...an' my sacred honor...to the preservation...protection...an' advancement of the white race...an' to that great order...the Knights of the Ku Klux Klan. *(*BOBBY JOE *has answered antiphonally.)* Makes you about half legal.

BOBBY JOE: Golly! Say, we ain't gonna lynch the dentist are we, 'cause I got me two temporaries waitin' on final fillin's.

TRAVIS: You want some colored puttin' his fingers in yer mouth?

BOBBY JOE: Inside of his hands is white.

TRAVIS: That ain't the point.

BOBBY JOE: Only touches yer teeth with the inside part.

TRAVIS: Bobby Joe...

BOBBY JOE: So they ain't technically colored fingers.

TRAVIS: *(Confounded by his stupidity)* How the hell'd I git into this?

BOBBY JOE: Don't run off Dr. Kennedy, Uncle Travis, I'd have to git Doc Crasty outta retirement, an' he got the shakes so bad he drilled me right through the lip.

TRAVIS: You rather have teeth or white Christian culture, boy? This here's the barn-raisin', Sunday-quiltin', home-made ice cream, lung-guts a'America, an' we sure as hell shouldn't be gittin' our dentists from Africa.

BOBBY JOE: Ain't from Africa, he's from Detroit.

TRAVIS: It's the same damn thing. What the hell he come down here for.

TOOTH: 'Cause he wanted to be a barn-raisin', Sunday-quiltin', home-made ice cream Nigra. Shoot, Travis, ain't no white Christian dentist gonna move down here. We ain't even got a suburb. When Doc Crasty started seein' little green men in yer cavities an' talkin' to yer teeth, an' Mabel made him retire, how long it take us t'git another one?

(RYMAN *enters unseen. He is dressed in a polyester suit and thin tie and wears small, round, wire-framed glasses.*)

RYMAN: Took three years. *(He lays two shotguns down. He also carries his robe in a garbage bag, and an oddly-shaped tool box.)*

TOOTH: Three years!

TRAVIS: *(To* RYMAN*)* Where the hell you bin?

RYMAN: I'm here now, ain't I?

TOOTH: So what I'm sayin' is Sambo over there had him some work t'do when he got here 'cause our teeth was fallin' out of our heads. Hell, I had one tooth come out when I bit into a strawberry. Another three years, I'll be gummin' baby food. What say we overlook this one itty bitty measly Nigra on behalf of dental hygiene?

TRAVIS: *(Looking steadily at* TOOTH*)* There's somethin' wrong with you.

TOOTH: Shoot, we only got three coloreds left...Beulah, him, an' Beannie. Y'all run them off, yer gonna have ta put yer sheets back on the bed.

PRITCHARD: Y'all lay off Beannie.

RYMAN: *(Working on something in the tool box)* So's he can fetch yer Hershey bars?

PRITCHARD: Uh-huh, that's right.

RYMAN: Cryin' shame if you ask me...ex-associate of the great Colonel William Joseph Simmons, honored founder-honcho of the Ol' Original Klan, pallin' aroun' with the Nigra town drunk.

PRITCHARD: Listen here, boy. I'm the town drunk 'an don't you forget it. Thing's I've seen an' done in this life earned me my drinkin'. I'us drunk yesterday, drunk t'day, an' I'm sure as hell gonna be drunk t'morrow. Now yesterday you was an asshole, an' I'm sure yer jus' as reliable.

RYMAN: Day you go too far, ol' soldier, I'll let you know.

PRITCHARD: Day you let me know, chile, I'll send some friends over t'part yer hair. Now I don't want nobody troublin' Beannie. He's the only one in the God-forsaken town knows how t'play two-handed solitaire.

BOBBY JOE: I kin play two-handed solitaire.

PRITCHARD: With yer ding-dong maybe.

TRAVIS: Ain't tryin' to ruin yer card game, Pritch. Far as I'm concerned, Beannie's a white man in a jigaboo suit. But we let some college-educated Northern Nigra come in here, buy him the best house, drive him a Mercy Benz, shed his wife an' start tippin' his hat t'our women, they gonna flood in here. They gonna work cheap, vote each other in, buy yer granddaddy's land, an' end up sippin' sloe gin on the porch while we're wearin' bandannas, washin' clothes in the creek, munchin' chicken-necks an' dandelion greens, an' hoppin' roun' singin' "Doo-dah, Doo-dah."

RYMAN: *(Extremely animated, a fist in the air)* Right on, brother, you lay 'em to waste.

TRAVIS: *(Who considers* RYMAN *extremely strange)* O.K. Ryman.

RYMAN: Mother-humpin' Zionists, the whole bunch of 'em. Commie-faggot-Democratic-pro-busing-fetus-killing-miserable-piss-ants.

TRAVIS: You bet, Ryman.

RYMAN: *(Still tinkering with screwdriver and pliers inside the tool box, which contains a bomb)* White man's down to the last tick of the clock. Last mother tick. All a man's got is time. You don't have time, you don't have nothin' but rigor mortis. You see this here decade-calendar, stop-sequence, microselective, astro-chronometer, digital-watch? White man designed this. Time's only in the white man's mind. Ain't no colored ever designed a good watch. Why you think they call it "colored people's time"? 'Cause it's late. Why you think there ain't no colored people in Switzerland? 'Cause that's where they make the watches. They lettin' us live fast while they live slow so they can be here when we're gone, brothers! They screwin' aroun' with our life span. Stealin' the white man's time. Got them a warehouse full of our minutes. An' our only hope...the only hope is the microprocessor, so we'll know exactly where we are down to the millisecond, an' they know it.

Them spades made themselves up like Japanese an' snuck into I.B.M. t'steal that program, an' if the security guard hadn't noticed they was wearin' bright maroon platform shoes, that woulda' been all she wrote, brother! They ain't gonna get our time! Ain't gonna steal our life! I got a surprise for the colored, brothers. You see if I don't. *(He stands for a second. Nobody knows how to react. He bends back over his work; a pause.)*

TOOTH: What you doin' there, Ryman?

RYMAN: Jes' puttin the mustard on a dynamite sandwich.

BOBBY JOE: You kiddin' me?

PRITCHARD: *(To* BOBBY JOE*)* Git on back, boy.

RYMAN: Gonna be the space program's first Nigranaut. Put the coon on the moon.

TOOTH: But that ain't really dynamite, right?

RYMAN: Read about that asphalt company in Birmingham got their 'splosive shed robbed? Hey, was that my day in Birmingham er not?

TOOTH: This here's a cross burnin', Ryman, not a nuclear attack.

RYMAN: That coon called me crazy.

TOOTH: Only after you peed on his car.

RYMAN: Think he's so high an' mighty? Well, there's gonna be tarbaby in the treetops tonight. *(Returns his concentration to the bomb)*

TRAVIS: *(He and* TOOTH *exchange looks.* TRAVIS *walks over to* RYMAN.*)* How'd the Pac-Man go, Ryman?

RYMAN: Got me three hundred thousand.

TRAVIS: On one quarter?

RYMAN: Didn't finish the game 'cause I knew y'all was waitin'.

TRAVIS: Man that good oughta git his quarter back.

RYMAN: Machine don't never give you yer quarter back.

TRAVIS: *(Tossing a quarter on the ground)* Well tha's the difference 'tween a man an' a machine, ain't it? Go on, pick it up.

RYMAN: Pick it up yourself, cowboy.

PRITCHARD: Y'really oughta pick that one up, Ryman. It's a silver one without any copper.

TOOTH: *(Smiling)* You scared t'pick it up, Ryman? *(*RYMAN *bends over to pick it up and* TRAVIS *kicks him in the butt and sends him sprawling.)*

TRAVIS: When it's time for the dynamite, Ryman, I 'magine you'll hear about it from the Grand Kludd.

RYMAN: *(Rising and brushing himself off)* I got that down in my book.

PRITCHARD: Mus' be a reg'lar historical novel by now.

BOBBY JOE: *(Serious and concerned, he picks up the quarter.)* Here, y'forgot yer quarter. (RYMAN *takes it.*) Want me t'pick up yer gold-plated pen? *(RYMAN picks up his pen and puts it away.)*

TRAVIS: Got the cross in yer pickup, Ryman? (RYMAN *nods yes.*) 'Leven footer? (RYMAN *nods yes.*) Well, go git it man. It ain't gonna walk over here by itself! (RYMAN *goes.* TRAVIS *turns to* BOBBY JOE.) Go on boy, make yerself useful. (BOBBY JOE *starts to go, then turns back.*)

BOBBY JOE: I'm in the Klan. In the Invisible Empire.

TOOTH: Yeah. You're some tough hombre now.

BOBBY JOE: Golly! *(He exits.)*

TOOTH: That Ryman's so mean he must spit formaldehyde.

PRITCHARD: When he was a boy, he'd sneak around the neighborhood at suppertime and stick them jalapeno peppers in ever'body's dog-dishes. Them hounds took off straight-up like helicopters. *(Indicates the dynamite sticks)* What we gonna do with them firecrackers, Trav?

TRAVIS: *(Moving them to one side)* I'll jes' take 'em on home with me.

TOOTH: Sure. A man cain't never have enough dynamite.

BOBBY JOE: *(Offstage)* Yo, Tooth. Give us a hand, will ya?

TOOTH: *(To* TRAVIS*)* You jes' cain't read between the lines, can ya?

TRAVIS: You gonna babysit me, you might's well give the man a hand.

TOOTH: *(Calling to* BOBBY JOE*)* I'm comin'. *(Starts off)* You know how many Klansmen it takes to unload a cross?

PRITCHARD: How many?

TOOTH: Jes' two, but then you got t'rub 'em together t'start the fire. (PRITCHARD *laughs.* TOOTH *exits.*)

TRAVIS: Hey, you think we're dumb?

PRITCHARD: You mean can we tell a hawk from a handsaw?

TRAVIS: *(Hits himself)* I mean I mus' be a damn Mongoloid moron if I'm in the same damn world with Ryman Stoner.

PRITCHARD: Ol' Ryman, he's purt near smart, so I'd say we're better off dumb. Shotguns, dynamite, pipe bombs, chemicals. Like a bunch a' two-bit A-rab go-rillas. Ol' days all we had was a rope.

TRAVIS: Ever seen you a lynchin', Pritch?

PRITCHARD: One. Wahalak, Mississippi in Twenty-two. Tossed my cookies for three days. When that neck snaps, it's louder 'an a twenty-two calibre. Blood spurt fifteen feet out the nose. After he's dead, he'll twitch two hours. Oh, I wasn't in on it...musta been about twelve. My daddy held me up so's I could see. There was four men fainted an' one man threw his hat in the air. Tried t'sing "Onward Christian Soldiers," but din't nobody know all the words. Daddy asked me did I want the man's shoelaces for a souvenir...but I didn't want 'em. Yeah. I only seen one lynchin'.

TRAVIS: How long you been Klannin'?

PRITCHARD: 'Smite over fifty years.

TRAVIS: That long, huh? How come we ain't never won the sum'bitch?

PRITCHARD: Cain't say.

TRAVIS: *(Putting on his robes)* Well, it's sumpin' to do. Wears me out though.

PRITCHARD: Saw Essie in the Parade. *(TRAVIS hits himself.)* Heard she slep' over to Lurlene's two, three days last week. *(TRAVIS hits himself.)* Trouble in the bed, or in the head?

TRAVIS: Says she's read me twice an' she knows how I come out.

PRITCHARD: Yeah, I had three wives an' they were all hell for variety.

TRAVIS: When it goes bad, can ya git it back?

PRITCHARD: Well, I couldn't. 'Course I'm dumber than a banana pizza so it don't signify. My first wife was in the female Klan.

TRAVIS: No kiddin'?

PRITCHARD: Sure. Called it the S.A.C.: Sambo Amusement Company. She was the Queen Cyclops of the Yazoo City Chickadee Klavern. First all-female Klavern an' marchin' band in the state. All'us carried honey an' sand in her purse t'pour in the colored's gas tanks. We were there in Carolina in Thirty-six when they burned them a hunnert an' sixteen foot cross. Set the record. Later on, we'd work the truck stops t'gether, order some coffee, read the paper, then she'd slap it down an' holler out, "Gawdamighty, honey, the Nigras is takin' over everythin'." Some truck jockey cross the room'd say "Amen," and we'd git him fer a ten-dollar donation. Nice when the husban' an' wife has the same hobby.

TRAVIS: How'd you lose her?

PRITCHARD: Ran off with an Imperial Wizard at a Klan Bake. Heard she died of pneumonia runnin' the bottle toss booth at the Fargo, North Dakota state fair.

TRAVIS: Essie don't like the Klan.

PRITCHARD: Lotta the women don't.

TRAVIS: She says one night some Nigra's gonna send me home in a Jello mold.

PRITCHARD: *(Indicating dentist's house)* They say this one's got him more guns than the Muslins.

TRAVIS: Yeah, he's a real humdinger.

(RYMAN, TOOTH, and BOBBY JOE enter, carrying the cross. It is at least ten feet long.)

BOBBY JOE: Hold 'er, hold 'er, gotta change my grip.

RYMAN: Lay it here, anyroad. It ain't doused.

TOOTH: *(Putting it down)* Breakin' my damn back.

RYMAN: *(Heads out)* I'll git the kerosene.

BOBBY JOE: *(To TRAVIS and PRITCHARD)* You know what's in his truck? Four rifles, a pistol, eight wooden clubs, a blackjack, brass-knuckles, and a hypodermic syringe!

TOOTH: Prob'ly the only way he kin git a goodnight kiss.

BOBBY JOE: *(Holding up a joint)* This was on the dash. You think it's Mary-juana?

TRAVIS: Hell, bein' it's Ryman, he prob'ly smokes used kitty-litter. *(RYMAN re-enters, now in his robe.)*

RYMAN: Any you boys got some kerosene?

TRAVIS: Got what?

PRITCHARD: You mean you ain't got any?

RYMAN: Musta drove off without her.

TOOTH: You got any kerosene, Trav?

TRAVIS: *(Shakes his head no)* Pritch?

PRITCHARD: I had any I'd drink it.

TRAVIS: Well, damn it t'hell...

TOOTH: Ryman, if the las' woman on Earth was waitin' on you t'come by an' procreate up another human race, you'd forget t'bring yer pecker.

RYMAN: You name's goin' in my book, Bigmouth.

BOBBY JOE: Got me a Bic lighter. We could break 'er open an' git that fluid on there.

TOOTH: Yer a thinkin' man's thinkin' man, Sunny Jim. *(BOBBY JOE starts to hand the lighter to TOOTH, but RYMAN reaches in.)* Hey!

RYMAN: S'my cross.

TRAVIS: Dang it Ryman...

RYMAN: S'my cross! *(Pulls at the lighter, trying to get it open)*

TOOTH: You gonna break it open, or jes' jerk it off?

RYMAN: Hard t'git a grip.

TOOTH: *(Gestures for it)* Here.

RYMAN: Jes' hold yer water.

BOBBY JOE: Let me do 'er. *(There is a lot of light pushing and jockeying for position.)*

TOOTH: Git offa me.

RYMAN: Git offa me.

BOBBY JOE: Melda says I got hands like a ape.

RYMAN: Piss-ant l'il thing.

TOOTH: Gimme the damn thing! *(Takes it)*

PRITCHARD: Hey Tooth...

TOOTH: Lemme be.

PRITCHARD: Oughta snap the top off.

TOOTH: *(Working with his teeth)* Huh?

PRITCHARD: Snap 'er.

TOOTH: Hell, I cracked a tooth.

BOBBY JOE: Says t'snap it.

TOOTH: Well shoot.

PRITCHARD: You hear me?

TOOTH: Say what?

PRITCHARD, BOBBY JOE, and TRAVIS: Snap it!!

TOOTH: *(Just as loudly)* Dammit, I cracked a tooth!!

TRAVIS: Shhhhhhhhhh!

PRITCHARD: Here, try m'buck knife.

TOOTH: I said cracked it, not extract it.

PRITCHARD: I mean use it on the...

BOBBY JOE: *(Overexcited)* I got it. I got it! *(Grabs lighter)*

TOOTH: Hey...

TRAVIS: Hol' on...

(BOBBY JOE throws it down.)

TOOTH: No, Bobby Joe! *(He stomps it. It breaks and liquid runs out.)*

PRITCHARD: He got 'er!

BOBBY JOE: *(Topping him)* I got 'er!

PRITCHARD: *(Slapping him on back)* Yesiree!

BOBBY JOE: We're gonna ride! *(TRAVIS, TOOTH, and RYMAN stare mournfully at him. He sees them; looks at the ground; gets the point.)* Oh-oh.

TOOTH: You bake all the brains in Alabama in a pie, you'd still have room fer all twenty-four blackbirds.

RYMAN: *(Pulls out another Bic)* I got one. *(Pulls a pistol out of the shoulder holster and aims at top of the Bic)*

TRAVIS: No! *(Pulls it out of RYMAN's hand)* Way you shoot, Ryman, we'll be up all night lookin' fer yer damn finger, plus you'll have the whole town all over us. *(TRAVIS snaps the Bic neatly in half.)* There. *(Starts the cross; RYMAN intercepts him.)*

RYMAN: It's my lighter. *(Takes it over and sprinkles fluid on the cross)* Y'all give me a hand here. *(BOBBY JOE, TRAVIS, and TOOTH go over to help.)* You down there. All right, le's do 'er. *(They lift the cross.)*

TRAVIS: Foot it.

BOBBY JOE: O.K., now.

TOOTH: Comin' on.

RYMAN: Easy.

TRAVIS: We got 'er. We got 'er. She straight, Pritch?

PRITCHARD: Little left.

TOOTH: O.K., now?

PRITCHARD: Little right.

TRAVIS: That it?

PRITCHARD: Little left.

TOOTH: *(Leaving the cross, walks over to look with* PRITCHARD*)* Good gravy, man, which way you want 'er?

RYMAN: Hey, this here's heavy, y'know?

PRITCHARD: Tol' ya, more left.

TOOTH: Lef', hell. Look at the pine tree. More right!

PRITCHARD: An' I tell ya more left!

TRAVIS: *(Leaving the cross and coming to them)* Gotta do ever' damn thing m'self. *(The cross is now too heavy for the two remaining men.)*

RYMAN: Hey.

BOBBY JOE: Hey.

RYMAN: Hey!

BOBBY JOE: Look out! *(The cross crashes to the ground.)*

(A brief pause)

TOOTH: Well, O.K., so tha's done.

PRITCHARD: Tol' ya' more left.

RYMAN: *(Starting for* PRITCHARD*)* You senile ol' idiot.

TRAVIS: Jes' cool off. Look, we'll jes' light 'er up lyin' on the ground.

TOOTH: What's the manual say on that, Pritch?

PRITCHARD: Manual says if y'd gone more left y'wouldn't have t'ask what the manual says.

TRAVIS: 'Member, we done 'er lyin' down at the library, lef' a real good scorch mark.

RYMAN: *(Frustrated)* Hell, whatever. *(All except* PRITCHARD *start for the cross.)*

PRITCHARD: Need a vote.

*(*TRAVIS *turns back.)*

TRAVIS: What's that?

PRITCHARD: Manual says we need a vote.

RYMAN: Ain't got the time, y'ol' fool.

PRITCHARD: *(Implacable)* Says in the sacred code.

RYMAN: Yer damn rulebook's the only thing in Alabama more decrepit than you are.

PRITCHARD: Whyn't you use a grenade fer a suppository?

TRAVIS: Awright, awright! All present wants t'light 'er up lyin' down, raise yer hands? *(All but* PRITCHARD *do so.)*

RYMAN: Let's do 'er! *(They all head for cross, except* PRITCHARD.*)*

PRITCHARD: S'posed to be a secret ballot.

TOOTH: *(To* TRAVIS*)* An' when we get through it says we gotta drink Lowenbrau beer.

TRAVIS: Ryman, gimme that handgun.

RYMAN: What for?

TRAVIS: So you can be alive fer another two minutes. *(*RYMAN *gives it to him.)* Pritch, I'm forty years old, been laid off six months, my wife's turned colored on me, m'oldest boy ran over m'neighbor's blue-ribbon Pekinese on his motorbike, I can only git it up once a week an' I'm goin' t'light that cross lyin' down. Now if that ain't in yer goddamn manual jes' go ahead an' shoot me. *(Gives pistol to* PRITCHARD *and goes to the cross; searches in pocket for matches; finds nothing.)* Somebody give me a light. *(A pause; they look at each other.)* Gimme a match. *(They look in their pockets.)* Gimme a lighter! *(They look at him.)* Gimme two goddamn sticks! *(*BOBBY JOE *does.* TRAVIS *breaks them and throws them at him.)* Colored, hell. We oughta run ourselves outta Alabama!

(Sound of an approaching car)

RYMAN: Car comin'.

TOOTH: Where?

(Flashing police beacon hits them from off.)

BOBBY JOE: State cops.

PRITCHARD: What'll I do with this gun?

RYMAN: Shoot fer the tires.

PRITCHARD: I ain't shootin' at the state cops.

TOOTH: Stick it in yer belt.

RYMAN: Dynamite. Where's the dynamite?

TRAVIS: Ryman....Hey, jes' look casual.

ZITS: *(From offstage)* How's it hangin'?

BOBBY JOE: Hey, aren't you...?

ZITS: *(Twenty-two years old, pock-marked face, high nasal voice, a recent graduate of the police academy)* Y'all havin' you a bang-up Fourth?

BOBBY JOE: Zat you, Zits?

ZITS: Dang it!

TOOTH: Zits?

ZITS: Aw, don't call me that. I got me a new face cream. Workin' real nice.

BOBBY JOE: *(A high-school cheer:)* We got the doughnut,
You got the hole (ZITS *joins him.*)
Les' go Rebels,
Roll, Roll, Roll!

ZITS: You Bobby Joe Bigun, ain't ya?

BOBBY JOE: Hell, yes! Hey, I was a freshman when you was a senior! Hey, y'all remember Zits dontcha? Had the lowest completion record of any quarterback in the history of Brine High.

TRAVIS: Good goin'.

ZITS: Well, I was playin' hurt.

BOBBY JOE: Got sacked fourteen times in one quarter.

TOOTH: Oh, yeah?

ZITS: I'm a state policeman now though.

TOOTH: That's a real scary thought.

ZITS: Evenin' Mr. Pritchard. Evenin' Mr. Scroggins. How you doin', Tooth?

BOBBY JOE: This here's Ryman B. Stoner, born in Brine but jes' moved back...sells them Apple computers.

ZITS: Hey, you ain't the Ryman Stoner put that seven-hundred-thousand on the Pac-Man at the Kinkler-Tutweiler Hotel over t'Hueytown, were ya?

RYMAN: Seven hunnert an' thirty.

ZITS: Gawdamn! Gawd Damn! Yer jes' a Lord-lovin' legend in yer own time! We retired that damn machine with a sixteen-pound sledge, in yer honor. You got the hands of a damn safecracker! You mind autographin' my undershirt?

RYMAN: Well...

ZITS: Gotta Magic Marker?

RYMAN: Well, sure.

ZITS: *(Tearing open his shirt, hands* RYMAN *the marker. Talks while* RYMAN *writes.)* Man, oh man, wait'll the boys see this! Jes' write "Happy Packin' to my ol' buddy Zits." Shoot, I'm a player. Won't even answer a burglary call if I got a good screen goin'.

RYMAN: *(Finishing)* There ya go.

ZITS: Fubbin'-fantasterrific, man! Lemme shake the king's joystick.

RYMAN: Say what?

ZITS: The hand that done seven-hundred-mother thousand. *(Shakes* RYMAN's *hand)* Say Mr. Scroggins, that your Toyota back over there?

TRAVIS: Might be.

ZITS: Right on! See, Mr. Scroggins, I'm pleased t'tell you, I'm givin' you my first ticket. First citation as a state po-liceman. See, this here's my first night on m'own. Fubbin' blast, man! You know what's funny? I got t'shoot me somebody last week, but I jes' ain't been privileged yet t'hand out a traffic violation. Seems like it should might go t'other way around. You know, give out a ticket first an' then shoot somebody. Well, life's funny, ain't it?

TOOTH: I'd say life was funny, wouldn't you Trav?

TRAVIS: *(To* ZITS*)* You got a match?

ZITS: Hey, I don' smoke man, that stuff kills ya. You know, it's funny first time y'shoot somebody. Goes down real easy. *(Pulls out pistol)* Truth is, I didn't even mean t'shoot this guy. It was real funny, see, they tol' me t'fire a warnin' shot so I aimed high, but I had the damn hiccups. Drilled that ol' boy clean. Bang. *(The gun fires accidentally.* ZITS *slaps it.)* Dumb ol' thang. M'partner said don't take it t'heart 'cause he was most likely a burglar...or somethin'. Hey, you know what? Dead people look real dead. I mean, it surprised me, you know, how dead they look. *(Puts gun in his holster; they all sigh in relief.)*

TRAVIS: What you givin' me a ticket for?

ZITS: Mr. Scroggins, I'm jes' pleased as punch t'tell you your Toyota is one hunnert percent illegal parked in a handicapped zone. Ain't that great? Purty good luck fer me. See, they tol' me I better git out there tonight an' jes' arrest the hell outta somebody's butt.

TRAVIS: You gonna arrest me at midnight on the Fourth of July fer parkin' in a handicapped zone?

ZITS: Them crips got a hard life, Mr. Scroggins. You didn't have any arms er legs you'd want a good place t'park. Now I called 'er in t'git ya towed off, but you got t'go anywhere I'd be right pleased to ride ya. Show y'all them gadgets in m'cruiser. *(Focusing on* BOBBY JOE's *outfit)* Say...what y'all up to out here?

TOOTH: Uhhh...

BOBBY JOE: Up to?

PRITCHRD: Uhhh...

TRAVIS: Well, we uh...

TOOTH: Jes', you know...

BOBBY JOE: Jes', you know...

PRITCHARD: Screwin' around.

TRAVIS: Yeah.

BOBBY JOE: Right!

TRAVIS: Jes' screwin' around.

ZITS: *(Noticing the cross)* An' watcha doin' with this here thing?

PRITCHARD: Lef' over from the Revival. Brother Thunder's travelin' tent savin'. You 'member that, dontcha Ryman?

RYMAN: Oh sure...sure.

TOOTH: Yeah, Brother Thunder. I got saved couple a' times that night. Had t'go out t'pee in the middle. Come back in, bang, they saved me again.

ZITS: This here's a ride, ain't she?

TOOTH: A ride?

PRITCHARD: Wha's a ride?

ZITS: Little Klan bang. Little sheet treat.

PRITCHARD: Now looky here, Zits...

TRAVIS: *(Cutting across him)* Yeah, that's right. The Klan. We gonna leave us a little callin' card on a Nigra's lawn, boy. Now jes' what you gonna do about it?

ZITS: *(A dramatic standoff)* A ride, huh? *(He and* TRAVIS *stare at each other.)* Hot damn! Got my robes in the car! *(He races off to the cruiser.)*

PRITCHARD: That boy got him zits on the brain.

RYMAN: He's all right.

TOOTH: You jes' like him 'cause he shook yer joystick.

TRAVIS: What Klan you figger that boy's in?

RYMAN: Ain't the Ol' Original, 'cause I'd know it. Could be the Dixie Knights or the Reconstituted. Read where they was workin' this part of the state.

TOOTH: Din't you have yer own Klan once, Pritch?

PRITCHARD: Called us the Emerald Rebs. Had us black hoods an' green satin bowlin' jackets. Tried t'git us some busin' started.

BOBBY JOE: Git it started?

PRITCHARD: All the Klans was hell on busin', but we din't have us none down here, so we figgered we git us some started so we could stop it.

Coloreds din't want it though, an' it was kindy embarrassin'. They'd picket us. Finally there wasn't enough Emerald Rebs fer a hand a' stud poker, an' we quit.

TRAVIS: Trouble with this damn country is everybody stays home 'steada participatin'. (ZITS *returns, carrying his robes and a big bowl of popcorn.*)

ZITS: Ready to ride! Any a'you gents want you some popcorn?

BOBBY JOE: Where's you git it this time of night?

ZITS: Got me a battery-operated popper in the cruiser, plus I got me a Sony T.V. an' some marital aids, case I run inta somethin' good. *(Claps his hands)* Man, I cain't wait till we git that fubbin' cross goin'!

BOBBY JOE: Ain't got a match.

ZITS: No fire huh? You jes' watch me. *(Heads up to* DR. KENNEDY's *front door)*

TRAVIS: Where the hell you goin'?

ZITS: Little Klangenuity. *(Rings door bell)*

TRAVIS: *(To the others)* Git back! *(They take cover.)*

ZITS: Hey, y'all scaredy-cats. (DR. KENNEDY *opens the door. He wears a summer-weight sport coat and slacks.*)

DR. KENNEDY: Yes?

ZITS: Officer Puckett, sir. State Highway Patrol. Sorry to disturb you, sir, but I saw some men of a suspicious nature near yer property, an' I found this...*(Shows* DR. KENNEDY *the robe over his arm)*...on yer lawn.

DR. KENNEDY: Uh-huh. Very kind of you to be concerned.

ZITS: Yes, sir. Well, I just wanted to let you know. And to assure you that we'll keep an eye open.

DR. KENNEDY: Well, I'd appreciate it Officer Puckett. The good ol' boys we have here tend to remember I was a Special Forces night weaponry expert in 'Nam, so they run through my flower beds every once in a while, but they're basically committed to stayin' live bigots 'stead of dead slipcovers.

ZITS: 'Nam, huh?

DR. KENNEDY: Right. 'Nam. Well, goodnight to you then.

ZITS: Say, uh, excuse me, but see, I got the cigs but no twigs, if you know what I mean. Need me a light t'git through the night.

DR. KENNEDY: Just what is it you want, Officer?

ZITS: Oh, jes' a match, mainly.

DR. KENNEDY: *(Reaches in his pocket)* Take the pack.

ZITS: Purely appreciate it. *(Turns to go)*

DR. KENNEDY: Officer? Is your first name Emory, by any chance?

ZITS: Hey. Yes sir. How'd you know that?

DR. KENNEDY: Well, for one thing, your name tag's sticking out of your robe. *(He closes the door on the astounded ZITS.)*

TRAVIS: Fooled him right down to the ground.

PRITCHARD: Your momma oughta sew a name tag on your pee-pee, so the toilet bowl'd know who you were.

ZITS: Got the matches, din't I?

RYMAN: Look, I got me a barn t'burn down, so I'd like t'git goin' here.

TRAVIS: Le's do 'er.

PRITCHARD: This a first warnin' or a second warnin'?

TRAVIS: Already nailed a cat to his door.

PRITCHARD: S'posed t'cut off a coon head an' stick it on the door handle.

TRAVIS: Damn it Pritch, it's late. I ain't chasin' no raccoons.

PRITCHARD: *(Adamant)* Gotta leave somethin' disgustin' on his front step.

BOBBY JOE: Got me some melted M&M's in my pocket.

TRAVIS: *(Irritated)* That's jes' fine! Light 'er up, Ryman.

PRITCHARD: S'posed t'sing "Ol' Rugged Cross."

TRAVIS: *(Crazed)* For Gawd's sake, sing it!

(PRITCHARD *starts. They join in. At the end,* RYMAN *leans down with the matches.*)

RYMAN: Well, turkey-turds-in-a-bowl-a-grits!

TRAVIS: *(In a quiet fury)* Now what?

RYMAN: These ain't matches, they're rubbers. Prophylactics!

TRAVIS: They are what?!

RYMAN: "Royal Sultan super sensitive. Money back guarantee." (TOOTH *falls down laughing.*) This ain't funny!

(TRAVIS *starts to laugh.*)

PRITCHARD: He jes' wanted ya t'have a good time, Ryman.

(The laughter is now general, with the exception of RYMAN.*)*

TOOTH: *(Looking at the pack)* "Extra small." Hell, Ryman, he knew they was for you! *(They all roar with laughter.)*

RYMAN: This ain't funny. *(Gales of laughter)* Y'all ain't s'posed t'laugh at a white man.

TOOTH: Put 'em on yer joystick. *(They fall about.)* This way yer sheep won't git pregnant.

RYMAN: *(Yelling at the house, pounding on the door)* Who you think you are? Who you think you are, Nigra? You think yer King Coon, dontcha? Yer screwin' with the white man, monkey-breath. *(Moves center in front of the door)*
"Black may be beautiful,
An' tan may be grand,
But white's still the color
Of the Big Boss Man." *(The door is opened and DR. KENNEDY hits RYMAN full in the face with a bucket of water.)* Son-of-a-bitch. *(RYMAN races across the stage to where the shotguns have been left.)*

TOOTH: *(The following dialogue overlaps right up to the shot.)* Hey, hol' on, Ryman.

TRAVIS: Git him.

TOOTH: Hey!

TRAVIS: Git him!

BOBBY JOE: Git that twelve gauge.

(ZITS grabs RYMAN but is shaken off.)

PRITCHARD: Plain crazy.

TOOTH: Watch it.

TRAVIS: Come on Ryman...

RYMAN: Lemme go.

TOOTH: Grab a holt a' that mother...

RYMAN: Lemme go.

PRITCHARD: Loaded. Look out!

TOOTH: Git it.

PRITCHARD: Git it.

(RYMAN breaks free.)

TOOTH: Je-sus!

BOBBY JOE: Hit the dirt.

TRAVIS: Rymannnnnnnnnn!

(RYMAN fires at the house, breaking the window. A woman's scream is heard.)

PRITCHARD: Somebody in there.

(RYMAN *levels the shotgun again.* TRAVIS *tackles him.*)

TRAVIS: You damn lunatic.

(DR. KENNEDY *appears at the door carrying an automatic weapon.*)

ZITS: Y'all git down!!

(DR. KENNEDY *lets go with a burst of automatic fire, raking the stage. The Klansmen flatten, faces in dirt. A moment; no one is hit.*)

DR. KENNEDY: All right, spooks. On your feet. Move it. *(They begin to rise.)* Hands on your head. Both hands. Kick that shotgun out of there. (TRAVIS *does.*) Move in where I can see you. Move! Now, a little light on the subject. *(Flips an outside switch; the yard floodlights come on)* Now, who we got here. *(To* TOOTH, *the only one without a robe)* Well, as I live an' breathe, it's Ashley Wilkes. All right, let's have a look. Get 'em off. *(No one moves.)* I said get 'em off. *(He fires a shot in the air. The men rip off their robes in a rush.* BOBBY JOE *is, of course, nude.* DR. KENNEDY *looks at him.)* For God's sake, put 'em back on! *(They do.)* There is nothing more depressing than a naked white man. Hands on heads! Move it. Say, weren't you boys singin' "Ol' Rugged Cross?" My momma used to sing that to me. I always did enjoy music. You got any other selections? A few tunes. "Swannee River?" "Ol' Black Joe?" No? Shoot. I'm a fool for harmony. Hey, you remember, "I'm A Little Teapot" from second grade? Yeah, you do.
"I'm a little teapot,
Short and stout.
This is my handle.
This is my spout."

BOBBY JOE: Shoot, I know that one.

DR. KENNEDY: Sure you do! Let's give it a try. *(He leads them in song.* TRAVIS *abstains.)*

ALL: "I'm a little teapot,
Short and stout.
This is my handle.
This is my spout.
When I get all steamed up,
Hear me shout.
Tip me over and pour me out." (TRAVIS *stands fixated on* DR. KENNEDY.)

DR. KENNEDY: Hey, there is just no doubt about it. You guys have got natural rhythm. One more time....*(Fires shot; they sing. He encourages them.)* Louder! *(They finish the second time.)* Very good. Now, with gestures! Move! *(He fires a shot. All dance but* TRAVIS.) Yes, sir! Motown sound! Uh-huh! Now spin! Go on, spin! *(Fires shots in the air as they spin; a woman appears in the doorway. It is* ESSIE, TRAVIS' *wife.)* That's real good...now...

ESSIE: You 'bout through funnin' with 'em, Harold?

DR. KENNEDY: Yeah. Just about.

(The Klansmen stop. They stare at ESSIE, *dumbfounded.* TOOTH *lets out an involuntary whistle and shakes his head.)*

ESSIE: Who you whistlin' at, Tooth Gannet?

TOOTH: *(Touches* TRAVIS' *shoulder)* I tried to tell you, Buddy. *(*TRAVIS *doesn't react.)*

DR. KENNEDY: Now boys, it's the Fourth of July, an' we all had us a real good time and I don't mind fooling with you as long as everybody's sure it's fooling.

TRAVIS: What the hell you doin', Essie?

DR. KENNEDY: *(Cutting across him)* Because it's not like it used to be, and it's never going to be that way again. See, the people you used to run out of town on a rail got them AR-15 semi-automatics with hollow-point ammunition, got them Imgrim Mach-10's hanging over their fireplaces equipped with infrared pathfinder night-scopes, got them eight-ply bulletproof glass in their Mercedes Benzes, .45 pistols in quick-draw vest holsters and...*(Takes something round out of his coat pocket)* when they go to pick up the paper in the morning, they are carrying an unpinned double-ought-three fragmentation grenade in their free hand. Hey, what used to be lynch-bait is now 'Nam-trained, half-nasty, and armed to our glow-in-the-dark teeth. Now what I want you to understand is that I don't care to take your jobs, mutilate your bodies, or steal your fraternal hand-shake. I just want to pull your teeth in a general atmosphere of wary, mutual respect. It's either that, or this. *(Squeezes off a shot)* And uh, listen up now, don't kid a kidder, O.K.? I am trained to hurt you. Got it? Now pick up your trash and get your Invisible Empire off my lawn.

RYMAN: I got you down in my book, Nigra.

DR. KENNEDY: You tell these boys you're in the F.B.I. yet, Ryman?

RYMAN: *(Petrified)* I ain't in the F.B.I.!

DR. KENNEDY: That's not what you told me out at the quarry.

RYMAN: Never went out to the quarry with him!

PRITCHARD: I got you down in my book, Ryman. *(They are picking up the lawn.* RYMAN *reaches for the shotgun.)*

TRAVIS: Hey...

DR. KENNEDY: *(Turning the gun on* RYMAN; *he freezes.)* Huh-uh. Oh, and leave me that big ol' cross. My momma'd like that. Go on.

BOBBY JOE: Dr. Kennedy, I dropped me a human glass eyeball somewhere on your lawn. Y'all better watch out it don't get throwed up by your lawn mower.

DR. KENNEDY: O.K., Son. I like your sheet.

BOBBY JOE: Onliest one she had.

ZITS: *(Taking off his hood)* Sir? I'm Officer Puckett, Sir? We met earlier? Well, I have successfully infiltrated this here Klavern, Sir.

DR. KENNEDY: You dance divinely, Officer Puckett.

ZITS: Yes, Sir. So anyway, Sir, I'll be puttin' these boys right in my cruiser an' takin' 'em into Hueytown, Sir. No fuss, no muss, Sir. You can count on me, Sir.

DR. KENNEDY: Officer Puckett, in my experience there is only one thing, historically, a black man absolutely cannot count on and that is the Alabama State Police. However, I would enjoy hearing you call me Sir one more time.

ZITS: Yes Sir, Sir.

(The churchbells begin striking twelve.)

DR. KENNEDY: 'Night boys. *(They don't move.)* Time to get on home now. *(They don't move.)* Slow learners. *(He pulls the pin on the grenade he's been holding.)* Bye, bye. *(He lobs the grenade out into the assemblage.)*

TOOTH: Grenade!

(The Klansmen scatter offstage in every direction. Only TRAVIS *stands stock still. The others are gone.* TRAVIS *calmly picks up the grenade and tosses it back to* DR. KENNEDY.*)*

TRAVIS: That ain't no live grenade. I was there, buddy. I-26 armored.

DR. KENNEDY: Special Forces. Junk Yard Dogs. Semi-detached.

TRAVIS: Sixty-six, sixty-seven.

DR. KENNEDY: Sixty-six, sixty-seven. *(In other words, they both served the same years.)*

TRAVIS: You boys was O.K....

DR. KENNEDY: *(He and* TRAVIS *eye each other.)* I was looking at your card the other day. It's time for you to come in and get your teeth cleaned.

TRAVIS: Like to talk to my wife, if you don't mind.

DR. KENNEDY: Sounds like one hell of a good idea to me. Goodnight, Essie.

Essie: Goodnight, Harold.

Dr. Kennedy: You know, I knew a guy once came home and caught his wife layin' under their car with a strange man, high noon, in his own damn driveway. Shot off three toes on her left foot, and then found out later they were just fixing the muffler. *(Looks up)* Hell of a nice night. *(Goes in and closes the door)*

Essie: *(There is a pause. Travis looks at her. First he nods his head yes, then he shakes it no. He slaps his fist into his hand several times.)* You're gonna do it, aren't you? *(He emits a low growl, punctuated by hitting his own shoulders.)* Told me on New Year's you weren't gonna do it no more. *(He yells a bloodcurdling yell. He hits his chest with a closed fist. He pounds on his thighs. He throws a couple of wild punches into the air and then socks himself a good one in the jaw. It knocks him down. He is up immediately, taking a barrage of blows. He switches to the midsection, grunting as he takes punches. He gets down on his knees and pounds his head on the ground. Leaps up, emits a bloodcurdling cry, and throws himself out full length, hitting the ground. He rolls over on his back, grabs himself by the hair, and swats his head on the ground three times. He rises groggily to his knees and unleashes a final corker to his jaw. He lies full length on the ground.)* I've been married to you nineteen years, an' it's still the goddamnedest thing I've ever seen.

Travis: Shoot! *(A rat-a-tat-tat of firecrackers in the distance)*

Essie: People still shootin' off fireworks. Come sit on the curb with me.

Travis: Boy, I tell you!

Essie: You're gonna be so sore. If I don't soak a flannel shirt in lard an' turpentine, you just won't be able to move a muscle tomorrow.

Travis: *(Still prone)* Who's with the damn kids?

Essie: Bitsy. Probably drinkin' our whiskey. Come on Travis, sit. You can beat me up later.

Travis: *(Not moving)* What the hell were you doin' in there?

Essie: Listenin' to music, talkin' about the parade...

Travis: Parade! *(He hits himself, still lying down, several times, but not as hard as before.)*

Essie: Travis! Oh, an' he read some to me.

Travis: Read to you what?

Essie: Ko-ran.

Travis: What the hell's that?

Essie: You hadn't shot up the place I mighta' found out.

TRAVIS: Whole damn Klavern saw you was in there.

ESSIE: After that dance they did, I don't think they'll tease you much. *(She laughs.)* Haven't seen those boys dance since Cotillion.

TRAVIS: *(Getting up)* That Nigra touch you?

ESSIE: No, sir.

TRAVIS: You damn sure?

ESSIE: I'm damn sure.

TRAVIS: You swear on your children's heads, your dead momma's grave, Christ your savior, your bodily health, an' Bear Bryant's hat?

ESSIE: He didn't touch me, Travis.

TRAVIS: What did he do?

ESSIE: Talked to me like a human being.

TRAVIS: I don't know, man. I was nineteen, they was all good days; got to be thirty, they was good days an' bad days; now I'm forty, an' it seems like I'm jes' alla time knee-deep in shit. I ain't got the hang of this thing no more.

ESSIE: Didn't teach us right.

TRAVIS: Yeah, maybe.

ESSIE: We started dumb, an' they taught us dumb, an' they kep' us dumb. Musta been somethin' in it for 'em. *(A pause)* You still like me, Travis? *(He doesn't react.)* Well, you didn't say no. You ever think about the mystery of life?

TRAVIS: He didn't make you take no drugs, did he?

ESSIE: *(Shakes her head no)* Some mornin's, when I'm scramblin' your brains an' eggs, jes' when I put the catsup on, I think, "This ain't it."

TRAVIS: Brings out the flavor.

ESSIE: No, this. *(Gestures at everything)* This.

TRAVIS: *(Trying to follow her)* You want me to put my own catsup on?

ESSIE: No, I....Travis...no, look, it's like...it's like when I read one a them Max Brand westerns you got...

TRAVIS: *Flamin' Irons?*

ESSIE: Yeah, that one...an' it's a good story, an' there's a whole lot happenin'...

TRAVIS: It's the best one.

ESSIE: But there's not much...shoot, I don't know...not much...

DR. KENNEDY: *(From inside the house — he has been listening by a window.)* Content.

TRAVIS: *(Springs up)* Goddamnit Kennedy, butt out! *(A venetian blind tumbles down.)*

ESSIE: Travis!

TRAVIS: Go stuff a watermelon in yer big damn mouth!

ESSIE: Travis!

TRAVIS: *(A mountain of frustration)* Flub-a-dub-a-dub-a-dub-a-dub.

ESSIE: Not enough content.

TRAVIS: Sittin' on a damn curb takin' thinkin' lessons from a Nigra.

ESSIE: Well, he's on it, don't you think? Must be somethin' better.

TRAVIS: Well hell, that's the dad-blamed, one-hunnert percent, mother-of-pearl, ever-lovin' truth.

ESSIE: You know, Harold played me a real nice record.

TRAVIS: Essie, you're callin' a colored by his first name.

ESSIE: Yes. *(A pause)* Second time you came courtin' you brought me stale candy an' sang "Scoundrels and Ramblers"...played yer brother I.W.'s guitar...more or less. Haven't sung to me since.

TRAVIS: Well, I forgot "Ace's Wild."

ESSIE: Want to learn a new tune? Travis? Huh?

TRAVIS: What tune?

ESSIE: Do you?

TRAVIS: I'm listenin'.

ESSIE: Now it's real different.

TRAVIS: I said I was listenin'.

ESSIE: All right now, get ready. *(Sings him the final "Ode to Joy" phrase of Beethoven's Ninth)* Do it.

TRAVIS: I cain't sing that.

ESSIE: You too dumb to learn a new tune? *(She repeats the phrase.)* Come on. *(He tries it grudgingly.)* Not too raggedy. *(She does a second phrase.)*

TRAVIS: Aw, come on Essie. This is nigger music.

ESSIE: No, you come on. *(She does the second phrase again. He repeats it.)* You got it, Baby Blue. *(A yellow flashing tow-truck beacon hits them from off.)*

TRAVIS: I cain't do this.

ESSIE: Come on, Travis. Yer learnin' some new tricks.

TRAVIS: *(Rising suddenly, looking off)* Damn. Dumb.

ESSIE: You're not dumb.

TRAVIS: I am dumb! *(Hits himself in chest)*

ESSIE: *(Furious)* Why do you say that?

TRAVIS: 'Cause it's one a.m. an' there's a State Police tow-truck haulin' off m'Toyota fer bein' parked in a handicapped zone!

ESSIE: That is dumb!

TRAVIS: That's right! *(Hits himself)*

ESSIE: You make me so damn mad! *(She hits herself.)*

TRAVIS: Hey. (ESSIE *hits herself again.)* Hey! *(Hits himself)* Knock it off. *(She hits herself several times. He grabs her. She struggles. He makes her stop. He stands holding her for a moment.)*

ESSIE: I have to sit down. *(He releases her, she sits on curb. A heavy metal clonk is heard offstage.)* What was that?

TRAVIS: *(Looking off)* Engine fell outta my car.

(Flashing yellow light fades. He sits by her. Silence; she begins to sing softly.)

ESSIE: "Oh don't let yer daughters love dealers.
For they'll sell both their soul an' yer child.
Oh Riverboat gamblers,
They're scoundrels and ramblers,
Gone at dawn and their game's Ace's Wild."
(She nudges him and he sings.)
"Ace's Wild, Ace's Wild, ain't no game fer yer child."
(They both sing.) "Gone at dawn and their game's Ace's Wild."
(They sit, silent. Firecrackers in distance. Lights fade.)

END OF PLAY

CRIMES OF THE HEART

Beth Henley

CRIMES OF THE HEART
Copyright © 1981, 1982 by Beth Henley. All rights reserved. Reprinted by permission of Viking Penguin Inc.

The stage production rights to this play are represented by Dramatists Play Service, 440 Park Ave South, NY NY 10016, 212 683-8960.

All other rights are represented by Gilbert Parker, William Morris Agency, 1350 Sixth Ave, NY NY 10019, 212 903-1328.

For Len, C.C., and Kayo

ABOUT THE AUTHOR

Beth Henley was awarded the Pulitzer Prize in Drama and the New York Drama Critics' Circle Award for Best American Play for her first full-length play, CRIMES OF THE HEART. CRIMES was also the 1979 co-winner of the Great American Play Contest, sponsored by the Actors Theatre of Louisville. CRIMES has since been produced in many leading resident theatres, on a major national tour, and in many countries throughout the world. Ms. Henley's second play, THE MISS FIRECRACKER CONTEST, has been produced in several regional theatres in the U.S. and in London at the Bush Theatre, and opened in the spring of 1984 at the Manhattan Theatre Club. It subsequently transferred for an extended run off-Broadway, and was published in the *Ten Best Plays of 1983-1984*. Ms. Henley's third play, THE WAKE OF JAMEY FOSTER, had its premiere at the Hartford Stage Company prior to its presentation on Broadway directed by Ulu Grosbard. Ms. Henley's one-act play AM I BLUE? has been seen at the Hartford Stage Company and the Circle Repertory Company in New York. It is included in the *Best Short Plays of 1983*. Her play THE DEBUTANTE BALL was presented in the spring of 1985 at South Coast Repertory in Costa Mesa, California, and was presented in a substantially revised version by the Manhattan Theatre Club and the New York Stage and Film Company in the spring and summer of 1988, respectively. Her newest play, THE LUCKY SPOT, was presented at the Williamstown Theatre Festival in the summer of 1986 and had its New York premiere at the Manhattan Theatre Club in the spring of 1987.

Ms. Henley wrote the screenplay for the acclaimed film version of CRIMES OF THE HEART, for which she was nominated for an Academy Award. The film was directed by Bruce Beresford, and starred Diane Keaton, Jessica Lange, Sissy Spacek, and Sam Shepard. She also has written the screenplay for THE MISS FIRECRACKER CONTEST, which will be released in 1989, starring Holly Hunter and Mary Steenburgen. She wrote the screenplay for NOBODY'S FOOL, which starred Rosanna Arquette and Eric Roberts, and another screenplay for Sissy Spacek entitled STRAWBERRY. She has written a teleplay for the PBS series TRYING TIMES.

Born and raised in Mississippi, Ms. Henley graduated from Southern Methodist University and presently lives in Los Angeles.

CRIMES OF THE HEART was first produced on 1 February 1979 at Actors Theatre of Louisville, with the following cast:

LENNY	Kathy Bates
CHICK	Nicola Sheara
DOC PORTER	Michael Kevin
MEG	Susan Kingsley
BABE	Lee Anne Fahey
BARNETTE LLOYD	William McNulty
Director	Jon Jory
Sets and lights	Paul Owen
Costumes	Kurt Wilhelm

The play opened on Broadway on 4 November 1981 at the John Golden Theater, with the following cast:

LENNY	Lizbeth Mackay
CHICK	Sharon Ullrick
DOC PORTER	Raymond Baker
MEG	Mary Beth Hurt
BABE	Mia Dillon
BARNETTE LLOYD	Peter MacNicol
Director	Melvin Bernhardt
Sets	John Lee Beatty
Costumes	Patricia McGourty
Lights	Dennis Parichy

CHARACTERS

LENNY MAGRATH, *thirty, the oldest sister*
CHICK BOYLE, *twenty-nine, the sisters' first cousin*
DOC PORTER, *thirty, Meg's old boyfriend*
MEG MAGRATH, *twenty-seven, the middle sister*
BABE BOTRELLE, *twenty-four, the youngest sister*
BARNETTE LLOYD, *twenty-six, Babe's lawyer*

Time: In the fall, five years after Hurricane Camille.

SETTING

The setting of the entire play is the kitchen in the MaGrath sisters' house in Hazlehurst, Mississippi, a small Southern town. The old-fashioned kitchen is unusually spacious, but there is a lived-in, cluttered look about it. There are four different entrances and exits to the kitchen: the back door, the door leading to the dining room and the front of the house, a door leading to the downstairs bedroom, and a staircase leading to the upstairs room. There is a table near the center of the room, and a cot has been set up in one of the corners.

ACT ONE

(The lights go up on the empty kitchen. It is late afternoon. LENNY MAGRATH, *a thirty-year-old woman with a round figure and face, enters from the back door carrying a white suitcase, a saxophone case, and a brown paper sack. She sets the suitcase and the sax case down and takes the brown sack to the kitchen table. After glancing quickly at the door, she gets the cookie jar from the kitchen counter, a box of matches from the stove, and then brings both objects back to the kitchen table. Excitedly, she reaches into the brown sack and pulls out a package of birthday candles. She quickly opens the package and removes a candle. She tries to stick the candle onto a cookie—it falls off. She sticks the candle in again, but the cookie is too hard and it crumbles. Frantically, she gets a second cookie from the jar. She strikes a match, lights the candle, and begins dripping wax onto the cookie. Just as she is beginning to smile we hear* CHICK'S *voice from offstage.)*

CHICK'S VOICE: Lenny! Oh, Lenny!

*(*LENNY *quickly blows out the candle and stuffs the cookie and candle into her dress pocket.* CHICK, *twenty-nine, enters from the back door. She is a brightly dressed matron with yellow hair and shiny red lips.)*

CHICK: Hi! I saw your car pull up.

LENNY: Hi.

CHICK: Well, did you see today's paper?

*(*LENNY *nods.)*

CHICK: It's just too awful! It's just way too awful! How I'm gonna continue holding my head up high in this community, I do not know. Did you remember to pick up those pantyhose for me?

LENNY: They're in the sack.

CHICK: Well thank goodness, at least I'm not gonna have to go into town wearing holes in my stockings.

(She gets the package, tears it open, and proceeds to take off one pair of stockings and put on another throughout the following scene. There should be something slightly grotesque about this woman changing her stockings in the kitchen.)

LENNY: Did Uncle Watson call?

CHICK: Yes, Daddy has called me twice already. He said Babe's ready to come home. We've got to get right over and pick her up before they change their simple minds.

LENNY: *(Hesitantly)* Oh, I know, of course, it's just—

CHICK: What?

LENNY: Well, I was hoping Meg would call.

CHICK: Meg?

LENNY: Yes, I sent her a telegram: about Babe, and—

CHICK: A telegram?! Couldn't you just phone her up?

LENNY: Well, no, 'cause her phone's...out of order.

CHICK: Out of order?

LENNY: Disconnected. I don't know what.

CHICK: Well, that sounds like Meg. My, these are snug. Are you sure you bought my right size?

LENNY: *(Looking at box)* Size extra-petite.

CHICK: Well, they're skimping on the nylon material. *(Struggling to pull up the stockings)* That's all there is to it. Skimping on the nylon. *(She finishes one leg and starts the other.)* Now, just what all did you say in this "telegram" to Meg?

LENNY: I don't recall exactly. I, well, I just told her to come on home.

CHICK: To come on home? Why, Lenora Josephine, have you lost your only brain, or what?

LENNY: *(Nervously, as she begins to pick up the mess of dirty stockings and plastic wrappings)* But Babe wants Meg home. She asked me to call her.

CHICK: I'm not talking about what Babe wants.

LENNY: Well, what then?

CHICK: Listen, Lenora, I think it's pretty accurate to assume that after this morning's paper, Babe's gonna be incurring some mighty negative publicity around this town. And Meg's appearance isn't gonna help out a bit.

LENNY: What's wrong with Meg?

CHICK: She had a loose reputation in high school.

LENNY: *(Weakly)* She was popular.

CHICK: She was known all over Copiah County as cheap Christmas trash, and that was the least of it. There was that whole sordid affair with Doc Porter, leaving him a cripple.

LENNY: A cripple—he's got a limp. Just kind of, barely a limp.

CHICK: Well, his mother was going to keep me out of the Ladies' Social League because of it.

LENNY: What?

CHICK: That's right. I never told you, but I had to go plead with that mean old woman and convince her that I was just as appalled with what Meg had done as she was, and that I was only a first cousin anyway and I could hardly be blamed for all the skeletons in the MaGraths' closet. It was humiliating. I tell you, she even brought up your mother's death. And that poor cat.

LENNY: Oh! Oh! Oh, please, Chick! I'm sorry. But you're in the Ladies' League now.

CHICK: Yes. That's true, I am. But frankly, if Mrs. Porter hadn't developed that tumor in her bladder, I wouldn't be in the club today, much less a committee head. *(As she brushes her hair)* Anyway, you be a sweet potato and wait right here for Meg to call, so's you can convince her not to come back home. It would make things a whole lot easier on everybody. Don't you think it really would?

LENNY: Probably.

CHICK: Good, then suit yourself. How's my hair?

LENNY: Fine.

CHICK: Not pooching out in the back, is it?

LENNY: No.

CHICK: *(Cleaning the hair from her brush)* All right then, I'm on my way. I've got Annie May over there keeping an eye on Peekay and Buck Jr., but I don't trust her with them for long periods of time. *(Dropping the ball of hair onto the floor)* Her mind is like a loose sieve. Honestly it is. *(As she puts the brush back into her purse.)* Oh! Oh! Oh! I almost forgot. Here's a present for you. Happy Birthday to Lenny, from the Buck Boyles! *(She takes a wrapped package from her bag and hands it to* LENNY.*)*

LENNY: Why, thank you, Chick. It's so nice to have you remember my birthday every year like you do.

CHICK: *(Modestly)* Oh, well, now, that's just the way I am, I suppose. That's just the way I was brought up to be. Well, why don't you go on and open up the present?

LENNY: All right. *(She starts to unwrap the gift.)*

CHICK: It's a box of candy—assorted cremes.

LENNY: Candy—that's always a nice gift.

CHICK: And you have a sweet tooth, don't you?

LENNY: I guess.

CHICK: Well, I'm glad you like it.

LENNY: I do.

CHICK: Oh, speaking of which, remember that little polka-dot dress you got Peekay for her fifth birthday last month?

LENNY: The red-and-white one?

CHICK: Yes; well, the first time I put it in the washing machine, I mean the very first time, it fell all to pieces. Those little polka-dots just dropped right off in the water.

LENNY: *(Crushed)* Oh, no. Well, I'll get something else for her, then—a little toy.

CHICK: Oh, no, no, no, no, no! We wouldn't hear of it! I just wanted to let you know so you wouldn't go and waste any more of your hard-earned money on that make of dress. Those inexpensive brands just don't hold up. I'm sorry, but not in these modern washing machines.

DOC PORTER'S VOICE: Hello! Hello, Lenny!

CHICK: *(Taking over)* Oh, look, it's Doc Porter! Come on in, Doc! Please come right on in!

(DOC PORTER *enters through the back door. He is carrying a large sack of pecans. Doc is an attractively worn man with a slight limp that adds rather than detracts from his quiet, seductive quality. He is thirty years old, but appears slightly older.*)

CHICK: Well, how are you doing? How in the world are you doing?

DOC: Just fine, Chick.

CHICK: And how are you liking it now that you're back in Hazlehurst?

DOC: Oh, I'm finding it somewhat enjoyable.

CHICK: Somewhat! Only somewhat! Will you listen to him! What a silly, silly, silly man! Well, I'm on my way. I've got some people waiting on me. *(Whispering to* DOC*)* It's Babe. I'm on my way to pick her up.

DOC: Oh.

CHICK: Well, goodbye! Farewell and goodbye!

LENNY: 'Bye.

(CHICK *exits.*)

DOC: Hello.

LENNY: Hi. I guess you heard about the thing with Babe.

DOC: Yeah.

LENNY: It was in the newspaper.

DOC: Uh huh.

LENNY: What a mess.

DOC: Yeah.

LENNY: Well, come on and sit down. I'll heat us up some coffee.

DOC: That's okay. I can only stay a minute. I have to pick up Scott; he's at the dentist.

LENNY: Oh; well, I'll heat some up for myself. I'm kinda thirsty for a cup of hot coffee. *(She puts the coffeepot on the burner.)*

DOC: Lenny—

LENNY: What?

DOC: *(Not able to go on)* Ah...

LENNY: Yes?

DOC: Here, some pecans for you. *(He hands her the sack.)*

LENNY: Why, thank you, Doc. I love pecans.

DOC: My wife and Scott picked them up around the yard.

LENNY: Well, I can use them to make a pie. A pecan pie.

DOC: Yeah. Look, Lenny, I've got some bad news for you.

LENNY: What?

DOC: Well, you know, you've been keeping Billy Boy out on our farm; he's been grazing out there.

LENNY: Yes—

DOC: Well, last night, Billy Boy died.

LENNY: He died?

DOC: Yeah. I'm sorry to tell you when you've got all this on you, but I thought you'd want to know.

LENNY: Well, yeah. I do. He died?

DOC: Uh huh. He was struck by lightning.

LENNY: Struck by lightning? In that storm yesterday?

DOC: That's what we think.

LENNY: Gosh, struck by lightning. I've had Billy Boy so long. You know. Ever since I was ten years old.

DOC: Yeah. He was a mighty old horse.

LENNY: *(Stung)* Mighty old.

DOC: Almost twenty years old.

LENNY: That's right, twenty years. 'Cause; ah, I'm thirty years old today. Did you know that?

DOC: No, Lenny, I didn't know. Happy birthday.

LENNY: Thanks. *(She begins to cry.)*

DOC: Oh, come on now, Lenny. Come on. Hey, hey, now. You know I can't stand it when you MaGrath women start to cry. You know it just gets me.

LENNY: Oh ho! Sure! You mean when Meg cries! Meg's the one you could never stand to watch cry! Not me! I could fill up a pig's trough!

DOC: Now, Lenny...stop it. Come on. Jesus!

LENNY: Okay! Okay! I don't know what's wrong with me. I don't mean to make a scene. I've been on this crying jag. *(She blows her nose.)* All this stuff with Babe, and Old Granddaddy's gotten worse in the hospital, and I can't get in touch with Meg.

DOC: You tried calling Meggy?

LENNY: Yes.

DOC: Is she coming home?

LENNY: Who knows. She hasn't called me. That's what I'm waiting here for—hoping she'll call.

DOC: She still living in California?

LENNY: Yes; in Hollywood.

DOC: Well, give me a call if she gets in. I'd like to see her.

LENNY: Oh, you would, huh?

DOC: Yeah, Lenny, sad to say, but I would.

LENNY: It is sad. It's very sad indeed.

(They stare at each other, then look away. There is a moment of tense silence.)

DOC: Hey, Jell-O Face, your coffee's boiling.

LENNY: *(Going to check)* Oh, it is? Thanks. *(After she checks the pot)* Look, you'd better go on and pick Scott up. You don't want him to have to wait for you.

Doc: Yeah, you're right. Poor kid. It's his first time at the dentist.

Lenny: Poor thing.

Doc: Well, bye. I'm sorry to have to tell you about your horse.

Lenny: Oh, I know. Tell Joan thanks for picking up the pecans.

Doc: I will. *(He starts to leave.)*

Lenny: Oh, how's the baby?

Doc: She's fine. Real pretty. She, ah, holds your finger in her hand; like this.

Lenny: Oh, that's cute.

Doc: Yeah. 'Bye, Lenny.

Lenny: 'Bye.

(Doc exits. Lenny stares after him for a moment, then goes and sits back down at the kitchen table. She reaches into her pocket and pulls out a somewhat crumbled cookie and a wax candle. She lights the candle again, lets the wax drip onto the cookie, then sticks the candle on top of the cookie. She begins to sing the "Happy Birthday" song to herself. At the end of the song she pauses, silently makes a wish, and blows out the candle. She waits a moment, then relights the candle, and repeats her actions, only this time making a different wish at the end of the song. She starts to repeat the procedure for the third time, as the phone rings. She goes to answer it.)

Lenny: Hello...Oh, hello, Lucille, how's Zackery?...Oh, no!...Oh, I'm so sorry. Of course, it must be grueling for you...Yes, I understand. Your only brother...No, she's not here yet. Chick just went to pick her up...Oh, now, Lucille, she's still his wife, I'm sure she'll be interested...Well, you can just tell me the information and I'll relate it all to her...Uh hum, his liver's saved. Oh, that's good news!...Well, of course, when you look at it like that... Breathing stabilized...Damage to the spinal column, not yet determined... Okay...Yes, Lucille, I've got it all down...Uh huh, I'll give her that message. 'Bye, 'bye.

(Lenny drops the pencil and paper. She sighs deeply, wipes her cheeks with the back of her hand, and goes to the stove to pour herself a cup of coffee. After a few moments, the front door is heard slamming. Lenny starts. A whistle is heard, then Meg's voice.)

Meg's Voice: I'm home! *(She whistles the family whistle.)* Anybody home?!

Lenny: Meg? Meg!

(Meg, twenty-seven, enters from the dining room. She has sad, magic eyes, and wears a hat. She carries a worn-out suitcase.)

Meg: *(Dropping her suitcase, running to hug Lenny)* Lenny—

LENNY: Well, Meg! Why, Meg! Oh, Meggy! Why didn't you call! Did you fly in? You didn't take a cab, did you? Why didn't you give us a call?

MEG: *(Overlapping)* Oh, Lenny! Why, Lenny! Dear Lenny! *(Then she looks at LENNY's face.)* My God, we're getting so old! Oh, I called, for heaven's sake. Of course, I called!

LENNY: Well, I never talked to you—

MEG: Well, I know! I let the phone ring right off the hook!

LENNY: Well, as a matter of fact, I was out most of the morning seeing to Babe.

MEG: Now, just what's all this business about Babe? How could you send me such a telegram about Babe? And Zackery! You say somebody's shot Zackery?

LENNY: Yes, they have.

MEG: Well, good Lord! Is he dead?

LENNY: No. But he's in the hospital. He was shot in his stomach.

MEG: In his stomach! How awful! Do they know who shot him? *(LENNY nods.)* Well, who? Who was it? Who? Who?

LENNY: Babe! They're all saying Babe shot him! They took her to jail! And they're saying she shot him! They're all saying it! It's horrible! It's awful!

MEG: *(Overlapping)* Jail! Good Lord, jail! Well, who? Who's saying it? Who?

LENNY: Everyone! The policemen, the sheriff, Zackery, even Babe's saying it! Even Babe herself!

MEG: Well, for God's sake. For God's sake.

LENNY: *(Overlapping, as she falls apart)* It's horrible! It's horrible! It's just horrible!

MEG: Now calm down, Lenny. Just calm down. Would you like a Coke? Here, I'll get you some Coke. *(She gets a Coke from the refrigerator. She opens it and downs a large swig.)* Why? Why would she shoot him? Why? *(She hands the Coke bottle to LENNY.)*

LENNY: I talked to her this morning and I asked her that very question. I said, "Babe, why would you shoot Zackery? He was your own husband. Why would you shoot him?" And do you know what she said? *(MEG shakes her head.)* She said, "'Cause I didn't like his looks. I just didn't like his looks."

MEG: *(After a pause)* Well, I don't like his looks.

LENNY: But you didn't shoot him! You wouldn't shoot a person 'cause you didn't like their looks! You wouldn't do that! Oh, I hate to say this—I do hate to say this—but I believe Babe is ill. I mean in-her-head ill.

MEG: Oh, now, Lenny, don't you say that! There're plenty of good sane reasons to shoot another person, and I'm sure that Babe had one. Now, what we've got to do is get her the best lawyer in town. Do you have any ideas on who's the best lawyer in town?

LENNY: Well, Zackery is, of course; but he's been shot!

MEG: Well, count him out! Just count him and his whole firm out!

LENNY: Anyway, you don't have to worry, she's already got her lawyer.

MEG: She does? Who?

LENNY: Barnette Lloyd. Annie Lloyd's boy. He just opened his office here in town. And Uncle Watson said we'd be doing Annie a favor by hiring him up.

MEG: Doing Annie a favor? Doing Annie a favor! Well, what about Babe? Have you thought about Babe? Do we want to do her a favor of thirty or forty years in jail? Have you thought about that?

LENNY: Now, don't snap at me! Just don't snap at me! I try to do what's right! All this responsibility keeps falling on my shoulders, and I try to do what's right!

MEG: Well, boo hoo, hoo, hoo! And how in the hell could you send me such a telegram about Babe!

LENNY: Well, if you had a phone, or if you didn't live way out there in Hollywood and not even come home for Christmas, maybe I wouldn't have to pay all that money to send you a telegram!

MEG: *(Overlapping)* BABE'S IN TERRIBLE TROUBLE—STOP! ZACKERY'S BEEN SHOT—STOP! COME HOME IMMEDIATELY—STOP! STOP! STOP!

LENNY: And what was that you said about how old we're getting? When you looked at my face, you said, "My God, we're getting so old!" But you didn't mean we—you meant me! Didn't you? I'm thirty years old today and my face is getting all pinched up and my hair is falling out in the comb.

MEG: Why, Lenny! It's your birthday, October 23. How could I forget. Happy Birthday!

LENNY: Well, it's not. I'm thirty years old and Billy Boy died last night. He was struck by lightning. He was struck dead.

MEG: *(Reaching for a cigarette)* Struck dead. Oh, what a mess. What a mess. Are you really thirty? Then I must be twenty-seven and Babe is twenty-four. My God, we're getting so old.

(They are silent for several moments as MEG drags on her cigarette and LENNY drinks her Coke.)

MEG: What's the cot doing in the kitchen?

LENNY: Well, I rolled it out when Old Granddaddy got sick. So I could be close and hear him at night if he needed something.

MEG: *(Glancing toward the door leading to the downstairs bedroom)* Is Old Granddaddy here?

LENNY: Why, no. Old Granddaddy's at the hospital.

MEG: Again?

LENNY: Meg!

MEG: What?

LENNY: I wrote you all about it. He's been in the hospital for over three months straight.

MEG: He has?

LENNY: Don't you remember? I wrote you about all those blood vessels popping in his brain?

MEG: Popping—

LENNY: And how he was so anxious to hear from you and to find out about your singing career. I wrote it all to you. How they have to feed him through those tubes now. Didn't you get my letters?

MEG: Oh, I don't know, Lenny. I guess I did. To tell you the truth, sometimes I kinda don't read your letters.

LENNY: What?

MEG: I'm sorry. I used to read them. It's just, since Christmas, reading them gives me these slicing pains right here in my chest.

LENNY: I see. I see. Is that why you didn't use that money Old Granddaddy sent you to come home Christmas—because you hate us so much? We never did all that much to make you hate us. We didn't!

MEG: Oh, Lenny! Do you think I'd be getting slicing pains in my chest if I didn't care about you? If I hated you? Honestly, now, do you think I would?

LENNY: No.

MEG: Okay, then. Let's drop it. I'm sorry I didn't read your letters. Okay?

LENNY: Okay.

MEG: Anyway, we've got this whole thing with Babe to deal with. The first thing is to get her a good lawyer and get her out of jail.

LENNY: Well, she's out of jail.

MEG: She is?

LENNY: That young lawyer, he's gotten her out.

MEG: Oh, he has?

LENNY: Yes, on bail. Uncle Watson's put it up. Chick's bringing her back right now—she's driving her home.

MEG: Oh; well, that's a relief.

LENNY: Yes, and they're due home any minute now; so we can just wait right here for 'em.

MEG: Well, good. That's good. *(As she leans against the counter)* So, Babe shot Zackery Botrelle, the richest and most powerful man in all of Hazlehurst, slap in the gut. It's hard to believe.

LENNY: It certainly is. Little Babe—shooting off a gun.

MEG: Little Babe.

LENNY: She was always the prettiest and most perfect of the three of us. Old Granddaddy used to call her his Dancing Sugar Plum. Why, remember how proud and happy he was the day she married Zackery?

MEG: Yes, I remember. It was his finest hour.

LENNY: He remarked how Babe was gonna skyrocket right to the heights of Hazlehurst society. And how Zackery was just the right man for her whether she knew it or not.

MEG: Oh, Lordy, Lordy. And what does Old Granddaddy say now?

LENNY: Well, I haven't had the courage to tell him all about this as yet. I thought maybe tonight we could go to visit him in the hospital, and you could talk to him and...

MEG: Yeah; well, we'll see. We'll see. Do we have anything to drink around here—to the tune of straight bourbon?

LENNY: No. There's no liquor.

MEG: Hell. *(She gets a Coke from the refrigerator and opens it.)*

LENNY: Then you will go with me to see Old Granddaddy at the hospital tonight?

MEG: Of course. *(She goes to her purse and gets out a bottle of Empirin. She takes out a tablet and puts it on her tongue.)* Brother, I know he's gonna go on about my singing career. Just like he always does.

LENNY: Well, how is your career going?

MEG: It's not.

LENNY: Why, aren't you still singing at that club down on Malibu beach?

MEG: No. Not since Christmas.

LENNY: Well, then, are you singing someplace new?

MEG: No, I'm not singing. I'm not singing at all.

LENNY: Oh. Well, what do you do then?

MEG: What I do is I pay cold-storage bills for a dog-food company. That's what I do.

LENNY: *(Trying to be helpful)* Gosh, don't you think it'd be a good idea to stay in the show business field?

MEG: Oh, maybe.

LENNY: Like Old Granddaddy's says, "With your talent, all you need is exposure. Then you can make your own breaks!" Did you hear his suggestion about your getting your foot put in one of those blocks of cement they've got out there? He thinks that's real important.

MEG: Yeah. I think I've heard that. And I'll probably hear it again when I go to visit him at the hospital tonight; so let's just drop it. Okay? *(She notices the sack of pecans.)* What's this? Pecans? Great, I love pecans! *(She takes out two pecans and tries to open them by cracking them together.)* Come on....Crack, you demons! Crack!

LENNY: We have a nutcracker!

MEG: *(Trying with her teeth)* Ah, where's the sport in a nutcracker? Where's the challenge?

LENNY: *(Getting the nutcracker)* It's over here in the utensil drawer.

(As LENNY *gets the nutcracker* MEG *opens the pecan by stepping on it with her shoe.)*

MEG: There! Open! *(She picks up the crumbled pecan and eats it.)* Mmmm, delicious. Delicious. Where'd you get the fresh pecans?

LENNY: Oh...I don't know.

MEG: They sure are tasty.

LENNY: Doc Porter brought them over.

MEG: Doc. What's Doc doing here in town?

LENNY: Well, his father died a couple of months ago. Now he's back home seeing to his property.

MEG: Gosh, the last I heard of Doc, he was up in the East painting the walls of houses to earn a living. *(Amused)* Heard he was living with some Yankee woman who made clay pots.

LENNY: Joan.

MEG: What?

LENNY: Her name's Joan. She came down here with him. That's one of her pots. Doc's married to her.

MEG: Married—

LENNY: Uh huh.

MEG: Doc married a Yankee?

LENNY: That's right; and they've got two kids.

MEG: Kids—

LENNY: A boy and a girl.

MEG: God. Then his kids must be half Yankee.

LENNY: I suppose.

MEG: God. That really gets me. I don't know why, but somehow that really gets me.

LENNY: I don't know why it should.

MEG: And what a stupid-looking pot! Who'd buy it, anyway?

LENNY: Wait—I think that's them. Yeah, that's Chick's car! Oh, there's Babe! Hello, Babe! They're home, Meg! They're home.

(MEG *hides.*)

BABE'S VOICE: Lenny! I'm home! I'm free!

(BABE, *twenty-four, enters exuberantly. She has an angelic face and fierce, volatile eyes. She carries a pink pocketbook.*)

BABE: I'm home!

(MEG *jumps out of hiding.*)

BABE: Oh, Meg—Look, it's Meg! *(Running to hug her)* Meg! When did you get home?

MEG: Just now!

BABE: Well, it's so good to see you! I'm so glad you're home! I'm so relieved.

(CHICK *enters.*)

MEG: Why, Chick; hello.

CHICK: Hello, Cousin Margaret. What brings you back to Hazlehurst?

MEG: Oh, I came on home...*(Turning to* BABE*)* I came on home to see about Babe.

BABE: *(Running to hug* MEG*)* Oh, Meg—

MEG: How are things with you, Babe?

CHICK: Well, they are dismal, if you want my opinion. She is refusing to cooperate with her lawyer, that nice-looking young Lloyd boy. She won't tell any of us why she committed this heinous crime, except to say that she didn't like Zackery's looks—

BABE: Oh, look, Lenny brought my suitcase from home! And my saxophone! Thank you! *(She runs over to the cot and gets out her saxophone.)*

CHICK: Now, that young lawyer is coming over here this afternoon, and when he gets here he expects to get some concrete answers! That's what he expects! No more of this nonsense and stubbornness from you, Rebecca MaGrath, or they'll put you in jail and throw away the key!

BABE: *(Overlapping, to* MEG*)* Meg, come look at my new saxophone. I went to Jackson and bought it used. Feel it. It's so heavy.

MEG: *(Overlapping* CHICK*)* It's beautiful.

(The room goes silent.)

CHICK: Isn't that right, won't they throw away the key?

LENNY: Well, honestly, I don't know about that—

CHICK: They will! And leave you there to rot. So, Rebecca, what are you going to tell Mr. Lloyd about shooting Zackery when he gets here? What are your reasons going to be?

BABE: *(Glaring)* That I didn't like his looks! I just didn't like his stinking looks! And I don't like yours much, either, Chick the Stick! So just leave me alone! I mean it! Leave me alone! Oooh!

*(*BABE *exits up the stairs. There is a long moment of silence.)*

CHICK: Well, I was only trying to warn her that she's going to have to help herself. It's just that she doesn't understand how serious the situation is. Does she? She doesn't have the vaguest idea. Does she, now?

LENNY: Well, it's true, she does seem a little confused.

CHICK: And that's putting it mildly, Lenny honey. That's putting it mighty mild. So, Margaret, how's your singing career going? We keep looking for your picture in the movie magazines.

*(*MEG *moves to light a cigarette.)*

CHICK: You know, you shouldn't smoke. It causes cancer. Cancer of the lungs. They say each cigarette is just a little stick of cancer. A little death stick.

MEG: That's what I like about it, Chick—taking a drag off of death. *(She takes a long, deep drag.)* Mmm! Gives me a sense of controlling my own destiny. What power! What exhilaration! Want a drag?

LENNY: *(Trying to break the tension)* Ah, Zackery's liver's been saved! His sister called up and said his liver was saved. Isn't that good news?

CHICK: Well, yes, that's fine news. Mighty fine news. Why, I've been told that the liver's a powerful important bodily organ. I believe it's used to absorb all of our excess bile.

LENNY: Yes—well—it's been saved.

(The phone rings. LENNY gets it.)

MEG: So! Did you hear all that good news about the liver, Little Chicken?

CHICK: I heard it. And don't you call me Chicken! *(MEG clucks like a chicken.)* I've told you a hundred times if I've told you once not to call me Chicken. You cannot call me Chicken.

LENNY: ...Oh no!...Of course, we'll be right over! 'Bye! *(She hangs up the phone.)* That was Annie May—Peekay and Buck Jr. have eaten paint!

CHICK: Oh, no! Are they all right? They're not sick? They're not sick, are they?

LENNY: I don't know. I don't know. Come on. We've got to run on next door.

CHICK: *(Overlapping)* Oh, God! Oh, please! Please let them be all right! Don't let them die! Please, don't let them die!

(CHICK runs off howling, with LENNY following after. MEG sits alone, finishing her cigarette. After a moment, BABE's voice is heard.)

BABE'S VOICE: Pst—Psst!

(MEG looks around. BABE comes tiptoeing down the stairs.)

BABE: Has she gone?

MEG: She's gone. Peekay and Buck Jr. just ate their paints.

BABE: What idiots.

MEG: Yeah.

BABE: You know, Chick's hated us ever since we had to move here from Vicksburg to live with Old Grandmama and Old Granddaddy.

MEG: She's an idiot.

BABE: Yeah. Do you know what she told me this morning while I was still behind bars and couldn't get away?

MEG: What?

BABE: She told me how embarrassing it was for her all those years ago, you know, when Mama—

MEG: Yeah, down in the cellar.

BABE: She said our mama had shamed the entire family, and we were known notoriously all through Hazlehurst. *(About to cry)* Then she went on to say how I would now be getting just as much bad publicity, and humiliating her and the family all over again.

MEG: Ah, forget it, Babe. Just forget it.

BABE: I told her, "Mama got national coverage! National!" And if Zackery wasn't a senator from Copiah County, I probably wouldn't even be getting statewide.

MEG: Of course you wouldn't.

BABE: *(After a pause)* Gosh, sometimes I wonder...

MEG: What?

BABE: Why she did it. Why Mama hung herself.

MEG: I don't know. She had a bad day. A real bad day. You know how it feels on a real bad day.

BABE: And that old yellow cat. It was sad about that old yellow cat.

BABE: I bet if Daddy hadn't of left us, they'd still be alive.

MEG: Oh, I don't know.

BABE: 'Cause it was after he left that she started spending whole days just sitting there and smoking on the back porch steps. She'd sling her ashes down onto the different bugs and ants that'd be passing by.

MEG: Yeah. Well, I'm glad he left.

BABE: That old yellow cat'd stay back there with her. I thought if she felt something for anyone it woulda been that old cat. Guess I musta been mistaken.

MEG: God, he was a bastard. Really, with his white teeth. Daddy was such a bastard.

BABE: Was he? I don't remember.

(MEG *blows out a mouthful of smoke.*)

BABE: *(After a moment, uneasily)* I think I'm gonna make some lemonade. You want some?

MEG: Sure.

(BABE *cuts lemons, dumps sugar, stirs ice cubes, etc., throughout the following exchange.*)

MEG: Babe. Why won't you talk? Why won't you tell anyone about shooting Zackery?

BABE: Oooh—

MEG: Why not? You must have had a good reason. Didn't you?

BABE: I guess I did.

MEG: Well, what was it?

BABE: I...I can't say.

MEG: Why not? *(Pause)* Babe, why not? You can tell me.

BABE: 'Cause...I'm sort of...protecting someone.

MEG: Protecting someone? Oh, Babe, then you really didn't shoot him! I knew you couldn't have done it! I knew it!

BABE: No, I shot him. I shot him all right. I meant to kill him. I was aiming for his heart, but I guess my hands were shaking and I—just got him in the stomach.

MEG: *(Collapsing)* I see.

BABE: *(Stirring the lemonade)* So I'm guilty. And I'm just gonna have to take my punishment and go on to jail.

MEG: Oh, Babe—

BABE: Don't worry, Meg, jail's gonna be a relief to me. I can learn to play my new saxophone. I won't have to live with Zackery anymore. And I won't have his snoopy old sister, Lucille, coming over and pushing me around. Jail will be a relief. Here's your lemonade.

MEG: Thanks.

BABE: It taste okay?

MEG: Perfect.

BABE: I like a lot of sugar in mine. I'm gonna add some more sugar.

(BABE *goes to add more sugar to her lemonade as* LENNY *bursts through the back door in a state of excitement and confusion.*)

LENNY: Well, it looks like the paint is primarily on their arms and faces, but Chick wants me to drive them all over to Dr. Winn's just to make sure. *(She grabs her car keys from the counter, and as she does so, she notices the mess of lemons and sugar.)* Oh, now, Babe, try not to make a mess here; and be careful with this sharp knife. Honestly, all that sugar's gonna get you sick. Well, 'bye, 'bye. I'll be back as soon as I can.

MEG: 'Bye, Lenny.

BABE: 'Bye.

(LENNY *exits.*)

BABE: Boy, I don't know what's happening to Lenny.

MEG: What do you mean?

BABE: "Don't make a mess; don't make yourself sick; don't cut yourself with that sharp knife." She's turning into Old Grandmama.

MEG: You think so?

BABE: More and more. Do you know she's taken to wearing Old Grandmama's torn sunhat and her green garden gloves?

MEG: Those old lime-green ones?

BABE: Yeah; she works out in the garden wearing the lime-green gloves of a dead woman. Imagine wearing those gloves on your hands.

MEG: Poor Lenny. She needs some love in her life. All she does is work out at that brick yard and take care of Old Granddaddy.

BABE: Yeah. But she's so shy with men.

MEG: *(Biting into apple)* Probably because of that *shrunken* ovary she has.

BABE: *(Slinging ice cubes)* Yeah, that *deformed* ovary.

MEG: Old Granddaddy's the one who's made her feel self-conscious about it. It's his fault. The old fool.

BABE: It's so sad.

MEG: God—you know what?

BABE: What?

MEG: I bet Lenny's never even slept with a man. Just think, thirty years old and never even had it once.

BABE: *(Slyly)* Oh, I don't know. Maybe she's...had it once.

MEG: She has?

BABE: Maybe. I think so.

MEG: When? When?

BABE: Well...maybe I shouldn't say—

MEG: Babe!

BABE: *(Rapidly telling the story)* All right, then. It was after Old Granddaddy went back to the hospital this second time. Lenny was really in a state of deep depression, I could tell that she was. Then one day she calls me up and asks me to come over and to bring along my Polaroid camera. Well, when I arrive she's waiting for me out there in the sun parlor wearing her powder-blue Sunday dress and this old curled-up wig. She confided that she was gonna try sending in her picture to one of those lonely-hearts clubs.

MEG: Oh, my God.

BABE: Lonely Hearts of the South. She'd seen their ad in a magazine.

MEG: Jesus.

BABE: Anyway, I take some snapshots and she sends them on in to the club, and about two weeks later she receives in the mail this whole load of pictures of available men, most of 'em fairly odd-looking. But of course she doesn't call any of 'em up 'cause she's real shy. But one of 'em, this Charlie Hill from Memphis, Tennessee, he calls her.

MEG: He does?

BABE: Yeah. And time goes on and she says he's real funny on the phone, so they decide to get together to meet.

MEG: Yeah?

BABE: Well, he drives down here to Hazlehurst 'bout three or four different times and has supper with her; then one weekend she goes up to Memphis to visit him, and I think that is where it happened.

MEG: What makes you think so?

BABE: Well, when I went to pick her up from the bus depot, she ran off the bus and threw her arms around me and started crying and sobbing as though she'd like to never stop. I asked her, I said, "Lenny, what's the matter?" And she said, "I've done it, Babe! Honey, I have done it!"

MEG: *(Whispering)* And you think she meant that she'd done *it?*

BABE: *(Whispering back, slyly)* I think so.

MEG: Well, goddamn!

(They laugh.)

BABE: But she didn't say anything else about it. She just went on to tell me about the boot factory where Charlie worked and what a nice city Memphis was.

MEG: So, what happened to this Charlie?

BABE: Well, he came to Hazlehurst just one more time. Lenny took him over to meet Old Granddaddy at the hospital, and after that they broke it off.

MEG: 'Cause of Old Granddaddy?

BABE: Well, she said it was on account of her missing ovary. That Charlie didn't want to marry her on account of it.

MEG: Ah, how mean. How hateful.

BABE: Oh, it was. He seemed like such a nice man, too—kinda chubby, with red hair and freckles, always telling these funny jokes.

MEG: Hmmm, that just doesn't seem right. Something about that doesn't seem exactly right. *(She paces about the kitchen and comes across the box of candy* LENNY *got for her birthday.)* Oh, God. "Happy Birthday to Lenny, from the Buck Boyles."

BABE: Oh, no! Today's Lenny's birthday!

MEG: That's right.

BABE: I forgot all about it!

MEG: I know. I did, too.

BABE: Gosh, we'll have to order up a big cake for her. She always loves to make those wishes on her birthday cake.

MEG: Yeah, let's get her a big cake! A huge one! *(Suddenly, noticing the plastic wrapper on the candy box)* Oh, God, that Chick's so cheap!

BABE: What do you mean?

MEG: This plastic has poinsettias on it!

BABE: *(Running to see)* Oh, let me see—*(She looks at the package with disgust.)* Boy, oh, boy! I'm calling that bakery and ordering the very largest cake size they have! That jumbo deluxe!

MEG: Good!

BABE: Why, I imagine they can make one up to be about *this* big. *(She demonstrates.)*

MEG: Oh, at least; at least that big. Why, maybe it'll even be *this* big. *(She makes a very, very, very large-size cake.)*

BABE: You think it could be *that* big?

MEG: Sure!

BABE: *(After a moment, getting the idea)* Or, or what if it were *this* big? *(She maps out a cake that covers the room.)* What if we get the cake and it's *this* big? *(She gulps down a fistful of cake.)* Gulp! Gulp! Gulp! Tasty treat!

MEG: Hmmm—I'll have me some more! Give me some more of that birthday cake!

(Suddenly there is a loud knock at the door.)

BARNETTE'S VOICE: Hello...Hello! May I come in?

BABE: *(To MEG, in a whisper, as she takes cover)* Who's that?

MEG: I don't know.

BARNETTE'S VOICE: *(He is still knocking.)* Hello! Hello, Mrs. Botrelle!

BABE: Oh, shoot! It's that lawyer. I don't want to see him.

MEG: Oh, Babe, come on. You've got to see him sometime.

BABE: No, I don't! *(She starts up the stairs.)* Just tell him I died. I'm going upstairs.

MEG: Oh, Babe! Will you come back here!

BABE: *(As she exits)* You talk to him, please, Meg. Please! I just don't want to see him—

MEG: Babe—Babe! Oh, shit...Ah, come on in! Door's open!

(BARNETTE LLOYD, *twenty-six, enters, carrying a briefcase. He is a slender, intelligent young man with an almost fanatical intensity that he subdues by sheer will.*)

BARNETTE: How do you do. I'm Barnette Lloyd.

MEG: Pleased to meet you. I'm Meg MaGrath, Babe's older sister.

BARNETTE: Yes, I know. You're the singer.

MEG: Well, yes...

BARNETTE: I came to hear you five different times when you were singing at that club in Biloxi. Greeny's, I believe was the name of it.

MEG: Yes, Greeny's.

BARNETTE: You were very good. There was something sad and moving about how you sang those songs. It was like you had some sort of vision. Some special sort of vision.

MEG: Well, thank you. You're very kind. Now...about Babe's case—

BARNETTE: Yes?

MEG: We've just got to win it.

BARNETTE: I intend to.

MEG: Of course. But, ah...*(She looks at him.)* Ah, you know, you're very young.

BARNETTE: Yes. I am. I'm young.

MEG: It's just I'm concerned, Mr. Lloyd—

BARNETTE: Barnette. Please.

MEG: Barnette; that, ah, just maybe we need someone with, well, with more experience. Someone totally familiar with all the ins and outs and the this and thats of the legal dealings and such. As that.

BARNETTE: Ah, you have reservations.

MEG: *(Relieved)* Reservations. Yes, I have...reservations.

BARNETTE: Well, possibly it would help you to know that I graduated first in my class from Ole Miss Law School. I also spent three different summers taking advanced courses in criminal law at Harvard Law School. I made A's in all the given courses. I was fascinated!

MEG: I'm sure.

BARNETTE: And even now, I've just completed one year working with Jackson's top criminal law firm, Manchester and Wayne. I was invaluable to them. Indispensable. They offered to double my percentage if I'd stay on; but I refused. I wanted to return to Hazlehurst and open my own office. The reason being, and this is a key point, that I have a personal vendetta to settle with one Zackery F. Botrelle.

MEG: A personal vendetta?

BARNETTE: Yes, ma'am. You are correct. Indeed, I do.

MEG: Hmmm. A personal vendetta...I think I like that. So you have some sort of a personal vendetta to settle with Zackery?

BARNETTE: Precisely. Just between the two of us, I not only intend to keep that sorry s.o.b. from ever being re-elected to the state senate by exposing his shady, criminal dealings; but I also intend to decimate his personal credibility by exposing him as a bully, a brute, and a red-neck thug!

MEG: Well; I can see that you're—fanatical about this.

BARNETTE: Yes, I am. I'm sorry if I seem outspoken. But for some reason I feel I can talk to you...those songs you sang. Excuse me; I feel like a jackass.

MEG: It's all right. Relax. Relax, Barnette. Let me think this out a minute. *(She takes out a cigarette. He lights it for her.)* Now just exactly how do you intend to get Babe off? You know, keep her out of jail.

BARNETTE: It seems to me that we can get her off with a plea of self-defense, or possibly we could go with innocent by reason of temporary insanity. But basically I intend to prove that Zackery Botrelle brutalized and tormented this poor woman to such an extent that she had no recourse but to defend herself in the only way she knew how!

MEG: I like that!

BARNETTE: Then, of course, I'm hoping this will break the ice and we'll be able to go on to prove that the man's a total criminal, as well as an abusive bully and contemptible slob!

MEG: That sounds good! To me that sounds very good!

BARNETTE: It's just our basic game plan.

MEG: But now, how are you going to prove all this about Babe being brutalized? We don't want anyone perjured. I mean to commit perjury.

BARNETTE: Perjury? According to my sources, the'll be no need for perjury.

MEG: You mean it's the truth?

BARNETTE: This is a small town, Miss MaGrath. The word gets out.

MEG: It's really the truth?

BARNETTE: *(Opening his briefcase)* Just look at this. It's a photostatic copy of Mrs. Botrelle's medical chart over the past four years. Take a good look at it, if you want your blood to boil!

MEG: *(Looking over the chart)* What! What! This is maddening. This is madness! Did he do this to her? I'll kill him; I will—I'll fry his blood! Did he do this?

BARNETTE: *(Alarmed)* To tell you the truth, I can't say for certain what was accidental and what was not. That's why I need to talk with Mrs. Botrelle. That's why it's very important that I see her!

MEG: *(Her eyes wild, as she shoves him toward the door)* Well, look, I've got to see her first. I've got to talk to her first. What I'll do is I'll give you a call. Maybe you can come back over later on—

BARNETTE: Well, then, here's my card—

MEG: Okay. Goodbye.

BARNETTE: 'Bye!

MEG: Oh, wait! Wait! There's one problem with you.

BARNETTE: What?

MEG: What if you get so fanatically obsessed with this vendetta thing that you forget about Babe? You forget about her and sell her down the river just to get at Zackery. What about that?

BARNETTE: I—wouldn't do that.

MEG: You wouldn't?

BARNETTE: No.

MEG: Why not?

BARNETTE: Because I'm—I'm fond of her.

MEG: What do you mean you're fond of her?

BARNETTE: Well, she...she sold me a pound cake at a bazaar once. And I'm fond of her.

MEG: All right; I believe you. Goodbye.

BARNETTE: Goodbye. *(He exits.)*

MEG: Babe! Babe, come down here! Babe!

(BABE comes hurrying down the stairs.)

BABE: What? What is it? I called about the cake—

MEG: What did Zackery do to you.

BABE: They can't have it for today.

MEG: Did he hurt you? Did he? Did he do that?

BABE: Oh, Meg, please—

MEG: Did he? Goddamnit, Babe—

BABE: Yes, he did.

MEG: Why? Why?

BABE: I don't know! He started hating me, 'cause I couldn't laugh at his jokes. I just started finding it impossible to laugh at his jokes the way I used to. And then the sound of his voice got to where it tired me out awful bad to hear it. I'd fall asleep just listening to him at the dinner table. He'd say, "Hand me some of that gravy!" Or, "This roast beef is too damn bloody." And suddenly I'd be out cold like a light.

MEG: Oh, Babe. Babe, this is very important. I want you to sit down here and tell me what all happened right before you shot Zackery. That's right, just sit down and tell me.

BABE: *(After a pause)* I told you, I can't tell you on account of I'm protecting someone.

MEG: But, Babe, you've just got to talk to someone about all this. You just do.

BABE: Why?

MEG: Because it's a human need. To talk about our lives. It's an important human need.

BABE: Oh. Well, I do feel like I want to talk to someone. I do.

MEG: Then talk to me; please.

BABE: *(Making a decision)* All right. *(After thinking a minute)* I don't know where to start.

MEG: Just start at the beginning. Just there at the beginning.

BABE: *(After a moment)* Well, do you remember Willie Jay? *(*MEG *shakes her head.)* Cora's youngest boy?

MEG: Oh, yeah, that little kid we used to pay a nickel to, to run down to the drugstore and bring us back a cherry Coke.

BABE: Right. Well, Cora irons at my place on Wednesdays now, and she just happened to mention that Willie Jay'd picked up this old stray dog and that he'd gotten real fond of him. But now they couldn't afford to feed him anymore. So she was gonna have to tell Willie Jay to set him loose in the woods.

MEG: *(Trying to be patient)* Uh huh.

BABE: Well, I said I liked dogs, and if he wanted to bring the dog over here, I'd take care of him. You see, I was alone by myself most of the time 'cause the Senate was in session and Zackery was up in Jackson.

MEG: Uh huh. *(She reaches for* LENNY's *box of birthday candy. She takes little nibbles out of each piece throughout the rest of the scene.)*

BABE: So the next day, Willie Jay brings over this skinny old dog with these little crossed eyes. Well, I asked Willie Jay what his name was, and he said they called him Dog. Well, I liked the name, so I thought I'd keep it.

MEG: *(Getting up)* Uh huh. I'm listening. I'm just gonna get me a glass of cold water. Do you want one?

BABE: Okay.

MEG: So you kept the name—Dog.

BABE: Yeah. Anyway, when Willie Jay was leaving he gave Dog a hug and said, "Goodbye, Dog. You're a fine ole dog." Well, I felt something for him, so I told Willie Jay he could come back and visit with Dog any time he wanted, and his face just kinda lit right up.

MEG: *(Offering the candy)* Candy—

BABE: No, thanks. Anyhow, time goes on and Willie Jay keeps coming over and over. And we talk about Dog and how fat he's getting, and then, well, you know, things start up.

MEG: No, I don't know. What things start up?

BABE: Well, things start up. Like sex. Like that.

MEG: Babe, wait a minute—Willie Jay's a boy. A small boy, about this tall. He's about this tall!

BABE: No! Oh no! He's taller now! He's fifteen now. When you knew him he was only about seven or eight.

MEG: But even so—fifteen. And he's a black boy; a colored boy; a Negro.

BABE: *(Flustered)* Well, I realize that, Meg. Why do you think I'm so worried about his getting public exposure? I don't want to ruin his reputation!

MEG: I'm amazed, Babe. I'm really completely amazed. I didn't even know you were a liberal.

BABE: Well, I'm not! I'm not a liberal! I'm a democratic! I was just lonely! I was so lonely. And he was good. Oh, he was so, so good. I'd never had it that good. We'd always go out in the garage and—

MEG: It's okay. I've got the picture; I've got the picture! Now, let's just get back to the story. To yesterday, when you shot Zackery.

BABE: All right, then. Let's see....Willie Jay was over. And it was after we'd—

MEG: Yeah! Yeah.

BABE: And we were just standing around on the back porch playing with Dog. Well, suddenly Zackery comes from around the side of the house. And he startled me 'cause he's supposed to be away at the office, and there he is coming from round the side of the house. Anyway, he says to Willie Jay, "Hey, boy, what are you doing back here?" And I say, "He's not doing anything. You just go on home, Willie Jay! You just run right on home." Well, before he can move, Zackery comes up and knocks him once right across the face and then shoves him down the porch steps, causing him to skin up his elbow real bad on that hard concrete. Then he says, "Don't you ever come around here again, or I'll have them cut out your gizzard!" Well, Willie Jay starts crying—these tears come streaming down his face—then he gets up real quick and runs away, with Dog following off after him. After that, I don't remember much too clearly; let's see...I went on into the living room, and I went right up to the davenport and opened the drawer where we keep the burglar gun...I took it out. Then I—I brought it up to my ear. That's right. I put it right inside my ear. Why, I was gonna shoot off my own head! That's what I was gonna do. Then I heard the back door slamming and suddenly, for some reason, I thought about Mama...how she'd hung herself. And here I was about ready to shoot myself. Then I realized—that's right, I realized how I didn't want to kill myself! And she—she probably didn't want to kill herself. She wanted to kill him, and I wanted to kill him, too. I wanted to kill Zackery, not myself. 'Cause I—I wanted to live! So I waited for him to come on into the living room. Then I held out the gun, and I pulled the trigger, aiming for his heart but getting him in the stomach. *(After a pause)* It's funny that I really did that.

MEG: It's a good thing that you did. It's a damn good thing that you did.

BABE: It was.

MEG: Please, Babe, talk to Barnette Lloyd. Just talk to him and see if he can help.

BABE: But how about Willie Jay?

MEG: *(Starting toward the phone)* Oh, he'll be all right. You just talk to that lawyer like you did to me. *(Looking at the number on the card, she begins dialing.)* See, 'cause he's gonna be on your side.

BABE: No! Stop, Meg, stop! Don't call him up! Please don't call him up! You can't! It's too awful. *(She runs over and jerks the bottom half of the phone away from* MEG.*)*

*(*MEG *stands, holding the receiver.)*

MEG: Babe!

*(*BABE *slams her half of the phone into the refrigerator.)*

BABE: I just can't tell some stranger all about my personal life. I just can't.

MEG: Well, hell, Babe; you're the one who said you wanted to live.

BABE: That's right. I did. *(She takes the phone out of the refrigerator and hands it to* MEG.*)* Here's the other part of the phone. *(She moves to sit at the kitchen table.)*

*(*MEG *takes the phone back to the counter.)*

BABE: *(As she fishes a piece of lemon out of her glass and begins sucking on it)* Meg.

MEG: What?

BABE: I called the bakery. They're gonna have Lenny's cake ready first thing tomorrow morning. That's the earliest they can get it.

MEG: All right.

BABE: I told them to write on it, "Happy Birthday, Lenny—A Day Late." That sound okay?

MEG: *(At the phone)* It sounds nice.

BABE: I ordered up the very largest size cake they have. I told them chocolate cake with white icing and red trim. Think she'll like that.

MEG: *(Dialing the phone)* Yeah, I'm sure she will. She'll like it.

BABE: I'm hoping.

CURTAIN

END OF ACT ONE

ACT TWO

(The lights go up on the kitchen. It is evening of the same day. MEG's *suitcase has been moved upstairs.* BABE's *saxophone has been taken out of the case and put together.* BABE *and* BARNETTE *are sitting at the kitchen table.* BARNETTE *is writing and rechecking notes with explosive intensity.* BABE, *who has changed into a casual shift, sits eating a bowl of oatmeal, slowly.)*

BARNETTE: *(To himself)* Mmm huh! Yes! I see, I see! Well, we can work on that! And of course, this is mere conjecture! Difficult, if not impossible, to prove. Ha! Yes, indeed. Indeed—

BABE: Sure you don't want any oatmeal?

BARNETTE: What? Oh, no. No, thank you. Let's see; ah, where were we?

BABE: I just shot Zackery.

BARNETTE: *(Looking at his notes)* Right. Correct. You've just pulled the trigger.

BABE: Tell me, do you think Willie Jay can stay out of all this?

BARNETTE: Believe me, it is in our interest to keep him as far out of this as possible.

BABE: Good.

BARNETTE: *(Throughout the following,* BARNETTE *stays glued to* BABE's *every word.)* All right, you've just shot one Zackery Botrelle, as a result of his continual physical and mental abuse—what happens now?

BABE: Well, after I shot him, I put the gun down on the piano bench, and then I went out into the kitchen and made up a pitcher of lemonade.

BARNETTE: Lemonade?

BABE: Yes, I was dying of thirst. My mouth was just as dry as a bone.

BARNETTE: So in order to quench this raging thirst that was choking you dry and preventing any possibility of you uttering intelligible sounds or phrases, you went out to the kitchen and made up a pitcher of lemonade?

BABE: Right. I made it just the way I like it, with lots of sugar and lots of lemon—about ten lemons in all. Then I added two trays of ice and stirred it up with my wooden stirring spoon.

BARNETTE: Then what?

BABE: Then I drank three glasses, one right after the other. They were large glasses—about this tall. Then suddenly my stomach kind of swole all up. I guess what caused it was all that sour lemon.

BARNETTE: Could be.

BABE: Then what I did was...I wiped my mouth off with the back of my hand, like this...*(She demonstrates.)*

BARNETTE: Hmmm.

BABE: I did it to clear off all those little beads of water that had settled there.

BARNETTE: I see.

BABE: Then I called out to Zackery. I said, "Zackery, I've made some lemonade. Can you use a glass?"

BARNETTE: Did he answer? Did you hear an answer?

BABE: No. He didn't answer.

BARNETTE: So what'd you do?

BABE: I poured him a glass anyway and took it out to him.

BARNETTE: You took it out to the living room?

BABE: I did. And there he was, lying on the rug. He was looking up at me trying to speak words. I said, "What?...Lemonade?...You don't want it? Would you like a Coke instead?" Then I got the idea—he was telling me to call on the phone for medical help. So I got on the phone and called up the hospital. I gave my name and address, and I told them my husband was shot and he was lying on the rug and there was plenty of blood. *(She pauses a minute, as BARNETTE works frantically on his notes.)* I guess that's gonna look kinda bad.

BARNETTE: What?

BABE: Me fixing that lemonade before I called the hospital.

BARNETTE: Well, not...necessarily.

BABE: I tell you, I think the reason I made up the lemonade, I mean besides the fact that my mouth was bone dry, was that I was afraid to call the authorities. I was afraid. I—I really think I was afraid they would see that I had tried to shoot Zackery, in fact, that I *had* shot him, and they would accuse me of possible murder and send me away to jail.

BARNETTE: Well, that's understandable.

BABE: I think so. I mean, in fact, that's what did happen. That's what is happening—'cause here I am just about ready to go right off to the

Parchment Prison Farm. Yes, here I am just practically on the brink of utter doom. Why, I feel so all alone.

BARNETTE: Now, now, look—Why, there's no reason for you to get yourself so all upset and worried. Please don't. Please.

(They look at each other for a moment.)

BARNETTE: You just keep filling in as much detailed information as you can about those incidents on the medical reports. That's all you need to think about. Don't you worry, Mrs. Botrelle, we're going to have a solid defense.

BABE: Please don't call me Mrs. Botrelle.

BARNETTE: All right.

BABE: My name's Becky. People in the family call me Babe, but my real name's Becky.

BARNETTE: All right, Becky.

(BARNETTE and BABE stare at each other for a long moment.)

BABE: Are you sure you didn't go to Hazlehurst High?

BARNETTE: No, I went away to a boarding school.

BABE: Gosh, you sure do look familiar. You sure do.

BARNETTE: Well, I—I doubt you'll remember, but I did meet you once.

BABE: You did? When?

BARNETTE: At the Christmas bazaar, year before last. You were selling cakes and cookies and...candy.

BABE: Oh, yes! You bought the orange pound cake!

BARNETTE: Right.

BABE: Of course, and then we talked for a while. We talked about the Christmas angel.

BARNETTE: You do remember.

BABE: I remember it very well. You were even thinner then than you are now.

BARNETTE: Well, I'm surprised. I'm certainly...surprised.

(The phone rings.)

BABE: *(As she goes to answer the phone)* This is quite a coincidence! Don't you think it is? Why, it's almost a fluke. *(She answers the phone.)* Hello...Oh, hello, Lucille...Oh, he is?...Oh, he does?...Okay. Oh, Lucille, wait! Has Dog come back to the house?...Oh, I see...Okay. Okay. *(After a brief pause)* Hello, Zackery? How are you doing?...Uh huh...uh huh....Oh, I'm sorry....Please don't scream....Uh huh...uh huh....You want what?...No, I can't come up there now....Well, for one thing, I don't even have the car. Lenny and Meg are up at the hospital right now, visiting with Old Granddaddy....What?...Oh, really?...Oh, really?...Well, I've got me a lawyer that's over here right now, and he's building me up a solid defense!...Wait just a minute, I'll see. *(To* BARNETTE*)* He wants to talk to you. He says he's got some blackening evidence that's gonna convict me of attempting to murder him in the first degree!

BARNETTE: *(Disgustedly)* Oh, bluff! He's bluffing! Here, hand me the phone. *(He takes the phone and becomes suddenly cool and suave.)* Hello, this is Mr. Barnette Lloyd speaking. I'm Mrs....ah, Becky's attorney....Why, certainly, Mr. Botrelle, I'd be more than glad to check out any pertinent information that you may have....Fine, then I'll be right on over. Goodbye. *(He hangs up the phone.)*

BABE: What did he say?

BARNETTE: He wants me to come see him at the hospital this evening. Says he's got some sort of evidence. Sounds highly suspect to me.

BABE: Ooooh! Didn't you just hate his voice? Doesn't he have the most awful voice? I just hate—I can't bear to hear it!

BARNETTE: Well, now—now wait. Wait just a minute.

BABE: What?

BARNETTE: I have a solution. From now on, I'll handle all communications between you two. You can simply refuse to speak with him.

BABE: All right—I will. I'll do that.

BARNETTE: *(Starting to pack his briefcase)* Well, I'd better get over there and see just what he's got up his sleeve.

BABE: *(After a pause)* Barnette.

BARNETTE: Yes?

BABE: What's the personal vendetta about? You know, the one you have to settle with Zackery.

BARNETTE: Oh, it's—it's complicated. It's a very complicated matter.

BABE: I see.

BARNETTE: The major thing he did was ruin my father's life. He took away his job, his home, his health, his respectability. I don't like to talk about it.

BABE: I'm sorry. I just wanted to say—I hope you win it. I hope you win your vendetta.

BARNETTE: Thank you.

BABE: I think it's an important thing that a person could win a lifelong vendetta.

BARNETTE: Yes. Well, I'd better be going.

BABE: All right. Let me know what happens.

BARNETTE: I will. I'll get back to you right away.

BABE: Thanks.

BARNETTE: Goodbye, Becky.

BABE: Goodbye, Barnette.

(BARNETTE *exits.* BABE *looks around the room for a moment, then goes over to her white suitcase and opens it up. She takes out her pink hair curlers and a brush. She begins brushing her hair.*)

BABE: Goodbye, Becky. Goodbye, Barnette. Goodbye, Becky. Oooh.

(LENNY *enters. She is fuming.* BABE *is rolling her hair throughout most of this scene.*)

BABE: Lenny, hi!

LENNY: Hi.

BABE: Where's Meg?

LENNY: Oh, she had to go by the store and pick some things up. I don't know what.

BABE: Well, how's Old Granddaddy?

LENNY: *(As she picks up* BABE's *bowl of oatmeal)* He's fine. Wonderful! Never been better!

BABE: Lenny, what's wrong? What's the matter?

LENNY: It's Meg! I could just wring her neck! I could just wring it!

BABE: Why? Wha'd she do?

LENNY: She lied! She sat in that hospital room and shamelessly lied to Old Granddaddy. She went on and on telling such untrue stories and lies.

BABE: Well, what? What did she say?

LENNY: Well, for one thing, she said she was gonna have an RCA record coming out with her picture on the cover, eating pineapples under a palm tree.

BABE: Well, gosh, Lenny, maybe she is! Don't you think she really is?

LENNY: Babe, she sat here this very afternoon and told me how all that she's done this whole year is work as a clerk for a dog-food company.

BABE: Oh, shoot. I'm disappointed.

LENNY: And then she goes on to say that she'll be appearing on the Johnny Carson show in two weeks' time. Two weeks' time. Why, Old Granddaddy's got a TV set in his room. Imagine what a letdown it's gonna be.

BABE: Why, mercy me.

LENNY: *(Slamming the coffeepot on)* Oh, and she told him the reason she didn't use the money he sent her to come home Christmas was that she was right in the middle of making a huge multimillion-dollar motion picture and was just under too much pressure.

BABE: My word!

LENNY: The movie's coming out this spring. It's called "Singing in a Shoe Factory." But she only has a small leading role—not a large leading role.

BABE: *(Laughing)* For heaven's sake—

LENNY: I'm sizzling. Oh, I just can't help it! I'm sizzling.

BABE: Sometimes Meg does such strange things.

LENNY: *(Slowly, as she picks up the opened box of birthday candy)* Who ate this candy?

BABE: *(Hesitantly)* Meg.

LENNY: My one birthday present, and look what she does! Why, she's taken one little bite out of each piece and then just put it back in! Oooh! That's just like her! That is just like her!

BABE: Lenny, please—

LENNY: I can't help it! It gets me mad! It gets me upset! Why, Meg's always run wild—she started smoking and drinking when she was fourteen years old; she never made good grades—never made her own bed! But somehow she always seemed to get what she wanted. She's the one who got singing and dancing lessons, and a store-bought dress to wear to her senior prom. Why, do you remember how Meg always got to wear twelve jingle bells on her petticoats, while we were only allowed to wear three apiece? Why?! Why should Old Grandmama let her sew twelve golden jingle bells on her petticoats and us only three?

BABE: *(Who has heard all this before)* I don't know! Maybe she didn't jingle them as much!

LENNY: I can't help it! It gets me mad! I resent it. I do.

BABE: Oh, don't resent Meg. Things have been hard for Meg. After all, she was the one who found Mama.

LENNY: Oh, I know; she's the one who found Mama. But that's always been the excuse.

BABE: But I tell you, Lenny, after it happened, Meg started doing all sorts of these strange things.

LENNY: She did? Like what?

BABE: Like things I never even wanted to tell you about.

LENNY: What sort of things?

BABE: Well, for instance, back when we used to go over to the library, Meg would spend all her time reading and looking through this old black book called *Diseases of the Skin*. It was full of the most sickening pictures you've ever seen. Things like rotting-away noses and eyeballs drooping off down the sides of people's faces, and scabs and sores and eaten-away places all over all parts of people's bodies.

LENNY: *(Trying to pour her coffee)* Babe, please! That's enough.

BABE: Anyway, she'd spend hours and hours just forcing herself to look through this book. Why, it was the same way she'd force herself to look at the poster of crippled children stuck up in the window at Dixieland Drugs. You know, that one where they want you to give a dime. Meg would stand there and stare at their eyes and look at the braces on their little crippled-up legs—then she'd purposely go and spend her dime on a double scoop ice cream cone and eat it all down. She'd say to me, "See, I can stand it. I can stand it. Just look how I'm gonna be able to stand it."

LENNY: That's awful.

BABE: She said she was afraid of being a weak person. I guess 'cause she cried in bed every night for such a long time.

LENNY: Goodness mercy. *(After a pause)* Well, I suppose you'd have to be a pretty hard person to be able to do what she did to Doc Porter.

BABE: *(Exasperated)* Oh, shoot! It wasn't Meg's fault that hurricane wiped Biloxi away. I never understood why people were blaming all that on Meg—just because that roof fell in and crunched Doc's leg. It wasn't her fault.

LENNY: Well, it was Meg who refused to evacuate. Jim Craig and some of Doc's other friends were all down there, and they kept trying to get everyone to evacuate. But Meg refused. She wanted to stay on because she thought a hurricane would be—oh, I don't know—a lot of fun. Then everyone says she baited Doc into staying there with her. She said she'd marry him if he'd stay.

BABE: *(Taken aback by this new information)* Well, he has a mind of his own. He could have gone.

LENNY: But he didn't. 'Cause...'cause he loved her. And then, after the roof caved in and they got Doc to the high school gym, Meg just left. She just left him there to leave for California—'cause of her career, she says. I think it was a shameful thing to do. It took almost a year for his leg to heal, and after that he gave up his medical career altogether. He said he was tired of hospitals. It's such a sad thing. Everyone always knew he was gonna be a doctor. We've called him Doc for years.

BABE: I don't know. I guess I don't have any room to talk; 'cause I just don't know. *(Pause)* Gosh, you look so tired.

LENNY: I feel tired.

BABE: They say women need a lot of iron...so they won't feel tired.

LENNY: What's got iron in it? Liver?

BABE: Yeah, liver's got it. And vitamin pills.

(After a moment, MEG enters. She carries a bottle of bourbon that is already minus a few slugs, and a newspaper. She is wearing black boots, a dark dress, and a hat. The room goes silent.)

MEG: Hello.

BABE: *(Fooling with her hair)* Hi, Meg.

(LENNY quietly sips her coffee.)

MEG: *(Handing the newspaper to BABE)* Here's your paper.

BABE: Thanks. *(She opens it.)* Oh, here it is, right on the front page.

(MEG lights a cigarette.)

BABE: Where's the scissors, Lenny?

LENNY: Look in there in the ribbon drawer.

BABE: Okay. *(She gets the scissors and glue out of the drawer and slowly begins cutting out the newspaper article.)*

MEG: *(After a few moments, filled only with the snipping of scissors)* All right—I lied! I lied! I couldn't help it...these stories just came pouring out of my mouth! When I saw how tired and sick Old Granddaddy'd gotten—they just flew out! All I wanted was to see him smiling and happy. I just wasn't going to sit there and look at him all miserable and sick and sad! I just wasn't!

BABE: Oh, Meg, he is sick, isn't he—

MEG: Why, he's gotten all white and milky—he's almost evaporated!

LENNY: *(Gasping and turning to MEG)* But still you shouldn't have lied! It just was wrong for you to tell such lies—

MEG: Well, I know that! Don't you think I know that? I hate myself when I lie for that old man. I do. I feel so weak. And then I have to go and do at least three or four things that I know he'd despise just to get even with that miserable, old, bossy man!

LENNY: Oh, Meg, please don't talk so about Old Granddaddy! It sounds so ungrateful. Why, he went out of his way to make a home for us, to treat us like we were his very own children. All he ever wanted was the best for us. That's all he ever wanted.

MEG: Well, I guess it was; but sometimes I wonder what we wanted.

BABE: *(Taking the newspaper article and glue over to her suitcase)* Well, one thing I wanted was a team of white horses to ride Mama's coffin to her grave. That's one thing I wanted.

(LENNY and MEG exchange looks.)

BABE: Lenny, did you remember to pack my photo album?

LENNY: It's down there at the bottom, under all that night stuff.

BABE: Oh, I found it.

LENNY: Really, Babe, I don't understand why you have to put in the articles that are about the unhappy things in your life. Why would you want to remember them?

BABE: *(Pasting the article in)* I don't know. I just like to keep an accurate record, I suppose. There. *(She begins flipping through the book.)* Look, here's a picture of me when I got married.

MEG: Let's see.

(They all look at the photo album.)

LENNY: My word, you look about twelve years old.

BABE: I was just eighteen.

MEG: You're smiling, Babe. Were you happy then?

BABE: *(Laughing)* Well, I was drunk on champagne punch. I remember that!

(They turn the page.)

LENNY: Oh, there's Meg singing at Greeny's!

BABE: Ooooh, I wish you were still singing at Greeny's! I wish you were!

LENNY: You're so beautiful!

BABE: Yes, you are. You're beautiful.

MEG: Oh, stop! I'm not—

LENNY: Look, Meg's starting to cry.

BABE: Oh, Meg—

MEG: I'm not—

BABE: Quick, better turn the page; we don't want Meg crying—*(She flips the pages.)*

LENNY: Why, it's Daddy.

MEG: Where'd you get that picture, Babe? I thought she burned them all.

BABE: Ah, I just found it around.

LENNY: What does it say here? What's that inscription?

BABE: It says "Jimmy—clowning at the beach—1952."

LENNY: Well, will you look at that smile.

MEG: Jesus, those white teeth—turn the page, will you; we can't do any worse than this!

(They turn the page. The room goes silent.)

BABE: It's Mama and the cat.

LENNY: Oh, turn the page—

BABE: That old yellow cat. You know, I bet if she hadn't of hung that old cat along with her, she wouldn't have gotten all that national coverage.

MEG: *(After a moment, hopelessly)* Why are we talking about this?

LENNY: Meg's right. It was so sad. It was awfully sad. I remember how we all three just sat up on that bed the day of the service all dressed up in our black velveteen suits crying the whole morning long.

BABE: We used up one whole big box of Kleenexes.

MEG: And then Old Granddaddy came in and said he was gonna take us out to breakfast. Remember, he told us not to cry anymore 'cause he was gonna take us out to get banana splits for breakfast.

BABE: That's right—banana splits for breakfast!

MEG: Why, Lenny was fourteen years old, and he thought that would make it all better—

BABE: Oh, I remember he said for us to eat all we wanted. I think I ate about five! He kept shoving them down us!

MEG: God, we were so sick!

LENNY: Oh, we were!

MEG: *(Laughing)* Lenny's face turned green—

LENNY: I was just as sick as a dog!

BABE: Old Grandmama was furious!

LENNY: Oh, she was!

MEG: The thing about Old Granddaddy is, he keeps trying to make us happy, and we end up getting stomachaches and turning green and throwing up in the flower arrangements.

BABE: Oh, that was me! I threw up in the flowers! Oh, no! How embarrassing!

LENNY: *(Laughing)* Oh, Babe—

BABE: *(Hugging her sisters)* Oh, Lenny! Oh, Meg!

MEG: Oh, Babe! Oh, Lenny! It's so good to be home!

LENNY: Hey, I have an idea—

BABE: What?

LENNY: Let's play cards!!

BABE: Oh, let's do!

MEG: All right!

LENNY: Oh, good! It'll be just like when we used to sit around the table playing hearts all night long.

BABE: I know! *(Getting up)* I'll fix us up some popcorn and hot chocolate—

MEG: *(Getting up)* Here, let me get out that old black popcorn pot.

LENNY: *(Getting up)* Oh, yes! Now, let's see, I think I have a deck of cards around here somewhere.

BABE: Gosh, I hope I remember all the rules—Are hearts good or bad?

MEG: Bad, I think. Aren't they, Lenny?

LENNY: That's right. Hearts are bad, but the Black Sister is the worst of all—

MEG: Oh, that's right! And the Black Sister is the Queen of Spades.

BABE: *(Figuring it out)* And spades are the black cards that aren't the puppy dog feet.

MEG: *(Thinking a moment)* Right. And she counts a lot of points.

BABE: And points are bad?

MEG: Right. Here, I'll get some paper so we can keep score.

(The phone rings.)

LENNY: Oh, here they are!

MEG: I'll get it—

LENNY: Why, look at these cards! They're years old!

BABE: Oh, let me see!

MEG: Hello....No, this is Meg MaGrath...Doc. How are you?...Well, good....You're where?...Well, sure. Come on over....Sure I'm sure....Yeah, come right on over....All right. 'Bye. *(She hangs up.)* That was Doc Porter. He's down the street at Al's Grill. He's gonna come on over.

LENNY: He is?

MEG: He said he wanted to come see me.

LENNY: Oh. *(After a pause)* Well, do you still want to play?

MEG: No, I don't think so.

LENNY: All right. *(She starts to shuffle the cards, as MEG brushes her hair.)* You know, it's really not much fun playing hearts with only two people.

MEG: I'm sorry; maybe after Doc leaves I'll join you.

LENNY: I know; maybe Doc'll want to play. Then we can have a game of bridge.

MEG: I don't think so. Doc never liked cards. Maybe we'll just go out somewhere.

LENNY: *(Putting down the cards; BABE picks them up.)* Meg—

MEG: What?

LENNY: Well, Doc's married now.

MEG: I know. You told me.

LENNY: Oh. Well, as long as you know that. *(Pause)* As long as you know that.

MEG: *(Still primping)* Yes, I know. She made the pot.

BABE: How many cards do I deal out?

LENNY: *(Leaving the table)* Excuse me.

BABE: All of 'em, or what?

LENNY: Ah, Meg, could I—could I ask you something?

(BABE *proceeds to deal out all the cards.*)

MEG: What?

LENNY: I just wanted to ask you—

MEG: What?

(Unable to go on with what she really wants to say, LENNY runs and picks up the box of candy.)

LENNY: Well, just why did you take one little bite out of each piece of candy in this box and then just put it back in?

MEG: Oh. Well, I was looking for the ones with nuts.

LENNY: The ones with nuts.

MEG: Yeah.

LENNY: But there are none with nuts. It's a box of assorted cremes—all it has in it are cremes!

MEG: Oh.

LENNY: Why couldn't you just read on the box? It says right here, "Assorted Cremes," not nuts! Besides, this was a birthday present to me! My one and only birthday present; my only one!

MEG: I'm sorry. I'll get you another box.

LENNY: I don't want another box. That's not the point!

MEG: What is the point?

LENNY: I don't know; it's—it's—You have no respect for other people's property! You just take whatever you want. You just take it! Why, remember how you had layers and layers of jingle bells sewed onto your petticoats while Babe and I only had three apiece?!

MEG: Oh, God! She's starting up about those stupid jingle bells!

LENNY: Well, it's an example! A specific example of how you always got what you wanted!

MEG: Oh, come on, Lenny, you're just upset because Doc called.

LENNY: Who said anything about Doc? Do you think I'm upset about Doc? Why, I've long since given up worrying about you and all your men.

MEG: *(Turning in anger)* Look, I know I've had too many men. Believe me, I've had way too many men. But it's not my fault you haven't had any—or maybe just that one from Memphis.

LENNY: *(Stopping)* What one from Memphis?

MEG: *(Slowly)* The one Babe told me about. From the—club.

LENNY: Babe!

BABE: Meg!

LENNY: How could you! I asked you not to tell anyone! I'm so ashamed! How could you? Who else have you told? Did you tell anyone else?

BABE: *(Overlapping, to* MEG*)* Why'd you have to open your big mouth?

MEG: *(Overlapping)* How am I supposed to know? You never said not to tell!

BABE: Can't you use your head just for once? *(To* LENNY*)* No, I never told anyone else. Somehow it just slipped out to Meg. Really, it just flew out of my mouth—

LENNY: What do you have—wings on your tongue?

BABE: I'm sorry, Lenny. Really sorry.

LENNY: I'll just never, never, never be able to trust you again—

MEG: *(Furiously coming to* BABE*'s defense)* Oh, for heaven's sake, Lenny, we were just worried about you! We wanted to find a way to make you happy!

LENNY: Happy! Happy! I'll never be happy!

MEG: Well, not if you keep living your life as Old Granddaddy's nursemaid—

BABE: Meg, shut up!

MEG: I can't help it! I just know that the reason you stopped seeing this man from Memphis was because of Old Granddaddy.

LENNY: What—Babe didn't tell you the rest of the story—

MEG: Oh, she said it was something about your shrunken ovary.

BABE: Meg!

LENNY: Babe!

BABE: I just mentioned it!

MEG: But I don't believe a word of that story!

LENNY: Oh, I don't care what you believe! It's so easy for you—you always have men falling in love with you! But I have this underdeveloped ovary and I can't have children and my hair is falling out in the comb—so what man can love me? What man's gonna love me?

MEG: A lot of men!

BABE: Yeah, a lot! A whole lot!

MEG: Old Granddaddy's the only one who seems to think otherwise.

LENNY: 'Cause he doesn't want to see me hurt! He doesn't want to see me rejected and humiliated.

MEG: Oh, come on now, Lenny, don't be so pathetic! God, you make me angry when you just stand there looking so pathetic! Just tell me, did you really ask the man from Memphis? Did you actually ask that man from Memphis all about it?

LENNY: *(Breaking apart)* No, I didn't. I didn't. Because I just didn't want him not to want me—

MEG: Lenny—

LENNY: *(Furious)* Don't talk to me anymore! Don't talk to me! I think I'm gonna vomit—I just hope all this doesn't cause me to vomit! *(She exits up the stairs, sobbing.)*

MEG: See! See! She didn't even ask him about her stupid ovary! She just broke it all off 'cause of Old Granddaddy! What a jackass fool!

BABE: Oh, Meg, shut up! Why do you have to make Lenny cry? I just hate it when you make Lenny cry! *(She runs up the stairs.)* Lenny! Oh, Lenny—

(MEG gives a long sigh and goes to get a cigarette and a drink.)

MEG: I feel like hell. *(She sits in despair, smoking and drinking bourbon. There is a knock at the back door. She starts. She brushes her hair out of her face and goes to answer the door. It is DOC.)*

DOC: Hello, Meggy.

MEG: Well, Doc. Well, it's Doc.

DOC: *(After a pause)* You're home, Meggy.

MEG: Yeah, I've come home. I've come on home to see about Babe.

DOC: And how's Babe?

MEG: Oh, fine. Well, fair. She's fair.

(DOC nods.)

MEG: Hey, do you want a drink?

DOC: Watcha got?

MEG: Bourbon.

DOC: Oh, don't tell me Lenny's stocking bourbon.

MEG: Well, no. I've been to the store. *(She gets him a glass and pours them each a drink. They click glasses.)*

MEG: So, how's your wife?

DOC: She's fine.

MEG: I hear ya got two kids.

DOC: Yeah. Yeah, I got two kids.

MEG: A boy and a girl.

DOC: That's right, Meggy, a boy and a girl.

MEG: That's what you always said you wanted, wasn't it? A boy and a girl.

DOC: Is that what I said?

MEG: I don't know. I thought it's what you said.

(They finish their drinks in silence.)

DOC: Whose cot?

MEG: Lenny's. She's taken to sleeping in the kitchen.

DOC: Ah. Where is Lenny?

MEG: She's in the upstairs room. I made her cry. Babe's up there seeing to her.

DOC: How'd you make her cry?

MEG: I don't know. Eating her birthday candy; talking on about her boyfriend from Memphis. I don't know. I'm upset about it. She's got a lot on her. Why can't I keep my mouth shut?

DOC: I don't know, Meggy. Maybe it's because you don't want to.

MEG: Maybe.

(They smile at each other. MEG *pours each of them another drink.)*

DOC: Well, it's been a long time.

MEG: It has been a long time.

DOC: Let's see—when was the last time we saw each other?

MEG: I can't quite recall.

DOC: Wasn't it in Biloxi?

MEG: Ah, Biloxi. I believe so.

DOC: And wasn't there a—a hurricane going on at the time?

MEG: Was there?

DOC: Yes, there was; one hell of a hurricane. Camille, I believe they called it. Hurricane Camille.

MEG: Yes, now I remember. It was a beautiful hurricane.

DOC: We had a time down there. We had quite a time. Drinking vodka, eating oysters on the half shell, dancing all night long. And the wind was blowing.

MEG: Oh, God, was it blowing.

DOC: Goddamn, was it blowing.

MEG: There never has been such a wind blowing.

DOC: Oh, God, Meggy. Oh, God.

MEG: I know, Doc. It was my fault to leave you. I was crazy. I thought I was choking. I felt choked!

DOC: I felt like a fool.

MEG: No.

DOC: I just kept on wondering why.

MEG: I don't know why....'Cause I didn't want to care. I don't know. I did care, though. I did.

DOC: *(After a pause)* Ah, hell—*(He pours them both another drink.)* Are you still singing those sad songs?

MEG: No.

DOC: Why not?

MEG: I don't know, Doc. Things got worse for me. After a while, I just couldn't sing anymore. I tell you, I had one hell of a time over Christmas.

DOC: What do you mean?

MEG: I went nuts. I went insane. Ended up in L.A. County Hospital. Psychiatric Ward.

DOC: Hell. Ah, hell, Meggy. What happened?

MEG: I don't really know. I couldn't sing anymore, so I lost my job. And I had a bad toothache. I had this incredibly painful toothache. For days I had it, but I wouldn't do anything about it. I just stayed inside my apartment. All I could do was sit around in chairs, chewing on my fingers. Then one afternoon I ran screaming out of the apartment with all my money and jewelry and valuables, and tried to stuff it all into one of those March of Dimes collection boxes. That was when they nabbed me. Sad story. Meg goes mad.

(DOC stares at her for a long moment. He pours them both another drink.)

DOC: *(After quite a pause)* There's a moon out.

MEG: Is there?

DOC: Wanna go take a ride in my truck and look out at the moon?

MEG: I don't know, Doc. I don't wanna start up. It'll be too hard if we start up.

DOC: Who says we're gonna start up? We're just gonna look at the moon. For one night just you and me are gonna go for a ride in the country and look out at the moon.

MEG: One night?

DOC: Right.

MEG: Look out at the moon?

DOC: You got it.

MEG: Well...all right. *(She gets up.)*

DOC: Better take your coat. *(He helps her into her coat.)* And the bottle—*(He takes the bottle.* MEG *picks up the glasses.)* Forget the glasses—

MEG: *(Laughing)* Yeah—forget the glasses. Forget the goddamn glasses.

(MEG *shuts off the kitchen lights, leaving the kitchen with only a dim light over the kitchen sink.* MEG *and* DOC *leave. After a moment,* BABE *comes down the stairs in her slip.)*

BABE: Meg—Meg? *(She stands for a moment in the moonlight wearing only a slip. She sees her saxophone, then moves to pick it up. She plays a few shrieking notes. There is a loud knock on the back door.)*

BARNETTE'S VOICE: Becky! Becky, is that you?

(BABE *puts down the saxophone.)*

BABE: Just a minute. I'm coming. *(She puts a raincoat on over her slip and goes to answer the door.)* Hello, Barnette. Come on in.

(BARNETTE *comes in. He is troubled but is making a great effort to hide the fact.)*

BARNETTE: Thank you.

BABE: What is it?

BARNETTE: I've, ah, I've just come from seeing Zackery at the hospital.

BABE: Oh?

BARNETTE: It seems....Well, it seems his sister, Lucille, was somewhat suspicious.

BABE: Suspicious?

BARNETTE: About you?

BABE: Me?

BARNETTE: She hired a private detective; he took these pictures.

(He hands BABE *a small envelope containing several photographs.* BABE *opens the envelope and begins looking at the pictures in stunned silence.)*

BARNETTE: They were taken about two weeks ago. It seems she wasn't going to show them to Botrelle straightaway. She, ah, wanted to wait till the time was right.

(The phone rings one and a half times. BARNETTE *glances uneasily toward the phone.)*

BARNETTE: Becky?

(The phone stops ringing.)

BABE: *(Looking up at* BARNETTE, *slowly)* These are pictures of Willie Jay and me...out in the garage.

BARNETTE: *(Looking away)* I know.

BABE: You looked at these pictures?

BARNETTE: Yes—I—well...professionally, I looked at them.

BABE: Oh, mercy. Oh, mercy! We can burn them, can't we? Quick, we can burn them—

BARNETTE: It won't do any good. They have the negatives.

BABE: *(Holding the pictures, as she bangs herself hopelessly into the stove, table, cabinets, etc.)* Oh, no; oh, no; oh, no! Oh, no—

BARNETTE: There—there, now—there—

LENNY'S VOICE: Babe? Are you all right? Babe—

BABE: *(Hiding the pictures)* What? I'm all right. Go on back to bed.

*(*BABE *hides the pictures as* LENNY *comes down the stairs. She is wearing a coat and wiping white night cream off of her face with a washrag.)*

LENNY: What's the matter? What's going on down here?

BABE: Nothing! *(Then, as she begins dancing ballet style around the room)* We're—we're just dancing. We were just dancing around down here. *(Signaling to* BARNETTE *to dance)*

LENNY: Well, you'd better get your shoes on, 'cause we've got—

BABE: All right, I will! That's a good idea! *(She goes to get her shoes.)* Now, you go on back to bed. It's pretty late and—

LENNY: Babe, will you listen a minute—

BABE: *(Holding up her shoes)* I'm putting 'em on—

LENNY: That was the hospital that just called. We've got to get over there. Old Granddaddy's had himself another stroke.

BABE: Oh. All right. My shoes are on. *(She stands.)*

(They all look at each other as the lights black out.)

CURTAIN

END OF ACT TWO

ACT THREE

(The lights go up on the empty kitchen. It is the following morning. After a few moments, BABE *enters from the back door. She is carrying her hair curlers in her hands. She lies down on the cot. A few moments later,* LENNY *enters. She is tired and weary.* CHICK's *voice is heard.)*

CHICK'S VOICE: Lenny! Oh, Lenny!

*(*LENNY *turns to the door.* CHICK *enters energetically.)*

CHICK: Well...how is he?

LENNY: He's stabilized; they say for now his functions are all stabilized.

CHICK: Well, is he still in the coma?

LENNY: Uh huh.

CHICK: Hmmm. So do they think he's gonna be...passing on?

LENNY: He may be. He doesn't look so good. They said they'd phone us if there were any sudden changes.

CHICK: Well, it seems to me we'd better get busy phoning on the phone ourselves. *(Removing a list from her pocket)* Now, I've made out this list of all the people we need to notify about Old Granddaddy's predicament. I'll phone half, if you'll phone half.

LENNY: But—what would we say?

CHICK: Just tell them the facts: that Old Granddaddy's got himself in a coma, and it could be he doesn't have long for this world.

LENNY: I—I don't know. I don't feel like phoning.

CHICK: Why, Lenora, I'm surprised; how can you be this way? I went to all the trouble of making up the list. And I offered to phone half the people on it, even though I'm only one-fourth of the granddaughters. I mean, I just get tired of doing more than my fair share, when people like Meg can suddenly disappear to where they can't even be reached in case of emergency!

LENNY: All right; give me the list. I'll phone half.

CHICK: Well, don't do it just to suit me.

LENNY: *(Wearily tearing the list in half)* I'll phone these here.

CHICK: *(Taking her half of the list)* Fine then. Suit yourself. Oh, wait—let me call Sally Bell. I need to talk to her, anyway.

LENNY: All right.

CHICK: So you add Great-uncle Spark Dude to your list.

LENNY: Okay.

CHICK: Fine. Well, I've got to get on back home and see to the kids. It is gonna be an uphill struggle till I can find someone to replace that good-for-nothing Annie May Jenkins. Well, you let me know if you hear any more.

LENNY: All right.

CHICK: Goodbye, Rebecca. I said goodbye. (BABE *blows her sax.* CHICK *starts to exit in a flurry, then pauses to add:)* And you really ought to try to get that phoning done before twelve noon. *(She exits.)*

LENNY: *(After a long pause)* Babe, I feel bad. I feel real bad.

BABE: Why, Lenny?

LENNY: Because yesterday I—I wished it.

BABE: You wished what?

LENNY: I wished that Old Granddaddy would be put out of his pain. I wished it on one of my birthday candles. I did. And now he's in this coma, and they say he's feeling no pain.

BABE: Well, when did you have a cake yesterday? I don't remember you having any cake.

LENNY: Well, I didn't...have a cake. But I just blew out the candles, anyway.

BABE: Oh. Well, those birthday wishes don't count, unless you have a cake.

LENNY: They don't?

BABE: No. A lot of times they don't even count when you do have a cake. It just depends.

LENNY: Depends on what?

BABE: On how deep your wish is, I suppose.

LENNY: Still, I just wish I hadn't of wished it. Gosh, I wonder when Meg's coming home.

BABE: Should be soon.

LENNY: I just wish we wouldn't fight all the time. I don't like it when we do.

BABE: Me, neither.

LENNY: I guess it hurts my feelings, a little, the way Old Granddaddy's always put so much stock in Meg and all her singing talent. I think I've been, well, envious of her 'cause I can't seem to do much.

BABE: Why, sure you can.

LENNY: I can?

BABE: Sure. You just have to put your mind to it, that's all. It's like how I went out and bought that saxophone, just hoping I'd be able to attend music school and start up my own career. I just went out and did it. Just on hope. Of course, now it looks like....Well, it just doesn't look like things are gonna work out for me. But I know they would for you.

LENNY: Well, they'll work out for you, too.

BABE: I doubt it.

LENNY: Listen, I heard up at the hospital that Zackery's already in fair condition. They say soon he'll probably be able to walk and everything.

BABE: Yeah. And life sure can be miserable.

LENNY: Well, I know, 'cause—day before yesterday, Billy Boy was struck down by lightning.

BABE: He was?

LENNY: *(Nearing sobs)* Yeah. He was struck dead.

BABE: *(Crushed)* Life sure can be miserable.

(They sit together for several moments in morbid silence. MEG is heard singing a loud, happy song. She suddenly enters through the dining room door. She is exuberant! Her hair is a mess, and the heel of one shoe has broken off. She is laughing radiantly and limping as she sings into the broken heel.)

MEG: *(Spotting her sisters)* Good morning! Good morning! Oh, it's a wonderful morning! I tell you, I am surprised I feel this good. I should feel like hell. By all accounts. I should feel like utter hell! *(She is looking for the glue.)* Where's that glue? This damn heel has broken off my shoe. La, la, la, la, la! Ah, here it is! Now, let me just get these shoes off. Zip, zip, zip, zip, zip! Well, what's wrong with you two? My God, you look like doom!

(BABE and LENNY stare helplessly at MEG.)

MEG: Oh, I know, you're mad at me 'cause I stayed out all night long. Well, I did.

LENNY: No, we're—we're not mad at you. We're just...depressed. *(She starts to sob.)*

MEG: Oh, Lenny, listen to me, now; everything's all right with Doc. I mean, nothing happened. Well, actually a lot did happen, but it didn't come to anything. Not because of me, I'm afraid. *(Smearing glue on her heel)* I mean, I was out there thinking, What will I say when he begs me to run away with him? Will I have pity on his wife and those two half-Yankee children? I mean, can I sacrifice their happiness for mine? Yes! Oh, yes! Yes, I can! But...he didn't ask me. He didn't even want to ask me. I could tell by this certain look in his eyes that he didn't even want to ask me. Why aren't I miserable! Why aren't I morbid! I should be humiliated! Devastated! Maybe these feelings are coming—I don't know. But for now it was...just such fun. I'm happy. I realized I could care about someone. I could want someone. And I sang! I sang all night long! I sang right up into the trees! But not for Old Granddaddy. None of it was to please Old Grandaddy!

(LENNY and BABE *look at each other.*)

BABE: Ah, Meg—

MEG: What—

BABE: Well, it's just—It's...

LENNY: It's about Old Granddaddy—

MEG: Oh, I know; I know. I told him all those stupid lies. Well, I'm gonna go right over there this morning and tell him the truth. I mean every horrible thing. I don't care if he wants to hear it or not. He's just gonna have to take me like I am. And if he can't take it, if it sends him into a coma, that's just too damn bad!

(BABE *and* LENNY *look at each other.* BABE *cracks a smile.* LENNY *cracks a smile.*)

BABE: You're too late—Ha, ha, ha!

(They both break up laughing.)

LENNY: Oh, stop! Please! Ha, ha, ha!

MEG: What is it? What's so funny?

BABE: *(Still laughing)* It's not—It's not funny!

LENNY: *(Still laughing)* No, it's not! It's not a bit funny!

MEG: Well, what is it, then? What?

BABE: *(Trying to calm down)* Well, it's just—it's just—

MEG: What?

BABE: Well, Old Granddaddy—he—he's in a coma!

(BABE *and* LENNY *break up again.*)

MEG: He's what?

BABE: *(Shrieking)* In a coma!

MEG: My God! That's not funny!

BABE: *(Calming down)* I know. I know. For some reason, it just struck us as funny.

LENNY: I'm sorry. It's—it's not funny. It's sad. It's very sad. We've been up all night long.

BABE: We're really tired.

MEG: Well, my God. How is he? Is he gonna live?

(BABE and LENNY look at each other.)

BABE: They don't think so!

(They both break up again.)

LENNY: Oh, I don't know why we're laughing like this. We're just sick! We're just awful!

BABE: We are—we're awful!

LENNY: *(As she collects herself)* Oh, good; now I feel bad. Now I feel like crying. I do; I feel like crying.

BABE: Me, too. Me, too.

MEG: Well, you've gotten me depressed!

LENNY: I'm sorry. I'm sorry. It, ah, happened last night. He had another stroke.

(They laugh again.)

MEG: I see.

LENNY: But he's stabilized now. *(She chokes up once more.)*

MEG: That's good. You two okay?

(BABE and LENNY nod.)

MEG: You look like you need some rest.

(BABE and LENNY nod again.)

MEG: *(Going on, about her heel)* I hope that'll stay. *(She puts the top back on the glue; a realization:)* Oh, of course, now I won't be able to tell him the truth about all those lies I told. I mean, finally I get my wits about me, and he conks out. It's just like him. Babe, can I wear your slippers till this glue dries?

BABE: Sure.

LENNY: *(After a pause)* Things sure are gonna be different around here...when Old Granddaddy dies. Well, not for you two really, but for me.

MEG: It'll work out.

BABE: *(Depressed)* Yeah. It'll work out.

LENNY: I hope so. I'm just afraid of being here all by myself. All alone.

MEG: Well, you don't have to be alone. Maybe Babe'll move back in here.

(LENNY *looks at* BABE *hopefully.*)

BABE: No, I don't think I'll be living here.

MEG: *(Realizing her mistake)* Well, anyway, you're your own woman. Invite some people over. Have some parties. Go out with strange men.

LENNY: I don't know any strange men.

MEG: Well...you know that Charlie.

LENNY: *(Shaking her head)* Not anymore.

MEG: Why not?

LENNY: *(Breaking down)* I told him we should never see each other again.

MEG: Well, if you told him, you can just untell him.

LENNY: Oh, no, I couldn't. I'd feel like a fool.

MEG: Oh, that's not a good enough reason! All people in love feel like fools. Don't they, Babe?

BABE: Sure.

MEG: Look, why don't you give him a call right now? See how things stand?

LENNY: Oh, no! I'd be too scared—

MEG: But what harm could it possibly do? I mean, it's not gonna make things any worse than this never seeing him again, at all, forever.

LENNY: I suppose that's true—

MEG: Of course it is; so call him up! Take a chance, will you? Just take some sort of chance!

LENNY: You think I should?

MEG: Of course! You've got to try—You do!

(LENNY *looks over at* BABE.)

BABE: You do, Lenny—I think you do.

LENNY: Really? Really, really?

MEG: Yes! Yes!

BABE: You should!

LENNY: All right. I will! I will!

MEG: Oh, good!

BABE: Good!

LENNY: I'll call him right now, while I've got my confidence up!

MEG: Have you got the number?

LENNY: Uh huh. But, ah, I think I wanna call him upstairs. It'll be more private.

MEG: Ah, good idea.

LENNY: I'm just gonna go on and call him up and see what happens—*(She has started up the stairs.)* Wish me good luck!

MEG: Good luck!

BABE: Good luck, Lenny!

LENNY: Thanks.

(LENNY *gets almost out of sight when the phone rings. She stops;* MEG *picks up the phone.)*

MEG: Hello? *(Then, in a whisper)* Oh, thank you very much...yes, I will. 'Bye, 'bye.

LENNY: Who was it?

MEG: Wrong number. They wanted Weed's Body Shop.

LENNY: Oh. Well, I'll be right back down in a minute. *(She exits.)*

MEG: *(After a moment, whispering to* BABE*)* That was the bakery; Lenny's cake is ready!

BABE: *(Who has become increasingly depressed)* Oh.

MEG: I think I'll sneak on down to the corner and pick it up. *(She starts to leave.)*

BABE: Meg—

MEG: What?

BABE: Nothing.

MEG: You okay?

(BABE *shakes her head.)*

MEG: What is it?

BABE: It's just—

MEG: What?

(BABE *gets the envelope containing the photographs.)*

BABE: Here. Take a look.

MEG: *(Taking the envelope)* What is it?

BABE: It's some evidence Zackery's collected against me. Looks like my goose is cooked.

(MEG *opens the envelope and looks at the photographs.*)

MEG: My God, it's you and...is *that* Willie Jay?

BABE: Yah.

MEG: Well, he certainly has grown. You were right about that. My, oh, my.

BABE: Please don't tell Lenny. She'd hate me.

MEG: I won't. I won't tell Lenny. *(Putting the pictures back into the envelope)* What are you gonna do?

BABE: What can I do?

(*There is a knock on the door.* BABE *grabs the envelope and hides it.*)

MEG: Who is it?

BARNETTE'S VOICE: It's Barnette Lloyd.

MEG: Oh. Come on in, Barnette.

(BARNETTE *enters. His eyes are ablaze with excitement.*)

BARNETTE: *(As he paces around the room)* Well, good morning! *(Shaking* MEG's *hand)* Good morning, Miss MaGrath. *(Touching* BABE *on the shoulder)* Becky. *(Moving away)* What I mean to say is, How are you doing this morning?

MEG: Ah—fine. Fine.

BARNETTE: Good. Good. I—I just had time to drop by for a minute.

MEG: Oh.

BARNETTE: So, ah, how's your granddad doing?

MEG: Well, not very, ah—ah, he's in this coma. *(She breaks up laughing.)*

BARNETTE: I see...I see. *(To* BABE*)* Actually, the primary reason I came by was to pick up that—envelope. I left it here last night in all the confusion. *(Pause)* You, ah, still do have it?

(BABE *hands him the envelope.*)

BARNETTE: Yes. *(Taking the envelope)* That's the one. I'm sure it'll be much better off in my office safe. *(He puts the envelope into his coat pocket.)*

MEG: I'm sure it will.

BARNETTE: Beg your pardon?

BABE: It's all right. I showed her the pictures.

BARNETTE: Ah; I see.

MEG: So what's going to happen now, Barnette? What are those pictures gonna mean?

BARNETTE: *(After pacing a moment)* Hmmm. May I speak frankly and openly?

BABE: Uh huh.

MEG: Please do.

BARNETTE: Well, I tell you now, at first glance, I admit those pictures had me considerably perturbed and upset. Perturbed to the point that I spent most of last night going over certain suspect papers and reports that had fallen into my hands—rather recklessly.

BABE: What papers do you mean?

BARNETTE: Papers that, pending word from three varied and unbiased experts, could prove graft, fraud, forgery, as well as a history of unethical behavior.

MEG: You mean about Zackery?

BARNETTE: Exactly. You see, I now intend to make this matter just as sticky and gritty for one Z. Botrelle as it is for us. Why, with the amount of scandal I'll dig up, Botrelle will be forced to settle this affair on our own terms!

MEG: Oh, Babe! Did you hear that?

BABE: Yes! Oh, yes! So you've won it! You've won your lifelong vendetta!

BARNETTE: Well...well, now of course it's problematic in that, well, in that we won't be able to expose him openly in the courts. That was the original game plan.

BABE: But why not? Why?

BARNETTE: Well, it's only that if, well, if a jury were to—to get, say, a glance at these, ah, photographs, well...well, possibly....

BABE: We could be sunk.

BARNETTE: In a sense. But! On the other hand, if a newspaper were to get hold of our little item, Mr. Zackery Botrelle could find himself boiling in some awfully hot water. So what I'm looking for, very simply, is—a deal.

BABE: A deal?

MEG: Thank you, Barnette. It's a sunny day, Babe. *(Realizing she is in the way)* Ooh, where's that broken shoe? *(She grabs her boots and runs upstairs.)*

BABE: So, you're having to give up your vendetta?

BARNETTE: Well, in a way. For the time. It, ah, seems to me you shouldn't always let your life be ruled by such things as, ah, personal vendettas. *(Looking at* BABE *with meaning)* Other things can be important.

BABE: I don't know, I don't exactly know. How 'bout Willie Jay? Will he be all right?

BARNETTE: Yes, it's all taken care of. He'll be leaving incognito on the midnight bus—heading north.

BABE: North.

BARNETTE: I'm sorry, it seemed the only...way.

*(*BARNETTE *moves to her; she moves away.)*

BABE: Look, you'd better be getting on back to your work.

BARNETTE: *(Awkwardly)* Right—'cause I—I've got those important calls out. *(Full of hope for her)* They'll be pouring in directly. *(He starts to leave, then says to her with love.)* We'll talk.

MEG: *(Reappearing in her boots)* Oh, Barnette—

BARNETTE: Yes?

MEG: Could you give me a ride just down to the corner? I need to stop at Helen's Bakery.

BARNETTE: Be glad to.

MEG: Thanks. Listen, Babe, I'll be right back with the cake. We're gonna have the best celebration! Now, ah, if Lenny asks where I've gone, just say I'm....Just say, I've gone out back to, ah, pick up some pawpaws! Okay?

BABE: Okay.

MEG: Fine; I'll be back in a bit. Goodbye.

BABE: 'Bye.

BARNETTE: Goodbye, Becky.

BABE: Goodbye, Barnette. Take care.

*(*MEG *and* BARNETTE *exit.* BABE *sits staring ahead, in a state of deep despair.)*

BABE: Goodbye, Becky. Goodbye, Barnette. Goodbye, Becky. *(She stops when* LENNY *comes down the stairs in a fluster.)*

LENNY: Oh! Oh! Oh! I'm so ashamed! I'm such a coward! I'm such a yellow-bellied chicken! I'm so ashamed! Where's Meg?

BABE: *(Suddenly bright)* She's, ah—gone out back—to pick up some pawpaws.

LENNY: Oh. Well, at least I don't have to face her! I just couldn't do it! I couldn't make the call! My heart was pounding like a hammer. Pound! Pound! Pound! Why, I looked down and I could actually see my blouse moving back and forth! Oh, Babe, you look so disappointed. Are you?

BABE: *(Despondently)* Uh huh.

LENNY: Oh, no! I've disappointed Babe! I can't stand it! I've gone and disappointed my little sister, Babe! Oh, no! I feel like howling like a dog!

CHICK'S VOICE: Oooh, Lenny! *(She enters dramatically, dripping with sympathy.)* Well, I just don't know what to say! I'm so sorry! I am so sorry for you! And for little Babe here, too. I mean, to have such a sister as that!

LENNY: What do you mean?

CHICK: Oh, you don't need to pretend with me. I saw it all from over there in my own back yard: I saw Meg stumbling out of Doc Porter's pickup truck, not fifteen minutes ago. And her looking such a disgusting mess. You must be so ashamed! You must just want to die! Why, I always said that girl was nothing but cheap Christmas trash!

LENNY: Don't talk that way about Meg.

CHICK: Oh, come on now, Lenny honey, I know exactly how you feel about Meg. Why, Meg's a low-class tramp and you need not have one more blessed thing to do with her and her disgusting behavior.

LENNY: I said, don't you ever talk that way about my sister Meg again.

CHICK: Well, my goodness gracious, Lenora, don't be such a noodle—it's the truth!

LENNY: I don't care if it's the Ten Commandments. I don't want to hear it in my home. Not ever again.

CHICK: In your home?! Why, I never in all my life—This is my grandfather's home! And you're just living here on his charity; so don't you get high-falutin' with me, Miss Lenora Josephine MaGrath!

LENNY: Get out of here—

CHICK: Don't you tell me to get out! What makes you think you can order me around? Why, I've had just about my fill of you trashy MaGrath's and your trashy ways: hanging yourselves in cellars; carrying on with married men; shooting your own husbands!

LENNY: Get out!

CHICK: *(To BABE)* And don't you think she's not gonna end up at the state prison farm or in some—mental institution. Why, it's a clear-cut case of manslaughter with intent to kill!

LENNY: Out! Get out!

CHICK: *(Running on)* That's what everyone's saying, deliberate intent to kill! And you'll pay for that! Do you hear me? You'll pay!

LENNY: *(Picking up a broom and threatening* CHICK *with it)* And I'm telling you to get out!

CHICK: You—you put that down this minute—Are you a raving lunatic?

LENNY: *(Beating* CHICK *with the broom)* I said for you to get out! That means out! And never, never, never come back!

CHICK: *(Overlapping, as she runs around the room)* Oh! Oh! Oh! You're crazy! You're crazy!

LENNY: *(Chasing* CHICK *out the door)* Do you hear me, Chick the Stick! This is my home! This is my house! Get out! Out!

CHICK: *(Overlapping)* Oh! Oh! Police! Police! You're crazy! Help! Help!

(LENNY *chases* CHICK *out of the house. They are both screaming. The phone rings.* BABE *goes and picks it up.)*

BABE: Hello?...Oh, hello, Zackery!...Yes, he showed them to me!...You're what!...What do you mean?...What!...You can't put me out to Whitfield... 'Cause I'm not crazy...I'm not! I'm not!...She wasn't crazy, either...Don't you call my mother crazy!...No, you're not! You're not gonna. You're not! *(She slams the phone down and stares wildly ahead.)* He's not. He's not. *(As she walks over to the ribbon drawer)* I'll do it. I will. And he won't...*(She opens the drawer, pulls out the rope, becomes terrified, throws the rope back in the drawer, slams it shut.)*

(LENNY *enters from the back door, swinging the broom and laughing.)*

LENNY: Oh, my! Oh, my! You should have seen us! Why, I chased Chick the Stick right up the mimosa tree. I did! I left her right up there screaming in the tree!

BABE: *(Laughing; she is insanely delighted)* Oh, you did!

LENNY: Yes, I did! And I feel so good! I do! I feel so good! I feel good!

BABE: *(Overlapping)* Good! Good, Lenny! Good for you!

(They dance around the kitchen.)

LENNY: *(Stopping)* You know what—

BABE: What?

LENNY: I'm gonna call Charlie! I'm gonna call him up right now!

BABE: You are?

LENNY: Yeah, I feel like I can really do it!

BABE: You do?

LENNY: My courage is up; my heart's in it; the time is right! No more beating around the bush! Let's strike while the iron is hot!

BABE: Right! Right! No more beating around the bush! Strike while the iron is hot!

(LENNY *goes to the phone.* BABE *rushes over to the ribbon drawer. She begins tearing through it.*)

LENNY: *(With the receiver in her hand)* I'm calling him up, Babe! I'm really gonna do it!

BABE: *(Still tearing through the drawer)* Good! Do it! Good!

LENNY: *(As she dials)* Look. My hands aren't even shaking.

BABE: *(Pulling out a red rope)* Don't we have any stronger rope than this?

LENNY: I guess not. All the rope we've got's in that drawer. *(About her hands)* Now they're shaking a little.

(BABE *takes the rope and goes up the stairs.* LENNY *finishes dialing the number. She waits for an answer.*)

LENNY: Hello?...Hello, Charlie. This is Lenny MaGrath....Well, I'm fine. I'm just fine. *(An awkward pause)* I was, ah, just calling to see—how you're getting on....Well, good. Good....Yes, I know I said that. Now I wish I didn't say it....Well, the reason I said that before, about not seeing each other again, was 'cause of me, not you....Well, it's just I—I can't have any children. I—have this ovary problem....Why, Charlie, what a thing to say!...Well, they're not all little snot-nosed pigs!...You think they are!...Oh, Charlie, stop, stop! You're making me laugh....Yes, I guess I was.... I can see now that I was....You are?...Well, I'm dying to see you, too....Well, I don't know when, Charlie...soon. How about, well, how about tonight?...You will?...Oh, you will!...All right, I'll be here. I'll be right here....Goodbye, then, Charlie. Goodbye for now. *(She hangs up the phone in a daze.)* Babe. Oh, Babe! He's coming. He's coming! Babe! Oh, Babe, where are you? Meg! Oh...out back—picking up pawpaws. *(As she exits through the back door:)* And those paw-paws are just ripe for picking up!

(*There is a moment of silence; then a loud, horrible thud is heard, coming from upstairs. The telephone begins ringing immediately. It rings five times before* BABE *comes hurrying down the stairs with a broken piece of rope hanging around her neck. The phone continues to ring.*)

BABE: *(To the phone)* Will you shut up! *(She is jerking the rope from around her neck. She grabs a knife to cut it off.)* Cheap! Miserable! I hate you! I hate you! *(She throws the rope violently across the room. The phone stops ringing.)* Thank God. *(She looks at the stove, goes over to it, and turns the gas on. The sound of gas escaping is heard. She sniffs at it.)* Come on. Come on....Hurry up....I beg of you—hurry up! *(Finally, she feels the oven is ready; she takes a deep breath and opens the oven door to stick her head into it. She spots the rack and furiously jerks it out. Taking another breath, she sticks her head into the oven. She stands for several moments, tapping her fingers furiously on top of the stove. She speaks from inside the oven.)* Oh, please. Please. *(After a few moments, she reaches for the box of matches with her head still in the oven. She tries to strike a match. It doesn't catch.)* Oh, Mama, please! *(She throws the match away and is getting a second one.)* Mama....Mama....So that's why you done it! *(In her excitement she starts to get up, bangs her head, and falls back in the oven.)*

(MEG enters from the back door, carrying a birthday cake in a pink box.)

MEG: Babe! *(She throws the box down and runs to pull BABE's head out of the oven.)* Oh, my God! What are you doing? What the hell are you doing?

BABE: *(Dizzily)* Nothing. I don't know. Nothing.

(MEG turns off the gas and moves BABE to a chair near the open door.)

MEG: Sit down. Sit down! Will you sit down!

BABE: I'm okay. I'm okay.

MEG: Put your head between your knees and breathe deep!

BABE: Meg—

MEG: Just do it! I'll get you some water. *(She gets some water for BABE.)* Here.

BABE: Thanks.

MEG: Are you okay?

BABE: Uh huh.

MEG: Are you sure?

BABE: Yeah, I'm sure. I'm okay.

MEG: *(Getting a damp rag and putting it over her own face)* Well, good. That's good.

BABE: Meg—

MEG: Yes?

BABE: I know why she did it?

MEG: What? Why who did what?

BABE: *(With joy)* Mama. I know why she hung that cat along with her.

MEG: You do?

BABE: *(With enlightenment)* It's 'cause she was afraid of dying all alone.

MEG: Was she?

BABE: She felt so unsure, you know, as to what was coming. It seems the best thing coming up would be a lot of angels and all of them singing. But I imagine they have high, scary voices and little gold pointed fingers that are as sharp as blades and you don't want to meet 'em all alone. You'd be afraid to meet 'em all alone. So it wasn't like what people were saying about her hating that cat. Fact is, she loved that cat. She needed him with her 'cause she felt so all alone.

MEG: Oh, Babe...Babe. Why, Babe? Why?

BABE: Why what?

MEG: Why did you stick your head into the oven?

BABE: I don't know, Meg. I'm having a bad day. It's been a real bad day; those pictures, and Barnette giving up his vendetta; then Willie Jay heading north; and—and Zackery called me up. *(Trembling with terror)* He says he's gonna have me classified insane and then send me on out to the Whitfield asylum.

MEG: What! Why, he could never do that!

BABE: Why not?

MEG: 'Cause you're not insane.

BABE: I'm not?

MEG: No! He's trying to bluff you. Don't you see it? Barnette's got him running scared.

BABE: Really?

MEG: Sure. He's scared to death—calling you insane. Ha! Why, you're just as perfectly sane as anyone walking the streets of Hazlehurst, Mississippi.

BABE: I am?

MEG: More so! A lot more so!

BABE: Good!

MEG: But, Babe, we've just got to learn how to get through these real bad days here. I mean, it's getting to be a thing in our family. *(Slight pause as she looks at* BABE*)* Come on, now. Look, we've got Lenny's cake right here. I mean, don't you wanna be around to give her her cake, watch her blow out the candles?

BABE: *(Realizing how much she wants to be here)* Yeah, I do, I do. 'Cause she always loves to make her birthday wishes on those candles.

MEG: Well, then, we'll give her her cake and maybe you won't be so miserable.

BABE: Okay.

MEG: Good. Go on and take it out of the box.

BABE: Okay. *(She takes the cake out of the box. It is a magical moment.)* Gosh, it's a pretty cake.

MEG: *(Handing her some matches)* Here now. You can go on and light up the candles.

BABE: All right. *(She starts to light the candles.)* I love to light up candles. And there are so many here. Thirty pink ones in all, plus one green one to grow on.

MEG: *(Watching her light the candles)* They're pretty.

BABE: They are. *(She stops lighting the candles.)* And I'm not like Mama. I'm not so all alone.

MEG: You're not.

BABE: *(As she goes back to lighting candles)* Well, you'd better keep an eye out for Lenny. She's supposed to be surprised.

MEG: All right. Do you know where she's gone?

BABE: Well, she's not here inside—so she must have gone on outside.

MEG: Oh, well, then, I'd better run and find her.

BABE: Okay; 'cause these candles are gonna melt down.

(MEG starts out the door.)

MEG: Wait—there she is coming. Lenny! Oh, Lenny! Come on! Hurry up!

BABE: *(Overlapping and improvising as she finishes lighting candles)* Oh, no! No! Well, yes—Yes! No, wait! Wait! Okay! Hurry up!

(LENNY enters. MEG covers LENNY's eyes with her hands.)

LENNY: *(Terrified)* What? What is it? What?

MEG and BABE: Surprise! Happy birthday! Happy birthday to Lenny!

LENNY: Oh, no! Oh, me! What a surprise! I could just cry! Oh, look: "*Happy Birthday, Lenny—A Day Late!*" How cute! My! Will you look at all those candles—it's absolutely frightening.

BABE: *(A spontaneous thought)* Oh, no, Lenny, it's good! 'Cause—'cause the more candles you have on your cake, the stronger your wish is.

LENNY: Really?

BABE: Sure!

LENNY: Mercy! *(MEG and BABE start to sing.)*

LENNY: *(Interrupting the song)* Oh, but wait! I—can't think of my wish! My body's gone all nervous inside.

MEG: For God's sake, Lenny—come on!

BABE: The wax is all melting!

LENNY: My mind is just a blank, a total blank!

MEG: Will you please just—

BABE: *(Overlapping)* Lenny, hurry! Come on!

LENNY: Okay! Okay! Just go!

(MEG and BABE *burst into the "Happy Birthday" song. As it ends,* LENNY *blows out all the candles on the cake.* MEG *and* BABE *applaud loudly.*)

MEG: Oh, you made it!

BABE: Hurray!

LENNY: Oh, me! Oh, me! I hope that wish comes true! I hope it does!

BABE: Why? What did you wish for?

LENNY: *(As she removes the candles from the cake)* Why, I can't tell you that.

BABE: Oh, sure you can—

LENNY: Oh, no! Then it won't come true.

BABE: Why, that's just superstition! Of course it will, if you made it deep enough.

MEG: Really? I didn't know that.

LENNY: Well, Babe's the regular expert on birthday wishes.

BABE: It's just I get these feelings. Now, come on and tell us. What was it you wished for?

MEG: Yes, tell us. What was it?

LENNY: Well, I guess it wasn't really a specific wish. This—this vision just sort of came into my mind.

BABE: A vision? What was it of?

LENNY: I don't know exactly. It was something about the three of us smiling and laughing together.

BABE: Well, when was it? Was it far away or near?

LENNY: I'm not sure; but it wasn't forever; it wasn't for every minute. Just this one moment and we were all laughing.

BABE: Then, what were we laughing about?

LENNY: I don't know. Just nothing, I guess.

MEG: Well, that's a nice wish to make.

(LENNY and MEG look at each other a moment.)

MEG: Here, now, I'll get a knife so we can go ahead and cut the cake in celebration of Lenny being born!

BABE: Oh, yes! And give each one of us a rose. A whole rose apiece!

LENNY: *(Cutting the cake nervously)* Well, I'll try—I'll try!

MEG: *(Licking the icing off a candle)* Mmmm—this icing is delicious! Here, try some!

BABE: Mmmmm! It's wonderful! Here, Lenny!

LENNY: *(Laughing joyously as she licks icing from her fingers and cuts huge pieces of cake that her sisters bite into ravenously)* Oh, how I do love having birthday cake for breakfast! How I do!

(The sisters freeze for a moment, laughing and catching cake. The lights change and frame them in a magical, golden, sparkling glimmer; saxophone music is heard. The lights dim to blackout, and the saxophone continues to play.)

CURTAIN

END OF PLAY

FOOD FROM TRASH
Gary Leon Hill

FOOD FROM TRASH
© Copyright 1983 by Gary Leon Hill

The stage production rights to this play are represented by Broadway Play Publishing Inc.

All other rights are represented by Mary Harden, Bret Adams Ltd, 448 W 44th St, NY NY 10036, 212 765-5630.

ABOUT THE AUTHOR

FOOD FROM TRASH was Gary Leon Hill's first produced play and was the 1982 winner of the Great American Play Contest sponsored by Actors Theatre of Louisville. His one-act THE BLACK BRANCH was produced in the 1985 Humana Festival of New American Plays. His other plays include WATCH YOUR BACK, PIVOT, and SOUNDBITE, as well as BLUESCROP, a feature film script. Mr. Hill has received two NEA grants and the TCG/HBO Award for Outstanding Achievement in Playwriting, as well as grants from the New York Foundation for the Arts, the Arthur Foundation, the Corporation for Public Broadcasting, and Sensory Overload, Inc.

FOOD FROM TRASH was first produced by Actors Theatre of Louisville on 26 March 1983, with the following cast:

SUDDEN PISANGER	Bill Smitrovich
LEATHA	Nora Chester
LOMAR	Amy Appleby
SON	Will Oldham
BOB	John Pielmeier
CB	Helen-Jean Arthur
PHIL COBB	Andy Backer
BUTCH COBB	Robert Schenkkan
SARGE	Ray Fry
RUNNING JOKE	Kent Broadhurst
FREDDY THE COP	Gary Leon Hill
ALMA	Helen-Jean Arthur
Director	Jon Jory
Set and Lighting	Paul Owen
Costumes	Karen Gerson
Sound	Richard L. Sirois and Larry Hickman

CHARACTERS

SUDDEN PISANGER, *muscled, older than his 36 years, garbageman, husband, father, and natural-born mechanic. Suffers partial neuropathy (nerve damage), arthritis of the upper arms, rash.*

LEATHA PISANGER, *35,* SUDDEN's *wife. Adult-onset diabetes with related symptoms — overweight, retinopathy (retinal damage), water retention, tingling of the hands and feet.*

LOMAR, *teenage foster daughter of* LEATHA *and* SUDDEN. *Bronchial congestion, rash, runny nose, watering eyes.*

SON, *9-year-old son of* LEATHA *and* SUDDEN.

BOB, *30, garbageman, husband, father. Drinks too much, rash, broken glasses, sores that don't heal.*

CB, BOB's *wife* FRANCINE *(never seen).*

PHIL COBB, *55, the boss, owner-operator of Domestic Refuge Inc. Chronic cough, candidate for hypertension, coronary stress.*

BUTCH COBB, *35, puffy son of* PHIL, *in line to take over the business. Developing ulcer.*

SARGE, *60, alcoholic, garbageman, lift on one shoe, liver damage, fine tremors.*

RUNNING JOKE, *30s, ex-garbageman.*

FREDDY THE COP, *dressed in county browns, hung with flashlight, bullhorn, portable phone, handcuffs, bullet belt, Smith & Wesson .38.*

ALMA, *50s, owner-operator of Alma's Bar & Grill.*

PISANGER *and* BOB *wear filthy green overalls.* BUTCH *wears clean green overalls.* PHIL *wears spotless dark blue overalls, white collar showing, tie knot, horn rims.*

The entire cast of characters suffer long range effects of close-up exposure to carcinogenic particles and fumes emanating from PHIL COBB's *Dump. These include recurring nosebleeds, nausea, dizziness, blurriness of vision, nasal, and bronchial congestion.*

LOCATIONS

Landfill Dump *and adjacent surroundings.*

Trailerhouse *platform SR — couch, TV, CB, bed, Coldspot refrigerator, wastebasket, back door, front door.*

Garbage Truck *— USL of* **Trailerhouse***, rear end facing DS, side wall perhaps serving as US wall of* **Trailerhouse***. Hopper holds trash, blade pushes it out.*

The Tanks *— USC, high platform with access to DSC. Five-inch pipe sticking out of the ground, assorted car parts and salvage.*

PHIL COBB's **Office** *— Platform SL of* **The Tanks** *and one step down. Desk, three chairs, phone.*

Alma's Bar & Grill *— Far SL to DSL, connected by steps to Phil's* **Office***. Bar counter, two tables, four chairs, a Wurlitzer jukebox.*

Each playing area has both DS and US access, with CS serving as common playing area. It is front yard for **Trailerhouse***, the bottom of B Street, the dump, the tanks, Phil Cobb's lot, and Alma's lot at different times.*

PHIL COBB's **Car** *— An abbreviated platform, front seat, steering wheel, grill with headlights, perhaps worked by a winch to drive in and out from under* **Office** *platform. Up at* **The Tanks***,* **Car** *can be just a grill with headlights.*

TIME: July

ACT ONE

(Pre-show music ends with Johnny Cash singing "Five Feet High and Rising":

"—rails are washed out north of town
We gotta head for higher ground
Can't come back til the water goes down
Five feet high and rising."

House out.

Scene One

(Hear gate slam shut in a chain-link fence. Hear distant diesel tractor-trailer humming up a grade.

Dim light comes up in **Trailerhouse** bedroom. Pre-dawn.

LEATHA *in her nightgown pounds slow motion on* SUDDEN PISANGER's *chest. His ribcage moans a slow percussion. He is rigid, numb, beyond emotion. He doesn't resist or respond as* LEATHA *pounds on him like a drum. She finally rolls off onto the bed, one side of him. Lights fade.*

Video spill comes up in the **Trailerhouse** *living room where* LOMAR *stares at the TV, rolled up in a sheet like an enchilada on the couch. Hear white noise.*

Dim light up in PHIL COBB's **Office**. BUTCH COBB *snores, slumped in a chair, an open yellow-bound report face down on his belly.*

LOMAR *stands, yawns, sheet draped from her outstretched arms for a moment, then falling to the floor as she crosses to the Coldspot refrigerator. Inside light illuminates her bare legs in a man's T-shirt as she pulls out four tall Cokes, kicks the door shut, uncaps one and lets it roll down her open throat.*

KABOOM! Pre-dawn sky opens up in a blast of orange.

LOMAR's *eyes bug.*

The yellow-bound report leaps high off BUTCH's *belly as he falls off his chair.*

LOMAR *crosses to the* **Trailerhouse** *door.*

Magnified sound: Loose change hits the bedroom floor. PISANGER's *arm drops out of bed.*

BUTCH *scrambles half asleep on all fours, stands, shoves the yellow-bound report into his back pocket and exits* **Office**.)

LOMAR *crosses back to the couch, punches off the TV, and rolls back up into her sheet.*

PHIL COBB's **Car**. BUTCH *and* BOB, BUTCH *driving*.)

BOB: You come down Mohawk?

BUTCH: That's right.

BOB: How's it look?

BUTCH: Dark.

BOB: Is it runnin heavy?

BUTCH: Bob, how long you worked for us?

BOB: Three years.

BUTCH: How's Monday run?

BOB: How heavy, though? Three loads?

BUTCH: Four.

BOB: Shit.

BUTCH: Whatsa matter, Bob? Don't you like hauling garbage?

BOB: Oh, I love it. It just don't lead to nothin.

BUTCH: Don't tell Dad that. He started out at sixteen with a wheelbarrow and a pair of gloves. Now look at us — fifteen men, ten trucks, a 48-acre sanitary landfill and a 19__ Lincoln Continental.

BOB: You can train a damn monkey to walk down the street and pick up garbage cans.

BUTCH: That's what he did.

(**Trailerhouse**. *Tight flashlight beam hits* PISANGER *in the face coming out of the bedroom — bag-eyed, in underpants, carrying his clothes. He squints, covers his face.*)

PISANGER: Dammit, Lomar. (LOMAR *shifts the beam to his crotch and wags it.*) DAMMIT! (*He turns his back, pulls on his pants.* LOMAR *throws the flashlight onto the couch, picks up three tall Cokes off the TV, and crosses to the door.*)

LOMAR: God, it's back.

PISANGER: What is?

LOMAR: The stench. Couldn't sleep for the trucks driving in and out of the dump all night, now a *bomb* goes off, and now this stink.

PISANGER: What trucks?

LOMAR: Those tractor-trailer trucks.

PISANGER: The dump don't open till seven.

LOMAR: You didn't hear that bomb go off?

PISANGER: You're dreaming, Lomar.

LOMAR: Not this stink.

(PISANGER *leans in for Cokes* LOMAR *holds behind her.*)

PISANGER: That's the smell of money. *(Grabs two Cokes)*

LOMAR: Not yours. Not mine. (PISANGER *is out the door.*) Phil's money!

(BUTCH *and* BOB *stand out front.*)

BUTCH: Morning, Pisanger.

BOB: 'Lo, Sudden.

LOMAR: *(Opens screen door)* Either you guys hear that explosion?

PISANGER: *(Lacing his boots on the stoop)* Get back inside.

LOMAR: *(Back inside)* Either of yuh?

BUTCH: *(Leers)* Either of us? (BOB *shakes his head no.*) Nice dress, Lomar.

PISANGER: *(Snaps)* Where's my boat trailer, Butch? I paid you for it. You said you'd bring it over.

BUTCH: What's your hurry? You don't have a boat so you can't use it. Your Chevy don't run so you can't pull it anywhere.

(LOMAR *flops back onto the couch.*)

PISANGER: I'll get the Chevy running. All I need is some parts.

BUTCH: You'll need a sled by then and a pickax to chop through the ice with.

BOB: At least he'll catch something.

BUTCH: Catch cold first, catch hell when he gets home. Ain't that right, Piss-Anger?

(*They cross toward* **Alma's Bar & Grill**.)

PISANGER: I don't know. I'd have to ask Freddy.

BUTCH: Ask Freddy about what?

PISANGER: About all those holes in the bottom of your boat.

BUTCH: *(Laughs hysterically)* Axe fishing!

BOB: Don't tell that again.

(BOB *tries* ALMA's *door. It's locked.*)

BUTCH: The day Freddy Cook got down on all fours in the bottom of my new boat and caught carp with his goddam hands!

BOB: You can't catch carp with your hands.

BUTCH: *You* can't. Freddy could. He *was*! He was down on all fours in the bottom of my boat —

BOB and BUTCH: *(In unison)* — scooping carp out of Branched Oak Lake —

BOB: — with his *hands*. And you got mad and started busting up the water with your goddam ax.

PISANGER: Catch anything?

BUTCH: Bluegill, carp, channel cat — Hell yes I hit em. And they come up bite size, too.

PISANGER: How many holes in the bottom of your boat?

(ALMA *unlocks her door. They enter.*)

BUTCH: I clobbered so goddam many fish you couldn't count the pieces.

ALMA: Morning Butch, boys.

BUTCH: Morning, Alma.

PISANGER: How long'd it take that boat to sink?

BUTCH: Bout as long as it took me to talk you into buying my boat trailer. For *twice* what I paid for it. I come outta that one pretty good, wouldn't you say, Pisanger? Huh?

PISANGER: Yeh.

BUTCH: Huh?

PISANGER: Yeh.

BUTCH: Wouldn't you say I come outta that one all right?

BOB: Let his turds roll, Sudden.

BUTCH: If you ever get your Chevy running, I might even sell you the boat!

BOB: He ain't like us. He don't work for a living. He don't know friendship.

PISANGER: What do you want, Bob?

(BUTCH *sits, then stands immediately to remove the yellow-bound report rolled up in his back pocket. He puts the report on the table in front of him.*)

BOB: *(Continuous)* Will you take my place when I finish up today? I gotta get somewhere.

PISANGER: She'll wait.

BOB: That ain't it. I don't see her anymore.

PISANGER: Since when?

BOB: Since that night you seen us out to the garage? Two days after that I went back to Francine.

PISANGER: Yeh?

BOB: Yeh. Francine used the kid on me. Had Aaron tell me he didn't wanna see me drunk or throw up in his sandbox. Kids. They pull at the heartstrings. Hell, you know that.

PISANGER: If it's Francine —

BOB: No.

PISANGER: — I *know* she can wait to see you.

BOB: There's a 'lectronics class at three-thirty over at Tech. I gotta get home, clean up, get there.

PISANGER: Electronics!

BOB: *(Pulls magazine from his pocket)* Yeh!

PISANGER: I thought you were gonna get a truck and steal a garbage route.

BOB: Shhhhhhh.

PISANGER: Run Cobbs outta business.

BOB: I said if they ever made me mad enough I would.

PISANGER: Ain't Butch runnin the route today?

BOB: That's what I mean. He'll be drivin round in circles. I'll never get off.

PISANGER: That oughta make you mad enough.

ALMA: *(Serves BOB a plate of food)* Everything eats and everything is eaten. What's eating you boys this morning?

BOB: *(Reads plate)* Three eggs, toast, hashbrowns, coffee. Thanks, Alma.

ALMA: You never change, Bob. How 'bout you, Sudden?

PISANGER: I'll drink my Coke.

ALMA: And rot your insides.

PISANGER: It starts my heart, Alma.

(ALMA shakes her head.)

BOB: *(Eats)* Sudden, it ain't me. Look, I've had worse jobs.

PISANGER: What's worsen haulin garbage?

BOB: Rippin cheeks offa pigs at the slaughterhouse. No, it's Francine, see. She don't wanna be married to a garbageman.

PISANGER: She got you the job.

BOB: *(Hits nerve)* The hell she did!

PISANGER: *(Hands BOB a matchbook)* Giver these.

BOB: *(Reads cover)* "No-fault divorce."

(Enter PHIL COBB, pleased with himself, unlit cigar in mouth.)

ALMA: Lo, Phil.

PHIL: *(Expansive)* Good morning, beautiful.

BUTCH: Hey, Dad.

PHIL: Son.

(BUTCH double takes on the yellow-bound report. He slides it underneath him on the seat of his chair, sits down.)

ALMA: *(Continuous)* What are you so happy about, Phil?

BOB: *(Hands matches back to PISANGER)* I give you my rod and reel.

ALMA: Got a bottle in the car or what?

PHIL: Alma, you know I can't drink. *(He coughs.)*

BOB: And my copper wire.

ALMA: You smokin somethin funny, Phil?

PHIL: *(Still coughing)* I haven't even lit it yet.

PISANGER: *(Tosses matches to PHIL)* Here, Phil.

PHIL: Thanks, Sudden. *(Reads matchbook)*

BOB: And I'll throw in all my aluminum.

PISANGER: I can't today, Bob.

ALMA: Did you get that government contract?

PISANGER: Leatha's got Weight Watchers.

ALMA: You're going to haul the schools.

PHIL: Schools, hell!

BOB: *(Throws his magazine open)* Shit.

BUTCH: Did K-Mart finally pay up, Dad?

PHIL: No, Butch. I'm sending you out to K-Mart this morning to shut that compactor off.

BUTCH: That'll put the screws to them. Wait'll their store fills up with garbage.

PHIL: Decided that last night, me and your mother, counting our money. *(He pulls out a wad of bills.)*

BUTCH: Holy shit, Dad!

PHIL: Intuition in the fifth!

BOB: *(Ears prick.)* That's MY horse! Phil! You bet him?

PHIL: Intuition? Damn right I did!

BUTCH: What he pay, Dad?

PHIL: *(Second thought, folds money away)* Overhead.

BOB: Where's my share?

PHIL: You get a new barrel.

BOB: I give you the tip!

PHIL: And I put a brand new carrying barrel on the truck for you.

BOB: Phil, I give you the goddam tip!

PHIL: Don't drag this one down the driveway. Put it on your shoulder. It's the last one you get.

(SARGE *enters. He is 60, dressed in a threadbare dark suit, white shirt, tie, a lift on one shoe, both shoes shined.)*

ALMA: Sarge!

PHIL: Goddam!

PISANGER: Hey!

BUTCH: Holy cow! Back from the dead!

PHIL: Sarge, where in hell you been?

SARGE: I been in the slammer, Phil.

PHIL: You want to work?

SARGE: I got two dimes in my pocket, Phil. I gotta work.

PISANGER: You rested up?

SARGE: Oh yeh. Dried out and everything else, I guess.

BOB: *(To* PISANGER*)* I asked Phil for two bucks to bet that horse and Phil wouldn't do it. Then HE bets the sonofabitch.

PHIL: I don't suppose you got too good a breakfast in jail.

SARGE: No, they kick you out before breakfast. Save that money.

PHIL: Well, I'll buy you breakfast. *(Pulls* BUTCH *out of his chair)* Son, let Sarge sit down. Alma, give Sarge something to eat.

ALMA: Ham and eggs, Sarge?

PHIL: *(Sits* SARGE *down)* There you go, Sarge.

ALMA: Short stack, coffee, toast?

SARGE: That'll fit, Alma.

PHIL: Butch, where's Running Joke?

BUTCH: Oh, ain't you heard, Dad? Running Joke's gone back up to the reservation.

PHIL: Butch —

BUTCH: Yeh, he's up there at Rosebud hanging from his tits over a pile of shit!

PHIL: I told you to go find him.

BUTCH: That's the famous Indian Shit Ritual! *(Laughs real hard)*

PHIL: You tell him we need him, Son.

BUTCH: We don't need him, Dad. We never did. And sure not now that Sarge is squeezed dry. Right, Sarge?

PHIL: Sarge lost his driver's license.

BUTCH: Well, you're not gonna let Running Joke *drive* again, are you?

PHIL: Go get him, Son.

BUTCH: Number twelve's not out of the shop yet and you're gonna put that dog eater behind the wheel again?

PHIL: *(Quiet authority)* Butch.

BUTCH: *(Resigns)* Jesus.

PHIL: Pisanger, quit scratching.

PISANGER: *(Rakes his arm with his nails)* It's gettin' worse, Phil.

PHIL: It'd go away if you stopped drinking all that Coke.

PISANGER: Doc Stewart says it comes from workin the route.

BUTCH: Hoo hah. Now I heard everything.

PISANGER: He says it's got to be an infection of some kind I'm gettin from the garbage.

BUTCH: If you could get diseased offa garbage route, don't you think I'd died of it a long time ago?

BOB: Maybe you can't get it just sittin in the truck.

PHIL: Butch. (BUTCH *exits.* PHIL *peels off more bills.*) Here, Sarge. Get some cigarettes.

SARGE: Thanks, Phil.

PHIL: I don't suppose you have any gloves.

SARGE: No.

PHIL: Alma, get this man some gloves. And here. *(Peels off more bills for* SARGE*)*

(*Outside* **Alma's Bar & Grill**, FREDDY THE COP *leans against* PHIL COBB's **Car** *and peers through binoculars toward* LOMAR *asleep in the* **Trailerhouse**.)

BUTCH: Freddy.

FREDDY: Butch.

(FREDDY *hands binoculars to* BUTCH, *who focuses in on* LOMAR.)

SARGE: *(Continuous)* I appreciate this, Phil.

PHIL: Just don't say nothing to my wife or the boys.

SARGE: How do you want me to pay you back?

PHIL: When you get it.

SARGE: I will as soon as I can.

PHIL: There's no hurry about it. I'll get it out of you.

(PHIL *stands, crosses to* ALMA *at the bar to settle accounts.*)

FREDDY: Kooser's trailerhouse exploded, Butch. (BUTCH *lowers binoculars.*) Some kinda fumes.

BUTCH: Does anybody know?

FREDDY: You mean was anybody hurt?

BUTCH: You know what I mean.

FREDDY: Better mean you got rid of that report, Butch.

BUTCH: *(Hand to back pocket)* I did.

FREDDY: Like you said you would.

BUTCH: *(Hand to other back pocket)* I will.

FREDDY: You better.

(FREDDY *exits.* BUTCH *turns 360° and frisks himself, then remembers where he left it. He moves to* ALMA's *door as* PHIL *turns to the assembled for a final word, blocking* BUTCH's *entrance.*)

PHIL: Gentlemen, three hundred garbage cans stand out there waiting on your gentle expertise.

SARGE: Thanks, Phil.

PHIL: Bye Alma. Bye boys.

ALMA: Bye, Phil.

PHIL: *(Turns)* Butch!

BUTCH: Dad I —

PHIL: Butch! GO!

(Exit BUTCH *and* PHIL.*)*

BOB: Seven hundred cans! A day! Sixteen thousand pounds! A day! Eight goddam tons of somebody else's shit!

ALMA: *(Serving* SARGE *breakfast)* Bob, don't talk like that.

SARGE: Thanks, Alma.

BOB: Alma, I haul two thousand houses and fifty downtown stops eight times a month for that sonofabitch. Now forget downtown, he takes in twenty-five, thirty grand a month. He takes in thirty grand a month, he gives me one hundred seventy-five dollars a week.

PISANGER: He gives you one hundred fifty dollars a week and takes half that back playing blackjack in the office. But what are you gonna do about it?

BOB: I'm gonna —

PISANGER and BOB: *(In unison)* — complain about it —

PISANGER: — real loud. What else?

BOB: Look, Sudden, I ain't dumb and I ain't dead and I ain't given up like *you* have.

PISANGER: I ain't given up.

BOB: Phil's got ten years of your life. So far. And what have you got? One sad-ass trailer down by the dump. This ain't no place to raise kids, have a family, support a wife. You ain't a man.

PISANGER: You are?

BOB: Damn right. I'm tryin.

PISANGER: Bob, you're me five years younger and if you don't know that, you're stupider than I was when I was your age.

BOB: I ain't *nothin* like you!

(BOB *stands scratching his arm in a gesture identical to* PISANGER's. PISANGER *scratches.*)

PISANGER: Oh no? *(Moves toward door)* See you out there, Sarge.

SARGE: Where at?

PISANGER: I'll pick up King Dollar. You meet me at the bottom of B.

SARGE: Okay.

(Exit PISANGER.*)*

ALMA: Bob —

BOB: *(On his way out)* What?

ALMA: Three eggs, toast, hashbrowns, and coffee.

BOB: Phil paid.

ALMA: Phil paid for Sarge. Not for every stoat in the hall.

BOB: That was *my* horse, Alma!

ALMA: Next time you give *me* the tip.

BOB: I give that man three years of my life and he ain't *never* bought me breakfast.

ALMA: You boys put together a union, you could be buying Phil breakfast. No union, no protection, no bargaining, no benefits, you won't stick together —

BOB: It's too late for a union, Alma.

ALMA: *(Hand out)* Two thirty-seven with tax. (BOB *pays, exits.* ALMA *turns to* SARGE, *smiles.*) Good to see you again, Dugan.

SARGE: Still alive, Alma. Thought a lot about you. Peter did, too.

ALMA: Him too, huh?

(ALMA *straddles* SARGE's *lap, facing him.*)

SARGE: Yep. *(They hold each other.)* Remember Branched Oak Lake?

ALMA: After the wreck? Or before?

(They crack up laughing.)

SARGE: How'd that happen again?

(ALMA *rotates slowly in* SARGE's *lap.* SARGE *matches her move. They laugh. Phone rings. She stands, moves back behind the bar, and* SARGE *gets up.*)

ALMA: I'll see *you* later.

(ALMA *answers phone.* SARGE *pulls on new gloves, is about to leave* —)

SARGE: See you later, Alma...

(—*when he sees the yellow-bound report on the seat of his chair. He picks it up. An accordion page flops out. He exits.*)

Scene Two

(**Garbage Truck** *idles at the bottom of B Street.* PISANGER *hooks the truck's chains to a container and hits the switch. The blade pulls back, the container lifts, and garbage slides out into the hopper.* PISANGER *reverses the switch, the blade comes forward, the container drops. He unchains it, rolls it out of the way as the blade shoves garbage high into the truck. The power take-off shuts off, truck idles.*

A mourning dove purrs. PISANGER *shivers and wheels around. He's heard something else, seen something in his blindspot.*

SARGE *drags his barrel round the back of the truck wearing clean green overalls, pulling on new gloves.*)

SARGE: Jimmy Plattsmouth says hello.

PISANGER: That goofy bastard back in jail?

SARGE: He bounced another check.

PISANGER: Insufficient brains. I heard he called the cops up and told them he was gonna drive a hundred miles an hour through downtown and they couldn't catch him.

(*They work the route, empty garbage cans into barrels either side of CS.*)

SARGE: He was doin ninety when he went off that little bridge. Yeh. He's still in. He don't want out. Funny how many people locked up in jail don't want out.

PISANGER: It's getting worse out here.

SARGE: Looks good to me. Smells good. Feels good.

PISANGER: I'm not talking about Alma.

SARGE: *(Laughs)* How you doin, though, Sudden? Really.

PISANGER: Fine.

SARGE: How fine?

PISANGER: All right.

SARGE: You get your Chevy runnin?

PISANGER: Not yet.

SARGE: You and Leatha? Workin things out?

PISANGER: Not really.

SARGE: You ever figure out what killed your trees?

PISANGER: Whatever it was killed the bushes, too.

SARGE: I saw Lomar's father in prison. He's one mean stupid sonofabitch. Musta been murder livin with him.

PISANGER: *(Pulls apple from pocket)* What's he in for? *(He already knows.)*

SARGE: Incest, ain't it? (PISANGER *bites into the apple — crack.*) Delinquency of a minor? You still eatin outta the hopper?

PISANGER: I got this offa tree.

SARGE: You don't change.

PISANGER: Come on, Sarge. I got this off that tree.

SARGE: Still eatin garbage and still won't admit it.

PISANGER: Bullshit.

SARGE: Remember eatin chicken out backa the Drumstick? Fillin' our bellies and greasin our hair at the same time? *(Runs fingers through his hair)*

PISANGER: I remember the summer you quit haulin that woman's cat shit.

SARGE: Well, Jesus. I told her to bag it. She wouldn't bag it. Just poured it down in the bottom of the can and put her other stuff on top. I took her other stuff.

PISANGER: *(Laughs)* Yeh, and you kept pullin her can around into the sun so it'd bake up real good.

SARGE: It kept gettin fuller and I kept not takin it. Finally built up to where even she couldn't stand it. One morning she came out with another box of cat shit, lifted the lid, and fell over. (PISANGER *dumps his barrel into the hopper, leans over into his empty barrel and pulls out a snapshot, wipes it on his leg.*) Catshit turns into industrial ammonia. It'll kill yuh.

PISANGER: *(Hands him the snapshot)* Look at this.

SARGE: Now if you only knew where she lived, huh?

PISANGER: She moved in over there. That yellow house.

SARGE: With this fellow?

PISANGER: No.

SARGE: Got a little one, don't he?

PISANGER: How's yer foot?

(SARGE *starts to tuck the snapshot into his back pocket, hits the rolled-up yellow-bound report.*)

SARGE: It's better.

(SARGE *pulls out the yellow-bound report.*)

PISANGER: You all right now?

(*The accordion page flops out.*)

SARGE: Yeh.

PISANGER: — I quit drinkin'.

SARGE: — Did you?

PISANGER: Day you got hurt.

SARGE: That wasn't your fault, Sudden. (PISANGER *shrugs.*) You told Butch not to put anybody on that truck. You hadn't finished with the brakes, you said. Butch knew that when he give it to Running Joke. He knew it when I got on. I knew it too.

PISANGER: So why'd you get on?

SARGE: *(Beat)* I don't remember. I was drunker than you were. *(They laugh.)* Tell you what, though, Sudden, here, you take this — *(Hands him report)* —and I'll take this — *(He wags the snapshot.)* — and you pull the truck up —

PISANGER: What *is* it?

SARGE: You tell me. I'm gonna go work this woman's side of the street.

(SARGE *laughs, exits.* PISANGER *opens the report. The accordion page flops out. His lips move, reading.*)

Scene Three

(**Trailerhouse**. *Early morning.*)

CB: Breaker one nine, we lookin for that one Queen Bee. You got your ears on, girl? Over. (LEATHA *in chenille bathrobe crosses to the CB radio.* LOMAR *on the couch*) Breaker one nine for the Queen Bee. You copy?

LEATHA: Ten four, Cotton Candy. You're hittin me with ten pounds over here and thanks for the pills.

CB: That's all I could get is two bottles. Go head.

LEATHA: *(Holds one bottle)* Two bottles?

CB: I'm sorry. I know how it is. I porked out after Aaron was born — uh, that slipped. I'm sorry.

LEATHA: I'm fat, Francine. I know it. These'll help.

CB: You get dizzy, you stretch out.

LEATHA: You have any fun last night?

CB: I was having fun when he passed out. Put it that way.

LEATHA: You gotta wean that man.

CB: Bob was born spittin up.

LEATHA: I did my time. I won't live with a drunk. Over.

CB: Tell you what, though, Leatha. Next time don't send Lomar over. Go head.

LEATHA: Why not?

CB: She sleep good?

LEATHA: Yeh. Still is.

CB: She ought to. She drank enough barley pop over here to flush a toilet.

LEATHA: You wanna ten-nine that?

CB: She wouldn't go home!

LEATHA: You got her hooked on your color TV.

CB: Negatory. She was eyeballing my Bob.

LOMAR: *(Sits up)* That dumb cow.

CB: You wanna ten-nine that?

(Alarm clock goes off.)

LEATHA: Lomar, get the clock. (LOMAR *layers her lips with blood-red lipstick.*) Get off your butt and shut off the clock!

(LOMAR *doesn't budge.* LEATHA *crosses back to the bed and punches the alarm clock.*)

CB: Queen Bee, you out there? Queen Bee, you copy?

(LEATHA *crosses back to the CB radio.*)

LEATHA: I gotta back out, Francine. I'll catch you on the flipflop.

CB: Threes to you and a buncha eighty-eights. We gone.

(LEATHA *cradles the CB mike and crosses to the couch, takes one end of* LOMAR's *sheet and whips her out onto the floor.*)

LEATHA: Get up. Get dressed. Get out of my sight.

(LEATHA *flops onto her bed.* LOMAR *makes a sullen cross to the Coldspot, pulls out a tall Coke and uncaps it. She pops a handful of pills into her mouth and draws slow on her Coke.*)

Scene Four

(**Garbage Truck**—*Landfill Dump. Early afternoon.*

SARGE *stands at rear of truck.* PISANGER's *legs stick out from underneath it. His red tool box sits open DS. Hear a ratchet wrench from underneath as* BOB *rounds the truck with a six pack: "R-r-r- itch, r-r-r-itch, r-r-r-itch.")*

BOB: Here, Sarge. Welcome back.

SARGE: You shouldn't of.

BOB: It was sittin on top of that Radar Range.

SARGE: Somebody lost their mind.

BOB: *(Pops open a can, hands one to* SARGE*)* Here's to you, Sarge. Here's to life outside the slammer.

(BOB *drinks.* SARGE *doesn't.*)

SARGE: I had a nice family one time I lost onna counta this shit. Kept gettin drunk, gettin mean with her. She finally wouldn't put up with it.

BOB: Hell, Francine drank moren I did. She was always gettin' *me* drunk.

SARGE: Not anymore?

BOB: Not since the kids. Now I gotta stop? Cause I got kids? Cause she stopped?

SARGE: Lotta people wonder why a man drinks. Why he grows old. There's a lotta things people don't know.

BOB: I know I ain't quittin.

SARGE: I'm like you. I'm stubborn. In 1976 Phil Cobb got me outta jail twenty-seven times for public intoxication. Finally said, you know, I think you're so hooked on that booze you can't quit. It made me angry. I didn't take a drink for eighteen months! Phil Cobb told me I couldn't quit. So I bust my ass to show him I did. *(He pops open his beer and draws hard.)*

BOB: So now you got a busted ass and a lift on one shoe. And what's Phil got?

SARGE: The leg was my fault. I come down wrong off the backa that truck.

BOB: Phil's truck. You were workin.

SARGE: My own fault.

BOB: The hell it was. Running Joke was drivin.

(PISANGER *slides out from under the truck, face spliced with crud.*)

SARGE: Running Joke got set up.

BOB: How much longer's this gonna take?

PISANGER: Gettin mad, Bob?

BOB: I been mad enough to quit since I started.

(PISANGER *moves DS to his red tool box.*)

PISANGER: You oughta look into the field of electronics.

BOB: Blew that. It's past noon. We still got half the route left.

PISANGER: What took you guys so long?

BOB: Butch took us out to K-Mart so we could watch him disconnect that compactor. Spent the rest of the morning driving round in circles looking for Running Joke.

PISANGER: You find him?

BOB: He don't wanna be found.

PISANGER: Butch don't wanna find him.

BOB: Hell, we spent the mornin—

PISANGER: Butch knows where he is.

BOB: Where?

PISANGER: Up at the tanks.

BOB: Phil's tanks?

PISANGER: Look up there at night sometime, Bob. Lights flashing, smoke signals.

BOB: What's he doing?

PISANGER: Livin like an animal. Has been.

BOB: Does Phil know that?

PISANGER: I know it.

BOB: Why would Phil let him up there and act like he don't know it?

PISANGER: Why'd Phil beg him not to quit in the first place? Why's he always tryin to hire him back? Why'd Phil try and give him a route?

BOB: What!

PISANGER: Day after the accident, Phil told Running Joke he could have the Air Base. Phil'd give him a truck. He could work that route himself.

BOB: *After* the accident?

PISANGER: Yeh.

BOB: I work three years I get nothin! Running Joke works one week, wrecks a truck, puts Sarge inna hospital —

PISANGER: What about *me*, Bob? *Ten years*! Work the route, fix the trucks, drop that tranny, put a new motor in. Do this. Do that. Come in early. Stay late. Go home. Come back. *Phil don't even know the route!*

BOB: *(Cowed)* — So what's he see in Running Joke?

PISANGER: *(Grudgingly)* He's smart, Bob. Running Joke knows something we don't know.

BOB: Like what?

PISANGER: *(Leans in, obvious)* Like I don't know, Bob.

BOB: I told Butch we could find the bastard better with a Geiger counter, whatever it was, you remember that time Butch had it out there looking for coins? Every time he'd point it in Running Joke's direction damn thing'd go off tick tick tick tick tick tick tick —

SARGE: *(To himself)* ...If it hadn't been for that little lady I was stayin with at that time, I'd been awful cold and awful hungry. (SARGE *peels a third beer out of the collar.* PISANGER *throws what's left of the six pack to hell and gone.)* Between her and her sister they kept me pretty well satisfied both physically and sexually and everything else, so —

PISANGER: Try it now, Sarge. Start it up. *(Approaches* SARGE*)*

(SARGE *pushes* PISANGER*'s hand away, throws beer can, stalks off around the truck.)*

PISANGER: Bob, you dumb fuck.

(Truck starter grinds. Engine turns over. Exit BOB. PISANGER *hits the lever on his way out and the Power Take Off kicks in. The blade clears the hopper. The hopper lifts on chrome hydraulics. The front wall shoves back, forcing out a truckload of garbage in a jerking peristalsis. The hopper drops. The PTO kicks out. Birds twirp. High idle. Taillights.*

From deep within this mountain of garbage, emerges RUNNING JOKE, *in boots, maroon sweat pants, a black shirt hanging in wide ribbons, a yellow shirt hanging in wide ribbons over that, a shredding denim jacket with large pockets outside and many more inside. Standing, he is vertical litter. Blackout.)*

Scene Five

(**Trailerhouse**. *Afternoon.* SON *explodes up out of a nightmare, hits the floor —* THUD *— screaming.*)

SON: Maaaaaaa! Maaaaaa! (LEATHA *rushes in.*) I saw Buddy, Ma —

(She lifts him into her arms.)

LEATHA: Shhhhhhhh, I'm here.

SON: He just kept comin at me, gettin bigger —

LEATHA: You're dreamin.

SON: — and his skin kept comin off him and his mouth was...

LEATHA: *(Rocks him)* Shhhhhhhhhh.

SON: He was spittin out his fur, Ma.... Turnin black and bleeding, he was...

LEATHA: Shhhhhhhhhhh.

Scene Six

(PHIL COBB's **Office**. *Afternoon.*)

FREDDY: Don't worry. Butch got rid of it.

PHIL: I did not *give* Butch that report to throw away, Fred. I gave it to him to *read*. I wouldn't have done *that* if you hadn't told him there *was* a report. I didn't tell him.

FREDDY: I thought we were in this together, Phil.

PHIL: We are *out* of it together, Fred. As of now. (PHIL *pulls dollar bills from his wad and gives them to* FREDDY.) I have plans.

FREDDY: *(Pockets money)* What plans?

PHIL: I will tell you when it's time.

FREDDY: What about Running Joke?

PHIL: What about him?

FREDDY: Yer not afraid of what he'll do?

PHIL: I don't *know* what he'll do. I don't know what he knows. Do you?

FREDDY: You want me to run him off your land?

(PHIL *lays one more dollar bill down in front of* FREDDY.)

PHIL: I want you to watch him.

(FREDDY *takes it.*)

Scene Seven

(**Landfill Dump**. Afternoon. LOMAR *sits in the pile of garbage where* RUNNING JOKE *was last seen. She sorts trash and sings to herself.*

The earth rumbles. She looks behind her, sees nothing. She rips open another bag and finds a rubber dildo. Brightening some, she uses it as a microphone.)

LOMAR: *(Sings)* She don't love you.
Like I love you.
If she did she wouldn't
Break my heart —

(RUNNING JOKE *appears.*)

RUNNING JOKE: Afternoon, Lomar.

LOMAR: Oooooooh! *(Stashes dildo in shoulder bag)* You give me chills creepin up on me like that!

RUNNING JOKE: You bring the boy?

LOMAR: I get tired him taggin after me everywhere I go. Sides, Leatha don't want him out here with you.

RUNNING JOKE: Leatha doesn't want *you* out here, either, does she?

LOMAR: She doesn't have that bigga say over me. I know too much.

RUNNING JOKE: About what?

LOMAR: Her. (RUNNING JOKE *hunkers down, starts sorting trash.*) You think I'm pretty?

(RUNNING JOKE *pulls a length of plastic tubing from a bag, coils it, puts it in his pocket.*)

RUNNING JOKE: You remind me of my sister.

LOMAR: She pretty?

RUNNING JOKE: Beautiful.

LOMAR: I mean not now with my eyes burnt holes inna blanket and a chest fulla crud, but —

RUNNING JOKE: Maybe too much makeup.

LOMAR: That's to cover up these splotches. I'm breakin out. Somethin's got me good. I think it's all this ree-pressed sex I'm not gettin. *(Laughs too loud)* She's nice, though, huh? Your sister?

RUNNING JOKE: She is sad like you. She misses Father.

(FREDDY enters with binoculars high SR. He focuses in on them.)

LOMAR: You hear that bomb go off?

RUNNING JOKE: This morning.

LOMAR: I *knew* it! Was it out here?

RUNNING JOKE: Sounded like the trailer court.

LOMAR: He lied to me.

RUNNING JOKE: Who did?

LOMAR: Everybody. *(She hands him an empty milk jug.)* This work?

RUNNING JOKE: Looks like it might. *(He sets it aside.*

The earth rumbles. RUNNING JOKE *cocks an ear.)*

LOMAR: You ever drink blood?

RUNNING JOKE: No, but I did pills, Lomar.

LOMAR: I heard of a person oncet usta work out to the slaughterhouse? He'd bring cow blood home in a mason jar and drink it.

RUNNING JOKE: *(Reads page he's pulled from his pocket)* " The level of your being attracts your life."

LOMAR: Where'd you get that?

RUNNING JOKE: I found it in the garbage.

LOMAR: What's it mean?

RUNNING JOKE: *(Hands her the page)* What do you think?

(She reads the page, she droops.)

LOMAR: *(Sighs)* I belong at the dump. I feel like a pile of shit.

RUNNING JOKE: *(Points) That* is a pile of shit.

LOMAR: I could *tell* that.

RUNNING JOKE: Some animal couldn't use that part of what it ate and got rid of it.

LOMAR: That's me.

RUNNING JOKE: You treat it right, that pile of shit will heat your home, it'll drive a car, lift a Lear jet right up off the ground and fly you — Where do you want to go?

LOMAR: *(Brightens)* Kansas! I told you. You gonna take me?

BUTCH: *(Offstage)* Running Joke!

LOMAR: You said you would!

RUNNING JOKE: I said I would *not*.

LOMAR: Goddammit!

BUTCH: *(Offstage)* Running Joke!

LOMAR: I gotta get outta here. You gotta help me.

(LOMAR *shoots offstage as* BUTCH *comes in with a shotgun and metal traps.*)

BUTCH: Running Joke. You're on our land.

RUNNING JOKE: Dad's land.

BUTCH: Mine too.

RUNNING JOKE: Mother Earth.

(The earth rumbles. They both hear it.)

BUTCH: Out checking your traps? *(Throws traps at* RUNNING JOKE'S *feet)*

RUNNING JOKE: Just listening to your ground fart.

BUTCH: That was a truck backfire.

RUNNING JOKE: Last week it backfired, took out that stinkweed tree.

BUTCH: What stinkweed tree?

RUNNING JOKE: I watched your tractor plow it under.

BUTCH: We got nothing to hide.

RUNNING JOKE: You got a lot you're ignoring.

BUTCH: Like what?

RUNNING JOKE: Like the fact that garbage packed this tight this long makes methane gas.

BUTCH: Like the fact this land is posted "No Trespassing" every fifty feet? *(Levels shotgun at* RUNNING JOKE*)* I could part your hair for good right now, no white man'd ever miss you.

RUNNING JOKE: Crippled Sarge last time you tried —

BUTCH: Including Dad won't miss you.

RUNNING JOKE: Wrecked a truck.

BUTCH: We don't need that truck and we don't need you. We got ten trucks and fifteen men without you. Plus we got the first sanitary landfill in America with a plastic liner. We had a centerfold in *Waste Age*.

RUNNING JOKE: *Waste Age*?

BUTCH: We are state-of-the-art in solid waste management.

RUNNING JOKE: Waste makes you great?

BUTCH: It makes us boss.

RUNNING JOKE: Of what?

BUTCH: Of shit like you. Hell, you know that. We wasted your people. Smashed your culture. Stole your land. We murdered your parents.

RUNNING JOKE: You did all that?

BUTCH: You're an Indian, ain't you?

RUNNING JOKE: Who told you that, Butch?

(LOMAR *hovers US.*)

BUTCH: *You* did.

RUNNING JOKE: I told you I was an alien, Butch. To the way you think. Alien.

(LOMAR *from behind shoves dildo between* BUTCH's *legs and wags it.* BUTCH *grabs it, sees what it is, yells out, lets go.*)

BUTCH: Put that down! You don't know where it's been.

LOMAR: I gotta pretty good idea.

BUTCH: Give it here!

LOMAR: Get yer own!

BUTCH: Dammit, Lomar! Give me the goddam —

(BUTCH *lunges.* LOMAR *sidesteps him and breaks USL, off.* BUTCH *chases after her.*

RUNNING JOKE *wraps copper wire around his hand, pockets it, then hunkers down to sort more trash.*

PHIL *approaches, unhurried.*)

PHIL: Looking for something?

RUNNING JOKE: All my life, Phil.

PHIL: Anything worth money the men already took.

RUNNING JOKE: *(Inventory)* Copper wire, plastic tubing —

PHIL: You still up at the tanks?

RUNNING JOKE: You know where I am, Phil.

PHIL: We had a incident happen this morning.

RUNNING JOKE: Something blew up.

PHIL: Which is under investigation.

RUNNING JOKE: Freddy looking into it?

PHIL: He may want to talk to you.

RUNNING JOKE: Was it methane?

PHIL: It was Kooser's trailerhouse. They're not sure what happened.

RUNNING JOKE: Methane.

PHIL: We don't know that for a fact.

RUNNING JOKE: There is power underground here. Phil.

PHIL: I *know* what's underground here. I put it there.

RUNNING JOKE: Let's mine it.

PHIL: What?

RUNNING JOKE: Let's bring the methane up.

PHIL: I am not digging up this landfill.

RUNNING JOKE: You won't have to. Just drop pipes down. We'll use fans.

PHIL: No.

RUNNING JOKE: It'll power your trucks. It'll drive that brand-ew car of yours.

PHIL: *(Proudly)* That's a Lincoln Continental.

RUNNING JOKE: I know. I saw it.

PHIL: You could be driving one like it.

RUNNING JOKE: *(Shakes head)* Lot of chrome on that car, Phil.

PHIL: My offer stands, Running Joke. You take the Air Base. Work that route. It's yours. You take a truck. We split the money.

RUNNING JOKE: And I shut up about what I know?

PHIL: What do you know?

RUNNING JOKE: I know as is your methane here won't burn in a combustion engine.

PHIL: Then leave it where it is.

RUNNING JOKE: It won't stay there. It keeps drifting, keeps exploding.

PHIL: But if it won't burn as fuel—

RUNNING JOKE: We have to separate it out.

PHIL: *(Measured)* Separate it out from what?

RUNNING JOKE: From whatever else besides garbage you've been dumping here, Phil.

(Their eyes lock. BUTCH *chases* LOMAR *back onstage. She's got the dildo. He's got the shotgun.)*

PHIL: Butch!

BUTCH: *(Surprised, caught, foolish)* Dad!

PHIL: Goddammit, Butch, what are you doing?

(BUTCH *throws a look at* LOMAR *and points his shotgun at the ground, squeezes trigger in denial —)*

BUTCH: Nothin. *(BLAM! The shotgun fires.)* Jesus Christ, my foot!

Scene Eight

(**Alma's Bar & Grill**. *Afternoon.* SON *sits monkeying with a toy gun.* ALMA *rounds the bar with a water dish.)*

SON: This here's suppose to light up and buzz and I think this is suppose to go round and round. The death ray don't work. The spontaneous combuster I don't think ever *did* work.

ALMA: You got your batteries in upside down?

SON: No.

(ALMA *places the water dish in the middle of the floor.)*

ALMA: They leaking?

SON: No.

ALMA: Let me see that thing. Where'd you get it? Out to the dump?

SON: No. I saved up for it. I paid eighteen dollars for it.

ALMA: Eighteen dollars! *(Shakes head, pulls out a screwdriver)*

SON: Frankie's got one.

ALMA: This isn't supposed to work.

SON: He's got a cosmic dissembler on his and everything.

ALMA: This was designed *not* to work. To break and not get fixed. It's junk. (ALMA *looks to the water dish, then looks around the bar.)* Where's Buddy? He must be dying for a drink.

SON: — No.

ALMA: Didn't Buddy come in with you? (SON *shakes head no.*) Child, where's your dog?

SON: He was swimmin at the pond.

ALMA: At the dump?

SON: *(Nods)* He stayed there.

ALMA: He didn't come back?

SON: He come back covered with tar, Alma. He couldn't pee. Just walked around with his leg up and nothin.

ALMA: When was this?

SON: *(Shakes head no)* His fur fell off.

ALMA: Sweetheart —

SON: His teeth fell out. Then he just wouldn't — I couldn't — (ALMA *embraces him.*) I tried to bury him in the backyard but —

Scene Nine

(**Trailerhouse** *livingroom. Afternoon. Piles of laundry.* LEATHA's *on the CB.*)

LEATHA: With Butch? She did? *(*LOMAR *comes in.)* Ten four, Cotton Candy.

CB: Threes to you. And a buncha 88s. We gone.

LEATHA: *(She cradles the CB mike.)* Where you been?

LOMAR: Up on Venus where men suck their penis.

LEATHA: You wanna go back to County?

LOMAR: Is it worse than this? I forget.

LEATHA: There's no married men to seduce.

LOMAR: Hell there ain't.

LEATHA: Why don't you go find a boy your own age?

LOMAR: There are no boys my age. There are only men my age.

LEATHA: Think of Sudden.

LOMAR: *(Does she know?)* I didn't mean him.

LEATHA: He's gotta work with Butch.

LOMAR: Who's stoppin him?

LEATHA: You don't make it easier, hittin on his boss.

LOMAR: I ain't hittin on Butch. Jesus, whatta expression. Sides, Butch ain't Sudden's boss anyway. Phil is.

LEATHA: Butch'll take over when Phil retires.

LOMAR: Butch will? God, I thought Sudden would.

LEATHA: Butch will.

LOMAR: Butch is kinda cute.

LEATHA: Lomar —

LOMAR: You jealous?

LEATHA: Of you?

LOMAR: It could happen.

LEATHA: Finish up with this. *(The laundry)* I gotta go.

LOMAR: *(Peels off shirt)* Butch is a teddy bear. Sudden is a goat.

LEATHA: Well, the goat's asleep, so keep the TV down. And put your shirt back on!

LOMAR: I don't have to.

LEATHA: In *my* house?

LOMAR: Whose house?

LEATHA: The hell you don't.

LOMAR: *(Kicks off her shoes)* You're not the boss of me!

LEATHA: The hell I'm not!

LOMAR: Sudden!

LEATHA: Hush up!

LOMAR: You get two hundred dollars a month to put up with your foster child. Why should I make it easy?

LEATHA: If I wasn't late for Weight Watchers, we'd settle this right now. *(She goes out door.)*

LOMAR: *(At door)* Weight Watchers meets at the mall. Not at the Terminal Hotel....*Mom!*

(LEATHA *exits.* LOMAR *moves into the bedroom where* PISANGER *snores in the blast of an electric fan.* LOMAR *punches off the fan.)*

PISANGER: *(One eye opens)* Lomar — turn the fan on.

LOMAR: You don't take me, I'm going anyway. I'll get Running Joke to do it.

PISANGER: Do what?

LOMAR: Take me cross into Kansas.

PISANGER: He'll take you up to Pine Ridge, trade you for a horse.

LOMAR: You think!

PISANGER: He's an Indian, ain't he? Turn the fan on.

LOMAR: I hate Leatha.

PISANGER: Well — She thinks a lot of you.

LOMAR: Shit she does. What would she do she knew about us?

PISANGER: Uhhh —

LOMAR: She'd go crazy, call the cops *and* the County.

PISANGER: Lomar, what we did — with you — what I —

LOMAR: *(Over)* Wouldn't she?

PISANGER: It was wrong.

LOMAR: Then we'd have to go.

PISANGER: You and me we —

LOMAR: And I won't hitchhike. I won't take no goddam bus.

PISANGER: — You'd go bareback with Running Joke.

LOMAR: Hell I did. Did you say did or would? I am goin in a car.

PISANGER: He don't have a car.

LOMAR: He can get one.

PISANGER: How? Steal it?

LOMAR: If he had to.

PISANGER: Who's gonna make him? He can't even keep a job.

LOMAR: Maybe he don't wanna work for Phil. Maybe he's too smart of a person that should be hauling garbage.

PISANGER: He's a freak.

LOMAR: He don't need that job.

PISANGER: Who needs it? I need it? I could quit tomorrow.

LOMAR: And jump a goddam train.

PISANGER: No. Drive.

LOMAR: When?

PISANGER: Soon as I don't know when.

LOMAR: Or how.

PISANGER: When I get the Chevy runnin is how. When I get the money for the parts for the Chevy.

LOMAR: Trick'll be yankin it out of that tar pool it's sunk in. It's up over the wheels now.

PISANGER: I know.

LOMAR: Gets hot like this that whole back yard heaves up and down like a hairy water bed.

PISANGER: Somethin will happen.

LOMAR: You wish. *(Phone rings. LOMAR crosses, answers it, into phone.)* Hello. Hi, Phil. Yeh, he's here. No, he's asleep. He told me not to. Yes I will. *(Puts hand over phone)* It's Phil! He says if you don't go back out to the garage and grease the trucks, you're fired!

PISANGER: Tell him then I'm fired then cause *I'm not goin back out there*!

LOMAR: *(Into phone)* Hello, Phil? Phooey. *(Yells to* PISANGER*)* Phil's not there!

PISANGER: I *been* out there!

*(*PISANGER *rolls out of bed, starts pulling on his clothes.)*

LOMAR: *(Into phone)* Well, Butch, Phil said Sudden's fired if he don't go back out and grease the trucks and Sudden says he ain't going back out there so Phil — Phil never fired Sudden? Well, by God he did over the phone. *(Yells to* PISANGER*)* Sudden! Butch don't know if you're fired or not! *(Into phone)* Butch? Uh huh. Yeh I will only no he won't. *(*PISANGER *grabs his boots and sneaks out back door.)* He says he's staying here with me. Not coming in. Okay, 'bye.

*(*LOMAR *hangs up and hurries back into the bedroom.* PISANGER*'s gone.)*

Scene Ten

*(*PHIL COBB's **Office**. *Late afternoon. Top of scene dovetails previous action.* PHIL, BUTCH, *and* BOB *play blackjack at the desk.* BOB *is drunk and drinking.* BUTCH *drinks from a flask but isn't drunk yet. His foot is encased in an oversized plaster cast.* BUTCH *hangs up the phone.)*

BOB: Not a damn thing!

PHIL: Quitcher bitchin, Bob.

BOB: It ain't fair, Phil.

PHIL: Who said it would be?

BOB: You treat us all different.

PHIL: I respect your differences.

BUTCH: Hell, you *count* on em — heheheh.

BOB: All I want is a fair shake.

PHIL: That's a low goal, Bob. I'll take a hit.

(BUTCH *deals* PHIL *a card.*)

BOB: I'll take a hit.

BUTCH: *(Deals)* You'll shit and fall back in it.

(Phone rings.)

BOB: What I'm talkin about Phil is I don't care if I never make another nickel more in wages. Forget it.

(Phone rings.)

BUTCH: You're gone now, aren't you?

PHIL: Yeh, I'm gone.

BOB: What I want is benefits.

BUTCH: *(Into phone)* Domestic Refuge.

BOB: It's no moren fair.

BUTCH: May I say who's calling? *(Hand over phone)* Uric Salts from the K-Mart Company in Minneapolis!

(Laughter, shouts from BUTCH *and* PHIL*)*

PHIL: We want the money! We want the money, Butch!

BUTCH: *(Can't believe it)* Minneapolis! *(Hands phone to* PHIL*)*

PHIL: You take it, Son.

BUTCH: Me!?

PHIL: *(Puts money down for a bet)* He'll talk you out of it. I bet he does.

BUTCH: *(Matches* PHIL*'s bet)* I bet he don't. *(Drops his voice, into phone)* Hello.

BOB: Like if I get sick on the job this winter or somebody else gets sick on the job so that he has to go to the hospital for ammonia, heart attack, or anything else —

BUTCH: *(Into phone)* Uh huh. Well I just took it out of service temporarily until I receive some money on it.

BOB: I just want him to be able to support his family.

BUTCH: If he does that there'll be no problem. I'll turn the compactor right back on.

BOB: I want to be able to be a human being like everybody else.

BUTCH: The store *was* notified.

BOB: To hell with the wages, forget it.

PHIL: Three or four times we told them!

BOB: What I want is the benefits. It's no moren fair.

BUTCH: The store was notified about three or four times.

BOB: I mean if we go out there —

PHIL: Bob —

BOB: — in the middle of winter —

PHIL: Bob.

BOB: — thirty degrees below zero —

PHIL: Shuttup.

BUTCH: *(To* PHIL*)* A personal check?

PHIL: No! Cash or a certified check.

BUTCH: *(Into phone)* It'll have to be cash or a certified check.

BOB: — and if we go out there middle of summer, a hundred and thirty degrees *above* zero —

PHIL: Goddammit!

BUTCH: Yeh.

BOB: If we're not appreciated that much then we're not appreciated at all.

BUTCH: The only way I could take anything other than that would be to have a board meeting and some of the board members aren't here right now and I'm sure I can't get hold of them.

(PHIL *cracks up laughing.* BUTCH *beams.*)

BOB: Then somebody else better start taking over and hauling the garbage altogether.

BUTCH: I'm just taking orders.

BOB: All of it!

BUTCH: I — and you remember the kind of problem we got into there because we had nothing in writing and it was verbal.

BOB: All of it!

BUTCH: And I'm sure you can understand my point.

(PHIL *grabs phone and yells into it.*)

PHIL: NOT UNTIL WE GET THE MONEY.

(PHIL *hands phone back to* BUTCH.)

BUTCH: *(Into phone)* Not until we get the — Hello? *(To* PHIL*)* He hung up. *(He hangs up.)*

PHIL: *(Collecting his bet)* What he say?

BUTCH: *(With relish)* He's gonna meet me at seven-fifteen with a certified check for nine thousand dollars! *(Takes bet back from* PHIL*)*

BOB: Phil —

PHIL: *(Punches* BUTCH*)* Wheee! I told you we'd get it.

BOB: Phil —

BUTCH: *(Punches* PHIL *twice as hard)* I *told* you I could do it!

BOB: *(Holding a card)* Phil, you're over. You were sitting on a queen.

PHIL: Ahhh! I didn't know I had a queen!

BUTCH: Well, don't you look at your cards, Dad?

BOB: *(Raking in the money)* You were thinking about all that money.

(**Office** *door swings open.* SARGE *limps in.*)

PHIL: Wouldn't you worry about nine thousand dollars?

BOB: Phil, I worry about *nine* dollars.

BUTCH: *(Shows cards to* BOB*)* Bob — I think I gotcha beat, Bob.

BOB: *(Reads cards)* Ah shit.

SARGE: Well, see you tomorrow, Phil.

(BUTCH *rakes in money from his winning hand.* BOB's *forehead hits the table.*)

BUTCH: You still in the game, Bob?

PHIL: How'd you get along out there, Sarge?

SARGE: Fine.

PHIL: Easy as fallin offa log, ain't it?

SARGE: Yeh.

PHIL: Bullshit. *(Gets up)* I know better than that. It's hard work.

SARGE: You seen Sudden?

BUTCH: He's greasin the trucks.

PHIL: *(Throws arm around* SARGE*)* You know what, you old bastard?

SARGE: What, Phil?

PHIL: I want you to stay with me till you die.

SARGE: Great. I got a job till I die.

PHIL: If you want it.

SARGE: Well, if I'm gonna stay with you till I die, Phil, you're workin me to death.

PHIL: Ahhhhh! *(Laughs)* Sarge, you guys are all my family. If it wasn't for you guys, I wouldn't have nothing.

SARGE: Thanks, Phil. I'll get that money back to you.

PHIL: Don't worry about it, Sarge. I'll get it out of you.

(PHIL *shoves cigar into* SARGE's *mouth.* SARGE *leaves.* PHIL *sits down,* BUTCH *gets up.)*

BUTCH: Dad, I gotta talk to Sarge.

PHIL: Sit down, Butch. Deal. (BUTCH *sits.)* You got any money left, Bob?

(BOB, *drunk, slides off chair, hits floor.)*

(Outside PHIL COBB's **Office**, PISANGER *enters, wiping grease from his hands into a rag. He stretches, exhausted. He eyes* PHIL's **Car**. *It rivets him. He walks a wide arc, drops rag into open red tool box DS, and approaches the* **Car** *from the driver's side. He hesitates, spits. Nervous, as if being watched, he puts one hand on the door handle, looks around, inhales, holds it, opens the door. The buzzer goes off. He slams the door, jumps back.)*

PISANGER: What are you doing in there?

RUNNING JOKE: *(Sits up inside* **Car***)* I scare you?

PISANGER: You don't scare me.

RUNNING JOKE: *(Gets out far side)* Good. *(Crosses to tool box)* I came to borrow some tools from Daddy Phil.

PISANGER: They're not Phil's. They're mine.

RUNNING JOKE: All of them?

PISANGER: Damn near. The ones that aren't broke are.

RUNNING JOKE: *(Hunkers down, looks into box)* You have everything you need.

PISANGER: People forget that around here. They take em out, they don't put em back.

RUNNING JOKE: You could open your own garage —

PISANGER: *(Closes toolbox with his foot)* I'm keeping my tools at home now.

RUNNING JOKE: — if you wanted to.

PISANGER: I still can't find my five-eighths socket.

RUNNING JOKE: *(Pulls socket wrench out of his pocket)* This it?

PISANGER: Where'd you get that?

RUNNING JOKE: Lomar gave it to me.

PISANGER: *(Takes it)* It ain't hers to give it.

RUNNING JOKE: What about that box end combination there, your quarter inch?

PISANGER: What were you gonna do with Phil's car?

RUNNING JOKE: Steal it.

PISANGER: I don't want you seeing Lomar.

RUNNING JOKE: I won't hurt Lomar.

PISANGER: She don't need help getting into trouble.

RUNNING JOKE: I know. She needs a father.

PISANGER: Yer not her father.

RUNNING JOKE: I'm not trying to be. Are you?

PISANGER: No. Yeh! I'm her foster father.

RUNNING JOKE: *(Pulls valve out of pocket)* What is this?

PISANGER: You don't know?

RUNNING JOKE: No.

PISANGER: It's a valve off a carburetor.

RUNNING JOKE: Is that a valve you'd use if you weren't burning gasoline?

PISANGER: If *what*?

RUNNING JOKE: If you weren't using gasoline to run a car, would a jet like that be —

PISANGER: What you gonna burn? Horseshit?

RUNNING JOKE: Maybe chickenshit. But in a vapor state.

PISANGER: Where at?

RUNNING JOKE: I want to run methane from a tank in the trunk through a line to —

PISANGER: Methane?

RUNNING JOKE: Yeh.

PISANGER: What's that — like propane?

RUNNING JOKE: Only lighter.

PISANGER: You wanna feed it through the air cleaner? Mix it with gas?

RUNNING JOKE: Into the carburetor. No, just straight. No gas.

PISANGER: You can't use the carburetor. You'd hafta go straight into the manifold and jet it down. You can't — See, it don't go in at the same rate gas does. You gotta shoot a finer spray. You'd — Well. It'd be a carburetor in a way, but — *(He pictures it.)* you'd need a tube comin off the engine vacuum. The throttle plate assembly'd have to be a little smaller. You need a pressure regulator of some kind. You'd uh —

RUNNING JOKE: *(Smiles)* Thanks. *(Squats at tool box)* I'll get this box end back to you.

PISANGER: *No!*

(Slams foot down on tool box)

PISANGER: You can't have it! It's mine! They're all mine! And I'm gonna need them!

RUNNING JOKE: *(Stands)* When you steal Phil's car?

(PISANGER *glares.* RUNNING JOKE *nods, exits.*)

PISANGER: Shit!

(Inside **Office**, PHIL *and* BUTCH *turn off the lights and leave.)*

PISANGER *spits, scratches, turns 360°. He crosses back to* PHIL's **Car**, *opens door, puts toolbox on seat, climbs in, shuts door.)*

PISANGER: Here goes, Sugar.

(He turns the key. Hear starter grind, engine rev, tires screech.

SARGE *weaves in. He steadies himself on his carrying barrel and sees* PISANGER *driving off.)*

SARGE: *(Waving yellow-bound report)* Sudden! You left this in the truck! Sudden!

(SARGE *inhales, hoists the loaded barrel to his shoulder, takes one step and doubles under — one leg gives way, he drops to one knee, falls sideways. Glass breaks, garbage leaps out of his barrel.*

Tires squeal. **Car** *door kicked open.* PISANGER *rushes back onstage. He straddles* SARGE.)

PISANGER: *Sarge!*

SARGE: *(Gasping)* Be good to the little boy in you. Good seed, Sudden, your boy, Lomar —

PISANGER: *(Takes report)* Don't talk.

SARGE: Call Alma.

PISANGER: Shuttup.

SARGE: Don't die in jail, Sudden.

(The yellow-bound report in his fist, PISANGER *pounds on* SARGE's *chest like a drum.* SARGE *dies.*

As lights fade and the sound of drums comes up, hear a car door shut, ignition, engine revving, clutch popping, then rubber rip across asphalt. Headlights sweep the stage. The sound of acceleration through three gears, two high speed corners, and gradual fade out as the car leaves reach of the senses.

PISANGER *throws a look over his shoulder —)*

PISANGER: Running Joke, you sonofabitch!

BLACKOUT

END OF ACT ONE

ACT TWO

Scene One

*(PHIL COBB's **Office**. Early evening.)*

BUTCH: *(On phone)* Dammit, Freddy, answer the goddam phone.

(Far side of stage, FREDDY THE COP *ignores phone beeping on his belt as he focuses in on unseen parties with binoculars. Hear: beep beep beep beep beep beep beep.*

Trailerhouse. PISANGER *sits on the front stoop, lips moving, sounding out words in the yellow-bound report.)*

PISANGER: ...uncontrained...dispose—all...tock...sick...

BUTCH: Dammit, Freddy!

PISANGER: ..ever-mental...rezeal...soul...vents...

BUTCH: *Freddy!*

FREDDY: Beep beep beep beep beep beep beep — Goddammit. *(Answers phone)* Mobile two.

BUTCH: Put your pants on, Freddy.

FREDDY: My pants are on.

BUTCH: Well, pull em up and get over here.

FREDDY: What's the occasion, Butch? You set your truck on fire again?

BUTCH: No, Freddy.

FREDDY: You dump another hot load in the middle of O Street I'm gonna have to help you clean up?

BUTCH: No, Freddy.

FREDDY: When King Dollar puts out ashes, you hose them down first, Butch, I told you —

BUTCH: *(Over)* Running Joke stole my car, Fred!

FREDDY: — you don't have to haul their ashes.

BUTCH: *Running Joke stole my car!*

FREDDY: Who'd want your car?

BUTCH: A 28 thousand-dollar Lincoln Continental?

FREDDY: *Phil's* car!

BUTCH: Dammit, Freddy!

FREDDY: Hell, that's different!

BUTCH: Get over here!

*(*FREDDY *exits.* BUTCH *hangs up, leaves office.)*

LEATHA *drags a bulging trash bag through the* **Trailerhouse** *out onto the stoop where* SUDDEN *sits, absorbed. She drops the bag into the open can by the stoop.)*

LEATHA: Lomar's gone.

PISANGER: Sarge is dead.

LEATHA: He's dead?

PISANGER: Where'd she go?

LEATHA: In jail?

PISANGER: He got out of jail this morning. He worked the route.

LEATHA: What of?

PISANGER: Where'd she go?

LEATHA: I dunno. I came back from Weight Watcher's wasn't nobody here. Then the kid came back from the dump which I told him not to go there. He said Lomar's there.

PISANGER: With Running Joke?

LEATHA: I guess. *(Beat)* Well, aren't you going to do something? *(*PISANGER *moves into the* **Trailerhouse***.* LEATHA *follows him in.)* She knows she's not supposed to be there or with him or leave the kid.

PISANGER: Every light's on in this place. The CB, the TV, it's six o'clock in the middle of July and every goddam light is on! *(Punches off CB, TV)*

LEATHA: It was like this when I got here.

PISANGER: I bust my ass —

LEATHA: I told her a million times.

PISANGER: Leatha, Jesus Christ, the stereo!

LEATHA: Why won't you go get her!

PISANGER: Cause I just got home, I been up since five, hauled garbage, fixed the jimmy, came home —

LEATHA: *(Over)* What are you afraid of?

PISANGER: — couldn't sleep, went back out there, greased six more trucks, and *Sarge is dead!*

LEATHA: Sarge was an alcoholic. Their throats explode.

PISANGER: He worked too hard.

LEATHA: He drank too much.

PISANGER: His whole damn life.

LEATHA: And so do you.

PISANGER: I haven't had a drink in three months!

LEATHA: You *work* too hard, I said.

PISANGER: *(Amused)* Sarge still owes Phil money. Four or five hundred dollars.

LEATHA: Daddy Phil.

PISANGER: Phil'd say, don't worry, I'll get it out of you. He didn't this time.

LEATHA: He got enough out it killed the man.

PISANGER: His heart popped out of his mouth.

LEATHA: Go get Lomar.

PISANGER: *(Peels off shirt)* I'm gonna take a shower.

LEATHA: You watch the kid, then, cause I'm gonna go get her.

PISANGER: You take the kid.

(LEATHA *leaves the* **Trailerhouse**, *exits.* PISANGER *pulls off his clothes in the bedroom.*

FREDDY THE COP *comes in CS, speaks through a portable bullhorn.*)

FREDDY: *(Through bullhorn)* SUDDEN PISANGER?

(PISANGER *wraps a towel around himself and goes to the door.*)

PISANGER: How long you known me, Fred?

FREDDY: *(Through bullhorn)* ALL YOUR LIFE.

PISANGER: What do you want? I'm takin a shower.

FREDDY: Not right now, you're answering questions.

PISANGER: I don't know nothin.

FREDDY: About what?

PISANGER: Anything you'd be interested in.

FREDDY: Oh, we're interested, Pisanger.

PISANGER: In what?

FREDDY: In where's that foster kid of yours?

PISANGER: Lomar's my adopted daughter.

FREDDY: She's yer foster kid. The county pays you to watch her.

PISANGER: So what?

FREDDY: So, you been watching her?

PISANGER: Yeh.

FREDDY: How good? Somebody said they seen her and Running Joke coming outta Tebo's chicken shed on their hands and knees all covered with chicken shit, grinning like coyotes.

PISANGER: That's a lie.

FREDDY: *(Grins)* Where is she?

PISANGER: What do you want her for?

FREDDY: We want her boyfriend. Running Joke just stole Phil's car.

PISANGER: I didn't see nothin.

FREDDY: You were there.

PISANGER: I was helpin Sarge.

FREDDY: Were they both in the car?

PISANGER: No.

FREDDY: Where is she?

PISANGER: She's with the kid.

(FREDDY *throws a look around the* **Trailerhouse** *where* SON *sits in the dirt with a football.* FREDDY *smiles, steps toward the door.*)

FREDDY: I'll take a look. (PISANGER *blocks his entrance.*) We gonna need a warrant? After all these years?

PISANGER: *(Steps aside)* She ain't here.

FREDDY: You told me.

(FREDDY *comes in, looks around, moves into the bedroom, opens drawers —* LOMAR *comes in front door.*)

LOMAR: Sudden!

PISANGER: Shhhhh!

LOMAR: *(Flat up against him)* Call me your bitch, Sudden.

PISANGER: Don't do that.

LOMAR: Suhh-denn —

(He shoves her down behind the couch and sits down, fidgets. FREDDY lifts the laundry on the bed and finds the yellow-bound report. PISANGER crosses to the bedroom.)

FREDDY: *(Looks up, leafing through it)* Where'd you get this?

PISANGER: Sarge give it to me.

FREDDY: Where'd he get it?

PISANGER: I don't even know what it is. *(FREDDY tucks it under his arm.)* Is it important?

FREDDY: *(Starts out)* Probably not —

PISANGER: You can't take it. No warrant.

FREDDY: All right. *(Tosses report onto bed)* Pisanger. *(Nods)* When Lomar gets back here, you call me first thing — you got that?

PISANGER: Yeh.

FREDDY: You don't, your ass is grass.

PISANGER: Sure, Freddy. *(PISANGER watches FREDDY cross off and out. LOMAR pops up. He wheels on her.)* You're not goin with him.

LOMAR: Goin where with who?

PISANGER: You're not leavin town with Running Joke.

LOMAR: I don't wanna leave town with him.

FREDDY: *(Back onstage)* Sudden!

PISANGER: Jesus Christ!

FREDDY: One more thing!

LOMAR: *(Hiding)* I wanna go with you.

PISANGER: *What?*

FREDDY: WHEN YOU GONNA HAUL MY TREE LIMBS OUT FROM IN FRONT OF MY HOUSE?

PISANGER: *When you cut 'em down into three-foot lengths like the law says! Now get the fuck outta here!*

(Exit FREDDY. PISANGER *starts pulling on his clothes.)*

PISANGER: I was better offa alcoholic.

LOMAR: That's before I got here.

PISANGER: That's what I mean.

LOMAR: So I wouldn't know.

PISANGER: Never home. Just workin and drinkin. I didn't have time to get into trouble.

LOMAR: Aren't you gonna take a shower? *(Moves in close)* I need one, too.

PISANGER: *(Shaking head)* I sober up and get into this.

LOMAR: Shit! Here comes Leatha!

(LOMAR shoots out back door, it slams, she exits.)

PISANGER: *(Hushed)* Lomar!

*(LEATHA crosses toward the **Trailerhouse**. PISANGER shoves the report into his back pocket and goes out to meet her.)*

LEATHA: What Freddy want?

PISANGER: Nothin.

SON: Dad!

(SON DS, cocks the football, ready to throw.)

LEATHA: Lomar wasn't at the dump.

(SON throws. PISANGER catches it. LEATHA goes inside. PISANGER throws the football back to SON and sits down on the stoop to tie his boots. SON approaches.)

SON: *(Finally)* Do you love Mom?

PISANGER: Sure I love your mom.

SON: Do you love Lomar?

PISANGER: Yeh. I care about her. We take care of her.

SON: Do you love her?

PISANGER: Do you love me?

SON: Yeh.

PISANGER: Then go out for a long one.

*(SON backs off. PISANGER stands, moves out, throws him a pass. SON fumbles, ball bounces, SON retrieves it. They walk back toward **Trailerhouse**.)*

SON: You didn't answer my question, Dad.

*(PISANGER playfully cuffs his SON's head. A patch of hair comes off in his hand. SON crosses into **Trailerhouse**. PISANGER drops to his knees.)*

PISANGER: Jesus, his hair, Jesus.

(PISANGER *pulls out his handkerchief, spreads it out, and carefully transfers each hair into it. He turns toward the* **Trailerhouse** *where* SON *settles in on couch, turns on the TV.*

Headlights come on up at **The Tanks**. *Go off.*

PISANGER *stands, exits, handkerchief in hand.)*

Scene Two

(**The Tanks**. *Night. Meat sizzles in a skillet on the open end of a five-inch pipe sticking out of the ground. Plastic tubing, copper wire, and plastic milk jugs hang US.*

DCS, RUNNING JOKE *stands bent over, hands on knees, coughing.* PISANGER *enters over US rise, handkerchief in hand, still dazed.* RUNNING JOKE *straightens, speaks without turning.)*

RUNNING JOKE: You ready now?

PISANGER: *(Eyeing skillet)* What's that?

RUNNING JOKE: That's dinner.

PISANGER: It stinks.

RUNNING JOKE: You come up here to eat?

(PISANGER *shoves handkerchief into his pocket.)*

PISANGER: This whole place stinks.

RUNNING JOKE: Like knowledge.

PISANGER: Like the dump.

RUNNING JOKE: *(Points to separated piles)* Copper. Aluminum. Brass. Lead. Plastic. Cardboard. Kitchen slop and manure: dog, cat, chicken, cow —

PISANGER: You are a running joke. *(*RUNNING JOKE *smiles, shrugs.)* What kind of name is that?

RUNNING JOKE: Not mine. My name is Alex Slicing Lightning.

PISANGER: Who give you Running Joke?

RUNNING JOKE: White man. Railroad. Actually, Butch Cobb gave it to me. But I aim to give it back.

PISANGER: You Indians really hang from your tits up there?

RUNNING JOKE: In the Sun Dance.

PISANGER: What's that?

RUNNING JOKE: Sacred ceremony of my people, the one Leonard holds.

PISANGER: Leonard Nimoy?

RUNNING JOKE: No. One time up there, the FBI came down in helicopters. They broke up our meeting, scattered our fire, arrested the Roadman and Leonard and Grandmother. They didn't catch me. They won't. They paid. The wind swallowed up one copter and spit it out on the courthouse lawn in Valentine. Roadman and Grandmother were let go finally. Leonard's out now, too. Three years in the pen. They couldn't break him. The ones who did that, who still live, never stop hearing our drums. They turn on their CBs, breaker broke for a short stroke, all they get is drums. They turn on their radios for hog futures and the swapshop: drums. Five-point eight to sixteen hundred, AM, FM. *(Beat)* There is a power that you could not make no law for the power.

(RUNNING JOKE *pulls back a tarp to reveal* PHIL COBB's **Car**. PISANGER *looks at him, a long look.*)

PISANGER: You're not taking Lomar.

RUNNING JOKE: No, I'm not.

PISANGER: Then why'd you steal Phil's car?

RUNNING JOKE: I'm going to clean the machine, get it running right.

PISANGER: Then where you going?

RUNNING JOKE: No place to go.

PISANGER: You stole Phil's car to give him a tune-up?

RUNNING JOKE: I stole Phil's car to modify it. Make it run on methane gas. Derived from shit. Phil's shit. I thought you came to help me.

PISANGER: I ain't helpin you. And I'm *through* helpin Phil.

RUNNING JOKE: Why?

PISANGER: Phil killed Sarge.

RUNNING JOKE: Sarge never blamed Phil. Why should you?

PISANGER: Cause Phil's a greedy sonofabitch gettin rich off me.

RUNNING JOKE: You agree to it.

PISANGER: I developed the habit of eating. So's my wife. So's my kid.

RUNNING JOKE: So you work for Phil. You make him your boss. He takes your time, he takes your money, you feel cheated, so you hate him.

PISANGER: I don't exactly hate him.

RUNNING JOKE: No. Part of you loves him like a father. But he's not your father. You're not his child. And he's only your boss because you won't be your own boss.

PISANGER: I don't wanna be my own boss.

RUNNING JOKE: I know.

PISANGER: I wanna be *his* boss —

RUNNING JOKE: Sure. Boss him.

PISANGER: — boss *him* for a change. Make him work for me!

RUNNING JOKE: But you have to be your own boss first.

PISANGER: Why?

RUNNING JOKE: Because you have to know what you want. Do you know what you want?

PISANGER: *Yeh!*

RUNNING JOKE: What?

PISANGER: *(Beat)* — I usta wanna just get out, quit, ditch Leatha, take off, steal a car —

RUNNING JOKE: Drive out West O at a hundred miles an hour and go sailing offa bridge?

PISANGER: Only I wouldn't get caught.

RUNNING JOKE: Or killed?

PISANGER: Hell, what's the difference? I'm half dead now. I can't breathe, my joints swell up, get stiff. My whole left side is numb now. Can't think straight. I get headaches. Sometimes I have to just stop work and sit down I get so dizzy. *(Pulls handkerchief out to wipe his brow)* Probably die of cancer...*(He stares at the handkerchief.)*

RUNNING JOKE: You ever jump?

PISANGER: Off what?

RUNNING JOKE: Into a nuclear power generator. People who go down into that slop to clean that out they call jumpers. We called ourselves sponges, cause that's what you do. You soak up radiation. They give you a badge to wear tells you how much you've taken in. If you go the whole hog, you get two hundred dollars extra. I went in three times, took the bonus three times. My father died digging uranium and I did it anyway. My toenails fell off. I broke out, couldn't breathe, shit blood. My hair fell out. I threw up for weeks.

PISANGER: Why'd you do it?

RUNNING JOKE: Thought I had to. Like you. I didn't know I had a choice.

PISANGER: Your hair fell out?

(RUNNING JOKE *eats from the skillet. He nods.*)

PISANGER: How can you eat that shit?

RUNNING JOKE: I am immune. I'm dead to damn near everything you give your life to, Sudden.

PISANGER: Fuck you.

RUNNING JOKE: Stop hiding your tools.

PISANGER: They're *mine*!

RUNNING JOKE: So *use* them!

PISANGER: Look Cochise, I gotta right to —

RUNNING JOKE: Die stupid?

PISANGER: I'm stupid?

RUNNING JOKE: Do you know what you want?

PISANGER: And you're the smart one? Shit! I usta drink with Indians couldn't stand up after a six pack. You think you're something? You're nothing.

RUNNING JOKE: You think you're nothing? You're something.

PISANGER: What?

RUNNING JOKE: You think you're nothing, a machine. You think you deserve what you get, that you're no better than you are. You're more than that.

PISANGER: What am I?

RUNNING JOKE: You're a natural-born mechanic. And this is a mechanical problem.

(RUNNING JOKE *drops* PISANGER's *red tool box at his feet.*)

Scene Three

(*Outside* PHIL COBB's **Office**. *Moonlit night.* LOMAR, *apparently alone, tosses pills into the air and catches them in her mouth like popcorn.*

Inside **Office**, *drunken* BOB *struggles to his feet. He's been unconscious since Act One, Scene 10. He comes up ass first, finds balance, sees* LOMAR *DS. His eyes strain to focus. He moves toward her.*

LOMAR *whirls, startled, then recognizes* BOB. *She draws herself up straight and executes a perfect curtsey fit for an Elizabethan court.* BOB *produces a mason jar half-filled with blood-red fluid from behind his back and grins broadly.* LOMAR *whinnies, delighted. They drink. First* LOMAR, *then* BOB. LOMAR's *lip curls, she growls.* BOB *growls. She backs away, shifting weight from foot to foot like an animal.)*

BOB: Comere. I'll hit you with a stick.

LOMAR: *(Mood shifts)* That's ugly.

BOB: *(Convinced of his appeal)* Come on. I'll beat you with my hose, my rubber hose.

LOMAR: Don't talk like that. *(*BOB *reaches for her breast.)* Don't grab at me.

BOB: *(Squeezing* LOMAR's *breast)* Honk honk!

LOMAR: *(Pulls away)* Don't *do* that! Don't you — *(She knocks him down.)* I am not your rubber ducky! I am not some pot to piss in! *(She kicks his groin.)*

BUTCH: *(Yells coming in)* Hang on! Hang on! R-r- r-r-ring! I'll get it! *(Split wide,* BOB *doubled over in pain and* LOMAR *fuming, they both freeze as* BUTCH *answers an unringing phone in the* **Office***. They move in close to eavesdrop.* BUTCH, *into phone, drunk)* Domestic Refuge Incorp — No. *(Second thought, hangs up)* R-r-r-r-ring! R-r-r-r-ring! *(Answers)* Butch Cobb Unlimited. It's forty bucks a month twice a week on Tuesdays and Fridays and I want my money in advance. Where do you work? How much money you got? Hahahaha. *(Hangs up)* R-r-r-r- ring! *(Answers)* Butch Cobb Unlimited. Yes it is. Running *who?* No he don't. Not anymore he don't. No kikes, nips, niggers, dagos, spicks, slopes, slants, geeks, gooks, micks, mau maus, frogs, faggots, little girls, or Indians. *(Hangs up, then picks it up again, yelling)* Or ALIENS! *(He hangs up. Instantly, the phone rings.* BUTCH *nearly falls over. He answers.)* Butch Cobb Un — er — Domestic Refuge. Freddy! Yeh, yeh, it's me. What report?

FREDDY: *(SL, into phone)* That environmental thing you told me you got rid of, Butch.

BUTCH: So?

FREDDY: So, what did you do with it?

BUTCH: I got rid of it.

FREDDY: Pisanger's got it.

BUTCH: How'd he get it?

FREDDY: You tell me, Butch. I saw it over his place this afternoon. *(Open hole of silence)* Butch — you there?

BUTCH: *(Drinks from flask)* Don't worry, Freddy. Monkeys can't read. *(He laughs.)*

FREDDY: You better hope they don't. Your ass is hanging fire here, too.

BUTCH: I ain't worried.

FREDDY: Phil would.

BUTCH: You didn't tell him.

FREDDY: Not yet.

BUTCH: Well don't!

FREDDY: We'll see.

BUTCH: Just do your job, you sonofabitch! Go pick up Running Joke!

FREDDY: When we're ready, Butch. We will.

BUTCH: When *who's* ready? I'm ready!

FREDDY: When Phil and I are ready, Butch.

BUTCH: Fuck you, Freddy!

FREDDY: Night, Butch.

(FREDDY *hangs up.* BUTCH *slams the phone down and collapses in his chair.*)

Scene Four

(Video spill comes up in **Trailerhouse** *living room where* SON *sleeps balled up on the couch in a twisted sheet.*

Dim light comes up in the bedroom. LEATHA *in her nightgown pounds slow motion on* PISANGER's *chest like a drum. His ribcage moans. He doesn't respond. She finally rolls off onto the bed and he sits up, exhausted. His feet hit the floor. First light of day.)*

PISANGER: *(Finally)* Was that good for you?

LEATHA: Yeh. How bout you?

PISANGER: Yeah. Great. *(Stands to dress)* What are you gonna do today?

LEATHA: I got Weight Watchers at three.

PISANGER: You went yesterday.

LEATHA: He changed it.

PISANGER: I thought it was all women over there. They still meet at the mall?

LEATHA: *(Dangerous)* Will you please hold me?

PISANGER: What?

LEATHA: Just hold me.

PISANGER: Why should I?

LEATHA: I need you to.

PISANGER: What about what I need?

LEATHA: You gotta tell me what you need. *(No answer)* What do you need?

PISANGER: *(Sits down on bed)* Work on my back.

LEATHA: Where at?

PISANGER: Yeh.

LEATHA: Does that feel good?

PISANGER: Yeh.

LEATHA: This rash is worse.

PISANGER: Sarge is dead.

LEATHA: It's too bad.

PISANGER: Lomar's gone.

LEATHA: Again.

PISANGER: Forty years old, body fallin apart, shit jobs all my life, nine dollars in the bank...

LEATHA: We got five dollars in the bank. King Dollar wouldn't take food stamps for the bottled water.

PISANGER: Great.

LEATHA: I love you, Sudden.

PISANGER: *(Stands)* Bullshit.

LEATHA: It's not bullshit. I love you.

PISANGER: You say that.

LEATHA: You want me to dance it? I will.

PISANGER: Leatha, you say you love me, you cry, you get mad, you show your emotions. I'm numb. You're there crying and I'm way over here. Behind glass. I don't feel a thing.

LEATHA: You don't love me?

PISANGER: I don't believe you.

LEATHA: You don't believe I love you?

PISANGER: Not like I love our son. I never loved anything like I love him. When he popped out, I knew what love is. It's blood.

LEATHA: I love you like you love our son.

PISANGER: Is that why you go to the Terminal Hotel?

(He grabs his shirt, shoots out the door.)

LEATHA: Yes.

*(LEATHA grabs her robe and moves out past him, exits off as PISANGER swings around, charging back into the **Trailerhouse** for his boots —)*

PISANGER: *Leatha!*

(She's gone. He storms offstage, boots in hand.

SON *sits up on the couch in a twisted sheet.)*

SON: Buddy?

*(He stands and moves through **Trailerhouse** out back door as BOB and LOMAR cross from far SR. LOMAR swats at BOB, who's moving backwards, blocking her path, talking nonstop.)*

BOB: Motors! Lasers! Computers! Radar!

LOMAR: Get away from me! Get offa me!

BOB: Missile trackers! Video games! Traffic signals! Pacemakers! Price scanners! Seeing eye doors! Look around. Hearing aids! Anything electric I'll know how to fix!

LOMAR: When you grow up?

BOB: I'll take the static outta your CB.

LOMAR: When Francine lets you.

BOB: Francine's got nothin to do with it.

LOMAR: Bob, you're pussy whipped.

BOB: How many strands in a standard stranded cable?

LOMAR: She's had her foot on your throat since before I came.

BOB: Nineteen.

LOMAR: Always, probably!

BOB: What's the resistance of a three-six-kilowatt heater wired one-twenty? Do you know? Do you know what a rheostat is? *(LOMAR breaks away, dashes into* **Trailerhouse**.*)* Or a polyphase induction squirrel cage? *(LOMAR dives onto the couch.* BOB *corners her.)* If a four-pole two-twenty-volt sixty-cycle induction motor has a slip of five percent, what's the speed of the shaft? Do you know?

LOMAR: *Who gives a shit!*

BOB: Do you think Sudden could even *say* it? Let alone know what it means? Or Butch? Or Running Joke? Even Phil'd get lost here, see, but not me. Cause I don't breathe this air. I think my own thoughts. I gotta plan. I gotta future. And the long range picture is good for me, too, see, cause war goes on and the military'll always need electrical engineers.

LOMAR: *(Pulling out from under him)* Cow blood my ass!

BOB: I didn't say it was cow blood.

(PISANGER *storms toward* **Trailerhouse**.)

LOMAR: *(Swinging at* BOB*)* Goddam tomato juice!

BOB: I never said what it was!

LOMAR: Goddam V-8 shit fulla celery! Git away from me! Git away from me! Git! Git!

PISANGER: *(Enters* **Trailerhouse**) Leatha?

LOMAR: Sudden!

PISANGER: Where you been?

LOMAR: Looking everywhere for you.

PISANGER: Last night where were you?

LOMAR: Out to the garage. Don't look at Bob like that. Nothin happened.

PISANGER: Where's Leatha?

LOMAR: I don't know.

BOB: Sudden, I —

PISANGER: Bob, yer dead.

LOMAR: Sudden! Where you goin? (PISANGER *storms out front door.* LOMAR *chases after him.)* What'll I tell Leatha?

PISANGER: Tell her the truth.

LOMAR: *(Blocks his path)* I'll tell her *everything*!

PISANGER: You don't know everything.

LOMAR: I'll tell the *cops*! *(He knocks her down.)* I'll tell the *county*! (PISANGER *exits.)* I'll spill my guts!

(Livid, LOMAR *peels off her shirt and chugs back into the* **Trailerhouse***, pushes* BOB *onto the bed and throws herself on top of him, kissing, grinding.*

SON *rounds DSL end of* **Trailerhouse** *and moves to the pile of rocks, Buddy's grave.)*

CB: Breaker one nine. Breaker one nine. Queen Bee, you copy? *(LEATHA comes in back door, sees LOMAR and BOB on bed.)* Breaker one nine, this is Cotton Candy lookin for that one Queen Bee, come on?

LEATHA: *(Lifts mike)* Go ahead, Cotton Candy. Queen Bee here.

CB: Hi, Leatha. Lomar still gone? Any sign of her? Over.

(LOMAR sits up, flushed, eyes flaming, limbs pounding.)

LEATHA: No, Francine. I don't know where she is. Over.

CB: I hate to trouble you, Leatha, but Bob's gone off. You seen him? Come on?

(BOB cowers in a pile of laundry on the bed.)

LEATHA: Negatory. You call the garage?

CB: Nobody answers out there.

LEATHA: Ten four.

CB: You see my Bob or hear anything, you give me a buzz, ten four?

LEATHA: Ten four. *(Hangs up)*

CB: Threes to you.

LEATHA: Bob —

BOB: *(Moves toward door)* Thanks, Leatha.

LEATHA: You shit.

(BOB exits. LOMAR snags her shirt from the floor and insolently exits out past LEATHA. LEATHA moves out front door and sits on the stoop, drained. DS side of stoop sits SUDDEN's red tool box. LEATHA slowly fills with the realization that her SON is on his knees at the pile of rocks DSL. Deliberate, with great care, SON unstacks the rocks one by one.)

LEATHA: *(Finally)* Sweetheart? Maybe you better leave Buddy alone.

SON: I gotta tell him something, Ma.

LEATHA: Not now, son, you put those rocks back and come over here. *(Her arms go out to him. He sadly rises, crosses into her arms with a rock in his hand. They hug.)* Now go inside, get something to eat.

*(SON moves into the **Trailerhouse** and crosses to the Coldspot. Light hits him when he opens the door and LEATHA looks up.)*

LEATHA: Running Joke.

RUNNING JOKE: How are you, Leatha?

LEATHA: Sick to death of that goddam dump.

RUNNING JOKE: Hard living downwind. Maybe you should move.

LEATHA: Up on the hill?

RUNNING JOKE: Better view.

LEATHA: Same dump.

RUNNING JOKE: I have something for you.

LEATHA: We don't have the money to live here. Let alone leave.

RUNNING JOKE: Something I found.

LEATHA: I don't need more garbage.

(RUNNING JOKE *hands* LEATHA *three balls of twisted paper. She unfolds them. He turns from her, starts picking up toys scattered in the front yard.*)

RUNNING JOKE: They're poems Lomar wrote and threw away.

(LEATHA *reads one, then the next. Finished, she looks up at* RUNNING JOKE, *who has piled most of the scattered toys into a wagon. He cradles a rubber doll in his arms and as* LEATHA *looks into his face for help,* RUNNING JOKE *slowly rocks the baby. Inside,* SON *screams into the refrigerator.*)

SON: Maaaaaaa!

(*Hear sound of* **Garbage Truck** *pulling in. Rear lights blink on. It idles.*)

LEATHA: You better get out of here.

(RUNNING JOKE *gives the rubber doll to* LEATHA.)

SON: Maaaaaaa!

(RUNNING JOKE *exits.* LEATHA *puts the poems in her pocket and turns to go inside as* PISANGER *rounds the* **Garbage Truck** *and rushes toward her.*)

PISANGER: Leatha!

LEATHA: I gotta go in.

PISANGER: Wait a minute, wait — (*He grabs her.*) I wanna talk to you.

SON: Maaaaaaaaah!

PISANGER: I just come back from the Terminal Hotel. Room 309. I kicked the goddam door in.

(*Inside,* SON *slams the Coldspot door. He leans against it.*)

LEATHA: Congratulations.

PISANGER: And there he was. Sittin' with his legs crossed, smokin a woman's cigarette. You shoulda seen the look on his face when his door caved in.

LEATHA: Why didn't you just turn the knob?

PISANGER: Why didn't you tell me you were seein a shrink?

LEATHA: I was afraid of what you'd do.

PISANGER: What would I do?

LEATHA: What you just did, I guess. Maybe to me.

PISANGER: I haven't hit you since I quit drinkin.

(*Inside,* SON *slams his rock against the Coldspot door. BOOM.*)

LEATHA: I know.

PISANGER: And I been going to work every day.

(*BOOM.* SON *pounds again.*)

LEATHA: I need to talk to somebody, Sudden.

(*BOOM*)

PISANGER: Well, I give him somethin to talk about.

(*BOOM*)

LEATHA: You are not the center of the universe.

PISANGER: What do you talk about — sex?

(*BOOM*)

LEATHA: Yeh.

PISANGER: About how you hate sex?

(*BOOM*)

LEATHA: I don't hate it. (*BOOM*) I just can't make it work.

(*BOOM*)

PISANGER: It ain't work. It's fun.

(*BOOM. BOOM. BOOM. BOOM.*)

LEATHA: For you it's fun. For me it's never been!

(*Drums start in as* SON *keeps pounding.*)

PISANGER: (*Turning away from* LEATHA) Oh, shit, not this again! (LEATHA *hurries into the* **Trailerhouse**.) You tell him that? You tell him I can't satisfy you? (LEATHA *stops* SON's *pounding hand, embraces him.*) You pay him *my* money to agree with you that I'm no good? That it's *my* fucking fault?

What's this costing me!? *(He rages toward the* **Truck***.)* What's this costing me! What's this costing me!

(Drums beat louder, faster. LEATHA *carries* SON *to bed.)*

PISANGER *hits the lever and the* **Truck** *blade lurches forward.*

Shrill eagle-bone whistle sounds as RUNNING JOKE *emerges from the shadows DSR and moves unseen toward* SUDDEN. *He grabs him, lifts him off his feet and throws him into the hopper of the* **Truck** *as the blade comes down, gears grinding.* PISANGER *disappears behind the blade, is shoved up high into compacted garbage.* RUNNING JOKE *crosses past the* **Trailerhouse***, takes* SUDDEN's *red tool box and exits off.*

Blade stops at the end of its cycle. Drums cut out. Power take-off shuts off. The Truck idles. Unseen cats screw. Rear lights flash. Expanding metal ticks. Moments pass.

PISANGER *pulls himself up out of the hopper — shaken, bleeding. He drops down onto the stage, one knee doubles under, he goes down, comes up, weaves off. Slow fade to black.)*

Scene Five

*(*PHIL COBB's **Office**. *Late afternoon.* FREDDY *leans against the desk as* PHIL *changes out of a dirty jumpsuit.)*

FREDDY: We shoulda done it this morning.

PHIL: I had to *work* this morning, Fred. Bob didn't show up til noon. Butch came in drunk. Then Sudden takes off.

FREDDY: Hell, I coulda did it.

PHIL: *(Shakes head)* This business is like a farmer with milking cows. He can't just leave unless there's somebody there to milk em. *(He lights a cigar.)* Now, what about Sarge?

FREDDY: It's arranged.

PHIL: And Kooser's trailerhouse?

FREDDY: It was a blowback in the oil burner. Explosion caused by — *(Reads)* "— the spontaneous combustion of dust in the furnace ducts."

PHIL: No methane?

FREDDY: Not to our official knowledge. *(Grins)*

PHIL: Thank God no one was hurt.

FREDDY: Can we go now?

PHIL: I'm waiting for a phone call, Fred.

FREDDY: Running Joke is sitting up there on your land, Phil. With your car. Which he stole. And you won't let me get him?

PHIL: I don't need the trouble.

FREDDY: Oh, it's no trouble, Phil.

PHIL: Fred, in two years that landfill will be covered with condominiums. Families will be living there. With tennis courts. And bike trails. And a shopping mall.

FREDDY: You're selling it?

PHIL: It's sold. The zoning change is already on the Master Plan.

FREDDY: But what about the report?

PHIL: What kind of tax revenue do you think this town is going to get off a development like that? How many jobs will it mean? And what will that do for business here? *(Phone rings.* PHIL *smiles, reaches for it. Blackout.)*

Scene Six

*(Dim light comes up in the **Trailerhouse** bedroom.* LEATHA *eases off the bed, tucking covers in around her sleeping* SON, *and crosses to the Coldspot. She opens the door, pulls out a Coke, uncaps it, crosses to the couch. She sits, punches on the TV. Video spill comes up as* LEATHA *opens a bottle of diet pills, takes several, puts the bottle on the TV, and drinks her Coke. Moments pass with only the drone of the television show.* LEATHA *turns to the screen door.* LOMAR *watches her.)*

LOMAR: Leatha, I gotta talk to you.

LEATHA: *(Turns to the TV)* I'm listening, Lomar.

*(*LOMAR *steps in.)*

LOMAR: It's about Sudden. It's about Running Joke. I love them both and they love me.

LEATHA: Of course you do. *(Staring at the TV)* Well, maybe not Running Joke.

LOMAR: Yes, Running Joke. *And* Sudden. They love me. They both want me. Not like a father wants you, either. They want to fuck me. They want to marry me. They want to run off with me, take me anywhere I want to go — Cuba, Ceylon, Zaire *(zie-ear)*, Kansas. It don't matter to them, it's whatever I want. That's why they stole Phil's car.

LEATHA: Who stole Phil's car?

LOMAR: Sudden stole it first I made him. Then Running Joke stole it from Sudden. They're both crazy about me. And super jealous. They both want me so bad I'm afraid what they might do. I'm scared they'll kill each other maybe over me. You gotta *do* something!

(LOMAR *charges* LEATHA, *throws her arms around her, buries her head against her breasts, and* LEATHA *turns to stone. Her arms grow rigid in the air. She can't give* LOMAR *what she needs.* LOMAR *bolts, grabs* LEATHA's *bottle of pills off the TV, and shoots out the* **Trailerhouse** *door, runs OS.* LEATHA, *arms still in the air, stares at the fading TV screen.*)

Scene Seven

(**The Tanks**. *Evening.* RUNNING JOKE *works on* PHIL COBB's **Car** *with the hood up. He tinkers, coughs. He moves like an old man. DS sits* SUDDEN's *red tool box.*

PISANGER *enters over Upstage rise. He jumps* RUNNING JOKE. *They fight — like animals of the strongest kind, splattering junk, kicking and punching, scattering ordered piles of trash, finally rolling like logs until they're both nearly dead from exhaustion. They lay on the ground. The play nearly stops. Finally,* PISANGER *rolls over, slowly, body heaving, something broken.* RUNNING JOKE *stumbles up and slides in behind the wheel of* PHIL COBB's **Car**, *turns the key, revs it, gets out. The* **Car** *idles.*)

RUNNING JOKE: *(Exhausted)* There's no gasoline in that car.

PISANGER: *(Exhausted)* Tank was full when I took it.

RUNNING JOKE: I drained the tank. It's empty.

PISANGER: And it runs.

RUNNING JOKE: It runs.

PISANGER: Witchcraft.

RUNNING JOKE: Methane. I brewed it myself. Three buckets of shit airtight in this barrel. Keep it at eighty degrees with this heater under there, and two microbes inside eat each other. That makes gas. Put the gas in the milk jug, feed it through a tube into the carburetor through this adapter and — (*The* **Car** *farts out, stops running.*) I'm having trouble with the adapter.

PISANGER: I told you take the carburetor off, it wouldn't work with the — (*Stops himself*) Why'd you throw me in the garbage truck?

RUNNING JOKE: Somebody did it for me. Shook me up. It's faster than peyote.

PISANGER: I don't understand that.

RUNNING JOKE: You eat peyote, you eat earth. You're never the same with that inside you. But that takes time, work. This way, throwing you in the hopper, is a shortcut.

PISANGER: A shortcut to where?

RUNNING JOKE: To wherever you can get from the shock of seeing yourself. Once. Straight. From the outside. This way there's no water drums, no little wind, no sweat lodge, no messiah talk, no white man paranoia. Just real fear and the face of your own death.

PISANGER: What gives you the right to mess with me?

RUNNING JOKE: If you don't get smarter, I don't get smarter.

PISANGER: I'm not working on that car!

RUNNING JOKE: I cannot do it by myself. (PISANGER *sits down on his red tool box.*) Sarge didn't convince you?

PISANGER: Sarge is dead.

RUNNING JOKE: What he tell you before he died?

PISANGER: That my kid is good. I should protect him.

RUNNING JOKE: He told you not to die in jail. His dying words. To you. *(Beat)* Are you going to the funeral?

PISANGER: Yeh.

RUNNING JOKE: You going to the cemetery?

PISANGER: Yeh.

RUNNING JOKE: You going to piss on Sarge's grave?

PISANGER: Yeh. While you light a fart in his memory! *(He laughs.)* That's all you're doing making methane.

(Silence opens up between them. Long beat.)

RUNNING JOKE: *(Dead on.)* How's your boy?

(PISANGER *looks away, looks up, looks down. His chest heaves. He turns.*)

PISANGER: Alex. What's a car-sin-notion?

RUNNING JOKE: What's what?

PISANGER: Car-sin-notion?

RUNNING JOKE: Carcinogen?

PISANGER: What is it?

RUNNING JOKE: Something that causes cancer.

PISANGER: *(Pulls out report)* What's — what is ahh — die mental suffoxide?

RUNNING JOKE: A carcinogen.

PISANGER: What is dibb-row-mow-chloropropane?

RUNNING JOKE: A carcinogen.

PISANGER: Die oxen?

RUNNING JOKE: Agent Orange. What have you got there?

PISANGER: *(Hands him report)* You tell me. *(Crosses to* **Car** *with tool box)*

RUNNING JOKE: *(Reads)* "....biochemical profile...."

PISANGER: Yeh.

RUNNING JOKE: On Phil's dump. Results of research. Lists the chemicals they found in the earth, in the air, in the water.... *(Accordion page flops out.)* Jesus.

PISANGER: There's a lot of them. *(Starts in on* **Car***)*

RUNNING JOKE: "Remedial Action."

PISANGER: Read that part.

*(*RUNNING JOKE *leafs through the report, reading, under, to himself as* PISANGER *works on* PHIL COBB's *car.)*

RUNNING JOKE: "...ditches, dikes, check dams...dredge the pond...."

PISANGER: *(Under the hood)* Shit, how'd you think *this* was gonna work?

RUNNING JOKE: "...lower water table...flush into treatment beds...."

PISANGER: Nig-rigged sonofabitch.

RUNNING JOKE: "Drill holes into bedrock...fill holes with concrete..."

PISANGER: Does it say there how to clean it up?

RUNNING JOKE: No.

PISANGER: There's all kind of actions they say you can take, but they all cost millions and they don't say it'll work.

RUNNING JOKE: It won't.

PISANGER: One place says to dig up the whole damn dump and seal it in a plastic bag or something, take it somewhere. But they don't say where.

RUNNING JOKE: There is no where.

PISANGER: *(Back to work)* Well, there's gotta be somewhere. *(*RUNNING JOKE *reads.* PISANGER *works on* **Car***.)* There's gotta be something we can do. *(Lights fade. Hear* SUDDEN's *ratchet wrench: r-r-r-itch, r-r-r-itch, r-r-r-itch....)* Gotta be a solution — don't you think? — Alex? *(R-r-r-itch, r-r- r-itch, r-r-r-itch....)* Alex?

Scene Eight

(**Trailerhouse** *bedroom. Early morning.* LEATHA, *dressed for funeral, folds the last of the laundry.*)

Trailerhouse *front yard.* LOMAR *stumbles in — leaden, wasted, half dancing.*)

LOMAR: *(Sings)* How high's the water, Mama?
Five feet high and risin.
How high's the water —
Papa! You had me!
But I never had youuuuuuuu!
I-I-I-I-I-I!
(LEATHA *cocks an ear.* LOMAR *drops to her knees, spits poem:*)
Clean up my bleeding streets!
Make a park of night sweats!
Some cure for continents of flesh!

(LOMAR *falls sideways, pulls herself back up onto one knee, crawls toward stoop, collapses.*)

LEATHA: *(Crosses to door)* Lomar! Lomar! *(Kneels, tries to lift her)* Oh my God. Wake up. Wake up! *(Slaps her)* How many did you take? *(Slaps her)* Sudden! Help me! Sudden! (LEATHA *struggles* LOMAR *to her feet, half drags, half carries her inside onto the couch. She gets wastebasket from bedroom, puts it on the floor between* LOMAR'S *legs, leans over and triggers the gag reflex.* LOMAR *gags once audibly, then—*) Cough em up, Lomar. Spit out the ugly ones. Get rid of the monsters, baby. Ohhhhhh, baby —

(LEATHA *cradles* LOMAR *in her arms.* LEATHA *gently rocking.* LOMAR *rooting. Blackout.*)

Scene Nine

(**Alma's Bar & Grill**. *Morning.* BOB, *dressed in a borrowed suit, stands silhouetted in the neon glow of the Wurlitzer jukebox. Magnified sound: Coin drops into machine.*)

BOB: Here's to you, Sarge.

(BOB *punches a button. Wurlitzer plays Hank Williams'* "May You Never Be Alone".

VOICE OF HANK WILLIAMS: *(On jukebox)*
Like a bird that's lost its mate in flight
I'm alone and oh so blue tonight.

Like a piece of driftwood on the sea
May you never be alone like me —

(Lights bloom. ALMA, *dressed in black, polishes a glass behind the bar across from* RUNNING JOKE.)

ALMA: *(In reaction to* BOB's *selection)* Bob —

(BOB *kicks the Wurlitzer. Song cuts out. He drops another coin, punches button. Wurlitzer doesn't play.* BOB *kicks it. Wurlitzer plays Merle Haggard's "Everybody's Had the Blues".)*

VOICE OF MERLE HAGGARD: *(On jukebox)*
— love, hate, a want, a wait
Til misery fills your mind.
Everybody knows the way I'm feeling
Cause everybody's had the blues —

(ALMA *shakes her head at* BOB's *selection.* RUNNING JOKE *squeezes her arm with affection and crosses to Wurlitzer. He kicks it hard. The song cuts out.* RUNNING JOKE *kicks Wurlitzer a second time. Wurlitzer plays Aaron Neville's "Tell It Like It Is".)*

VOICE OF AARON NEVILLE: *(On jukebox)*
Tell it like it is!
Don't be ashamed!
Let your conscience be your guide!

("Tell It Like It Is" continues to play over—)

PISANGER, *dressed for funeral, enters* **Alma's**: RUNNING JOKE *catches his eye.* BOB *nods. They're in on something.* RUNNING JOKE *exits out* **Alma's** *back way as* PHIL *comes in the front door, coughing, dressed in suit and tie. Nobody looks his way.)*

PHIL: Well, it was a beautiful funeral, wasn't it? Was I all right? What I said? My little statement? *(Shrugs)* It was the least I could do. Nice man. *Good* man. Man like Sarge could work for me anytime.

ALMA: He had a job til he died.

PHIL: It meant a lot to him. A lot of employers won't hire a convict.

PISANGER: What was he convicted of?

PHIL: It's the same for alcoholics. A lot of them cannot get hired.

ALMA: That's right, Phil. You even bought him drinks.

PHIL: True.

ALMA: And you bought him gloves and cigarettes and breakfast and you gave him spending money —

PHIL: I'd forgotten that.

ALMA: — and you took his body and had him embalmed like he *had no kin*, Phil! Like nobody loved him!

PHIL: I loved him, Alma.

ALMA: Why did Freddy take the body?

PHIL: He was *indigent*, Alma.

ALMA: He had *family*, Phil! *(PHIL looks from ALMA to BOB to PISANGER.)* How much does Sarge still owe you?

PHIL: Five hundred and eleven dollars.

ALMA: You're sure?

PHIL: *(Catching himself)* — Roughly.

ALMA: Then that's what I owe you.

PHIL: No, Alma —

ALMA: Sarge would have paid you back.

PHIL: Call me sentimental, I —

ALMA: He'd want me to.

PHIL: I feel like I owe Sarge that much.

ALMA: Phil —

PHIL: That's how I feel.

ALMA: Good. You put five hundred dollars on the counter and I'll put five hundred dollars on the counter next to it. That's a thousand dollars in Sarge's name to start an insurance fund to cover your workers.

PHIL: Alma —

ALMA: How bout it, Phil?

PHIL: It's the end of the month.

ALMA: And a full moon.

PHIL: I'm not made of money, Alma.

ALMA: We know what you're made out of, Phil. We want to see what you're going to do with it.

PHIL: It can wait until after they've run the route. We'll talk about it then. You boys get started now you can be done before dark. *(No one moves.)* Men, I gave you time off for the funeral. I didn't complain. But Sarge is buried now and this is a work day. There's no days off when it comes to trash on this planet, heh heh heh —

PISANGER: When it comes to trashing the planet?

PHIL: Only Christmas.

PISANGER: Trashing people on this planet?

BOB: What killed Sarge, Phil?

PHIL: Let me buy you all drinks.

PISANGER: I ain't starting.

BOB: I'm stopping.

PHIL: Wait, think about your families. You've *got* to work.

BOB: Why?

PHIL: Because *I don't know the route*!

BOB: *(Beat)* Fuck you.

*(Magnified sound: Starter motor, ignition. PHIL COBB's **Car** turns over, pulls up out front. RUNNING JOKE, behind the wheel, revs it. PHIL spins around.)*

PHIL: Running Joke. *(PHIL exits **Alma's**. RUNNING JOKE slides out of the **Car**. It idles.)* What is this?

RUNNING JOKE: Living proof, Phil. You pack garbage tight enough for long enough and apply enough pressure, you get power, heat, gold, light.

PISANGER: Phil's driving a shit-eating car!

(They laugh.)

RUNNING JOKE: It's running on methane, Phil. I brewed it myself.

*(PHIL laughs, doubles over laughing, starts to cough. RUNNING JOKE steps back into **Alma's** as FREDDY shoulders in from behind the bar with his .38 Smith & Wesson out.)*

FREDDY: Freeze!

(BOB, ALMA, and PISANGER fan back, make room. RUNNING JOKE stands exposed.)

PISANGER: Damn you, Freddy.

ALMA: Freddy Cook, you put that gun away in here.

*(BUTCH rounds the **Car**, moves past PHIL with his 10-gauge shotgun leveled at RUNNING JOKE, enters **Alma's**.)*

BUTCH: Party's over.

PHIL: *(Comes in behind him)* Dammit, Butch, gimme that gun.

BUTCH: *No!*

PHIL: *Butch!*

BUTCH: He stole my car!

PHIL: *My* car, Butch. He stole *my car*! (PHIL *jerks the shotgun out of* BUTCH'S *hands and backs off, takes a breath.*) And it's running on *shit*!

(PHIL *laughs.* BUTCH *doesn't.* **Car** *idles.* PISANGER *pulls the yellow-bound report out, holds it up for* PHIL *to see.*)

PISANGER: Now. What do we do about this, Phil?

(PHIL *looks toward* BUTCH.)

FREDDY: *(Lowers gun)* Great, Butch.

ALMA: What is that, Sudden?

PISANGER: It's a report on Phil's dump. It says his dump is a municipal landfill. That means he's got a permit to bury household garbage. That's it. But Phil's been taking money to let tanker trucks go in and dump toxic chemicals and industrial wastes there how long, Phil? Dead Man's Run is tarred shut. Ground water's poison. Kooser's trailerhouse exploded. Kids are born deaf, blind. My kid's — his dog died.

BUTCH: We got methane moving, Sudden. That's natural.

PISANGER: You got *cyanide* moving, Butch.

BUTCH: Running Joke said that himself.

PISANGER: And asbestos. And toxafeen.

BUTCH: But it's under legal limits, cause we ran tests.

PISANGER: What tests?

BUTCH: Our *own* tests, didn't we, Dad?

RUNNING JOKE: What are legal limits for benzene?

BUTCH: Hell, I don't —

RUNNING JOKE: And chlorobenzene? And dichlorobenzene?

BUTCH: You'd hafta —

RUNNING JOKE: And hexachlorobenzene? And chlordane? And vinyl chloride? Kepone. Mirex. Carbon tetrachloride. (This becomes a chant, like drums, as if the chemicals name themselves through him.) Strontium. Dieldrin. Diethyl ether. Heptachlor epoxide. Chromium. Nitroglycerin. Orthobenzyl parachlorophenol. Orthonitroaniline. Dimethyl sulfoxide. Dibromochloropropane. Ethanol. Ethyl acetate. Sulphur dioxide. Hydrogen sulfide. Nitric acid. Nickel. Napthalene. Lithium. Tritium. Zylene. Zirconium. Tetrachloroethylene. Trichlorophenol. Trichloroethane. Hexachlorocyclopentadiene.

PHIL: *(Shakes head)* Butch.

(BUTCH *crouches at his father's side, his hand on the shotgun.*)

BUTCH: Dad, I didn't dump that stuff. I never took any money. Wasn't me stood by and waved them through like Freddy did. *(He stands.)* Nobody asked me. *(He holds the shotgun.)* You shoulda *asked* me. *(He levels his gun at* RUNNING JOKE.*)* I'm *flesh and fucking bone*!

(BLAM! The shotgun fires.)

PISANGER: *(Leaps toward* RUNNING JOKE*)* Jesus Christ!

ALMA: Alex!

*(*FREDDY *pummels* BUTCH *behind the ear with the butt of his gun.* BUTCH *falls flat.*

RUNNING JOKE *sprawls half-standing against the Wurlitzer. Its neon facade blinks through a hole in his chest.)*

ALMA: Bob! Call nine one one! Call Doc Stewart! Get towels! There's towels under the sink back there, Bob! *Bob! Bob!!!*

BOB: *(Beat)* He's dead, Alma.

ALMA: Noooooooooo!

BOB: Yeh I — he — *(Silence fills the stage.* BOB *looks from* RUNNING JOKE *to* SUDDEN.*)* What happens now?

PISANGER: *(Dazed, fixed on* RUNNING JOKE*)* We cap it.

BOB: We do what?

PISANGER: We cap the landfill. We spread broken brick and a layer of sand, then flyash mixed with clay and lime'll set like cement and stop the runoff into Dead Man's Run. We close the well. We dredge the pond. We lower the water table, move it out around the toxic shit and use the water here to flush lechate into treatment beds. Eight-inch perforated clay-fired pipe in trenches eighteen feet deep backfilled with gravel. We build a slurry wall. Drill staggered double row of holes to bedrock. Inject Wyoming Bentonite in water, forms a gel, makes a wall. Then. We mine methane. Drop six-inch PVC to the bottom of the landfill every fifty feet. Each pipe vents into a header hooked to a manifold connected to a fan. Each branch takeoff's got a butterfly valve.... Molecular sieves'll separate it out. We can sweeten it. It'll run a car. It'll heat your home. Lift a Lear jet right up off the ground.... And then...what's left...we excavate! *(As if possessed)* We incinerate! We wet air oxidate it! Macrame detoxicate it! I'll solidify the fuck out of it! I can turn that landfill into *glass,* Alex! Plastic! Asphalt! Concrete! I can change it into cinderblocks and build a hundred houses with it! Banks! Jails! Lawyers! Doctors! Landlords! Flying buses! Space shudders! Bombs! Dogs! I can inject it fulla vinyl ester styroids and put it on a railgun and *shoot it to the sun*!

(Light narrows in on PISANGER *as he pulls his white handkerchief from his pocket and carefully unfolds it.)*

PISANGER: But I cannot put one hair...back...in.

(Lights pop out in the Wurlitzer. RUNNING JOKE *collapses in* PISANGER's *arms. Blackout.*

Video spill comes up on the couch in the **Trailerhouse** *living room where* SON *sits motionless in a twist of sheets, staring.)*

BLACKOUT

END OF PLAY

GETTING OUT

Marsha Norman

GETTING OUT
© Copyright 1978, 1979 by Marsha Norman

The stage production rights to this play are represented by Dramatists Play Service, 440 Park Ave South, NY NY 10016, 212 683-8960.

All other rights are represented by Larry Shire, Paul Weiss Rifkind Wharton & Garrison, 1285 Sixth Ave, NY NY 10019, 212 373-3363.

ABOUT THE AUTHOR

Marsha Norman's playwriting career began in 1977 with the premiere of GETTING OUT at Actors Theatre of Louisville, where her play was the co-winner of the Great American Play Contest. GETTING OUT was later produced off-Broadway and received the John Gassner Playwriting Medallion from the NY Outer Critics Circle and the George Oppenheimer Newsday Award. Her Pulitzer Prize-winning 'NIGHT, MOTHER opened at the American Repertory Theatre before moving to Broadway in 1983. Thus far it has been translated into twenty-three languages. Her other plays include THE HOLDUP, TRAVELER IN THE DARK, CIRCUS VALENTINE (produced in the 1979 Humana Festival of New American Plays), and two one-acts: THIRD AND OAK: THE LAUNDROMAT and THE POOL HALL (produced by Actors Theatre in 1978). Ms. Norman's SARAH AND ABRAHAM received a workshop production in the 1988 Humana Festival of New American Plays.

Ms. Norman was the recipient of the Literature Award from the American Academy and Institute of Arts and Letters, and has been awarded playwriting grants from the Rockefeller Foundation and the National Endowment for the Arts. She also serves on the Dramatists Guild Council. She has written two teleplays for Lorimar Production and PBS, and several screenplays, including her adaptation of 'NIGHT, MOTHER. Her first novel, THE FORTUNE TELLER, was published by Random House in 1987. Ms. Norman grew up in Louisville, Kentucky, and now makes her home in New York City.

GETTING OUT premiered at Actors Theatre of Louisville on 3 November 1977. The original cast was as follows:

ARLENE	Susan Kingley
ARLIE	Denny Dillon
BENNIE	Bob Burrus
GUARDS	Bryan Lynner and Jim Baker
DOCTOR	Thurman Scott
MOTHER	Anne Pitoniak
SCHOOL PRINCIPAL	Maggie Riley
CARL	Leo Burmester
WARDEN	Ray Fry
RUBY	Lynn Cohen
TEACHER	Nan Wray
WOMAN	Jeanne Cullen
MALE TEACHER	Michael Kevin

Director	Jon Jory
Sets and Lights	Paul Owen
Costumes	Kurt Wilhelm
Props	Cynthia Lee Beeman

The first New York production of GETTING OUT opened at The Phoenix Theatre on October 19, 1978. The cast of that production (in order of appearance) was as follows:

ARLIE	Pamela Reed
ARLENE	Susan Kingsley
GUARD (1)	John C. Capodice
BENNIE	Barry Corbin
GUARD (2)	David Berman
DOCTOR	William Jay
MOTHER	Madeleine Thorton-Sherwood
SCHOOL PRINCIPAL	Anna Minot
RONNIE	Kevin Bacon
CARL	Leo Burmester
WARDEN	Hansford Rowe
RUBY	Joan Pape

Director	Jon Jory
Scenery and Lighting	James Tilton
Costumes	Kurt Wilhelm

CHARACTERS

ARLENE, *a thin, drawn woman in her late twenties who has just served an eight-year prison term for murder*
ARLIE, ARLENE *at various times earlier in her life*
BENNIE, *an Alabama prison guard in his fifties*
GUARD (EVANS)
GUARD (CALDWELL)
DOCTOR, *a psychiatrist in a juvenile institution*
MOTHER, ARLENE'S *mother*
SCHOOL PRINCIPAL, **female**
RONNIE, *a teenager in a juvenile institution*
CARL, ARLENE'S *former pimp and partner in various crimes, in his late twenties*
WARDEN, *superintendent of Pine Ridge Correctional Institute for Women*
RUBY, ARLENE'S *upstairs neighbor, a cook in a diner, also an ex-con, in her late thirties*

PLAYWRIGHT'S NOTES

Arlie is the violent kid Arlene was until her last stretch in prison. Arlie may walk through the apartment quite freely, but no one there will acknowledge her presence. Most of her scenes take place in the prison areas.

Arlie, in a sense, is Arlene's memory of herself, called up by fears, needs, and even simple word cues. The memory haunts, attacks, and warns. But mainly, the memory will not go away.

Arlie's life should be as vivid as Arlene's, if not as continuous. There must be hints in both physical type and gesture that Arlie and Arlene are the same person, though seen at different times in her life. They both speak with a country twang, but Arlene is suspicious and guarded—withdrawal is always a possibility. Arlie is unpredictable and incorrigible. The change seen in Arlie during the second act represents a movement toward the adult Arlene, but the transition should never be complete. Only in the final scene are they enjoyably aware of each other.

The life in the prison "surround" needs to convince without distracting. The guards do not belong to any specific insitution, but rather to all the places where Arlene has done time.

PROLOGUE

(Beginning five minutes before the houselights come down, the following announcements are broadcast over the loudspeaker. A woman's voice is preferred; a droning tone is essential.)

LOUDSPEAKER VOICE: Kitchen workers, all kitchen workers report immediately to the kitchen. Kitchen workers to the kitchen. The library will not be open today. Those scheduled for book checkout should remain in morning work assignments. Kitchen workers to the kitchen. No library hours today. Library hours resume tomorrow as usual. All kitchen workers to the kitchen.

Frances Mills, you have a visitor at the front gate. All residents and staff, all residents and staff....Do not, repeat, do not, walk on the front lawn today or use the picnic tables on the front lawn during your break after lunch or dinner.

Your attention please. The exercise class for Dorm A residents has been cancelled. Mrs. Fischer should be back at work in another month. She thanks you for your cards and wants all her girls to know she had an eight-pound baby girl.

Doris Creech, see Mrs. Adams at the library before lunch. Frances Mills, you have a visitor at the front gate. The Women's Associates' picnic for the beauty school class has been postponed until Friday. As picnic lunches have already been prepared, any beauty school member who so wishes may pick up a picnic lunch and eat it at her assigned lunch table during the regular lunch period.

Frances Mills, you have a visitor at the front gate. Doris Creech to see Mrs. Adams at the library before lunch. I'm sorry, that's Frankie Hill, you have a visitor at the front gate. Repeat, Frankie Hill, not Frances Mills, you have a visitor at the front gate.

ACT ONE

(The play is set in a dingy one-room apartment in a rundown section of downtown Louisville, Kentucky. There is a twin bed and one chair. There is a sink, an apartment-sized combination stove and refrigerator, and a counter with cabinets above. Dirty curtains conceal the bars on the outside of the single window. There is one closet and a door to the bathroom. The door to the apartment opens into a hall. A catwalk stretches above the apartment and a prison cell, stage right, connects to it by stairways. An area downstage and another stage left complete the enclosure of the apartment by playing areas for the past. The apartment must seem imprisoned. Following the prologue, lights fade to black and the warden's voice is heard on tape.)

WARDEN'S VOICE: The Alabama State Parole Board hereby grants parole to Holsclaw, Arlene, subject having served eight years at Pine Ridge Correctional Institute for the second-degree murder of a cab driver in conjunction with a filling station robbery involving attempted kidnapping of attendant. Crime occurred during escape from Lakewood State Prison where subject Holsclaw was serving three years for forgery and prostitution. Extensive juvenile records from the state of Kentucky appended hereto.

(As the warden continues, light comes up on ARLENE, *walking around the cell, waiting to be picked up for the ride home.* ARLIE *is visible, but just barely, down center.)*

WARDEN'S VOICE: Subject now considered completely rehabilitated is returned to Kentucky under interstate parole agreement in consideration of family residence and appropriate support personnel in the area. Subject will remain under the supervision of Kentucky parole officers for a period of five years. Prospects for successful integration into community rated good. Psychological evaluation, institutional history, and health records attached in Appendix C, this document.

BENNIE'S VOICE: Arlie!

*(*ARLENE *leaves the cell as light comes up on* ARLIE, *seated down center. She tells this story rather simply. She enjoys it, but its horror is not lost on her. She may be doing some semi-absorbing activity such as painting her toenails.)*

ARLIE: So, there was this little kid, see, this creepy little fucker next door. Had glasses an' somethin' wrong with his foot. I don't know, seven, maybe. Anyhow, ever time his daddy went fishin', he'd bring this kid back some frogs. They built this little fence around 'em in the backyard like they was pets or somethin'. An' we'd try to go over an' see 'em but he'd start screamin' to his mother to come out an' git rid of us. Real snotty like. So we got sick of him bein' such a goody-goody an' one night me an' June snuck over there an' put all his dumb ol' frogs in this sack. You never heared such a fuss. *(Makes croaking sounds)* Slimy bastards, frogs. We was plannin' to let 'em go all over the place, but when they started jumpin' an' all, we just figured they was askin' for it. So, we taken 'em out front to the porch an' we throwed 'em, one at a time, into the street. *(Laughs)* Some of 'em hit cars goin' by but most of 'em jus' got squashed, you know, runned over? It was great, seein' how far we could throw 'em, over back of our backs an' under our legs an' God, it was really fun watchin' 'em fly through the air then splat *(Claps hands)* all over somebody's car window or somethin'. Then the next day, we was waitin' an' this little kid come out in his backyard lookin' for his stupid frogs an' he don't see any an' he gets so crazy, cryin' an' everything. So me and June goes over an' tells him we seen this big mess out in the street, an' he goes out an' sees all them frogs' legs an' bodies an' shit all over the everwhere, an', man, it was so funny. We 'bout killed ourselves laughin'. Then his mother come out an' she wouldn't let him go out an' pick up all the pieces, so he jus' had to stand there watchin' all the cars go by smush his little babies right into the street. I's gonna run out an' git him a frog's head, but June yellin' at me "Arlie, git over here 'fore some car slips on them frog guts an' crashes into you." *(Pause)* I never had so much fun in one day in my whole life.

(ARLIE *remains seated as* ARLENE *enters the apartment. It is late evening. Two sets of footsteps are heard coming up the stairs.* ARLENE *opens the door and walks into the room. She stands still, surveying the littered apartment.* BENNIE *is heard dragging a heavy trunk up the stairs.* BENNIE *is wearing his guard uniform. He is a heavy man, but obviously used to physical work.)*

BENNIE: *(From outside)* Arlie?

ARLENE: Arlene.

BENNIE: Arlene? *(Bringing the trunk just inside the door)*

ARLENE: Leave it. I'll git it later.

BENNIE: Oh, now, let me bring it in for you. You ain't as strong as you was.

ARLENE: I ain't as mean as I was. I'm strong as ever. You go on now. *(Beginning to walk around the room)*

ARLIE: *(Irritated, as though someone is calling her)* Lay off! *(Gets up and walks past* BENNIE*)*

BENNIE: *(Scoots the trunk into the room a little further)* Go on where, Arlie?

ARLENE: I don't know where. How'd I know where you'd be goin'?

BENNIE: I can't go till I know you're gonna do all right.

ARLENE: Look, I'm gonna do all right. I done all right before Pine Ridge, an' I done all right at Pine Ridge. An' I'm gonna do all right here.

BENNIE: But you don't know nobody. I mean, nobody nice.

ARLENE: Lay off.

BENNIE: Nobody to take care of you.

ARLENE: *(Picking up old newspapers and other trash from the floor)* I kin take care of myself. I been doin' it long enough.

BENNIE: Sure you have, an' you landed yourself in prison doin' it, Arlie girl.

ARLENE: *(Wheels around)* Arlie girl landed herself in prison. Arlene is out, okay?

BENNIE: Hey, now, I know we said we wasn't gonna say nuthin' about that, but I been lookin' after you for a long time. I been watchin' you eat your dinner for eight years now. I got used to it, you know?

ARLENE: Well, you kin jus' git unused to it.

BENNIE: Then why'd you ask me to drive you all the way up here?

ARLENE: I didn't, now. That was all your big ideal.

BENNIE: And what were you gonna do? Ride the bus, pick up some soldier, git yourself in another mess of trouble?

(ARLIE *struts back into the apartment, speaking as if to a soldier in a bar.*)

ARLIE: Okay, who's gonna buy me a beer?

ARLENE: You oughta go by Fort Knox on your way home.

ARLIE: Fuckin' soldiers, don't care where they get theirself drunk.

ARLENE: You'd like it.

ARLIE: Well, Arlie girl, take your pick.

ARLENE: They got tanks right out on the grass to look at.

ARLIE: *(Now appears to lean on a bar rail)* You git that haircut today, honey?

BENNIE: I just didn't want you given your twenty dollars the warden gave you to the first pusher you come across.

(ARLIE *laughs.*)

ARLENE: That's what you think I been waitin' for?

(A GUARD *appears and motions for* ARLIE *to follow him.)*

ARLIE: Yeah! I heard ya.

(The GUARD *takes* ARLIE *to the cell and slams the door.)*

BENNIE: But God almighty, I hate to think what you'd done to the first ol' bugger tried to make you in that bus station. You got grit, Arlie girl. I gotta credit you for that.

ARLIE: *(From the cell, as she dumps a plate of food on the floor)* Officer!

BENNIE: The screamin' you'd do. Wake the dead.

ARLENE: Uh-huh.

BENNIE: *(Proudly)* An' there ain't nobody can beat you for throwin' plates.

ARLIE: Are you gonna clean up this shit or do I have to sit here and look at it till I vomit?

(A GUARD comes in to clean it up.)

BENNIE: Listen, ever prison in Alabama's usin' plastic forks now on account of what you done.

ARLENE: You can quit talkin' just anytime now.

ARLIE: Some life you got, fatso. Bringin' me my dinner then wipin' it off the walls. *(Laughs)*

BENNIE: Some of them officers was pretty leery of you. Even the chaplain.

ARLENE: No he wasn't either.

BENNIE: Not me, though. You was just wild, that's all.

ARLENE: Animals is wild, not people. That's what he said.

ARLIE: *(Mocking)* Good behavior, good behavior. Shit.

BENNIE: Now what could that four-eyes chaplain know about wild? (ARLENE *looks up sharply.*) Okay. Not wild, then...

ARLIE: I kin git outta here anytime I want. *(Leaves the cell)*

BENNIE: But you got grit, Arlie.

ARLENE: I have said for you to call me Arlene.

BENNIE: Okay okay.

ARLENE: Huh?

BENNIE: Don't get riled. You want me to call you Arlene, then Arlene it is. Yes ma'am. Now, *(Slapping the trunk)* where do you want this? *(No response)* Arlene, I said, where do you want this trunk?

ARLENE: I don't care. (BENNIE *starts to put it at the foot of the bed.*) No! *(Then calmer)* I seen it there too long. (BENNIE *is irritated.*) Maybe over here. *(Points to a spot near the window)* I could put a cloth on it an' sit an' look out the... *(She pulls the curtains apart, sees the bars on the window.)* What's these bars doin' here?

BENNIE: *(Stops moving the trunk)* I think they're to keep out burglars, you know. *(Sits on the trunk)*

ARLENE: Yeah, I know.

(ARLIE *appears on the catwalk, as if stopped during a break-in.*)

ARLIE: We ain't breakin' in, cop, we're just admirin' this beautiful window.

ARLENE: I don't want them there. Pull them out.

BENNIE: You can't go tearin' up the place, Arlene. Landlord wouldn't like it.

ARLIE: *(To the unseen policeman)* Maybe I got a brick in my hand and maybe I don't.

BENNIE: Not one bit.

ARLIE: An' I'm standin' on this garbage can because I like to, all right?

ARLENE: *(Walking back toward BENNIE)* I ain't gonna let no landlord tell me what to do.

BENNIE: The landlord owns the building. You gotta do what he says or he'll throw you out right on your pretty little be-hind. *(Gives her a familiar pat)*

ARLENE: *(Slaps his hand away)* You watch your mouth. I won't have no dirty talk.

ARLIE: Just shut the fuck up, cop! Go bust a wino or somethin'. *(Returns to the cell)*

ARLENE: *(Points down right)* Here, put the trunk over here.

BENNIE: *(Carrying the trunk over to the spot she has picked)* What you got in here, anyhow? Rocks? Rocks from the rock pile?

ARLENE: That ain't funny.

BENNIE: Oh sweetie, I didn't mean nuthin' by that.

ARLENE: And I ain't your sweetie.

BENNIE: We really did have us a rock pile, you know, at the old men's prison, yes we did. And those boys, time they did nine or ten years carryin' rocks around, they was pret-ty mean, I'm here to tell you. And strong? God.

ARLENE: Well, what did you expect? *(Beginning to unpack the trunk)*

BENNIE: You're tellin' me. It was dumb, I kept tellin' the warden that. They coulda kill us all, easy, anytime, that outfit. Except, we did have the guns.

ARLENE: Uh-huh.

BENNIE: One old bastard sailed a throwin' rock at me one day, woulda took my eye out if I hadn't turned around just then. Still got the scar, see? *(Reaches up to the back of his head)*

ARLENE: You shoot him?

BENNIE: Nope. Somebody else did. I forget who. Hey! *(Walking over to the window)* These bars won't be so bad. Maybe you could get you some plants so's you don't even see them. Yeah, plants'd do it up just fine. Just fine.

ARLENE: *(Pulls a cheaply framed picture of Jesus out of the trunk)* Chaplain give me this.

BENNIE: He got it for free, I bet.

ARLENE: Now, look here. That chaplain was good to me, so you can shut up about him.

BENNIE: *(Backing down)* Fine. Fine.

ARLENE: Here. *(Handing him the picture)* You might as well be useful 'fore you go.

BENNIE: Where you want it?

ARLENE: Don't matter.

BENNIE: Course it matters. Wouldn't want me puttin' it inside the closet, would you? You gotta make decisions now, Arlene. Gotta decide things.

ARLENE: I don't care.

BENNIE: *(Insisting)* Arlene.

ARLENE: *(Pointing to a prominent position on the apartment wall, center)* There.

BENNIE: Yeah. Good place. See it first thing when you get up.

(ARLENE *lights a cigarette, as* ARLIE *retrieves a hidden lighter from the toilet in the cell.*)

ARLIE: There's ways...gettin' outta bars....*(Lights a fire in the cell, catching her blouse on fire too)*

BENNIE: *(As* ARLIE *is lighting the fire)* This ol' nail's pretty loose. I'll find something better to hang it with...somewhere or other....

(ARLIE *screams and the* DOCTOR *runs toward her, getting the attention of a* GUARD *who has been goofing off on the catwalk.*)

ARLIE: Let me outta here! There's a fuckin' fire in here!

(The DOCTOR *arrives at the cell, pats his pockets as if looking for the keys.)*

ARLIE: Officer!

DOCTOR: Guard!

(GUARD *begins his run to the cell.*)

ARLIE: It's burnin' me!

DOCTOR: Hurry!

GUARD (EVANS): I'm comin'! I'm comin'!

DOCTOR: What the hell were you—

GUARD (EVANS): *(Fumbling for the right key)* Come on, come on.

DOCTOR: *(Urgent)* For Chrissake!

(The GUARD gets the door open, they rush in. The DOCTOR, wrestling ARLIE to the ground, opens his bag.)

DOCTOR: Lay still, dammit.

(ARLIE collapses. The DOCTOR gives an injection.)

DOCTOR: *(Grabbing his hand)* Ow!

GUARD (EVANS): *(Lifting ARLIE up to the bed)* Get bit, Doc?

DOCTOR: You going to let her burn this place down before you start payin' attention up there?

GUARD (EVANS): *(Walks to the toilet, feels under the rim)* Uh-huh.

BENNIE: There, that what you had in mind?

ARLENE: Yeah, thanks.

GUARD (EVANS): She musta had them matches hid right here.

BENNIE: *(Staring at the picture he's hung)* How you think he kept his beard trimmed all nice?

ARLENE: *(Preoccupied with unloading the trunk)* Who?

BENNIE: *(Pointing to the picture)* Jesus.

DOCTOR: I'll have to report you for this, Evans.

ARLENE: I don't know.

DOCTOR: That injection should hold her. I'll check back later. *(Leaves)*

GUARD (EVANS): *(Walking over to the bed)* Report me, my ass. We got cells don't have potties, Holsclaw. *(Begins to search her and the bed, handling her very roughly)* So where is it now? Got it up your pookie, I bet. Oh, that'd be good. Doc comin' back in an' me with my fingers up your...roll over...don't weigh hardly nuthin', do you, dollie?

BENNIE: Never seen him without a moustache either.

ARLENE: Huh?

BENNIE: The picture.

GUARD (EVANS): Aw now....*(Finding the lighter under the mattress)* That wasn't hard at all. Don't you know 'bout hide an' seek, Arlie, girl? Gonna hide somethin', hide it where it's fun to find it. *(Standing up, going to the door)* Crazy fuckin' someday-we-ain't-gonna-come-save-you bitch!

(GUARD *slams cell door and leaves.*)

BENNIE: Well, Arlie girl, that ol' trunk's 'bout as empty as my belly.

ARLENE: You have been talkin' 'bout your belly ever since we left this mornin'.

BENNIE: You hungry? Them hot dogs we had give out around Nashville.

ARLENE: No. Not really.

BENNIE: You gotta eat, Arlene.

ARLENE: Says who?

BENNIE: *(Laughs)* How 'bout I pick us up some chicken, give you time to clean yourself up. We'll have a nice little dinner, just the two of us.

ARLENE: I git sick if I eat this late. Besides, I'm tired.

BENNIE: You'll feel better soon's you git somethin' on your stomach. Like I always said, "Can't plow less'n you feed the mule."

ARLENE: I ain't never heard you say that.

BENNIE: There's lot's you don't know about me, Arlene. You been seein' me ever day, but you ain't been payin' attention. You'll get to like me now we're out.

ARLENE: You...was always out.

BENNIE: Yes sir, I'm gonna like bein' retired. I kin tell already. An' I can take care of you, like I been, only now—

ARLENE: You tol' me you was jus' takin' a vacation.

BENNIE: I was gonna tell you.

ARLENE: You had some time off an' nothin' to do...

BENNIE: Figured you knew already.

ARLENE: You said you ain't never seen Kentucky like you always wanted to. Now you tell me you done quit at the prison?

BENNIE: They wouldn't let me drive you up here if I was still on the payroll, you know. Rules, against the rules. Coulda got me in big trouble doin' that.

ARLENE: You ain't goin' back to Pine Ridge?

BENNIE: Nope.

ARLENE: And you drove me all the way up here plannin' to stay here?

BENNIE: I was thinkin' on it.

ARLENE: Well what are you gonna do?

BENNIE: *(Not positive, just a possibility)* Hardware.

ARLENE: Sell guns?

BENNIE: *(Laughs)* Nails. Always wanted to. Some little store with bins and barrels full of nails and screws. Count 'em out. Put 'em in little sacks.

ARLENE: I don't need nobody hangin' around remindin' me where I been.

BENNIE: We had us a good time drivin' up here, didn't we? You throwin' that tomato outta the car...hit that no litterin' sign square in the middle. *(Grabs her arm as if to feel the muscle)* Good arm you got.

ARLENE: *(Pulling away sharply)* Don't you go grabbin' me.

BENNIE: Listen, you take off them clothes and have yourself a nice hot bath. *(Heading for the bathroom)* See, I'll start the water. And me, I'll go get us some chicken. *(Coming out of the bathroom)* You like slaw or potato salad?

ARLENE: Don't matter.

BENNIE: *(Asking her to decide)* Arlene...

ARLENE: Slaw.

BENNIE: One big bucket of slaw comin' right up. An' extra rolls. You have a nice bath, now, you hear? I'll take my time so's you don't have to hurry fixin' yourself up.

ARLENE: I ain't gonna do no fixin'.

BENNIE: *(A knowing smile)* I know how you gals are when you get in the tub. You got any bubbles?

ARLENE: What?

BENNIE: Bubbles. You know, stuff to make bubbles with. Bubble bath.

ARLENE: I thought you was goin'.

BENNIE: Right. Right. Goin' right now.

(BENNIE *leaves, locking the door behind him. He has left his hat on the bed.* ARLENE *checks the stove and refrigerator.*)

GUARD (CALDWELL): *(Opening the cell door, carrying a plastic dinner carton)* Got your grub, girlie.

ARLIE: Get out!

GUARD (CALDWELL): Can't. Doc says you gotta take the sun today.

ARLIE: You take it! I ain't hungry.

(*The* GUARD *and* ARLIE *begin to walk to the downstage table area.*)

GUARD (CALDWELL): You gotta eat, Arlie.

ARLIE: Says who?

GUARD (CALDWELL): Says me. Says the warden. Says the Department of Corrections. Brung you two rolls.

ARLIE: And you know what you can do with your—

GUARD (CALDWELL): Stuff 'em in your bra, why don't you?

ARLIE: Ain't you got somebody to go beat up somewhere?

GUARD (CALDWELL): Gotta see you get fattened up.

ARLIE: What do you care?

(ARLENE *goes into the bathroom.*)

GUARD (CALDWELL): Oh, we care all right. *(Setting the food down on the table)* Got us a two-way mirror in the shower room. *(She looks up, hostile.)* And you don't know which one it is, do you? *(He forces her onto the seat.)* Yes ma'am. Eat. *(Pointing to the food)* We sure do care if you go gittin' too skinny. *(Walks away but continues to watch her)* Yes ma'am. We care a hog-lickin' lot.

ARLIE: *(Throws the whole carton at him)* Sons-a-bitches!

(MOTHER'*s knock is heard on the apartment door.*)

MOTHER'S VOICE: Arlie? Arlie girl you in there?

(ARLENE *walks out of the bathroom. She stands still, looking at the door.* ARLIE *hears the knock at the same time and slips into the apartment and over to the bed, putting the pillow between her legs and holding the yellow teddy bear* ARLENE *has unpacked. The knocking gets louder.*)

MOTHER'S VOICE: Arlie?

ARLIE: *(Pulling herself up weakly on one elbow, speaking with the voice of a very young child)* Mama? Mama?

(ARLENE *walks slowly toward the door.*)

MOTHER'S VOICE: *(Now pulling the doorknob from the outside, angry that the door is locked)* Arlie? I know you're in there.

ARLIE: I can't git up, Mama. *(Hands between her legs)* My legs is hurt.

MOTHER'S VOICE: What's takin' you so long?

ARLENE: *(Smoothing out her dress)* Yeah, I'm comin'. *(Puts* BENNIE'*s hat out of sight under the bed)* Hold on.

MOTHER'S VOICE: I brung you some stuff but I ain't gonna stand here all night.

(ARLENE *opens the door and stands back.* MOTHER *looks strong but badly worn. She is wearing her cab driver's uniform and is carrying a plastic laundry basket stuffed with cleaning fluids, towels, bug spray, etc.*)

ARLENE: I didn't know if you'd come.

MOTHER: Ain't I always?

ARLENE: How are you?

(ARLENE *moves as if to hug her.* MOTHER *stands still,* ARLENE *backs off.*)

MOTHER: 'Bout the same. *(Walking into the room)*

ARLENE: I'm glad to see you.

MOTHER: *(Not looking at* ARLENE*)* You look tired.

ARLENE: It was a long drive.

MOTHER: *(Putting the laundry basket on the trunk)* Didn't fatten you up none, I see. *(Walks around the room, looking the place over)* You always was too skinny. *(*ARLENE *straightens her clothes again.)* Shoulda beat you like your daddy said. Make you eat.

ARLIE: Nobody done this to me, Mama. *(Protesting, in pain)* No! No!

MOTHER: He weren't a mean man, though, your daddy.

ARLIE: Was...*(Quickly)* My bike. My bike hurt me. The seat bumped me.

MOTHER: You remember that black chewing gum he got you when you was sick?

ARLENE: I remember he beat up on you.

MOTHER: Yeah. *(Proudly)* And he was real sorry a coupla times. *(Looking in the closet)* Filthy dirty. Hey! *(Slamming the closet door;* ARLENE *jumps at the noise.)* I brung you all kinda stuff. Just like Candy not leavin' you nuthin'. *(Walking back to the basket)* Some kids I got.

ARLIE: *(Curling up into a ball)* No, Mama, don't touch it. It'll git well. It git well before.

ARLENE: Where is Candy?

MOTHER: You got her place so what do you care? I got her outta my house so whatta I care? This'll be a good place for you.

ARLENE: *(Going to the window)* Wish there was a yard, here.

MOTHER: *(Beginning to empty the basket)* Nice things, see? Bet you ain't had no colored towels where you been.

ARLENE: No.

MOTHER: *(Putting some things away in cabinets)* No place like home. Got that up on the kitchen wall now.

ARLIE: I don't want no tea, Mama.

ARLENE: Yeah?

MOTHER: *(Repeating* ARLENE's *answers)* No....Yeah?...You forgit how to talk? I ain't gonna be here all that long. Least you can talk to me while I'm here.

ARLENE: You ever git that swing you wanted?

MOTHER: Dish towels, an' see here? June sent along this teapot. You drink tea, Arlie?

ARLENE: No.

MOTHER: June's havin' another baby. Don't know when to quit, that girl. Course, I ain't one to talk. *(Starting to pick up trash on the floor)*

ARLENE: Have you seen Joey?

ARLIE: I'm tellin' you the truth.

MOTHER: An' Ray...

ARLIE: *(Pleading)* Daddy didn't do nuthin' to me.

MOTHER: Ray ain't had a day of luck in his life.

ARLIE: Ask him. He saw me fall on my bike.

MOTHER: Least bein' locked up now, he'll keep off June till the baby gits here.

ARLENE: Have you seen Joey?

MOTHER: Your daddy ain't doin' too good right now. Man's been dyin' for ten years, to hear him tell it. You'd think he'd git tired of it an' jus' go ahead...pass on.

ARLENE: *(Wanting an answer)* Mother...

MOTHER: Yeah, I seen 'im. 'Bout two years ago. Got your stringy hair.

ARLENE: You got a picture?

MOTHER: You was right to give him up. Foster homes is good for some kids.

ARLIE: Where's my Joey-bear? Yellow Joey-bear? Mama?

ARLENE: How'd you see him?

MOTHER: I was down at the Detention Center pickin' up Pete. *(Beginning her serious cleaning now)*

ARLENE: *(Less than interested)* How is he?

MOTHER: I could be workin' at the Detention Center I been there so much. All I gotta do's have somethin' big goin' on an' I git a call to come after one of you. Can't jus' have kids, no, gotta be pickin' 'em up all over town.

ARLENE: You was just tellin' me—

MOTHER: Pete is taller, that's all.

ARLENE: You was just tellin' me how you saw Joey.

MOTHER: I'm comin' back in the cab an' I seen him waitin' for the bus.

ARLENE: What'd he say?

MOTHER: Oh, I didn't stop. (ARLENE *looks up quickly, hurt and angry.*) If the kid don't even know you, Arlie, he sure ain't gonna know who I am.

ARLENE: How come he couldn't stay at Shirley's?

MOTHER: 'Cause Shirley never was crazy about washin' more diapers. She's the only smart kid I got. anyway, social worker only put him there till she could find him a foster home.

ARLENE: But I coulda seen him.

MOTHER: Thatta been trouble, him bein' in the family. Kid wouldn't have known who to listen to, Shirley or you.

ARLENE: But I'm his mother.

MOTHER: See, now you won't have to be worryin' about him. No kids, no worryin'.

ARLENE: He just had his birthday, you know.

ARLIE: Don't let Daddy come in here, Mama. Just you an' me. Mama?

ARLENE: When I git workin', I'll git a nice rug for this place. He could come live here with me.

MOTHER: Fat chance.

ARLENE: I done my time.

MOTHER: You never really got attached to him anyway.

ARLENE: How do you know that?

MOTHER: Now don't go gettin' het up. I'm telling you...

ARLENE: But...

MOTHER: Kids need rules to go by an' he'll get 'em over there.

ARLIE: (*Screaming*) No Daddy! I didn't tell her nuthin'. I didn't! I didn't! (*Gets up from the bed, terrified*)

MOTHER: Here, help me with these sheets. (*Hands* ARLENE *the sheets from the laundry basket.*) Even got you a spread. Kinda goes with them curtains. (ARLENE *is silent.*) You ain't thanked me, Arlie girl.

ARLENE: (*Going to the other side of the bed*) They don't call me Arlie no more. It's Arlene now.

(ARLENE *and* MOTHER *make up the bed.* ARLIE *jumps up, looks around, and goes over to* MOTHER's *purse. She looks through it hurriedly and pulls out the wallet.*

She takes some money and runs down left, where she is caught by a school PRINCIPAL.)

PRINCIPAL: Arlie? You're in an awfully big hurry for such a little girl. *(Brushes at* ARLIE's *hair)* That is you under all that hair, isn't it? (ARLIE *resists this gesture.)* Now, you can watch where you're going.

ARLIE: Gotta git home.

PRINCIPAL: But school isn't over for another three hours. And there's peanut butter and chili today.

ARLIE: Ain't hungry. *(Struggling free)*

(The PRINCIPAL *now sees* ARLIE's *hands clenched behind her back.)*

PRINCIPAL: What do we have in our hands, Arlie?

ARLIE: Nuthin'.

PRINCIPAL: Let me see your hands, Arlie. Open up your hands.

(ARLIE *brings her hands around in front, opening them, showing crumpled dollars.)*

ARLIE: It's my money. I earned it.

PRINCIPAL: *(Taking the money)* And how did we earn this money?

ARLIE: Doin' things.

PRINCIPAL: What kind of things?

ARLIE: For my daddy.

PRINCIPAL: Well, we'll see about that. You'll have to come with me.

(ARLIE *resists as the* PRINCIPAL *pulls her.)*

ARLIE: No.

PRINCIPAL: Your mother was right after all. She said put you in a special school. *(Quickly)* No, what she said was put you away somewhere and I said, no, she's too young, well I was wrong. I have four hundred other children to take care of here and what have I been doing? Breaking up your fights, talking to your truant officer, and washing your writing off the bathroom wall. Well, I've had enough. You've made your choice. You want out of regular school and you're going to get out of regular school.

ARLIE: *(Becoming more violent)* You can't make me go nowhere, bitch!

PRINCIPAL: *(Backing off in cold anger)* I'm not making you go. You've earned it. You've worked hard for this, well, they're used to your type over there. They'll know exactly what to do with you. *(She stalks off, leaving* ARLIE *alone.)*

MOTHER: *(Smoothing out the spread)* Spread ain't new, but it don't look so bad. Think we got it right after we got you. No, I remember now. I was pregnant with you an' been real sick the whole time.

(ARLENE *lights a cigarette,* MOTHER *takes one,* ARLENE *retrieves the pack quickly.*)

MOTHER: Your daddy brung me home this big bowl of chili an' some jelly doughnuts. Some fare from the airport gave him a big tip. Anyway, I'd been eatin' peanut brittle all day, only thing that tasted any good. Then in he come with this chili and no sooner'n I got in bed I thrown up all over everwhere. Lucky I didn't throw you up, Arlie girl. Anyhow, that's how come us to get a new spread. This one here. *(Sits on the bed)*

ARLENE: You drivin' the cab any?

MOTHER: Any? Your daddy ain't drove it at all a long time now. Six years, seven maybe.

ARLENE: You meet anybody nice?

MOTHER: Not anymore. Mostly drivin' old ladies to get their shoes. Guess it got around the nursin' homes I was reliable. *(Sounds funny to her)* You remember that time I took you drivin' with me that night after you been in a fight an' that soldier bought us a beer? Shitty place, hole in the wall?

ARLENE: You made me wait in the car.

MOTHER: *(Standing up)* Think I'd take a child of mine into a dump like that?

ARLENE: You went in.

MOTHER: Weren't no harm in it. *(Walking over for the bug spray)* I didn't always look so bad, you know.

ARLENE: You was pretty.

MOTHER: *(Beginning to spray the floor)* You could look better'n you do. Do somethin' with your hair. I always thought if you'd looked better you wouldn't have got in so much trouble.

ARLENE: *(Pleased and curious)* Joey got my hair?

MOTHER: And skinny.

ARLENE: I took some beauty school at Pine Ridge.

MOTHER: Yeah, a beautician?

ARLENE: I don't guess so.

MOTHER: Said you was gonna work.

ARLENE: They got a law here. Ex-cons can't get no license.

MOTHER: Shoulda stayed in Alabama, then. Worked there.

ARLENE: They got a law there, too.

MOTHER: Then why'd they give you the trainin'?

ARLENE: I don't know.

MOTHER: Maybe they thought it'd straighten you out.

ARLENE: Yeah.

MOTHER: But you are gonna work, right?

ARLENE: Yeah. Cookin' maybe. Somethin' that pays good.

MOTHER: You? Cook? *(Laughs)*

ARLENE: I could learn it.

MOTHER: Your daddy ain't never forgive you for that bologna sandwich. (ARLENE *laughs a little, finally enjoying a memory.*) Oh, I wish I'd seen you spreadin' that Colgate on that bread. He'd have smelled that toothpaste if he hadn't been so sloshed. Little snotty-nosed kid tryin' to kill her daddy with a bologna sandwich. An' him bein' so pleased when you brung it to him....*(Laughing)*

ARLENE: He beat me good.

MOTHER: Well, now, Arlie, you gotta admit you had it comin' to you. *(Wiping tears from laughing)*

ARLENE: I guess.

MOTHER: You got a broom?

ARLENE: No.

MOTHER: Well, I got one in the cab I brung just in case. I can't leave it here, but I'll sweep up fore I go. *(Walking toward the door)* You jus' rest till I git back. Won't find no work lookin' the way you do.

(MOTHER *leaves.* ARLENE *finds some lipstick and a mirror in her purse, makes an attempt to look better while her mother is gone.*)

ARLIE: *(Jumps up, as if talking to another kid)* She is not skinny!

ARLENE: *(Looking at herself in the mirror)* I guess I could...

ARLIE: And she don't have to git them stinky permanents. Her hair just comes outta her head curly.

ARLENE: Some lipstick.

ARLIE: *(Serious)* She drives the cab to buy us stuff, 'cause we don't take no charity from nobody, 'cause we got money 'cause she earned it.

ARLENE: *(Closing the mirror, dejected, afraid* MOTHER *might be right)* But you're too skinny and you got stringy hair. *(Sitting on the floor)*

ARLIE: *(More angry)* She drives at night 'cause people needs rides at night. People goin' to see their friends that are sick, or people's cars broken down an' they gotta get to work at the...nobody calls my mama a whore!

MOTHER: *(Coming back in with the broom)* If I'd known you were gonna sweep up with your butt, I wouldn't have got this broom. Get up! *(Sweeps at* ARLENE *to get her to move)*

ARLIE: You're gonna take that back or I'm gonna rip out all your ugly hair and stuff it down your ugly throat.

ARLENE: *(Tugging at her own hair)* You still cut hair?

MOTHER: *(Noticing some spot on the floor)* Gonna take a razor blade to get out this paint.

ARLENE: Nail polish.

ARLIE: Wanna know what I know about your mama? She's dyin'. Somethin's eatin' up her insides piece by piece, only she don't want you to know it.

MOTHER: *(Continuing to sweep)* So, you're callin' yourself Arlene, now?

ARLENE: Yes.

MOTHER: Don't want your girlie name no more?

ARLENE: Somethin' like that.

MOTHER: They call you Arlene in prison?

ARLENE: Not at first when I was being hateful. Just my number then.

MOTHER: You always been hateful.

ARLENE: There was this chaplain, he called me Arlene from the first day he come to talk to me. Here, let me help you. *(She reaches for the broom.)*

MOTHER: I'll do it.

ARLENE: You kin rest.

MOTHER: Since when? *(*ARLENE *backs off.)* I ain't hateful, how come I got so many hateful kids? *(Sweeping harder now)* Poor dumb-as-hell Pat, stealin' them wigs, Candy screwin' since day one, Pete cuttin' up ol' Mac down at the grocery, June sellin' dope like it was Girl Scout cookies, and you...thank God I can't remember it all.

ARLENE: *(A very serious request)* Maybe I could come out on Sunday for...you still make that pot roast?

MOTHER: *(Now sweeping over by the picture of Jesus)* That your picture?

ARLENE: That chaplain give it to me.

MOTHER: The one that give you your "new name"?

ARLENE: Yes.

MOTHER: It's crooked. *(Doesn't straighten it)*

ARLENE: I like those potatoes with no skins. An' that ketchup squirter we had, jus' like in a real restaurant.

MOTHER: People that run them institutions now, they jus' don't know how to teach kids right. Let 'em run around an' get in more trouble. They should get you up at the crack of dawn an' set you to scrubbin' the floor. That's what kids need. Trainin'. Hard work.

ARLENE: *(A clear request)* I'll probably git my Sundays off.

MOTHER: Sunday...is my day to clean house now.

(ARLENE *gets the message, finally walks over to straighten the picture.* MOTHER *now feels a little bad about this rejection, stops sweeping for a moment.*)

MOTHER: I woulda wrote you but I didn't have nuthin' to say. An' no money to send, so what's the use?

ARLENE: I made out.

MOTHER: They pay you for workin'?

ARLENE: 'Bout three dollars a month.

MOTHER: How'd you make it on three dollars a month? *(Answers her own question)* You do some favors?

ARLENE: *(Sitting down in the chair under the picture, a somewhat smug look)* You jus' can't make it by yourself.

MOTHER: *(Pauses, suspicious, then contemptuous)* You play, Arlie?

ARLENE: You don't know nuthin' about that.

MOTHER: I hear things. Girls callin' each other "mommy" and bringin' things back from the canteen for their "husbands." Makes me sick. You got family, Arlie, what you want with that playin'? Don't want nobody like that in my house.

ARLENE: You don't know what you're talkin' about.

MOTHER: I still got two kids at home. Don't want no bad example. *(Not finishing the sweeping; has all the dirt in one place, but doesn't get it up off the floor yet)*

ARLENE: I could tell them some things.

MOTHER: *(Vicious)* Like about that cab driver.

ARLENE: Look, that was a long time ago. I wanna work, now, make somethin' of myself. I learned to knit. People'll buy nice sweaters. Make some extra money.

MOTHER: We sure could use it.

ARLENE: An' then if I have money, maybe they'd let me take Joey to the fair, buy him hot dogs and talk to him. Make sure he ain't foolin' around.

MOTHER: What makes you think he'd listen to you? Alice, across the street? Her sister took care her kids while she was at Lexington. You think they pay any attention to her now? Ashamed, that's what. One of 'em told me his mother done died. Gone to see a friend and died there.

ARLENE: Be different with me and Joey.

MOTHER: He don't even know who you are, Arlie.

ARLENE: *(Wearily)* Arlene.

MOTHER: You forgot already what you was like as a kid. At Waverly, tellin' them lies about that campin' trip we took, sayin' your daddy made you watch while he an' me...you know. I'd have killed you then if them social workers hadn't been watchin'.

ARLENE: Yeah.

MOTHER: Didn't want them thinkin' I weren't fit. Well, what do they know? Each time you'd get out of one of them places, you'd be actin' worse than ever. Go right back to that junkie, pimp, Carl, sellin' the stuff he steals, savin' his ass from the police. He follow you home this time, too?

ARLENE: He's got four more years at Bricktown.

MOTHER: Glad to hear it. Here...*(Handing her a bucket)* water.

(ARLENE *fills up the bucket and* MOTHER *washes several dirty spots on the walls, floor, and furniture.* ARLENE *knows better than to try to help. The* DOCTOR *walks downstage to find* ARLIE *for their counseling session.)*

DOCTOR: So you refuse to go to camp?

ARLIE: Now why'd I want to go to your fuckin' camp? Camp's for babies. You can go shit in the woods if you want to, but I ain't goin'.

DOCTOR: Oh, you're goin'.

ARLIE: Wanna bet?

MOTHER: Arlie, I'm waitin'. *(For the water)*

ARLIE: 'Sides, I'm waitin'.

DOCTOR: Waiting for what?

ARLIE: For Carl to come git me.

DOCTOR: And who is Carl?

ARLIE: Jus' some guy. We're goin' to Alabama.

DOCTOR: You don't go till we say you can go.

ARLIE: Carl's got a car.

DOCTOR: Does he have a driver's license to go with it?

ARLIE: *(Enraged, impatient)* I'm goin' now.

(ARLIE *stalks away, then backs up toward the* DOCTOR *again. He has information she wants.*)

DOCTOR: Hey!

ARLENE: June picked out a name for the baby?

MOTHER: Clara...or Clarence. Got it from this fancy shampoo she bought.

ARLIE: I don't feel good. I'm pregnant, you know.

DOCTOR: The test was negative.

ARLIE: Well I should know, shouldn't I?

DOCTOR: No. You want to be pregnant, is that it?

ARLIE: I wouldn't mind. Kids need somebody to bring 'em up right.

DOCTOR: Raising children is a big responsibility, you know.

ARLIE: Yeah, I know it. I ain't dumb. Everybody always thinks I'm so dumb.

DOCTOR: You could learn if you wanted to. That's what the teachers are here for.

ARLIE: Shit.

DOCTOR: Or so they say.

ARLIE: All they teach us is about geography. Why'd I need to know about Africa. Jungles and shit.

DOCTOR: They want you to know about other parts of the world.

ARLIE: Well, I ain't goin' there so whatta I care?

DOCTOR: What's this about Cindy?

ARLIE: *(Hostile)* She told Mr. Dawson some lies about me.

DOCTOR: I bet.

ARLIE: She said I fuck my daddy for money.

DOCTOR: And what did you do when she said that?

ARLIE: What do you think I did? I beat the shit out of her.

DOCTOR: And that's a good way to work out your problem?

ARLIE: *(Proudly)* She ain't done it since.

DOCTOR: She's been in traction, since.

ARLIE: So, whatta I care? She say it again, I'll do it again. Bitch!

ARLENE: *(Looking down at the dirt* MOTHER *is gathering on the floor)* I ain't got a can. Just leave it.

MOTHER: And have you sweep it under the bed after I go? *(Wraps the dirt in a piece of newspaper and puts it in her laundry basket)*

DOCTOR: *(Looking at his clipboard)* You're on unit clean up this week.

ARLIE: I done it last week!

DOCTOR: Then you should remember what to do. The session is over. *(Getting up, walking away)* And stand up straight! And take off that hat!

(DOCTOR *and* ARLIE *go offstage as* MOTHER *finds* BENNIE's *hat.*)

MOTHER: This your hat?

ARLENE: No.

MOTHER: Guess Candy left it here.

ARLENE: Candy didn't leave nuthin'.

MOTHER: Then whose is it? (ARLENE *doesn't answer.*) Do you know whose hat is this? (ARLENE *knows she has made a mistake.*) I'm askin' you a question and I want an answer. (ARLENE *turns her back.*) Whose hat is this? You tell me right now, whose hat this is?

ARLENE: It's Bennie's.

MOTHER: And who's Bennie?

ARLENE: Guy drove me home from Pine Ridge. A guard.

MOTHER: *(Upset)* I knew it. You been screwin' a goddamn guard. *(Throws the hat on the bed)*

ARLENE: He jus' drove me up here, that's all.

MOTHER: Sure.

ARLENE: I git sick on the bus.

MOTHER: You expect me to believe that?

ARLENE: I'm tellin' you, he jus'—

MOTHER: No man alive gonna drive a girl five hundred miles for nuthin'.

ARLENE: He ain't never seen Kentucky.

MOTHER: It ain't Kentucky he wants to see.

ARLENE: He ain't gettin' nuthin' from me.

MOTHER: That's what you think.

ARLENE: He done some nice things for me at Pine Ridge. Gum, funny stories.

MOTHER: He'd be tellin' stories all right, tellin' his buddies where to find you.

ARLENE: He's gettin' us some dinner right now.

MOTHER: And how're you gonna pay him? Huh? Tell me that.

ARLENE: I ain't like that no more.

MOTHER: Oh you ain't. I'm your mother. I know what you'll do.

ARLENE: I tell you I ain't.

MOTHER: I knew it. Well, when you got another bastard in you, don't come cryin' to me, 'cause I done told you.

ARLENE: Don't worry.

MOTHER: An' I'm gettin' myself outta here 'fore your boyfriend comes back.

ARLENE: *(Increasing anger)* He ain't my boyfriend.

MOTHER: I been a lotta things, but I ain't dumb, Arlene. *("Arlene" is mocking.)*

ARLENE: I didn't say you was. *(Beginning to know how this is going to turn out)*

MOTHER: Oh no? You lied to me!

ARLENE: How?

MOTHER: You took my spread without even sayin' thank you. You're hintin' at comin' to my house for pot roast just like nuthin' ever happened, an' all the time you're hidin' a goddamn guard under your bed. *(Furious)* Uh-huh.

ARLENE: *(Quietly)* Mama?

MOTHER: *(Cold, fierce)* What?

ARLENE: What kind of meat makes a pot roast?

MOTHER: A roast makes a pot roast. Buy a roast. Shoulder, chuck...

ARLENE: Are you comin' back?

MOTHER: You ain't got no need for me.

ARLENE: I gotta ask you to come see me?

MOTHER: I come tonight, didn't I, an' nobody asked me?

ARLENE: Just forgit it.

MOTHER: *(Getting her things together)* An' if I hadn't told them about this apartment, you wouldn't be out at all, how 'bout that!

ARLENE: Forgit it!

MOTHER: Don't you go talkin' back to me that way. You remember who I am. I'm the one took you back after all you done all them years. I brung you that teapot. I scrubbed your place. You remember that when you talk to me.

ARLENE: Sure.

MOTHER: Uh-huh. *(Now goes to the bed, rips off the spread, and stuffs it in her basket)* I knowed I shouldn't have come. You ain't changed a bit.

ARLENE: Same hateful brat, right?

MOTHER: *(Arms full, heading for the door)* Same hateful brat. Right.

ARLENE: *(Rushing toward her)* Mama...

MOTHER: Don't you touch me.

(MOTHER *leaves.* ARLENE *stares out the door, stunned and hurt. Finally she slams the door and turns back into the room.)*

ARLENE: No! Don't you touch Mama, Arlie!

(RONNIE, *a fellow juvenile offender, runs across the catwalk, waving a necklace and being chased by* ARLIE.)

RONNIE: Arlie got a boyfriend, Arlie got a boyfriend. *(Throws the necklace downstage)* Whoo!

ARLIE: *(Chasing him)* Ronnie, you ugly mother, I'll smash your fuckin'—

ARLENE: *(Getting more angry)* You might steal all—

RONNIE: *(Running down the stairs)* Arlie got a boyfriend...

ARLIE: Gimme that necklace or I'll—

ARLENE: —or eat all Mama's precious pot roast.

RONNIE: *(As they wrestle downstage.)* You'll tell the doctor on me? And get your private room back? *(Laughing)*

ARLENE: *(Cold and hostile)* No, don't touch Mama, Arlie. 'Cause you might slit Mama's throat. *(Goes into the bathroom)*

ARLIE: You wanna swallow all them dirty teeth?

RONNIE: Tell me who give it to you.

ARLIE: No, you tell me where it's at.

(RONNIE *breaks away, pushing* ARLIE *in the opposite direction, and runs for the necklace.)*

RONNIE: It's right here. *(Drops it down his pants)* Come an' git it.

ARLIE: Oh, now, that was really ignorant, you stupid pig.

RONNIE: *(Backing away, daring her)* Jus' reach right in. First come, first served.

ARLIE: Now, how you gonna pee after I throw your weenie over the fence?

RONNIE: You ain't gonna do that, girl. You gonna fall in love.

(ARLIE *turns vicious, pins* RONNIE *down, attacking. This is no longer play. He screams. The* DOCTOR *appears on the catwalk.*)

DOCTOR: Arlie! *(Heads down the stairs to stop this)*

CARL'S VOICE: *(From outside the apartment door)* Arlie!

DOCTOR: Arlie!

ARLIE: Stupid, ugly—

RONNIE: Help!

(ARLIE *runs away and hides down left.*)

DOCTOR: That's three more weeks of isolation, Arlie. *(Bending down to* RONNIE*)* You all right? Can you walk?

RONNIE: *(Looking back to* ARLIE *as he gets up in great pain.)* She was tryin' to kill me.

DOCTOR: Yeah. Easy now. You should've known, Ronnie.

ARLIE: *(Yelling at* RONNIE*)* You'll get yours, crybaby.

CARL'S VOICE: Arlie...

ARLIE: Yeah, I'm comin'!

CARL'S VOICE: Bad-lookin' dude says move your ass an' open up this here door, girl.

(ARLENE *does not come out of the bathroom.* CARL *twists the door knob violently, then kicks in the door and walks in.* CARL *is thin and cheaply dressed.* CARL'S *walk and manner are imitative of black pimps, but he can't quite carry it off.*)

CARL: Where you at, mama?

ARLENE: Carl?

CARL: Who else? You 'spectin' Leroy Brown?

ARLENE: I'm takin' a bath!

CARL: *(Walking toward the bathroom)* I like my ladies clean. Matter of professional pride.

ARLENE: Don't come in here.

CARL: *(Mocking her tone)* Don't come in here. I seen it all before, girl.

ARLENE: I'm gittin' out. Sit down or somethin'.

CARL: *(Talking loud enough for her to hear him through the door)* Ain't got the time. *(Opens her purse, then searches the trunk)* Jus' come by to tell you it's tomorrow. We be takin' our feet to the New York street. *(As though she will be pleased)* No more fuckin' around with these jiveass southern turkeys. We're goin' to the big city, baby. Get you some red shades and some red shorts an' the johns be linin' up 'fore we hit town. Four tricks a night. How's that sound? No use wearin' out that cute ass you got. Way I hear it, only way to git busted up there's be stupid, and I ain't lived this long bein' stupid.

ARLENE: *(Coming out of the bathroom wearing a towel)* That's exactly how you lived your whole life— bein' stupid.

CARL: Arlie...*(Moving in on her)* Be sweet, sugar.

ARLENE: Still got your curls.

CARL: *(Trying to bug her)* You're looking okay yourself.

ARLENE: Oh, Carl. *(Noticing the damage to the door, breaking away from any closeness he might try to force)*

CARL: *(Amused)* Bent up your door, some.

ARLENE: How come you're out?

CARL: Sweetheart, you done broke out once, been nabbed and sent to Pine Ridge and got yourself paroled since I been in. I got a right to a little free time too, ain't that right?

ARLENE: You escape?

CARL: Am I standin' here or am I standin' here? They been fuckin' with you, I can tell.

ARLENE: They gonna catch you.

CARL: *(Going to the window)* Not where we're going. Not a chance.

ARLENE: Where you goin' they won't git you?

CARL: Remember that green hat you picked out for me down in Birmingham? Well, I ain't ever wore it yet, but I kin wear it in New York 'cause New York's where you wear whatever you feel like. One guy tol' me he saw this dude wearin' a whole ring of feathers roun' his leg, right here *(Grabs his leg above the knee)* An' he weren't in no circus nor no Indian neither.

ARLENE: I ain't seen you since Birmingham. How come you think I wanna see you now?

(ARLIE appears suddenly, confronts CARL.)

ARLIE: *(Pointing as if there is a trick waiting)* Carl, I ain't goin' with that dude, he's weird.

CARL: 'Cause we gotta go collect the johns' money, that's "how come."

ARLIE: I don't need you pimpin' for me.

ARLENE: *(Very strong)* I'm gonna work.

CARL: Work?

ARLENE: Yeah.

CARL: What's this "work?"

ARLIE: You always sendin' me to them ol' droolers...

CARL: You kin do two things, girl—

ARLIE: They slobberin' all over me...

CARL: Breakin' out and hookin'.

ARLIE: They tyin' me to the bed!

ARLENE: I mean real work.

ARLIE: *(Now screaming, gets further away from him)* I could git killed working for you. Some sicko, some crazy drunk...

(ARLIE *goes offstage. A* GUARD *puts her in the cell some time before* BENNIE's *entrance.*)

CARL: You forget, we seen it all on TV in the day room, you bustin' outta Lakewood like that. Fakin' that palsy fit, then beatin' that guard half to death with his own key ring. Whoo-ee! Then that spree you went on...stoppin' at that fillin' station for some cash, then kidnappin' the old dude pumpin' the gas.

ARLENE: Yeah.

CARL: Then that cab driver comes outta the bathroom an' tries to mess with you and you shoots him with his own piece. *(Fires an imaginary pistol)* That there's nice work, mama. *(Going over to her, putting his arms around her)*

ARLENE: That gun...it went off, Carl.

CARL: *(Getting more determined with his affection)* That's what guns do, doll. They go off.

BENNIE'S VOICE: Arlene? Arlene?

CARL: Arlene? *(Jumping up)* Well la-de-da.

(BENNIE *opens the door, carrying the chicken dinners. He is confused, seeing* ARLENE *wearing a towel and talking to* CARL.)

ARLENE: Bennie, this here's Carl.

CARL: You're interruptin', Jack. Me an' Arlie got business.

BENNIE: She's callin' herself Arlene.

CARL: I call my ladies what I feel like, chicken man, an' you call yourself "gone."

BENNIE: I don't take orders from you.

CARL: Well, you been takin' orders from somebody, or did you git that outfit at the army surplus store?

ARLENE: Bennie brung me home from Pine Ridge.

CARL: *(Walking toward him)* Oh, it's a guard now, is it? That chicken break out or what? *(Grabs the chicken)*

BENNIE: I don't know what you're doin' here, but—

CARL: What you gonna do about it, huh? Lock me up in the toilet? You an' who else, Batman?

BENNIE: *(Taking the chicken back, walking calmly to the counter)* Watch your mouth, punk.

CARL: *(Kicks a chair toward BENNIE)* Punk!

ARLENE: *(Trying to stop this)* I'm hungry.

BENNIE: You heard her, she's hungry.

CARL: *(Vicious)* Shut up! *(Mocking)* Ossifer.

BENNIE: Arlene, tell this guy if he knows what's good for him...

CARL: *(Walking to the counter where BENNIE has left the chicken)* Why don't you write me a parkin' ticket? *(Shoves the chicken on the floor)* Don't fuck with me, dad. It ain't healthy.

(BENNIE *pauses. A real standoff; finally,* BENNIE *bends down and picks up the chicken.*)

BENNIE: You ain't worth dirtyin' my hands.

(CARL *walks by him, laughing.*)

CARL: Hey, Arlie. I got some dude to see. *(For BENNIE's benefit as he struts to the door.)* What I need with another beat-up guard? All that blood, jus' ugly up my threads. *(Very sarcastic)* Bye y'all.

ARLENE: Bye, Carl.

(CARL *turns back quickly at the door, stopping* BENNIE, *who was following him.*)

CARL: You really oughta shine them shoes, man. *(Vindictive laugh, slams the door in BENNIE's face)*

BENNIE: *(Relieved, trying to change the atmosphere)* Well, how 'bout if we eat? You'll catch your death dressed like that.

ARLENE: Turn around then.

(ARLENE *gets a shabby housecoat from the closet. She puts it on over her towel, buttons it up, then pulls the towel out from under it. This has the look of a prison ritual.*)

BENNIE: (*As she is dressing*) Your parole officer's gonna tell you to keep away from guys like that...for your own good, you know. Those types, just like the suckers on my tomatoes back home. Take everything right outta you. Gotta pull 'em off, Arlie, uh, Arlene.

ARLENE: Now, I'm decent now.

BENNIE: You hear what I said?

ARLENE: (*Going to the bathroom for her hairbrush*) I told him that. That's exactly what I did tell him.

BENNIE: Who was that anyhow? (*Sits down on the bed, opens up the chicken*)

ARLENE: (*From the bathroom*) Long time ago, me an' Carl took a trip together.

BENNIE: When you was a kid, you mean?

ARLENE: I was at this place for kids.

BENNIE: And Carl was there?

ARLENE: No, he picked me up an' we went to Alabama. There was this wreck an' all. I ended up at Lakewood for forgery. It was him that done it. Got me pregnant too.

BENNIE: That was Joey's father?

ARLENE: Yeah, but he don't know that. (*Sits down*)

BENNIE: Just as well. Guy like that, don't know what they'd do.

ARLENE: Mother was here while ago. Says she's seen Joey. (*Taking a napkin from* BENNIE)

BENNIE: Wish I had a kid. Life ain't, well, complete, without no kids to play ball with an' take fishin'. Dorrie, though, she had them backaches an' that neuralgia, day I married her to the day she died. Good woman though. No drinkin', no card playin', real sweet voice...what was that song she used to sing?...Oh, yeah...

ARLENE: She says Joey's a real good-lookin' kid.

BENNIE: Well, his mom ain't bad.

ARLENE: At Lakewood, they tried to git me to have an abortion.

BENNIE: They was just thinkin' of you, Arlene.

ARLENE: (*Matter-of-fact, no self-pity*) I told 'em I'd kill myself if they done that. I would have too.

BENNIE: But they took him away after he was born.

ARLENE: Yeah. *(BENNIE waits, knowing she is about to say more.)* An' I guess I went crazy after that. Thought if I could jus' git out an' find him...

BENNIE: I don't remember any of that on the TV.

ARLENE: No.

BENNIE: Just remember you smilin' at the cameras, yellin' how you tol' that cab driver not to touch you.

ARLENE: I never seen his cab. *(Forces herself to eat)*

ARLIE: *(In the cell, holding a pillow and singing)* Rock-a-bye baby, in the tree top, when the wind blows, the cradle will....*(Not remembering)*...cradle will...*(Now talking)* What you gonna be when you grow up, pretty boy baby? You gonna be a doctor? You gonna give people medicine and take out they...no, don't be no doctor...be...be a preacher....Sayin' Our Father who is in heaven...heaven, that's where people go when they dies, when doctors can't save 'em or somebody kills 'em 'fore they even git a chance to...no, don't be no preacher neither...be...go to school and learn good *(Tone begins to change)* so you kin...make everybody else feel so stupid all the time. Best thing you to be is stay a baby 'cause nobody beats up on babies or puts them....*(Much more quiet)* That ain't true, baby. People is mean to babies, so you stay right here with me so nobody kin git you an' make you cry an' they lay one finger on you *(Hostile)* an' I'll beat the screamin' shit right out of 'em. They even blow on you an' I'll kill 'em.

(BENNIE and ARLENE have finished their dinner. BENNIE puts one carton of slaw in the refrigerator, then picks up all the paper, making a garbage bag out of one of the sacks.)

BENNIE: Ain't got a can, I guess. Jus' use this ol' sack for now.

ARLENE: I ain't never emptyin' another garbage can.

BENNIE: Yeah, I reckon you know how by now. *(Yawns)* You 'bout ready for bed?

ARLENE: *(Stands up)* I s'pose.

BENNIE: *(Stretches)* Little tired myself.

ARLENE: *(Dusting the crumbs off the bed)* Thanks for the chicken.

BENNIE: You're right welcome. You look beat. How 'bout I rub your back. *(Grabs her shoulders)*

ARLENE: *(Pulling away)* No. *(Walking to the sink)* You go on now.

BENNIE: Oh come on. *(Wiping his hands on his pants)* I ain't all that tired.

ARLENE: I'm tired.

BENNIE: Well, see then, a back rub is just what the doctor ordered.

ARLENE: No. I don't...*(Pulling away)*

(BENNIE *grabs her shoulders and turns her around, sits her down hard on the trunk, starts rubbing her back and neck.*)

BENNIE: Muscles git real tightlike, right in here.

ARLENE: You hurtin' me.

BENNIE: Has to hurt a little or it won't do no good.

ARLENE: *(Jumps—he has hurt her.)* Oh, stop it! *(She slips away from him and out into the room. She is frightened.)*

BENNIE: *(Smiling, coming after her, toward the bed)* Be lot nicer if you was layin' down. Wouldn't hurt as much.

ARLENE: Now, I ain't gonna start yellin'. I'm jus' tellin' you to go.

BENNIE: *(Straightens up, as though he's going to cooperate)* Okay then, I'll jus' git my hat.

(He reaches for the hat, then turns quickly, grabs her and throws her down on the bed. He starts rubbing again.)

BENNIE: Now, you just relax. Don't you go bein' scared of me.

ARLENE: You ain't gettin' nuthin' from me.

BENNIE: I don't want nuthin', honey. Jus' tryin' to help you sleep.

ARLENE: *(Struggling)* Don't you call me honey.

(BENNIE *stops rubbing, but keeps one hand on her back. He rubs her hair with his free hand.*)

BENNIE: See? Don't that feel better?

ARLENE: Let me up.

BENNIE: Why, I ain't holdin' you down.

ARLENE: Then let me up.

BENNIE: *(Takes hands off)* Okay. Git up.

(ARLENE *turns over slowly, begins to lift herself up on her elbows.* BENNIE *puts one hand on her leg.*)

ARLENE: Move your hand. *(She gets up, moves across the room.)*

BENNIE: I'd be happy to stay here with you tonight. Make sure you'll be all right. You ain't spent a night by yourself for a long time.

ARLENE: I remember how.

BENNIE: Well how you gonna git up? You got a alarm?

ARLENE: It ain't all that hard.

BENNIE: *(Puts one hand in his pocket, leers a little)* Oh yeah it is. *(Walks toward her again)* Gimme a kiss. Then I'll go.

ARLENE: *(Edging along the counter, seeing she's trapped)* You stay away from me.

(BENNIE *reaches for her, clamping her hands behind her, pressing up against her.*)

BENNIE: Now what's it going to hurt you to give me a little ol' kiss?

ARLENE: *(Struggling)* Git out! I said git out!

BENNIE: You don't want me to go. You're jus' beginning to get interested. Your ol' girlie temper's flarin' up. I like that in a woman.

ARLENE: Yeah, you'd love it if I'd swat you one. *(Getting away from him)*

BENNIE: I been hit by you before. I kin take anything you got.

ARLENE: I could mess you up good.

BENNIE: Now, Arlie. You ain't had a man in a long time. And the ones you had been no-count.

ARLENE: Git out!

(She slaps him. He returns the slap.)

BENNIE: *(Moving in)* Ain't natural goin' without it too long. Young thing like you. Git all shriveled up.

ARLENE: All right, you sunuvabitch, you asked for it!

(She goes into a violent rage, hitting and kicking him. BENNIE *overpowers her capably, prison-guard style.)*

BENNIE: *(Amused)* Little outta practice, ain't you?

ARLENE: *(Screaming)* I'll kill you, you creep!

(The struggle continues, BENNIE *pinning her arms under his legs as he kneels over her on the bed.* ARLENE *is terrified and in pain.)*

BENNIE: You will? You'll kill ol' Bennie...kill ol' Bennie like you done that cab driver?

(A cruel reminder he employs to stun and mock her. ARLENE *looks as though she has been hit.* BENNIE, *still fired up, unzips his pants.)*

ARLENE: *(Passive, cold and bitter)* This how you got your Dorrie, rapin'?

BENNIE: *(Unbuttoning his shirt)* That what you think this is, rape?

ARLENE: I oughta know.

BENNIE: Uh-huh.

ARLENE: First they unzip their pants.

(BENNIE *pulls his shirttail out.*)

ARLENE: Sometimes they take off their shirt.

BENNIE: They do huh?

ARLENE: But mostly, they just pull it out and stick it in.

(BENNIE *stops, finally hearing what she has been saying. He straightens up, obviously shocked. He puts his arms back in his shirt.*)

BENNIE: Don't you call me no rapist. *(Pause, then insistently)* No, I ain't no rapist, Arlie. *(Gets up, begins to tuck his shirt back in, and zips up his pants)*

ARLENE: And I ain't Arlie.

(ARLENE *remains on the bed as he continues dressing.*)

BENNIE: No I guess you ain't.

ARLENE: *(Quietly and painfully)* Arlie coulda killed you.

END OF ACT ONE

PROLOGUE

(These announcements are heard during the last five minutes of the intermission.)

LOUDSPEAKER VOICE: Garden workers will, repeat, will, report for work this afternoon. Bring a hat and raincoat and wear boots. All raincoats will be checked at the front gate at the end of work period and returned to you after supper.

Your attention please. A checkerboard was not returned to the recreation area after dinner last night. Anyone with information regarding the black and red checkerboard missing from the recreation area will please contact Mrs. Duvall after lunch. No checkerboards or checkers will be distributed until this board is returned.

Betty Rickey and Mary Alice Wolf report to the laundry. Doris Creech and Arlie Holsclaw report immediately to the superintendent's office. The movie this evening will be "Dirty Harry" starring Clint Eastwood. Doris Creech and Arlie Holsclaw report to the superintendent's office immediately.

The bus from St. Mary's this Sunday will arrive at 1:00 pm as usual. Those residents expecting visitors on that bus will gather on the front steps promptly at 1:20 and proceed with the duty officer to the visiting area after it has been confirmed that you have a visitor on the bus.

Attention all residents. Attention all residents. *(Pause)* Mrs. Helen Carson has taught needlework classes here at Pine Ridge for thirty years. She will be retiring at the end of this month and moving to Florida where her husband has bought a trailer park. The Resident Council and the superintendent's staff has decided on a suitable retirement present. We want every resident to participate in this project— which is— a quilt, made from scraps of material collected from the residents and sewn together by residents and staff alike. The procedure will be as follows. A quilting room has been set up in an empty storage area just off the infirmary. Scraps of fabric will be collected as officers do evening count. Those residents who would enjoy cutting up old uniforms and bedding no longer in use should sign up for this detail with your dorm officer. If you would like to sign your name or send Mrs. Carson some special message on your square of fabric, the officers will have tubes of embroidery paint for that purpose. The backing for the quilt has been donated by the Women's Associates as well as the refreshments for the retirement party to be held after lunch on the thirtieth. Thank you very much for your attention and participation in this worthwhile tribute to someone we are all very fond of here. You may resume work at this time. Doris Creech and Arlie Holsclaw report to the superintendent's office immediately.

ACT TWO

(Lights fade. When they come up, it is the next morning. ARLENE *is asleep in the bed.* ARLIE *is locked in a maximum-security cell. We do not see the officer to whom she speaks.)*

ARLIE: No, I don't have to shut up, neither. You already got me in seg-re-ga-tion, what else you gonna do? I got all day to sleep, while everybody else is out bustin' ass in the laundry. *(Laughs)* Hey! I know...you ain't gotta go do no dorm count, I'll just tell you an you jus' sit. Huh? You 'preciate that? Ease them corns you been moanin' about...yeah...okay. Write this down. *(Pride, mixed with alternating contempt and amusement)* Startin' down by the john on the back side, we got Mary Alice. Sleeps with her pillow stuffed in her mouth. Says her mom says it'd keep her from grindin' down her teeth or somethin'. She be suckin' that pillow like she gettin' paid for it. *(Laughs)* Next, it's Betty the Frog. Got her legs all opened out like some fuckin'...*(Makes croaking noises)* Then it's Doris eatin' pork rinds. Thinks somebody gonna grab 'em outta her mouth if she eats 'em during the day. Doris ain't dumb. She fat, but she ain't dumb. Hey! You notice how many girls is fat here? Then it be Rhonda, snorin', Marvene, wheezin', and Suzanne, coughin'. Then Clara an' Ellie be still whisperin'. Family shit, who's gettin' outta line, which girls is gittin' a new work 'signment, an' who kin git extra desserts an' for how much. Them's the two really run this place. My bed right next to Ellie, for sure it's got some of her shit hid in it by now. Crackers or some crap gonna leak out all over my sheets. Last time I found a fuckin' grilled cheese in my pillow. Even had two of them little warty pickles. Christ! Okay. Linda and Lucille. They be real quiet, but they ain't sleepin'. Prayin', that's them. Linda be sayin' them Hell Marys till you kin just about scream. An' Lucille, she tol' me once she didn't believe in no God, jus' some stupid spirits whooshin' aroun' everwhere makin' people do stuff. Weird. Now, I'm goin' back down the other side, there's...*(Screams)* I'd like to see you try it! I been listenin' at you for the last three hours. Your husband's gettin' laid off an' you lettuce is gettin' eat by rabbits. Crap City. You shut up! Whadda I care if I wake everybody up? I want the nurse...I'm gittin' sick in here...an' there's bugs in here!

(The lights come up in the apartment. Faint morning traffic sounds are heard. ARLENE *does not wake up. The* WARDEN *walks across the catwalk. A* GUARD *catches up with him near* ARLIE's *cell.* BENNIE *is stationed at the far end of the walk.)*

LOUDSPEAKER VOICE: Dorm A may now eat lunch.

GUARD (EVANS): Warden, I thought 456...(*Nodding in* ARLIE's *direction*) was leavin' here.

WARDEN: Is there some problem?

GUARD (EVANS): Oh, we can take care of her all right. We're just tired of takin' her shit, if you'll pardon the expression.

ARLIE: You ain't seen nuthin' yet, you mother.

WARDEN: Washington will decide on her transfer. Till then, you do your job.

GUARD (EVANS): She don't belong here. Rest of—

LOUDSPEAKER VOICE: Betty Rickey and Mary Alice Wolf report to the laundry.

GUARD (EVANS): Most of these girls are mostly nice people, go along with things. She needs a cage.

ARLIE: *(Vicious)* I need a knife.

WARDEN: *(Very curt)* Had it occurred to you that we could send the rest of them home and just keep her? *(Walks away)*

LOUDSPEAKER VOICE: Dorm A may now eat lunch. Dorm A to lunch.

GUARD (EVANS): *(Turning around, muttering to himself)* Oh, that's a swell idea. Let everybody out except bitches like Holsclaw. *(She makes an obscene gesture at him, he turns back toward the catwalk.)* Smartass warden, thinks he's runnin' a hotel.

BENNIE: Give you some trouble, did she?

GUARD (EVANS): I can wait.

BENNIE: For what?

GUARD (EVANS): For the day she tries gettin' out an' I'm here by myself. I'll show that screechin' slut a thing or two.

BENNIE: That ain't the way, Evans.

GUARD (EVANS): The hell it ain't. Beat the livin'—

BENNIE: Outta a little thing like her? Gotta do her like all the rest. You got your shorts washed by givin' Betty Rickey Milky Ways. You git your chairs fixed givin' Frankie Hill extra time in the shower with Lucille Smith. An' you git ol' Arlie girl to behave herself with a stick of gum. Gotta have her brand, though.

GUARD (EVANS): You screwin' that wildcat?

BENNIE: *(Starts to walk to* ARLIE's *cell)* Watch. (ARLIE *is silent for a moment as he approaches, but is watching intently.)* Now *(To nobody in particular)*, where was that piece of Juicy Fruit I had in this pocket. Gotta be here somewhere. *(Takes a piece of gum and drops it within* ARLIE's *reach)* Well, *(Feigning disappointment)* I guess I already chewed it. (ARLIE *reaches for the gum and gets it.)* Oh, *(Looking down at her now)* how's it goin', kid?

(ARLIE *says nothing more, but unwraps the gum and chews it.* BENNIE *leaves the cell area, motioning to the other* GUARD *as if to say, "See, that's how it's done." A loud siren goes by in the street below the apartment.* ARLENE *bolts up out of bed, then turns back to it quickly, making it up in a frenzied, ritual manner. As she tucks the spread under the pillow, the siren stops and so does she. For the first time, now, she realizes where she is and the inappropriateness of the habit she has just played out. A jackhammer noise gets louder. She walks over to the window and looks out. There is a wolf-whistle from a worker below. She shuts the window in a fury. She looks around the room as if trying to remember what she is doing there. She looks at her watch, now aware that it is late and she has slept in her clothes.)*

ARLENE: People don't sleep in their clothes, Arlene. An' people git up 'fore noon.

(ARLENE *makes a still-disoriented attempt to pull herself together— changing shoes, combing her hair, washing her face— as prison life continues on the catwalk. The* WARDEN *walks toward* ARLIE, *stopping some distance from her but talking directly to her, as he checks files or papers.)*

WARDEN: Good afternoon, Arlie.

ARLIE: Fuck you. *(*WARDEN *walks away.)* Wait! I wanna talk to you.

WARDEN: I'm listening.

ARLIE: When am I gittin' outta here?

WARDEN: That's up to you.

ARLIE: The hell it is.

WARDEN: When you can show that you can be with the other girls, you can get out.

ARLIE: How'm I supposed to prove that bein' in here?

WARDEN: And then you can have mail again and visitors.

ARLIE: You're just fuckin' with me. You ain't never gonna let me out. I been in this ad-just-ment room four months, I think.

WARDEN: Arlie, you see the other girls in the dorm walking around, free to do whatever they want? If we felt the way you seem to think we do, everyone would be in lockup. When you get out of segregation, you can go to the records office and have your time explained to you.

ARLIE: It won't make no sense.

WARDEN: They'll go through it all very slowly....When you're eligible for parole, how many days of good time you have, how many industrial days you've earned, what constitutes meritorious good time...and how many days you're set back for your write-ups and all your time in segregration.

ARLIE: I don't even remember what I done to git this lockup.

WARDEN: Well, I do. And if you ever do it again, or anything like it again, you'll be right back in lockup where you will stay until you forget how to do it.

ARLIE: What was it?

WARDEN: You just remember what I said.

ARLENE: Now then...*(Sounds as if she has something in mind to do; looks as though she doesn't)*

ARLIE: What was it?

WARDEN: Oh, and Arlie, the prison chaplain will be coming by to visit you today.

ARLIE: I don't want to see no chaplain!

WARDEN: Did I ask you if you wanted to see the chaplain? No, I did not. I said, the chaplain will be coming by to visit you today. *(To an unseen guard)* Mrs. Roberts, why hasn't this light bulb been replaced?

ARLIE: *(Screaming)* Get out of my hall!

(The WARDEN walks away. ARLENE walks to the refrigerator and opens it. She picks out the carton of slaw BENNIE put there last night. She walks away from the door, then turns around, remembering to close it. She looks at the slaw, as a GUARD comes up to ARLIE's cell with a plate.)

ARLENE: I ain't never eatin' no more scrambled eggs.

GUARD (CALDWELL): Chow time, cutie pie.

ARLIE: These eggs ain't scrambled, they's throwed up! And I want a fork!

(ARLENE realizes she has no fork, then fishes one out of the garbage sack from last night. She returns to the bed, takes a bite of slaw and gets her wallet out of her purse. She lays the bills out on the bed one at a time.)

ARLENE: That's for coffee...and that's for milk and bread...an' that's cookies...an' cheese and crackers...and shampoo an' soap...and bacon and livercheese. No, pickle loaf...an' ketchup and some onions...an' peanut butter an' jelly...and shoe polish. Well, ain't no need gettin' everything all at once. Coffee, milk, ketchup, cookies, cheese, onions, jelly. Coffee, milk...oh, shampoo...

(There is a banging on the door.)

RUBY'S VOICE: *(Yelling)* Candy, I gotta have my five dollars back.

ARLENE: *(Quickly stuffing her money back in her wallet)* Candy ain't here!

RUBY'S VOICE: It's Ruby, upstairs. She's got five dollars I loaned her....Arlie? That Arlie? Candy told me her sister be...

(ARLENE *opens the door hesitantly.*)

RUBY: It is Arlie, right?

ARLENE: It's Arlene. *(Does not extend her hand)*

RUBY: See, I got these shoes in layaway...*(Puts her hand back in her pocket)* She said you been...you just got...you seen my money?

ARLENE: No.

RUBY: I don't get 'em out today they go back on the shelf.

ARLENE: *(Doesn't understand)* They sell your shoes?

RUBY: Yeah. Welcome back.

ARLENE: Thank you.

RUBY: She coulda put it in my mailbox.

(RUBY *starts to leave.* ARLENE *is closing the door when* RUBY *turns around.*)

RUBY: Uh...listen...if you need a phone, I got one most of the time.

ARLENE: I do have to make this call.

RUBY: Ain't got a book though...well, I got one but it's holdin' up my bed. *(Laughs)*

ARLENE: I got the number.

RUBY: Well, then...

ARLENE: Would you...wanna come in?

RUBY: You sure I'm not interruptin' anything?

ARLENE: I'm s'posed to call my parole officer.

RUBY: Good girl. Most of them can't talk but you call 'em anyway. (ARLENE *does not laugh.*) Candy go back to that creep?

ARLENE: I guess.

RUBY: I's afraid of that. *(Looking around)* Maybe an envelope with my name on it? Really cleaned out the place, didn't she?

ARLENE: Yeah. Took everything.

(*They laugh a little.*)

RUBY: Didn't have much. Didn't do nuthin' here 'cept...sleep.

ARLENE: Least the rent's paid till the end of the month. I'll be workin' by then.

RUBY: You ain't seen Candy in a while.

ARLENE: No. Think she was in the seventh grade when—

RUBY: She's growed up now, you know.

ARLENE: Yeah, I was thinkin' she might come by.

RUBY: Honey, she won't be comin' by. He keeps all his...*(Starting over)* His place is pretty far from here. But...*(Stops, trying to decide what to say)*

ARLENE: But what?

RUBY: But she had a lot of friends, you know. They might be comin' by.

ARLENE: Men, you mean.

RUBY: Yeah. *(Quietly, waiting for ARLENE's reaction)*

ARLENE: *(Realizing the truth)* Mother said he was her boyfriend.

RUBY: I shouldn't have said nuthin'. I jus' didn't want you to be surprised if some john showed up, his tongue hangin' out an' all. *(Sits down on the bed)*

ARLENE: It's okay. I shoulda known anyway. *(Now suddenly angry)* No, it ain't okay. Guys got their dirty fingernails all over her. Some pimp's out buyin' green pants while she....Goddamn her.

RUBY: Hey now, that ain't your problem. *(Moves toward her; ARLENE backs away)*

ARLIE: You stick your hand in here again Doris an' I'll bite it off.

RUBY: She'll figure it out soon enough.

ARLIE: *(Pointing to another person)* An' you, you ain't my mama, so you can cut the mama crap.

ARLENE: I wasn't gonna cuss no more.

RUBY: Nuthin' in the parole rules says you can't get pissed. My first day outta Gilbertsville I done the damn craziest....(ARLENE *looks around, surprised to hear she has done time.)* Oh yeah, a long time ago, but...hell, I heaved a whole gallon of milk right out the window my first day.

ARLENE: *(Somewhat cheered)* It hit anybody?

RUBY: It bounced! Made me feel a helluva lot better. I said, "Ruby, if a gallon of milk can bounce back, so kin you."

ARLENE: That's really what you thought?

RUBY: Well, not exactly. I had to keep sayin' it for 'bout a year 'fore I finally believed it. I's moppin' this lady's floor once an' she come in an' heard my sayin' "gallon a milk, gallon a milk," fired me. She did. Thought I was too crazy to mop her floors.

(RUBY *laughs, but is still bitter.* ARLENE *wasn't listening.* RUBY *wants to change the subject now.*)

RUBY: Hey! You have a good trip? Candy said you was in Arkansas.

ARLENE: Alabama. It was okay. This guard, well, he used to be a guard, he just quit. He ain't never seen Kentucky, so he drove me. *(Watching for* RUBY's *response)*

RUBY: Pine Ridge?

ARLENE: Yeah.

RUBY: It's coed now, ain't it?

ARLENE: Yeah. That's dumb, you know. They put you with the men so's they can git you if you're seen with 'em.

RUBY: S'posed to be more natural, I guess.

ARLENE: I guess.

RUBY: Well, I say it sucks. Still a prison. No matter how many pictures they stick up on the walls or how many dirty movies they show, you still gotta be counted five times a day. *(Now beginning to worry about* ARLENE's *silence)* You don't seem like Candy said.

ARLENE: She tell you I was a killer?

RUBY: More like the meanest bitch that ever walked. I seen lots worse than you.

ARLENE: I been lots worse.

RUBY: Got to you, didn't it?

(ARLENE *doesn't respond, but* RUBY *knows she's right.*)

RUBY: Well, you jus' gotta git over it. Bein' out, you gotta—

ARLENE: Don't you start in on me.

RUBY: *(Realizing her tone)* Right, sorry.

ARLENE: It's okay.

RUBY: Ex-cons is the worst. I'm sorry.

ARLENE: It's okay.

RUBY: Done that about a year ago. New waitress we had. Gave my little goin'-straight speech, "No booze, no men, no buyin' on credit," shit like that, she quit that very night. Stole my fuckin' raincoat on her way out. Some speech, huh? *(Laughs, no longer resenting this theft)*

ARLENE: You a waitress?

RUBY: I am the Queen of Grease. Make the finest french fries you ever did see.

ARLENE: You make a lot of money?

RUBY: I sure know how to. But I ain't about to go back inside for doin' it. Cookin' out's better'n eatin' in, I say.

ARLENE: You think up all these things you say?

RUBY: Know what I hate? Makin' salads— cuttin' up all that stuff'n floppin' it in a bowl. Some day...some day...I'm gonna hear "tossed salad" an' I'm gonna do jus' that. Toss out a tomato, toss out a head a lettuce, toss out a big ol' carrot. *(Miming the throwing and enjoying herself immensely)*

ARLENE: *(Laughing)* Be funny seein' all that stuff flyin' outta the kitchen.

RUBY: Hey Arlene! *(Gives her a friendly pat)* You had your lunch yet?

ARLENE: *(Pulling away immediately)* I ain't hungry.

RUBY: *(Carefully)* I got raisin toast.

ARLENE: No. *(Goes over to the sink, twists knobs as if to stop a leak)*

ARLIE: Whaddaya mean, what did she do to me? You got eyes or is they broke? You only seein' what you feel like seein'. I git ready to protect myself from a bunch of weirdos an' then you look.

ARLENE: Sink's stopped up. *(Begins to work on it)*

ARLIE: You ain't seein' when they's leavin' packs of cigarettes on my bed an' then thinking I owe 'em or somethin'.

RUBY: Stopped up, huh? *(Squashing a bug on the floor)*

ARLIE: You ain't lookin' when them kitchen workers lets up their mommies in line nights they know they only baked half enough brownies.

RUBY: Let me try.

ARLIE: You ain't seein' all the letters comin' in an' goin' out with visitors. I'll tell you somethin'. One of them workmen buries dope for Betty Rickey in little plastic bottles under them sticker bushes at the water tower. You see that? No, you only seein' me. Well, you don't see shit.

RUBY: *(A quiet attempt)* Gotta git you some Drano if you're gonna stay here.

ARLIE: I'll tell you what she done. Doris brung me some rollers from the beauty-school class. Three fuckin' pink rollers. Them plastic ones with the little holes. I didn't ask her. She jus' done it.

RUBY: Let me give her a try.

ARLENE: I can fix my own sink.

ARLIE: I's stupid. I's thinkin' maybe she were different from all them others. Then that night everybody disappears from the john and she's wantin' to brush my hair. Sure, brush my hair. How'd I know she was gonna crack her head open on the sink. I jus' barely even touched her.

RUBY: *(Walking to the bed now, digging through her purse)* Want a Chiclet?

ARLIE: You ain't asked what she was gonna do to me. Huh? When you gonna ask that? You don't give a shit about that 'cause Doris such a good girl.

ARLENE: *(Giving up)* Don't work.

RUBY: We got a dishwasher quittin' this week if you're interested.

ARLENE: I need somethin' that pays good.

RUBY: You type?

ARLENE: No.

RUBY: Do any clerk work?

ARLENE: No.

RUBY: Any keypunch?

ARLENE: No.

RUBY: Well, then I hate to tell you, but all us old-timers already got all the good cookin' and cleanin' jobs. *(Smashes another bug, goes to the cabinet to look for the bug spray)* She even took the can of Raid! Just as well, empty anyway. (ARLENE *doesn't respond.*) She hit the bugs with it. *(Still no response)* Now, there's that phone call you was talkin' about.

ARLENE: Yeah.

RUBY: *(Walking toward the door)* An' I'll git you that number for the dishwashin' job, just in case. (ARLENE *backs off.*) How 'bout cards? You play any cards? Course you do. I get sick of beatin' myself all the time at solitaire. Damn borin' bein' so good at it.

ARLENE: *(Goes for her purse)* Maybe I'll jus' walk to the corner an' make my call from there.

RUBY: It's always broke.

ARLENE: What?

RUBY: The phone...at the corner. Only it ain't at the corner. It's inside the A&P.

ARLENE: Maybe it'll be fixed.

RUBY: Look, I ain't gonna force you to play cards with me. It's time for my programs anyway.

ARLENE: I gotta git some pickle loaf an'...things.

RUBY: Suit yourself. I'll be there if you change your mind.

ARLENE: I have some things I gotta do here first.

RUBY: *(Trying to leave on a friendly basis)* Look, I'll charge you a dime if it'll make you feel better.

ARLENE: *(Takes her seriously)* Okay.

RUBY: *(Laughs, then realizes* ARLENE *is serious)* Mine's the one with the little picture of Johnny Cash on the door.

(RUBY *leaves. Singing to the tune of* "I'll Toe the Line," BENNIE *walks across the catwalk carrying a tray with cups and a pitcher of water.* ARLENE *walks toward the closet. She is delaying going to the store, but is determined to go. She checks little things in the room, remembers to get a scarf, changes shoes, checks her wallet. Finally, as she is walking out, she stops and looks at the picture of Jesus, then moves closer, having noticed a dirty spot. She goes back into the bathroom for a tissue, wets it in her mouth, then dabs at the offending spot. She puts the tissue in her purse, then leaves the room when noted, below.)*

BENNIE: I keep my pants up with a piece of twine. I keep my eyes wide open all the time. Da da da da-da da da da da da. If you'll be mine, please pull the twine.

ARLIE: You can't sing for shit.

BENNIE: *(Starts down the stairs toward* ARLIE's *cell)* You know what elephants got between their toes?

ARLIE: I don't care.

BENNIE: Slow natives. *(Laughs)*

ARLIE: That ain't funny.

GUARD (EVANS): *(As* BENNIE *opens* ARLIE's *door)* Hey, Davis.

BENNIE: Conversation is rehabilitatin', Evans. Want some water?

ARLIE: Okay.

BENNIE: How about some Kool-Aid to go in it? *(Gives her a glass of water)*

ARLIE: When does the chaplain come?

BENNIE: Want some gum?

ARLIE: Is it today?

BENNIE: Kool-Aid's gone up, you know. Fifteen cents and tax. You get out, you'll learn all about that.

ARLIE: Does the chaplain come today?

BENNIE: *(Going back up the catwalk)* Income tax, sales tax, property tax, gas and electric, water, rent—

ARLIE: Hey!

BENNIE: Yeah, he's comin', so don't mess up.

ARLIE: I ain't.

BENNIE: What's he tell you anyway, get you so starry-eyed?

ARLIE: He jus' talks to me.

BENNIE: I talk to you.

ARLIE: Where's Frankie Hill?

BENNIE: Gone.

ARLIE: Out?

BENNIE: Pretty soon.

ARLIE: When.

BENNIE: Miss her don't you? Ain't got nobody to bullshit with you. Stories you gals tell...whoo-e!

ARLIE: Get to cut that grass now, Frankie, honey.

BENNIE: Huh?

ARLIE: Stupidest thing she said. *(Gently)* Said first thing she was gonna do when she got out—

(ARLENE *leaves the apartment.*)

BENNIE: Get laid.

ARLIE: Shut up. First thing was gonna be going to the garage. Said it always smelled like car grease an' turpur...somethin'.

BENNIE: Turpentine.

ARLIE: Yeah, an' gasoline, wet. An' she'll bend down an' squirt oil in the lawnmower, red can with a long pointy spout. Then cut the grass in the backyard, up an' back. They got this grass catcher on it. Says she likes scoopin' all that cut grass an' spreadin' it out under the trees. Says it makes her real hungry for some lunch. *(A quiet curiosity about all this)*

BENNIE: I got a power mower, myself.

ARLIE: They done somethin' to her. Took out her nerves or somethin'. She...

BENNIE: She jus' got better, that's all.

ARLIE: Hah. Know what else? They give her a fork to eat with last week. A fork. A fuckin' fork. Now how long's it been since I had a fork to eat with?

BENNIE: *(Getting ready to leave the cell)* Wish I could help you with that, honey.

ARLIE: *(Loud)* Don't call me honey.

BENNIE: *(Locks the door behind him)* That's my girl.

ARLIE: I ain't your girl.

BENNIE: *(On his way back up the stairs)* Screechin' wildcat.

ARLIE: *(Very quiet)* What time is it?

(ARLENE *walks back into the apartment. She is out of breath and has some trouble getting the door open. She is carrying a big sack of groceries. As she sets the bag on the counter, it breaks open, spilling cans and packages all over the floor. She just stands and looks at the mess. She takes off her scarf and sets down her purse, still looking at the spilled groceries. Finally, she bends down and picks up the package of pickle loaf. She starts to put it on the counter, then turns suddenly and throws it at the door. She stares at it as it falls.*)

ARLENE: Bounce? *(In disgust)* Shit.

(ARLENE *sinks to the floor. She tears open the package of pickle loaf and eats a piece of it. She is still angry, but is competely unable to do anything about her anger.*)

ARLIE: Who's out there? Is anybody out there? *(Reading)* Depart from evil and do good. *(Yelling)* Now, you pay attention out there 'cause this is right out of the Lord's mouth. *(Reading)* and dwell, that means live, dwell for-ever-more. *(Speaking)* That's like for longer than I've been in here or longer than...this Bible the chaplain give me's got my name right in the front of it. Hey! Somebody's s'posed to be out there watchin' me. Wanna hear some more? *(Reading)* For the Lord for...*(The word is "forsaketh".)* I can't read in here, you turn on my light, you hear me? Or let me out and I'll go read it in the TV room. Please let me out. I won't scream or nuthin'? I'll just go right to sleep, okay? Somebody! I'll go right to sleep. Okay? You won't even know I'm there. Hey! Goddammit, somebody let me out of here, I can't stand it in here anymore. Somebody! *(Her spirit finally broken)*

ARLENE: *(She draws her knees up, wraps her arms around them and rests her head on her arms.)* Jus' gotta git a job an' make some money an' everything will be all right. You hear me, Arlene? You git yourself up and go find a job. *(Continues to sit)* An' you kin start by cleanin' up this mess you made 'cause food don't belong on the floor.

(ARLENE *still doesn't get up.* CARL *appears in the doorway of the apartment. When he sees* ARLENE *on the floor, he goes into a fit of vicious, sadistic laughter.*)

CARL: What's happenin', mama? You havin' lunch with the bugs?

ARLENE: *(Quietly)* Fuck off.

CARL: *(Threatening)* What'd you say?

ARLENE: *(Reconsidering)* Go away.

CARL: You watch your mouth or I'll close it up for you.

(ARLENE *stands up now.* CARL *goes to the window and looks out, as if checking for someone.*)

ARLENE: They after you, ain't they?

(CARL *sniffs, scratches at his arm. He finds a plastic bag near the bed, stuffed with brightly colored knitted things. He pulls out baby sweaters, booties and caps.*)

CARL: What the fuck is this?

ARLENE: You leave them be.

CARL: You got a baby hid here somewhere? I found its little shoes. *(Laughs, dangling them in front of him)*

ARLENE: *(Chasing him)* Them's mine.

CARL: Aw sugar, I ain't botherin' nuthin'. Just lookin'. *(Pulls more out of the sack, dropping one or two booties on the floor, kicking them away)*

ARLENE: *(Picking up what he's dropped)* I ain't tellin' you again. Give me them.

CARL: *(Turns around quickly, walking away with a few of the sweaters)* How much these go for?

ARLENE: I don't know yet.

CARL: I'll jus' take care of 'em for you— a few coin for the trip. You are gonna have to pay your share, you know.

ARLENE: You give me them. I ain't goin' with you. *(She walks toward him.)*

CARL: You ain't?

(Mocking, ARLENE *walks up close to him now, taking the bag in her hands. He knocks her away and onto the bed.)*

CARL: Straighten up, girlie. *(Now kneels over her)* You done forgot how to behave yourself. *(Moves as if to threaten her, but kisses her on the forehead, then moves out into the room)*

ARLENE: *(Sitting up)* I worked hard on them things. They's nice, too, for babies and little kids.

CARL: I bet you fooled them officers good, doin' this shit. *(Throws the bag in the sink)*

ARLENE: I weren't—

CARL: I kin see that scene. They sayin'....*(Puts on a high southern voice)* "I'd jus' love one a them nice yella sweaters."

ARLENE: They liked them.

CARL: Those turkeys, sure they did. Where else you gonna git your free sweaters an' free washin' an' free step-right-up-git-your-convict-special-shoe-shine. No, don't give me no money, officer. I's jus' doin' this 'cause I likes you.

ARLENE: They give 'em for Christmas presents.

CARL: *(Checks the window again, then peers into the grocery sack)* What you got sweet, mama? *(Pulls out a box of cookies and begins to eat them)*

ARLIE: I'm sweepin', Doris, 'cause it's like a pigpen in here. So you might like it, but I don't, so if you got some mops, I'll take one of them too.

ARLENE: You caught another habit, didn't you?

CARL: You turned into a narc or what?

ARLENE: You scratchin' an' sniffin' like crazy.

CARL: I see a man eatin' cookies an' that's what you see too.

ARLENE: An' you was laughin' at me sittin' on the floor! You got cops lookin' for you an' you ain't scored yet this morning. You better get yourself back to prison where you can git all you need.

CARL: Since when Carl couldn't find it if he really wanted it?

ARLENE: An' I bought them cookies for me.

CARL: An' I wouldn't come no closer if I's you.

ARLENE: *(Stops, then walks to the door)* Then take the cookies an' git out.

CARL: *(Imitating BENNIE)* Oh, please, Miss Arlene, come go with Carl to the big city. We'll jus' have us the best time.

ARLENE: I'm gonna stay here an' git a job an' save up money so's I kin git Joey. *(Opening the door)* Now, I ain't s'posed to see no ex-cons.

CARL: *(Big laugh)* You don't know nobody else. Huh, Arlie? Who you know ain't a con-vict?

ARLENE: I'll meet 'em.

CARL: And what if they don't wanna meet you? You ain't exactly a nice girl, you know. An' you gotta be jivin' about that job shit. *(Throws the sack of cookies on the floor)*

ARLENE: *(Retrieving the cookies)* I kin work.

CARL: Doin' what?

ARLENE: I don't know. Cookin', cleanin', somethin' that pays good.

CARL: You got your choice, honey. You can do cookin' an' cleanin' or you can do somethin' that pays good. You ain't gonna git rich working on your knees. You come with me an' you'll have money. You stay here, you won't have shit.

ARLENE: Ruby works and she does okay.

CARL: You got any Kool-Aid? *(Looking in the cabinets, moving* ARLENE *out of his way)* Ruby who?

ARLENE: Upstairs. She cooks. Works nights an' has all day to do jus' what she wants.

CARL: And what, exactly, does she do? See flicks take rides in cabs to pick up see-through shoes?

ARLENE: She watches TV, plays cards, you know.

CARL: Yeah, I know. Sounds just like the day room in the fuckin' joint.

ARLENE: She likes it.

CARL: *(Exasperated)* All right. Say you stay here an' finally find yourself some job. *(Grabs the picture of Jesus off the wall)* This your boyfriend?

ARLENE: The chaplain give it to me.

CARL: Say it's dishwashin', okay? *(*ARLENE *doesn't answer.)* Okay?

ARLENE: Okay. *(Takes the picture, hangs it back up)*

CARL: An' you git maybe seventy-five a week. Seventy-five for standin' over a sink full of greasy, grey water, fishin' out blobs of bread an' lettuce. People puttin' pieces of chewed-up meat in their napkins an' you gotta pick it out. Eight hours a day, six days a week, to make seventy-five lousy pictures of Big Daddy George. Now, how long it'll take you to make seventy-five workin' for me?

ARLENE: A night.

(She sits on the bed, CARL *pacing in front of her.)*

CARL: Less than a night. Two hours maybe. Now, it's the same fuckin' seventy-five bills. You can either work all week for it or make it in two hours. You work two hours a night for me an' how much you got in a week? *(*ARLENE *looks puzzled by the multiplication required. He sits down beside her, even more disgusted.)* Two seventy-five's a hundred and fifty. Three hundred-and-fifties is four hundred and fifty. You stay here you git seventy-five a week. You come with me an' you git four hundred and fifty a week. Now, four hundred and fifty, Arlie, is more than seventy-five. You stay here you gotta work eight hours a day and your hands git wrinkled and your feet swell up. *(Suddenly distracted)* There was this guy at Bricktown had webby toes like a duck. *(Back now)* You come home with me you work two hours a night an' you kin sleep all mornin' an' spend the day buyin' eyelashes and tryin' out perfume. Come home, have some guy openin' the door for you sayin', "Good evenin', Miss Holsclaw, nice night now ain't it?" *(Puts his arm around her)*

ARLENE: It's Joey I'm thinkin' about.

CARL: If you was a kid, would you want your mom to git so dragged out washin' dishes she don't have no time for you an' no money to spend on you? You come with me, you kin send him big orange bears an' Sting-Ray bikes with his name wrote on the fenders. He'll like that. Holsclaw. *(Amused)* Kinda sounds like coleslaw, don't it? Joey be tellin' all his friends 'bout his mom livin' up in New York City an' bein' so rich an' sendin' him stuff all the time.

ARLENE: I want to be with him.

CARL: *(Now stretches out on the bed, his head in her lap)* So, fly him up to see you. Take him on that boat they got goes roun' the island. Take him up to the Empire State Building, let him play King Kong. *(Rubs her hair, unstudied tenderness)* He be talkin' 'bout that trip his whole life.

ARLENE: *(Smoothing his hair)* I don't want to go back to prison, Carl.

CARL: *(Jumps up, moves toward the refrigerator)* There any chocolate milk? *(Distracted again)* You know they got this motel down in Mexico named after me? Carlsbad Cabins. *(Proudly)* Who said anything about goin' back to prison? *(Slams the refrigerator door, really hostile)* What do you think I'm gonna be doin'? Keepin' you out, that's what!

ARLENE: *(Stands up)* Like last time? Like you gettin' drunk? Like you lookin' for kid junkies to beat up?

CARL: God, ain't it hot in this dump. You gonna come or not? You wanna wash dishes, I could give a shit. *(Yelling)* But you comin' with me, you say it right now, lady! *(Grabs her by the arm)* Huh?

(There is a knock on the door.)

RUBY'S VOICE: Arlene?

CARL: *(Yelling)* She ain't here!

RUBY'S VOICE: *(Alarmed)* Arlene! You all right?

ARLENE: That's Ruby I was tellin' you about.

CARL: *(Catches* ARLENE's *arm again, very roughly)* We ain't through!

RUBY: *(Opening the door)* Hey! *(Seeing the rough treatment)* Goin' to the store. *(Very firm)* Thought maybe you forgot somethin'.

CARL: *(Turns* ARLENE *loose)* You this cook I been hearin' about?

RUBY: I cook. So what?

CARL: Buys you nice shoes, don't it, cookin'? Why don't you hock your watch and have somethin' done to your hair? If you got a watch.

RUBY: Why don't you drop by the coffee shop. I'll spit in your eggs.

CARL: They let you bring home the half-eat chili dogs?

RUBY: You...you got half-eat chili dogs for brains. *(To* ARLENE*)* I'll stop by later. *(Contemptuous look for* CARL*)*

ARLENE: No. Stay.

*(*CARL *gets the message. He goes over to the sink to get a drink of water out of the faucet, then looks down at his watch.)*

CARL: Piece a shit. *(Thumps it with his finger)* Shoulda took the dude's hat, Jack. Guys preachin' about the end of the world ain't gonna own a watch that works.

ARLENE: *(Walks over to the sink, bends over* CARL*)* You don't need me. I'm gittin' too old for it, anyway.

CARL: I don't discuss my business with strangers in the room. (He heads for the door.) Arlene, when you leavin'? (CARL sits.) *You wanna come, meet me at this bar. (Gives her a brightly colored matchbook)* I'm havin' my wheels delivered.

ARLENE: You stealin' a car?

CARL: Take a cab. *(Gives her a dollar)* You don't come...well, I already laid it out for you. I ain't never lied to you, have I, girl?

ARLENE: No.

CARL: Then you be there. That's all the words I got. *(Makes an unconscious move toward her)* I don't beg nobody. *(Backs off)* Be there.

(He turns abruptly and leaves. ARLENE *watches him go, folding up the money in the matchbook. The door remains open.)*

ARLIE: *(Reading, or trying to, from a small Testament)* For the Lord forsaketh not his saints, but the seed of the wicked shall be cut off.

*(*RUBY *walks over to the counter, starts to pick up some of the groceries lying on the floor, then stops.)*

RUBY: I 'magine you'll want to be puttin' these up yourself. *(*ARLENE *continues to stare out the door.)* He do this?

ARLENE: No.

RUBY: Can't trust these sacks. I seen bag boys punchin' holes in 'em at the store.

ARLENE: Can't trust anybody. *(Finally turning around)*

RUBY: Well, you don't want to trust him, that's for sure.

ARLENE: We spent a lot of time together, me an' Carl.

RUBY: He live here?

ARLENE: No, he jus' broke outta Bricktown near where I was. I got word there sayin' he'd meet me. I didn't believe it then, but he don't lie, Carl don't.

RUBY: You thinkin' of goin' with him?

ARLENE: They'll catch him. I told him but he don't listen.

RUBY: Funny ain't it, the number a men come without ears.

ARLENE: How much that dishwashin' job pay?

RUBY: I don't know. Maybe seventy-five.

ARLENE: That's what he said.

RUBY: He tell you you was gonna wear out your hands and knees grubbin' for nuthin', git old an' be broke an' never have a nice dress to wear? *(Sitting down)*

ARLENE: Yeah.

RUBY: He tell you nobody's gonna wanna be with you 'cause you done time?

ARLENE: Yeah.

RUBY: He tell you your kid gonna be ashamed of you an' nobody's gonna believe you if you tell 'em you changed?

ARLENE: Yeah.

RUBY: Then he was right. *(Pauses)* But when you make your two nickels, you can keep both of 'em.

ARLENE: *(Shattered by these words)* Well, I can't do that.

RUBY: Can't do what?

ARLENE: Live like that. Be like bein' dead.

RUBY: You kin always call in sick...stay home, send out for pizza an' watch your Johnny Carson on TV...or git a bus way out Preston Street an' go bowlin'.

ARLENE: *(Anger building)* What am I gonna do? I can't git no work that will pay good 'cause I can't do nuthin'. It'll be years 'fore I have a nice rug for this place. I'll never even have some ol' Ford to drive around, I'll never take Joey to no fair. I won't be invited home for pot roast and I'll have to wear this fuckin' dress for the rest of my life. What kind of life is that?

RUBY: It's outside.

ARLENE: Outside? Honey I'll either be inside this apartment or inside some kitchen sweatin' over a sink. Outside's where you get to do what you want, not where you gotta do some shit job jus' so's you can eat worse than you did in prison. That ain't why I quit bein' so hateful, so I could come back and rot in some slum.

RUBY: *(Word "slum" hits hard)* Well, you can wash dishes to pay the rent on your "slum," or you can spread your legs for any shit that's got the ten dollars.

ARLENE: *(Not hostile)* I don't need you agitatin' me.

RUBY: An' I don't live in no slum.

ARLENE: *(Sensing RUBY's hurt)* Well, I'm sorry...it's just...I thought... *(Increasingly upset)*

RUBY: *(Finishing her sentence)* ...it was gonna be different. Well, it ain't. And the sooner you believe it, the better off you'll be.

(A GUARD enters ARLIE's cell.)

ARLIE: Where's the chaplain? I got somethin' to tell him.

ARLENE: They said I's...

GUARD (CALDWELL): He ain't comin'.

ARLENE: ...he tol' me if...I thought once Arlie...

ARLIE: It's Tuesday. He comes to see me on Tuesday.

GUARD (CALDWELL): Chaplain's been transferred, Dollie. Gone. Bye-bye. You know.

ARLENE: He said the meek, meek, them that's quiet and good...the meek...as soon as Arlie...

RUBY: What, Arlene? Who said what?

ARLIE: He's not comin' back?

ARLENE: At Pine Ridge there was...

ARLIE: He woulda told me if he couldn't come back.

ARLENE: I was...

GUARD (CALDWELL): He left this for you.

ARLENE: I was...

GUARD (CALDWELL): Picture of Jesus, looks like.

ARLENE: ...this chaplain...

RUBY: *(Trying to call her back from this hysteria)* Arlene...

ARLIE: *(Hysterical)* I need to talk to him.

ARLENE: This chaplain...

ARLIE: You tell him to come back and see me.

ARLENE: I was in lockup...

ARLIE: *(A final, anguished plea)* I want the chaplain!

ARLENE: I don't know...years...

RUBY: And...

ARLENE: This chaplain said I had...said Arlie was my hateful self and she was hurtin' me and God would find some way to take her away...and it was God's will so I could be the meek...the meek, them that's quiet and good an' git whatever they want...I forgit the word...they git the earth.

RUBY: Inherit.

ARLENE: Yeah. And that's why I done it.

RUBY: Done what?

ARLENE: What I done. 'Cause the chaplain he said...I'd sit up nights waitin' for him to come talk to me.

RUBY: Arlene, what did you do? What are you talkin' about?

ARLENE: They tol' me... after I's out an' it was all over...they said after the chaplain got transferred...I didn't know why he didn't come no more till after...they said it was three whole nights at first, me screamin' to God to come git Arlie an' kill her. They give me this medicine an' thought I's better...then that night it happened, the officer was in the dorm doin' count...an' they didn't hear nuthin' but they come back out where I was an' I'm standin' there tellin' 'em to come see, real quiet I'm tellin' 'em, but there's all this blood all over my shirt an' I got this fork I'm holdin' real tight in my hand...*(Clenches one hand now, the other hand fumbling with the front of her dress as if she's going to show* RUBY) this fork, they said Doris stole it from the kitchen an' give it to me so I'd kill myself and shut up botherin' her...an' there's all these holes all over me where I been stabbin' myself an' I'm sayin' Arlie is dead for what she done to me, Arlie is dead an' it's God's will...I didn't scream it, I was jus' sayin' it over and over...Arlie is dead, Arlie is dead...they couldn't git that fork outta my hand till...I woke up in the infirmary and they said I almost died. They said they's glad I didn't. *(Smiling)* They said did I feel better now an' they was real nice, bringing me chocolate puddin'...

RUBY: I'm sorry, Arlene.

(RUBY *reaches out for her, but* ARLENE *pulls away sharply.*)

ARLENE: I'd be eatin' or jus' lookin' at the ceiling an' git a tear in my eye, but it's jus' dry up, you know, it didn't run out or nuthin'. An' then pretty soon,

I's well, an' officers was sayin' they's seein' such a change in me an' givin' me yarn to knit sweaters an' how'd I like to have a new skirt to wear an' sometimes lettin' me chew gum. They said things ain't never been as clean as when I's doin' the housekeepin' at the dorm. *(So proud)* An' then I got in the honor cottage an' nobody was foolin' with me no more or nuthin'. an' I didn't git mad like before or nuthin'. I jus' done my work an' knit...an' I don't think about it, what happened, 'cept...*(Now losing control)* people here keep callin' me Arlie an'...*(Has trouble saying "Arlie")* I didn't mean to do it, what I done...

RUBY: Oh, honey...

ARLENE: I did...*(This is very difficult.)* I mean, Arlie was a pretty mean kid, but I did...*(Very quickly)* I didn't know what I...

(ARLENE *breaks down completely, screaming, crying, falling over into* RUBY's *lap.*)

ARLENE: *(Grieving for this lost self)* Arlie!

(RUBY *rubs her back, her hair, waiting for the calm she knows will come.*)

RUBY: *(Finally, but very quietly)* You can still...*(Stops to think of how to say it)*...you can still love people that's gone.

(RUBY *continues to hold her tenderly, rocking as with a baby. A terrible crash is heard on the steps outside the apartment.*)

BENNIE'S VOICE: Well, chicken-pluckin', hog-kickin' shit!

RUBY: Don't you move now, it's just somebody out in the hall.

ARLENE: That's—

RUBY: It's okay Arlene. Everything's gonna be just fine. Nice and quiet now.

ARLENE: That's Bennie that guard I told you about.

RUBY: I'll get it. You stay still now. *(She walks to the door and looks out into the hall, hands on hips.)* Why you dumpin' them flowers on the stairs like that? Won't git no sun at all! *(Turns back to* ARLENE*)* Arlene, there's a man plantin' a garden out in the hall. You think we should call the police or get him a waterin' can?

(BENNIE *appears in the doorway, carrying a box of dead-looking plants.*)

BENNIE: I didn't try to fall, you know.

RUBY: *(Blocking the door)* Well, when you git ready to try, I wanna watch!

ARLENE: I thought you's gone.

RUBY: *(To* BENNIE*)* You got a visitin' pass?

BENNIE: *(Coming into the room)* Arlie...*(Quickly)* Arlene. I brung you some plants. You know, plants for your window. Like we talked about, so's you don't see them bars.

RUBY: *(Picking up one of the plants)* They sure is scraggly-lookin' things. Next time, git plastic.

BENNIE: I'm sorry I dropped 'em, Arlene. We kin get 'em back together an' they'll do real good. *(Setting them down on the trunk)* These ones don't take the sun. I asked just to make sure. Arlene?

RUBY: You up for seein' this petunia killer?

ARLENE: It's okay. Bennie, this is Ruby, upstairs.

BENNIE: *(Bringing one flower over to show* ARLENE, *stuffing it back into its pot)* See? It ain't dead.

RUBY: Poor little plant. It comes from a broken home.

BENNIE: *(Walks over to the window, getting the box and holding it up)* That's gonna look real pretty. Cheerful-like.

RUBY: Arlene ain't gettin' the picture yet. *(Walking to the window and holding her plant up too, posing)* Now.

(ARLENE *looks, but is not amused.)*

BENNIE: *(Putting the plants back down)* I jus' thought, after what I done last night...I jus' wanted to do somethin' nice.

ARLENE: *(Calmer now)* They is nice. Thanks.

RUBY: Arlene says you're a guard.

BENNIE: I was. I quit. Retired.

ARLENE: Bennie's goin' back to Alabama.

BENNIE: Well, I ain't leavin' right away. There's this guy at the motel says the bass is hittin' pretty good right now. Thought I might fish some first.

ARLENE: Then he's goin' back.

BENNIE: *(To* RUBY, *as he washes his hands.)* I'm real fond of this little girl. I ain't goin' till I'm sure she's gonna do okay. Thought I might help some.

RUBY: Arlene's had about all the help she can stand.

BENNIE: I got a car, Arlene. And money. An'...*(Reaching into his pocket)* I brung you some gum.

ARLENE: That's real nice, too. An' I 'preciate what you done, bringin' me here an' all, but...

BENNIE: Well, look. Least you can take my number at the motel an' give me a ring if you need somethin'. *(Holds out a piece of paper)* Here, I wrote it down for you. (ARLENE *takes the paper.)* Oh, an' somethin' else, these towel things....*(Reaching into his pocket, pulling out a package of towelettes)* They was in the chicken last night. I thought I might be needin' 'em, but they give us new towels every day at the motel.

ARLENE: Okay then. I got your number.

BENNIE: *(Backing up toward the door)* Right. Right. any ol' thing, now. Jus' any ol' thing. You even run outta gum an' you call.

RUBY: Careful goin' down.

ARLENE: Bye Bennie.

BENNIE: Right. The number now. Don't lose it. You know, in case you need somethin'.

ARLENE: No.

(BENNIE *leaves.* ARLENE *gets up and picks up the matchbook* CARL *gave her and holds it with* BENNIE's *piece of paper.* RUBY *watches a moment, sees* ARLENE *trying to make this decision, knows that what she says now is very important.*)

RUBY: We had this waitress put her phone number in matchbooks, give 'em to guys left her nice tips. Anyway, one night this little ol' guy calls her and comes over and says he works at this museum an' he don't have any money but he's got this hat belonged to Queen Victoria. An' she felt real sorry for him so she screwed him for this little lacy ol' hat. Then she takes the hat back the next day to the museum thinkin' she'll git a reward or somethin' an' you know what they done? *(Pause)* Give her a free membership. Tellin' her thanks so much an' we're so grateful an' wouldn't she like to see this mummy they got downstairs...an' all the time jus' stallin'...waiting 'cause they called the police.

ARLENE: You do any time for that?

RUBY: *(Admitting the story was about her)* County jail.

ARLENE: *(Quietly, looking at the matchbook)* County jail. *(She tears up the matchbook and drops it in the sack of trash.)* You got any Old Maids?

RUBY: Huh?

ARLENE: You know.

RUBY: *(Surprised and pleased)* Cards?

ARLENE: *(Laughs a little)* It's the only one I know.

RUBY: Old Maid, huh? *(Not her favorite game)*

ARLENE: I gotta put my food up first.

RUBY: 'Bout an hour?

ARLENE: I'll come up.

RUBY: Great. *(Stops by the plants on her way to the door, smiles)* These plants is real ugly.

(RUBY exits. ARLENE watches her, then turns back to the groceries still on the floor. Slowly, but with great determination, she picks up the items one at a time and puts them away in the cabinet above the counter. ARLIE appears on the catwalk. There is one light on each of them.)

ARLIE: Hey! You 'member that time we was playin' policeman an' June locked me up in Mama's closet an' then took off swimmin'? An' I stood around with them dresses itchin' my ears an' crashin' into that door tryin' to get outta there? It was dark in there. So, finally *(Very proud)*, I went around an' peed in all Mama's shoes. But then she come home an' tried to git in the closet only June taken the key so she said, "Who's in there?" an' I said, "It's me!" an' she said, "What you doin' in there?" an' I started gigglin' an' she started pullin' on the door an' yellin', "Arlie, what you doin' in there?" *(Big laugh)*

(ARLENE has begun to smile during the story. Now they speak together, standing as Mama did, one hand on her hip.)

ARLIE and ARLENE: Arlie, what you doin' in there?

ARLENE: *(Still smiling and remembering, stage dark except for one light on her face)* Aw shoot.

(Lights dim on ARLENE's fond smile as ARLIE laughs once more.)

END OF PLAY

TALES OF THE LOST FORMICANS

Constance Congdon

TALES OF THE LOST FORMICANS
© Copyright 1989 by Constance Congdon

All rights to this play are represented by Peter Franklin, William Morris Agency, Inc, 1350 Sixth Ave, NY NY 10019, 212 903-1550.

O Crocodile Night (Song)
© Copyright 1989 by Melissa Shiflett, lyrics by Constance Congdon. All rights reserved

For my father, Ned Congdon

ABOUT THE AUTHOR

Constance Congdon's most recent plays include: NO MERCY (published in SEVEN DIFFERENT PLAYS, Broadway Play Publishing, 1988) which premiered at the Humana Festival in 1986 and was subsequently produced at the Berkshire Theatre Festival's Unicorn Theatre; THE GILDED AGE, which premiered at the Hartford Stage Company in 1986 and toured the U.S. with John Houseman's Acting Company; and an adaptation of Mark Strand's and Red Grooms' book REMBRANDT TAKES A WALK, to be produced at The Moscow Central Children's Theatre in Russia in 1989.

TALES OF THE LOST FORMICANS workshopped at The Sundance Institute and was produced at River Arts Rep. It will be produced at the 1989 Humana Festival and at the Eureka Theatre Company. An earlier play, NATIVE AMERICAN, was produced at the Lyric Hammersmith Studio in London in 1988.

Constance Congdon has been awarded a National Endowment for the Arts Playwriting Fellowship, a Rockefeller Playwriting Award, and is the first recipient of the Arnold Weissberger Playwriting Award. She is Resident Playwright at the Hartford Stage Company, and is a member of New Dramatists in New York.

TALES OF THE LOST FORMICANS was produced by Actors Theatre of Louisville starting on 19 March 1989, with the following cast:

CATHY	Lizbeth Mackay
ERIC	Jason O'Neill
JIM	Edward Seamon
EVELYN	Joanne Manley
JUDY	Jan Leslie Harding
JERRY	Bob Morrisey
ACTOR	Jonathan Fried
Director	Roberta Levitow
Sets	Paul Owen
Lights	Ralph Dressler
Costumes	Lewis D. Rampino
Sound	Mark Hendren

CHARACTERS

CATHY *(nee* MCKISSICK*), early thirties*
ERIC *(her son), 15*
JIM MCKISSICK *(her father), late fifties*
EVELYN MCKISSICK *(her mother), early fifties*
JUDY, *early thirties*
JERRY, *early thirties*
AN ACTOR, *male, younger than* JIM, *who plays the following roles:* HANK, TRUCKER, ALIEN TRUCKER, CARTOON ALIEN, *and* JACK

All ALIENS *are played by the human cast members.*

PLACE

A New York apartment (briefly)
A large middle-class subdivision somewhere in Colorado

TIME

The present

PRODUCTION NOTES

About the Staging and Style:

The staging should be relatively seamless, with the stage space shared by all the characters. Furniture and other objects in the world are minimal because they are artifacts.

With the exception of the actor who plays JERRY, the ALIENS are played by the human cast members wearing matching sunglasses. They are human in their demeanor except that they are slightly detached, overly pleasant, and sound a little like stewardesses. (The character of JIM is only effective as an ALIEN in Act One.)

The VOICEOVER speeches should be shared by the actors as ALIENS (with the exception of the actor who plays JERRY). They need not be hidden while they do the VOICEOVERS, although sometimes it might be interesting if they were.

ACT ONE

(As the audience files in, JERRY lies on the stage, in darkness, lit only by a hand-held fluorescent lamp beside him. He is looking at the night sky with binoculars. He's lying on a sleeping bag. The chair and table for the next scene are pre-set nearby. After the audience gets settled, the lights bump all the way up and three ALIENS enter. They are the actor playing EVELYN, the actor playing CATHY, and the actor playing JIM. [The ALIENS look just like the characters they play except they all are wearing matching sunglasses. This device will be used throughout to distinguish the ALIENS from the human characters]. Two of the ALIENS unfold a star map and the CATHY/ALIEN finds a small dot and points to it.)

CATHY/ALIEN: *(To audience)* You are here. *(As they roll up the map, JERRY gets up and exits, discouraged, crossing near them, dragging his sleeping bag and carrying his fluorescent lamp—he doesn't see them, but they see him. One of the ALIENS cues the music and "restaurant music" is piped in. ALIENS exit, leaving the stage bare except for a chair and table, part of a kitchen ensemble, typical in suburbia, but dated by a decade or so. The chair is upholstered with plastic and the legs of both chair and table are of bent chrome. The chair has a hole in the back rest—a design element common to chairs of this type.)*

VOICEOVER: First item. A situpon. *(Aside, softly)* What? *(Back to mike)* Chair. Chair. For sitting. Sitting and eating or some other ritual. Goes with table...which we'll see in a minute. Note the construction. Forward legs *(Aside)* —they call them legs? *(Back to mike)* Forward legs are made as one unit, curving up to provide the rear of the chair. Rear legs are constructed in a smaller curve unit which fits under the seat and inside the forward leg unit, providing a very strong system for the body pads—cushions—and then the body itself. The wobble that some of these chairs exhibit we attribute to climate changes...or some other entropic reality. *(An ALIEN enters and "shows" the chair—sort of like Vanna White on "Wheel of Fortune.")* Care was taken in beautifying the chair. The sleek surface of the legs reflects light except, of course, where there are spots of oxidation. And this surface is the substance *chrome*. We have several other examples of that substance—evidently a precious metal used as a surface to apportion many religious objects, specifically the numerous wheeled sarcaphogae used to carry spirits to the next world. The cushions of the chair are covered in a substance made to mimic the epidermis of the sitter, but treated to hold a sheen which is kept polished by friction of the buttocks against the surface.

The significance of the hole in the back rest is unknown to us at this time. It was, perhaps, symbolic. A breathing hole for the spirit of the sitter, or even the ever-present eye of god.

(ALIEN *exits.* JIM *enters, a middle-aged man in work clothes. He is wearing lipstick and has a bandage on his right index finger.*)

VOICEOVER: Next, the table. Four legs—the hard surface covered with geometric shapes—decoration or, perhaps, a code?

(JIM *lowers head, face down, staring until it slowly touches the table surface, stays there. After a beat, the table wobbles.*)

JIM: Hmmmm. *(He rests the side of his head on the table—pressing it gently against the cool of the surface.)* Ahhh.

VOICEOVER: The table legs also wobble—this leading us to theorize that perhaps both examples of the wobble phenomenon are not random but conscious built-in representations of the unreliable nature of existence for this particular...species.

JIM: *(To someone offstage)* I'm gonna finally fix the goddam toaster. Evelyn?

VOICEOVER: Wait. Reverse it, please. *(Pause)* Please reverse it—it's too early—something else goes here—

JIM: Nilava? Retsote moddag aw sif eelaknife annog mee. (JIM *reverses his movements very fast and exits.*)

VOICEOVER: There.

CATHY: *(To audience)* Why would I move back home?

VOICEOVER: This is right.

CATHY: *(To audience)* I mean, I have a perfectly nice home of my—wait a minute— *(Stops to listen to something offstage, then back to audience)* —anyway, it's a two-bedroom apartment, rent-controlled— *(Stops again)* Excuse me— *(To someone offstage)* Honey? Mike? Is that you? *(Exiting to check on "Mike")* Mike? Are you throwing up? *(Sticking her head back in to talk to the audience)* He's in the bathroom. *(Offstage, to "Mike")* I'm coming in. *(A beat) (Sticking her head back in to talk to the audience)* Bad news. Excuse me....*(Offstage, to "Mike")* What? You *what??!!* And she's *what???!!!! (Re-enters fully, talks to audience)* Life's funny. One minute you're married. The next minute, you're not. One of his students, eighteen years old, "Kimberly", plays the oboe, the baby is his. (CATHY *exits.*)

JUDY: *(From offstage)* Home!! I'm home!! Jason!! Jennifer!! Somebody help me get these groceries outta the car!! *(Enters and crosses, lugging bags of groceries, stops near her exit and speaks to audience)* Last week one of the neighbors ran her rid'em mower the entire length of the street, on the grass—one mowed swatch through eight or nine lawns—flowers, toys, garden hoses all mowed into teeny, tiny little pieces—looked like a party. Then she hit somebody's rotary sprinkler and it threw her off course, but she kept on going, her foot flat on the gas, screaming at the top of her lungs until she came to rest, violently, against a garbage truck. Her husband died last year—he used to do all their mowing. I—I—I gotta move outta here. (JUDY *exits.*)

VOICEOVER: They reproduce with difficulty.

ERIC: *(To* CATHY *offstage)* You hear me, Mom? Everything is completely fucked up! I didn't get the fucking divorce. It's not my fucking fault. And now my entire life is fucked! *Mooooommmmm!* (CATHY *enters and looks at* ERIC.)

VOICEOVER: They are grouped in loosely stuctured units called families. Ring.

ERIC: *(Picks up phone.)* Yo. *(To* CATHY*)* It's someone named Grandma. Wait—is this the Grandma we're supposed to live with? *(To person on phone)* Where is this place? *(Listens to answer—turns back to* CATHY*)* No. No fucking way. Fuck no. (CATHY *takes phone.*)

CATHY: *(On phone)* Mom? Yes, they all use that word. A lot.

VOICEOVER: The economic system is antiquated, but communication is excellent, in spite of primitive equipment.

CATHY: *(On phone)* Yes, everything is fine. He's excited about coming. Excuse me— *(To* ERIC, *sotte voce, handing* ERIC *the phone)* Now, for Chrissake be nicccccccce.

ERIC: *(Into phone)* Whatsup, Grandma. *(Can't do it, hands* CATHY *the phone)*

CATHY: I'll call you back, Mom?

EVELYN: *(On stage, on the phone)* No.

CATHY: *(On phone)* No?

EVELYN: It's your father. *(*JIM *wanders on.)*

CATHY: What?

EVELYN: He's...different. I don't know...

CATHY: Should we still come home?

ERIC: This is my home.

EVELYN: Please.

ERIC: This is my home!

EVELYN: Please.

ERIC: *This is my home.*

EVELYN: Please. *(They both hang up.* EVELYN *follows the wandering* JIM *off as he exits.)*

CATHY: Eric, we *have* to go home. We are going home. *And that's final!!!*

ERIC: You're outta control, Mom. You need to get some fucking help.

CATHY: *Listen!!!* I am the mother!! You are the child!! I am in control here!!! *I am the adult!!!*

ERIC: Mom. There are no adults in this world. I just figured that out this year. And this boy's not going to live in any fucking suburb. No way. *(He exits.)*

VOICEOVER: No way.

(JUDY *is standing, looking out over the audience's head, pointing out houses to* CATHY.)

JUDY: Twisted cape, raised ranch, then that split level—

CATHY: They're new, then.

JUDY: Ten years ago.

CATHY: That was our little hill.

JUDY: It was just leftover dirt from something else. It wasn't, like, a real hill or anything.

CATHY: So after split level—the rest of the street—

JUDY: Some new siding. Above-ground swimming pools. Trying to be, you know....*(Points at a house)* New garage. It's a kit.

CATHY: Really? Huh. *(About another house)* Boy, that lawn looks like hell. He used to keep it perfect.

JUDY: You don't know?

CATHY: What?

JUDY: Spread newspapers on the living room rug, lay down, and shot himself.

CATHY: Oh my God!

JUDY: Of course, it still soaked through.

CATHY: *(Still about the suicide)* Why?!

JUDY: He lay there all afternoon. Wall-to-wall carpeting. *(About another house)* And over there? She never leaves the house.

CATHY: That was a showplace inside.

JUDY: Still may be. We'll never know.

CATHY: *(Another house)* The...boys. Those wild boys...

JUDY: Killed in Vietnam. Killed in a car wreck. And the other one's a lawyer.

CATHY: Mom never wrote.

JUDY: I thought you knew, or I would've—

CATHY: Yeah.

JUDY: Nobody writes...

CATHY: No. *(A pleasant memory of someone)* Oh, whatever happened to Darryl?

JUDY: San Francisco.

CATHY: Is he still alive?

JUDY: I dunno.

CATHY: *(About the neighborhood)* Strange.

JUDY: Yeah, it's pure Mars. I had to move back. I couldn't afford my rent plus the day care. Mom's alright with the kids. I mean, that's the way families used to do it all the time. This is a nice place to live. We grew up here. It's not the subdivision that's the problem, it's the society. My mother and I... get along. *(Long pause, waiting for CATHY to say something about this—agree with her)* I mean, you're doing all right, aren't you?

CATHY: *(Realizing that JUDY wants to hear this)* Yeah.

JUDY: It's only temporary. Until I get a better-paying job. I think I'm gonna start at one of those learning centers they advertise on TV—you can put it on your Mastercard.

CATHY: What are you gonna learn?

JUDY: Radiology. I don't know about wearing all that lead. Can't be good for you. What are you going to do?

CATHY: Something'll come up.

JUDY: Remember that little dog that was in love with you?

CATHY: Oh, the humper.

JUDY: Why don't we call him up for Saturday night? Boy, uh. *(Beat)* Actually, he's dead. They get kidney problems, those dogs.

CATHY: *(Thinking about the suicide)* Why did he do it?

JUDY: *(Thinking about the dog)* He was a slave of love, humping your leg—his little pink thing reaching out...with no place to go. So sad.

CATHY: No, I meant Mr. Whatshisname. (CATHY *puts a finger to her forehead like a gun.* JUDY *moves the "gun" so that the "barrel" is in* CATHY's *mouth.)*

JUDY: Bang.

CATHY: Oh.

JUDY: Yeah, he meant it.

CATHY: But why?

JUDY: Seems so incredible to you? He wasn't happy!

CATHY: Well, who is?

JUDY: But in a house that nice! You know?

(JUDY *exits.* CATHY *stays on the "lawn."*)

(JIM *enters as before, wearing lipstick, and puts his head down on the table, just as before.*)

VOICEOVER: This is the correct placement. Thank you.

JIM: *(About the coolness of the table against his head)* "Ahhh." *(To someone offstage)* I'm gonna finally fix the goddam toaster. Evelyn? *(He exits, returns with the toaster, sits.)*

(CATHY *enters the scene and addresses the audience.*)

CATHY: *(To the audience)* I'd forgotten how small this house is.

(EVELYN *enters, holding a dish towel.*)

CATHY: *(To* EVELYN*)* What?

EVELYN: He's in the kitchen. He's just sitting there.

CATHY: *(To* EVELYN*)* What time is it?

EVELYN: Ten a.m.

(CATHY *enters* JIM's *space,* EVELYN *following.*)

CATHY: *(To* JIM*)* What are you doing home, Dad?

JIM: *(Pleasant, oblivious)* Hi. I fixed this damn thing again.

EVELYN: What are you doing home, Jim?

JIM: What's for supper?

CATHY: What you got on your mouth?

JIM: Chapstick.

EVELYN: It's an honest mistake.

(EVELYN *wipes lipstick off* JIM's *mouth.*)

(*Phone rings.*)

CATHY: *(On phone)* Hello. *(She hands receiver to* JIM.*)* Dad?

JIM: *(Takes receiver, then puts it to his ear)* Uh-huh?... Hello, old buddy... Home... What?! *(Looks at watch)* What??!! *(Stands, drops phone)* No. *(Starts to exit, looks at* CATHY*)*

CATHY: What is it, Dad?

EVELYN: He's supposed to be at work! Don't you see?! He's supposed to be at work!!

JIM: I—I don't understand.

CATHY: Want me to go with you?

JIM: To work with me? Why? It's all right. Doesn't anybody think it's all right?! *(He bolts out the door.)*

CATHY: Dad—come back. Daddy—wait!

*(*CATHY *exits after* JIM.*)*

*(*EVELYN *notices the phone receiver which hasn't been hung up—she picks it up.)*

EVELYN: Hello? Jack?... He's left. He'll be right there.... No, he's fine. Came home to get Cathy. She's...visiting.... I'm fine, Jack.... Bye-bye. *(She hangs up the phone. She looks at the paper towel with the lipstick in it. The toaster pops—it's fixed.* ERIC *enters in his jockey shorts—he's just gotten up.)*

ERIC: Toaster fixed finally? Get some frozen waffles today—okay, Grandma?

EVELYN: No.

ERIC: Jesus, I can't even eat what I want? *(Exiting)* I don't get to live where I want, I can't say what I fucking want to say—

EVELYN: What did you say? *(Exiting after him)* What did you say?

ERIC: *(Offstage)* What kind of fucking life is this, huh???

*(*JERRY *enters, sits in the kitchen chair, and talks to the audience.)*

JERRY: First off, they get a warehouse—doesn't have to be all that big. A Butler building, say, about the size of a Safeway. And the first thing they do is spray the walls and the ceiling flat black. And then they bring in about thirty loads of number ten gravel and they cover the floor with it. And then a couple, three loads of retaining wall rock—you know the size I mean—about as big as my fist. And they sprinkle that over this base of gravel. Now you know they've made some mounds here and there, so the floor isn't completely flat. They hand some lights from the girders and set up some big spots, and they got a control booth in a corner. Then they bring in the machines—the lunar lander and the L E M. And that's when they set up the cameras, shout "action!" and make a movie. Then they print it in black and white on crummy film in slow motion and pipe it onto all the television sets. And whammo—all the world sees a man land on the moon and plant the

American flag. I mean, "Moon Rocks"? Really. And don't talk to me about Voyager. They got a ride at Walt Disney World better than that. Think about it.

(JERRY *exits.*)

VOICEOVER: He loses three days—no—wait. This is the female bonding scene.

(JUDY *and* CATHY *are talking.*)

CATHY: The kids? Your mom?

JUDY: At the mall.

CATHY: But I could've—

JUDY: I wouldn't go near the house—are you kidding me? His apartment. Are you into this? You don't seem into this.

CATHY: Oh—*I love* it.

JUDY: Yeah.

CATHY: I *love* this.

JUDY: Yeah.

CATHY: It's too much.

JUDY: Yeah.

CATHY: God.

JUDY: Right.

(Long pause as they both smile and nod)

CATHY: We're talking the same guy.

JUDY: Right.

CATHY: The one.

JUDY: That's right.

CATHY: Amazing. Makes me crazy! Uh! You are my hero. You are definitely my *hero.*

JUDY: There's just one thing.

CATHY: What? What?

JUDY: *(Beat)* I said the L-word. *(Pause)*

CATHY: What?

JUDY: I said the L-word.

CATHY: No.

JUDY: Yes.

CATHY: Was he...there?

JUDY: Was he there.

CATHY: Are you sure he heard you?

JUDY: Oh yeah.

CATHY: What did he do?

JUDY: It seemed to throw him off rhythm slightly.

CATHY: Then? You said it then?

JUDY: I know.

CATHY: Boy.

JUDY: I know.

CATHY: Was there any discussion...later?

JUDY: Nope.

CATHY: An acknowledgment of any kind from him?

JUDY: Are you kidding? *(Beat) Are you kidding? (Beat)* It would've been easier if I'd farted, frankly. Oh God. Oh God.

CATHY: I know.

JUDY: It's just—been a long time for me.

CATHY: I know.

JUDY: I just sort of, like, lost it.

CATHY: I know.

JUDY: Oh God, what an amateur.

CATHY: It'll be all right.

JUDY: He heard me say it.

CATHY: He'll forget. Men have short memories. Particularly for emotional information.

JUDY: Oh boy.

CATHY: Don't worry about it.

JUDY: I'm fucked. I'm totally fucked. Can you tell me I'm not fucked?

CATHY: Maybe he's different.

JUDY: I wish I could take it back.

CATHY: *(To herself)* Oh my God. Starting from scratch.

JUDY: What?

CATHY: Nothing.

(CATHY *and* JUDY *exit in opposite directions.*)

VOICEOVER: The buying of food is a ritual.

(JIM *enters and sits at the kitchen table, and stirs his coffee very carefully, completely immersed in this action.* EVELYN *enters.*)

EVELYN: *(Ready to go)* Alright.

JIM: *(Pleasantly)* Okay.

EVELYN: Are you go to the ready store?

JIM: What?

EVELYN: *(Annoyed, as to a child)* Are—you—ready—to—go—to—the—erstoe?

JIM: I—I—

EVELYN: *Yaagh!! Yaagh!!* Are you ready to go to the Yaagh?

JIM: Alright!

(EVELYN *exits. After a long beat,* JIM *stands up and begins to look around for her.*)

JIM: *Evelyn? Baby?*

(ALIENS *enter and take his table and chair, so when he comes back to where he was sitting, everything is gone.* JIM *panics and begins to run around. Suddenly a pair of headlights appears right upstage from him—*JIM *freezes in their light. A loud diesel horn honk. A* TRUCKER *enters, having climbed down from the truck.*)

TRUCKER: *Whatthehelliswrongwithyou?*

JIM: Who are you?

TRUCKER: Are you *blind?!!*

(EVELYN *enters with groceries in a couple of bags.*)

EVELYN: *Jim!!* Good *God!!*

TRUCKER: Is this guy yours???

EVELYN: Jim—you were right there with me at the check out—I turn around and you were gone!!

TRUCKER: Keep him out of the street!!

JIM: *(To* TRUCKER*)* I'll be with you in a minute.

EVELYN: *(To* TRUCKER*)* We're sorry.

JIM: Nice truck. Peterbilt!

TRUCKER: *(Exiting)* Dickhead!

JIM: *(To* EVELYN*)* Where's my coffee?

EVELYN: Come on, Jim.

(EVELYN *exits and* JIM *starts to follow.* ALIENS *replace his table and chair, but not his coffee. He turns and notices his chair and table again, crosses to it and sits—the coffee is gone.* EVELYN *enters in different clothes.*)

EVELYN: Alright. What do you want to do today? *(About his clothes)* Wait—didn't I lay out some clean clothes for you? These are the same ones you wore yesterday, Jim.

JIM: I can't keep track of my damn coffee. Isn't that funny?

(EVELYN *gets a fresh cup and puts it down in front of him.* JIM *puts his hand in it and burns it.*)

JIM: It's hot. Owwwwww!!

EVELYN: *(In sympathy and fear)* Oh Jim! That's your hurt hand! *(She tries to get him up.)* Come to the sink—I'll pour cold water on it.

JIM: No. Every time I leave this chair, something happens.

EVELYN: I'll get a washcloth. *(She exits.* HANK *enters—he's a male relative of* JIM*'s.*)

JIM: *Hank!!*

HANK: Jimmy!!

(JIM *puts out his hand—*HANK *shakes it vigorously and it doesn't hurt.* JIM *looks at his hand in amazement.*)

HANK: How are you doing?

JIM: What are you doing here?

HANK: I'm collecting for the Sunday paper.

JIM: No kidding. Why?

HANK: That'll be three thirty-five.

JIM: *(Looking in his billfold)* I don't have it.

HANK: *(Whispers)* Get out while there's still time. *(Horn honk.* HANK *speaks in a normal voice.)* Gotta run. I'll be back.

JIM: That's what you always say. Hank? Hank!!

(EVELYN *enters, dressed differently again.*)

EVELYN: I was honking for you, Jim. Didn't you hear me?

JIM: Hank was here, Evelyn!!

EVELYN: Hank is dead, Jim. Jim?

JIM: But he was here.

EVELYN: Jim—the paperboy yesterday—you called him Hank.

JIM: The paperboy is Scott.

EVELYN: Yes, that's right. Scott.

JIM: Scott—I know. I know that.

EVELYN: The doctor wants to check your hand today— *(She looks at his burned hand—the same one that had the bandaged finger at the beginning of the play.)* Jim!! You took the bandage off again!! Dammit! Come on.

JIM: Wait.

EVELYN: What is it?

JIM: I—I have to find my insurance card.

EVELYN: I left the car running. Don't be long. *(She exits.)*

(JIM takes out his billfold and sits down at the table and goes through all the cards and the pictures. As he lays the cards out carefully in a row, an ALIEN enters and begins to pick them up. JIM doesn't notice—he's become too involved, distracted, looking at some of the pictures he's found in his billfold. The ALIEN exits with the cards— JIM turns back to go through them, notices that they are gone—pats the table where they were, looking for them. Sound of a car horn honking. The honking becomes a long hum. JIM stares ahead.)

(CATHY and JUDY are doing the L-Word scene as in the earlier part of the play—but the tape is running backwards. JIM exits.)

CATHY: *(To herself)* Cha-erks mumrf geentrats. Dog eyem ho.

JUDY: *(Backing in)* Kab ti kate dluk I heewa I.

CATHY: Tner-rerf-fid see eebyaim.

JUDY: Tuff tawn my eem illet ooya nak. Tuff eelatote my. Tuff my.

CATHY: Ti touba eerow tnode.

JUDY: Ooya vul I. Ee-ace I dnaa ereeya gnikuf alohwa a ni amite tsnif.

VOICEOVER: We've seen this.

CATHY: Notayem-rofni lanoyhs-tomee rof—

VOICEOVER: I said we've seen this. And X-load tape. It's a zoomer. Thank you.

(CATHY and JUDY exit.)

(After a beat, EVELYN enters, sits down at the table, and makes a phone call.)

(*In another space,* CATHY *and* JIM *are in the cab of his pick up.* JIM *is humming "That Old Black Magic."*)

CATHY: Where are we, Dad?

JIM: In the pick-up.

CATHY: I know that.

EVELYN: Hello? Yes.

CATHY: Where are we going? Where's the job?

EVELYN: This is Mrs. McKissick. The doctor saw my husband last—I'll hold.

JIM: Out...out.

CATHY: Another subdivision.

EVELYN: Yes, we have insurance.

JIM: No. It's a—a—great, big place where you shop—

CATHY: A mall?

JIM: A mall. And we're putting in the—the—*Goddammit!!*

EVELYN: When does he get back from his cruise, then?

(EVELYN *writes something down.*)

CATHY: Drainage?

JIM: Right.

EVELYN: Thanks. *(Dials another number)*

CATHY: But you're the foreman. What are you running errands for?

EVELYN: Yes. Our doctor gave me your—I'll hold.

JIM: Jack—Jack wants me to.

EVELYN: Yes. Yes, we have insurance.

JIM: You hear something? *(He stops the truck.)*

EVELYN: I'll hold.

CATHY: No. Where are we?

JIM: *(Still humming)* I hear something—a humming.

EVELYN: Yes, we have insurance.

CATHY: A humming?

JIM: Yeah.

EVELYN: Yes, we have insurance!

CATHY: We've got to get Jack this pipe, Dad. Dad?

(JIM *has phased out, hums again.*)

EVELYN: Blue Cross. *Yes.*

(TRUCKER *enters. Suddenly, he notices* JIM *and* CATHY *in the pick up. He stops immediately and crosses to them.*)

TRUCKER: Can I help you?

EVELYN: ALL RIGHT.

JIM: I'd like a large root beer. *(To* CATHY*)* What do you want?

CATHY: Dad— (To TRUCKER) We're delivering some pipe. He's the foreman of the pipe-laying crew.

TRUCKER: Oh shit! Not him again!

CATHY: Listen—this is my father.

TRUCKER: You letting him drive?

EVELYN: *I was just talking to somebody*—oh, sorry.

TRUCKER: You'll have to back out. The street is closed off.

CATHY: Yessir. *(To* JIM*)* Back out, Dad.

EVELYN: Something's wrong with him. He's...

JIM: What? Oh.

EVELYN: Confused or...

CATHY: We have to back out. Back out.

EVELYN: *Some*thing. He's not...

CATHY: We *have to* back out. *Please,* Dad.

EVELYN: Himself.

JIM: Oh. Oh. (JIM *seems to be having trouble with the gear shift.*)

EVELYN: Thank—you. *(They've hung up on her—she hangs up the phone and writes something down.)*

TRUCKER: Back this truck outta here!

CATHY: Reverse, Dad. *(Reaches over, gets the gear shift in)*

JIM: I got it—I got it. *(Gets it into reverse)*

CATHY: Press the gas.

JIM: Right. Right. (TRUCKER *exits.*)

(EVELYN *gets up and exits.*)

(A beat or two later)

JIM: Who the hell was he?

CATHY: Shouldn't we turn here, Dad?

JIM: What? Oh. Gotta get this watch fixed.

CATHY: What's wrong, Dad?

(JIM *is humming, doesn't answer.*)

(ERIC *enters, throws down his books.* CATHY *enters.*)

VOICEOVER: They study the words and lives of the Dead. These hold Great Meaning for them.

ERIC: Fucking stupid American History. Not even in English! Now, Mom, I ask you, I fucking ask you, what the hell good is this for me?

CATHY: *(Looking at the book)* This is in English. These are just parts of original documents, that's all.

ERIC: Look! All the fucking esses are effs! *(Reads)* "Feftember 19. He failed on hif courfe, and made twenty-fix leaguef, fince it waf calm. Thif day, to the fip came a booby, and in the evening they faw another, and the Fanta Maria failed Weft toward the fetting fun." No way. No way. Not this boy.

CATHY: Eric, you are not quitting.

ERIC: I hate the bus.

CATHY: But you took the bus in New York all the time. It's no different.

ERIC: It's a different bus.

CATHY: *Eric, you are not quitting school and I will not hear another word about it!! Do you hear me???*

ERIC: I'm not deaf. *(He exits.)*

(CATHY *sits and reads* ERIC's *history book*—EVELYN *enters, distraught.*)

EVELYN: *Where is God??!* *(She lurches through the space.)* Where is God where is God where is God??Where is He where is He where is He?? *Where is God??! Where is God??!!!* Where is He where is He where is... *(She exits, still distraught.)*

(JIM *enters.*)

JIM: Did your mother come through here?

CATHY: Yeah.

JIM: How did she seem?

CATHY: Better.

JIM: That's a.... That's a....

CATHY: Good?

JIM: Good. Good. Good. Good. *(He exits.)*

CATHY: *(Reading from* ERIC's *American history book)* At sunset, Martin Alonso mounted the poop of his ship and in great delight called the Admiral, asking for a reward from him because he had sighted land. The Admiral, hearing this stated postively, fell on his knees to give thanks to Our Lord, and Martin Alonso with his men said the Gloria in Excelsis Deo. And all those in the Nina climbed their mast and into the rigging, and all affirmed that it was land. And on this course they sailed until after midday of the next day, until it was found that what they had said was land was not land, but only cloud.... *(Introducing the next scene, to the audience, as* CATHY*)* "Possible Explanation Number One."

*(*JIM *enters with blueprints and a field book—he's working on a construction site and knows exactly what he's doing. The* ACTOR *enters, carrying an incomprehensible metal object—he is costumed as a* CARTOON ALIEN. CATHY *watches.)*

ALIEN: *(Approaching* JIM*)* Greetings. Your overlord said you could repair any object.

JIM: What?

ALIEN: It is very fucked up. We are...kinda stuck. Old pal.

*(*JIM *takes the object and looks at it carefully.)*

JIM: *(About a part of it)* This needs to be machined better, I can tell you that.

ALIEN: No problem. Way to go. Far out. My buddy. Give me some skin.

JIM: Do you have a—a—nevermind. *(Takes a small all-purpose knife-pipe tamper tool from his pocket and opens the "knife")*

ALIEN: I don't understand. Put away your weapon. We come in peace.

JIM: You're not from here, are you?

ALIEN: What do you mean? I am Earth through and through. I hail from Ohio.

JIM: *(Too involved in fixing the object to care)* No problem. Never—force—anything.

ALIEN: *(Repeats it into a small recording device)* Never force anything. *(The thing lights up.)*

JIM: There. *(Hands thing back to* ALIEN*)*

ALIEN: *(Into recorder)* There. *(To* JIM*)* What is your task here?

JIM: Oh, I'm laying some pipe over there.

ALIEN: Well, this is top secret. Know what I mean, butter bean?

JIM: Oh, sure—I'm used to that. Corps of Engineers, you know.

ALIEN: What's your name?

JIM: Jim McKissick.

ALIEN: Thanks so many.

JIM: Hell, I never even seen one before. I couldn't describe it if I had to.

(ALIEN *places his fingers on* JIM's *head—*JIM *is instantly paralyzed.*)

ALIEN: Forget. Forget. Forget. Forget. How many? (*Looks in notebook—can't find the answer—does a few extra to be sure*) Forget-forget-forget. (*He's overloaded a bit—burns his fingers.*) Whew! No problem. (ALIEN *exits with gadget.* JIM *looks blankly at his hand, then exits, nearly catatonic.*)

CATHY: (*To the audience*) And that night I had a dream.

(CATHY *sits next to* JIM—*they are in the pick-up again.*)

CATHY: Dad, where are we now? We're going around in circles.

JIM: It's the circle drives.

CATHY: Is this the way to the job?

JIM: (*Reading street names*) Kiowa, Iriquois, Quapaw, Huron—

CATHY: Where are we?

JIM: (*Reading street names*) Saturn, Jupiter, Uranus, Mercury—

CATHY: Dad—what's that ahead? Like a big wall of—

JIM: Dark.

CATHY: But it's daytime. It's noon!

JIM: We ran out of streets. (CATHY *gets out of the pick-up.*) Watch your step.

CATHY: Where are we?

JIM: This is where the mall goes. See?

CATHY: No, I can't see anything—it's dark.

JIM: They haven't put in the electrics.

CATHY: But what happened to the sky?

JIM: They'll be skylights. They're in the plans.

CATHY: Can we get out of here?

(TRUCKER *enters, but is wearing* ALIEN *sunglasses.*)

ALIEN TRUCKER: Perhaps the little lady would like to see a map? *(He snaps his fingers and two* ALIENS *enter with a large, clear drawing of a rock, a wall, and a large arrow like you see on mall directories. They hold up the drawing—*ALIEN TRUCKER *points.)* This is a rock. This is a hard place. You are here.

JIM: Alright. Thank you.

(ALIEN TRUCKER *snaps his fingers, and he and* ALIENS *exit with drawing.)*

VOICEOVER: Jim? Thanks for bringing the pipe. It's about time, Jim. You're fired. Please leave the company truck.

JIM: Alright. Thank you.

CATHY: *(To invisible* VOICE*) What????!! (To* JIM*)* Dad. Dad? Let's get out of here!!

JIM: *(Cheerful)* Alright. Thank you. *(He exits.)*

CATHY: *(To her exiting father)* Alright? Thank you? Alright? Thank you? How do we get home? Dad? *(To the audience)* And I woke up and it was true.

(EVELYN *enters, speaks to* CATHY.)

EVELYN: I can't believe it. I can't believe it. You believe in something and they just take it away from you—they jerk it out of your hand like a toy—like a toy from a baby. Years and years and years and years. Thinking you're part of something and you're *not*. Calling him by his first name—Jaaack. Christmas presents. Being nice to Louise—Loooweeeze, Loooweeze. It's not her fault. But I just always liked him better than her. I mean, are we just, just a pair of boobs? I mean—are we just horses?

CATHY: What happened? Mom?

EVELYN: Don't upset your dad.

(JIM *enters.)*

JIM: Jack doesn't want me any more.

CATHY: Oh no.

JIM: I need to get the rest of my tools out of the car.

(He exits. ERIC *enters.)*

ERIC: *(Surprised to see them)* Whooooops! *(Exits)*

CATHY: Eric!! Come here!!!

ERIC: *(Offstage)* Why?

CATHY: It's *noon.*

ERIC: *(Offstage)* I came home for lunch...*money!!* I forgot my lunch money. Yeah! I'm—going—back—to—school! *Bye!!*

EVELYN: *(To* CATHY*)* Well, what are you going to do!! Just sit there?? He's cut school! He's cut school! He's cut school!

CATHY: I know, Mom. What do you want me to do? *Kill him??*

EVELYN: *Yes!!!!* That's what I would've done to *you!!!* I'm going to help your father get his tools...or something. *Look* at *me.* I'm doing *something!!! (She exits.)*

CATHY: *(To her absent ex-husband)* Michael, you sonovabitch, where *are* you! You jerk! You asshole! *(Notices audience)* Excuse me. I don't know— I'm much nicer than that, really. Excuse me. Excuse me. 'Cuse me. *(She exits quickly.)*

VOICEOVER: What they call community is, in fact, random habitational clustering, but those in adjacent dwellings are labelled "neighbors" and are treated with tolerance.

(A phone rings at JERRY's *and keeps on ringing until it stops.* JERRY *just stares at it.* CATHY *enters, looks at* JERRY.*)*

CATHY: Excuse me. I was ringing the door bell. I kept ringing the door bell. Six, seven times. No one came, but I saw you standing in here, so I walked in. Excuse me.... Sorry.

JERRY: I was watching the phone.

CATHY: I wasn't on the phone. I was ringing the doorbell.

JERRY: But the phone was ringing.

CATHY: Who called?

JERRY: I don't know.

CATHY: It was me. At the door.

JERRY: They hung up.

CATHY: I'm looking for my father.

JERRY: Wow. Are you working it out in therapy?

CATHY: No. I'm asking around.

JERRY: Wow. Sort of street corner psychiatry? You just blurt things out and take whatever answers people give you?

CATHY: I don't have much choice. I am dependent on what other people have seen, you know.

JERRY: Oh—wow. Like using the wisdom of the world. No bullshit. Other people's experience. Would you like something—?

CATHY: He's been taking walks. He's wearing khaki pants.

JERRY: I love khaki pants.

CATHY: And a shirt. He's been taking walks for exercise and sometimes, he gets...confused.

JERRY: I know about that. Would you like something to—

CATHY: There's something wrong with this floor.

JERRY: —drink? I don't get company much, but I have a well-stocked refrigerator.

CATHY: I don't drink a lot of fluids.

JERRY: You should. I know. I'm a nurse. Have you ever had the feeling that something that's just happened has happened before?

CATHY: There's a name for that.

JERRY: Really?

CATHY: Déjà vu.

JERRY: I've heard that before! *(Gasps)* Wow.

CATHY: It's French.

JERRY: France. They know about it, too! See? It's all over the world! Things happen! Things happen!

CATHY: Yes, they do.

JERRY: Another world—but it's this world. I don't know, maybe it's the government, but why do we know these things, if they aren't true? Why do we feel, like, this force, unless it's out there or, maybe, right here in this living room?

CATHY: Why would it be in your living room?

JERRY: "It"! "It!" You know. You *know*. I knew you would. We feel things that disturb us—right? Right? But why would we *want* to do that? Why wouldn't we just feel the things that make sense? But nooooo, no, no—God forbid we should have a little peace of mind. If we had a little peace of mind, we might think clearly. Noooo—it's give you something, take it away. Give you something—Oooops! Dropped it. Bend over and pick it up now. Are we good and bent over? Gooooood. *(Mimes gleefully kicking someone in the butt)* Surprise!

CATHY: Do most people understand you?

JERRY: No, but you do.

CATHY: Not that much—

JERRY: I want to show you some pictures.

CATHY: I don't think so. I really have to—

JERRY: *(Takes photos from his pocket)* Here.

(CATHY *looks at them.*)

CATHY: Is this Viet Nam?

JERRY: No, it's my backyard. Look at the sky, see?

CATHY: It's all marked up.

JERRY: You see them!! I knew you would. Tiny, little metal kites in the sky?

CATHY: You drew them in.

JERRY: No, I didn't.

CATHY: I can tell.

JERRY: We're controlled by aliens. And they're idiots.

CATHY: I'm going now.

JERRY: Oh.

CATHY: You need to find some friends.

JERRY: *(Afraid to move his mouth for fear aliens will see him talk)* They're making you do this.

CATHY: No, they're not.

JERRY: *(Little mouth movement)* Yes, they are.

CATHY: I have to go. *(She exits.)*

JERRY: *(Looking up at the sky)* I see you. *I see you.* *(Flipping the bird to the sky)* How's that?

VOICEOVER: Hmmmm. There's that gesture again.

(JERRY *exits.*)

(JUDY *is waiting on the street—she is holding a screwdriver in one hand and watching intently.*)

VOICEOVER: Next segment: An object may have many uses. Offspring are born without wheels and must acquire their own. Vocal intensity is frequently necessary for effective communication.

(CATHY *enters.*)

CATHY: Judy! Hey, Judy! *Judy!!* (JUDY *nods to her.*) What are you waiting for?

JUDY: The skateboard hoard. I'm taking Jason's wheels. He won't use Jennifer's skateboard. It's pink.

CATHY: Sounds serious. What did he do?

JUDY: It's all about power, Hon. And they've figured it out. We never figured it out. We were stupid.

CATHY: It's so windy.

JUDY: Nothing stops them. Even rain. My Ex came by. He's got a new Corvette. And a new girlfriend. She's young. Of course. Her biggest problem is if her blow dryer shorts out. Nature uses us. When I think that if I were watching TV some night and this movie came on where a small head appears from between some woman's legs and then this thing that is all wet and bloody comes out, and begins to bleat, and there's this long slimy tube attached to its body that comes from inside this sobbing and amazed woman, I would run out of the room and loose my dinner. And then I would call up the TV station and say, "What the *hell* is this horror movie doing on TV where my kids can *see it!*" So how's the journal?

CATHY: I gave it up. I can't write about my daily life.

JUDY: Why? I liked that story about the ant.

(*Sound of a far-off beat box approaching—with about three kinds of music coming out of it at once*)

JUDY: Oh, Jesus.

CATHY: What's that?

JUDY: Jagger.

CATHY: *(Sees him)* Who's he?

JUDY: Brain surgeon's kid. He's the leader. He's thirteen.

CATHY: I hear the wheels. There they are!! My God, they've got a sail! They look like a big ship!!! *(Music is closer)* Who *are* they?

JUDY: *They are our children!!*

CATHY: *Who are they?!!!*

JUDY: *I don't know!!!*

CATHY: Is Eric with them?

JUDY: No, but there's Jason *and* Jennifer!

CATHY: That sail looks familiar.

JUDY: It's my mother's Elvis Presley bedspread!! *Jasonnnnnn!!!!!*

(JUDY *exits, running.* ERIC *enters, crosses to* CATHY.)

ERIC: *(About the kids on the skateboards)* Look at those little worms.

CATHY: Eric—I was looking for you.

ERIC: Yeah.

CATHY: Grandma gave me this phone bill. Here's a charge for— *(Reads)* —"$184.63—New York—3:45 p.m."

ERIC: Yeah.

CATHY: Did you call New York City at 3 o'clock in the afternoon and talk for this long?

ERIC: Yeah.

CATHY: Are you out of your mind?

ERIC: I needed to talk to Todd.

CATHY: At 3:45 in the daytime for two hours and twelve minutes???!!

ERIC: We always used to talk after school.

CATHY: But not *long distance!*

ERIC: Hey. I'm a long distance guy.

CATHY: One hundred and eighty-four dollars and sixty-three cents!!!

ERIC: Hey. I didn't get the divorce. I didn't ask to move here. I didn't make Grandpa sick or whatever the fuck is wrong with him. Matter of fact, I didn't ask to be born. You and "Mike" had all the fun when I was conceived. I was exploding. You think exploding is fun? Doubling and quadrupling and sixteenth-toopling or whatever the hell it is. You're a blob, you're a fish, you're some hairless tadpole weird-looking piece of flesh? Huh?

CATHY: Well, for your information, conceiving you wasn't all that much fun!

ERIC: Well, don't talk to me about it! Call Dr. Ruth. And if I can't talk to my friends, then *fuck this world*, you know? *(He exits.)*

CATHY: *(Trying to come up with a parting shot)* Well—Eric! You know.... *(Gives up)*

CATHY: *(To audience)* Eric. Possible Explanation. *(She watches the following scene.)*

(JIM *is reading* "The National Enquirer" *and* EVELYN *is knitting.)*

JIM: Says here that alien beings have been abducting young girls, having intercourse with them, and then returning them to society where they, these young girls, bear monstrous babies, fathered by these alien beings.

EVELYN: Hmmmmmm? Ouch!

JIM: What's wrong?

EVELYN: This aluminum is hard to knit. *(Holds up knitting)* Booties.

JIM: *(About booties)* Strange shape. *(Back to paper)* These alien babies grow up to look pretty much like humans but are monstrous in that they have no respect for anything, especially their parents. Or their parent's parents. They hold nothing dear, these alien offspring, except each other. *(He takes the newspaper and exits.)*

EVELYN: *(To the absent* JIM*)* Sounds too improbable. Why do you read that trash? She's naming him Fong Emo Six. It came to her in a dream. *(She exits after* JIM.*)*

(JIM *re-enters, without the newspaper, crosses the stage, stops, changes his direction, crosses briefly, stops, changes direction, talks to himself.)*

JIM: There's nothing wrong with me. *(He exits.)*

(CATHY *and* EVELYN *enter from opposite sides of the stage. They meet at the kitchen table and the argument begins.)*

EVELYN:
There's something wrong with that boy! All those years you've been sending those damn pictures—he looked fine! "Eric—fifth grade," "Eric—eighth grade" —big smile and all those thank-you notes. I don't think he wrote them at all— I think you wrote them for him. In the meantime, look at what he's becoming. He looks at me like I was from Mars! Does he appreciate his own grandmother? Noooooo. Of course not. And your friend Judy— *she's gone off the deep end.* She's a complete slut!! I don't know how her mother stands it. I don't know how we all stand anything. Am I the only one that sees that everything is going straight to hell? I talk, talk, talk, and no one listens. Noooo. I asked you to come home for your own good and because I wanted an *adult* to help me

CATHY:
I knew it!! I knew it!! You wonder why I haven't been home—you wonder why we haven't come home to visit? Because I knew it would be like this!! You have no idea what my life is like—what it's like raising a child in the world today. I was a *peach!!* When I think of how *easy* it was for you, it makes me *crazy!!* For your information I sat him down to write all those notes. And do you appreciate it? Noooooooo. Of course not. *You could have come visit!!* But no— you were scared of where we lived. *Great!* Makes me feel great! Makes me feel wanted! And Eric, too!! He looks at you that way because he doesn't know you. But you don't know him! And you *don't want to know him!* Can you see how lonely he is? Noooo. Eric was right. This isn't my home. *I gave up my home* to come *here.* Isn't

Constance Congdon

because things are completely *impossible, impossible,* do you hear me?	that a riot? I don't know who you are, I don't know who Dad is, I don't know—

(At EVELYN's line, "...do you hear me?" they both stop for a beat or two, then start back up. [CATHY's stopping line may vary—EVELYN's line is the only cue.])

But instead, you go to work, come home, and only think of your own problems. See? See? That's exactly what's wrong with the world today! It's *me, me, me* and to *hell* with anyone else! And *that's* why *Eric* is the way he is. *Who* are his models? Hmmmm? It's coming home to roost. It's coming home to roost. Believe me, the world got by when men thought only of themselves but when women do, we're *dead, dead, dead!*	—anything. And *now* you, my own mother hits me where it hurts the most!! But, of course you would—you're my *mother!! That's what mothers are for! Go ahead!! Kick me!! In the stomach!!* "Come home, Cathy—please." So I fall for it. And what do I get for it? I don't want to hear it!! Judy's right, no one really gives a *damn* about who is raising the kids as long as they don't have to put in the *fucking* time themselves!

EVELYN: There's that word again!! *See!!*

CATHY: I never use that word. *See what you drive me to?*

EVELYN: I brought you into this world—I can drive you wherever I *want!*

CATHY: I didn't ask to be born! You and Dad had the fun when I was conceived! *(Puzzled, suddenly)* Wait a minute—

EVELYN: It wasn't that much fun!

CATHY: Well, call Dr. Ruth!

EVELYN: What are you talking about?

CATHY: I don't know!!! *(She exits.)*

EVELYN: What am I—invisible?? *(She exits.)*

(ERIC *enters, dressed in a couple layers of clothing—he carries a pair of sweatpants which he puts on over his two pair of pants, and a full knapsack.* CATHY *enters with an empty suitcase.*)

CATHY: What is this? I found this in your room. What are you doing?

ERIC: Getting dressed.

CATHY: Have you gone *crazy???* You're putting on *layers of clothing!!!*

ERIC: Bag is too small. Cheap piece of shit—not even Samsonite—embarrassing.

CATHY: Eric, what...is...this.

ERIC: I'm outta here.

CATHY: You are *not!!!*

ERIC: Yep.

CATHY: *(Grabbing him)* You are *not!!! Not, not!!!* Take *offf* these clothes!!! Now!!! Take them *off* take them *off, take them offffff!!!!!*

ERIC: Mom, please. I'm much stronger than you. Just let me go. *(She holds on. He looks at her, then firmly, but gently, removes her arms from his body.)* I sold my stereo. Girl I met's taking me to the airport. I'll be at Dad's. This is his number— (Hands her a scrap of paper) —just in case you burned it or something. (Picks up knapsack. He then places his open hand on top of his mother's head in an awkward gesture of affection.) Bye. Say "bye" to Grandma and—him—for me. (ERIC waddles off—his bulk making him look like a toddler. CATHY sits on the floor for a beat, then gets up slowly. Horn honk—she runs to say goodbye—we see her wave, but weakly, because he's already gone and doesn't see her.)

(JIM wanders through.)

JIM: There's nothing wrong with me.

CATHY: *Then it must be us!!! Huh????* We must be *fucked up!!!* Because it can't be *you!!! Nooooooo!!* (Beat) Oh, Dad. *(She embraces him and breaks down.)*

JIM: Oh, Honey— Shhhhhh. Shhhhhhh. Shhhhhhh. *(Wipes away her tears)* Who was that fat kid that just went out the door? He go to your school? *(Resigned,* CATHY *exits.)*

JIM: Now where was I? Oh— *(Points, offstage)* There. *(He exits.)*

VOICEOVER: They are fascinated by tools, however primitive.

(It's dark. JUDY *enters, wearing clear plastic goggles and carrying a small propane torch—she turns on a flashlight, revealing* CATHY *also wearing goggles and carrying another small propane torch.* CATHY *and* JUDY *are trying to be quiet. [Real torches are unreliable on stage—the effect can work with small flashlights in torch bodies. Electric carving knives can also be used—with appropriate line changes.])*

CATHY: I don't know about this.

JUDY: He says to me—

CATHY: You talk to him?

JUDY: No. He was just standing in the hall.

CATHY: Your hall?

JUDY: My mother's hall—yeah, my hall, my hall...now.

CATHY: How did he get in?

JUDY: I don't know—he was waiting for Jason. Jason had his mirrored sunglasses.

CATHY: Jason's just a kid.

JUDY: Don't start with me! I can't pick my son's friends! I can't lock him up! Besides you know as well as I do—whatever is forbidden, they love!

CATHY: So Jagger's in the hall—

JUDY: "Fire is real." He says to me. "Fire is real." The kid is heavy.

CATHY: I can't talk about kids anymore.

JUDY: *(About what they're about to do)* Come on—it'll get your mind off of it. By the time we're done, you can call buttface— (CATHY *doesn't get who.*) —your Ex— (CATHY *still doesn't get it.*) —your Former Husband— (CATHY *gets it.*) —and then you can talk to Eric on the phone—and you'll feel better. Ready? (JUDY *lights their propane torches.*)

CATHY: What a beautiful little flame— *(Sudden realization)* Oh my *God!* What are we *doing?* Oh my *God!!*

JUDY: No problem.

CATHY: No *problem?*

JUDY: It's all fiberglass. It'll melt like sugar.

CATHY: Are you sure this is the right Corvette?

JUDY: Believe me, I know this Corvette. I've dogged him in it for weeks.

CATHY: Are you sure nobody will see us?

JUDY: Make any design you want. Be creative.

(JUDY *puts flame to Corvette body.* CATHY *watches, tries.*)

CATHY: It's melting!

JUDY: *(Working away)* The way I see it, they fucked up in the Sixties, you know? They, like, took away all the values and didn't put anything in its place. You know—so, like, everything just—the whole mess they left—just started to coagulate like it would—I mean, the laws of physcis apply to life—Carl Sagan or whoever—those PBS guys have shown us that. Anyway, it, what was left of society, just coagulated like bad pudding, spoiled pudding, you know, like when the eggs separated and can't be put together again completely right. So they make this globular pudding or sometimes it happens to clam chowder. Anyway, it must, like of *formed* and we're stuck with it. There's a piece of God and a clump of law and alot of lumpy, fucked-up pictures and words that don't hardly mean anything any more. And—ahh—I made a peace sign but the center fell out, so don't do that. *(Looking at* CATHY's *work)* Oh, like just a free-formed continuous line. That's great.

CATHY: Thanks. That's enough.

JUDY: No, as long as we're gonna do it. His insurance will pay for it. Just think of no child support payments for six months—and he's taking out his new girlfriend every night—took her to fucking Las Vegas! Restaurants I'll never see the inside of! Buys the kids toys, clothes, whatever shit they want, but no child support for me. He's Santa Claus—I'm the Wicked Witch of the West. Trying to teach values that *nobody believes in any more!!*

CATHY: Let's do the other side.

JUDY: I'm not into it any more.

CATHY: Come on. Watergate. And—and all the lies about everything.

JUDY: All the bullshit.

CATHY: Nixon.

JUDY: Marilyn Monroe and John F. Kennedy doing it. Martin Luther King's sex life.

CATHY: Backing dictators—calling them democrats.

JUDY: Fucking with the destinies of other countries. Pardoning each other for criminal acts!

CATHY: Killing presidents—our own!!

JUDY: Selling us!! Selling us!! *(Stops) Shit!!!* I'm out of propane!

CATHY: So am I.

JUDY: *See??!* Nothing fucking *works!!!*

(They exit.)

*(*JIM *is sitting on the couch, staring at the television.* EVELYN *enters and watches him.)*

VOICEOVER: They watch hours of television.

*(*EVELYN *crosses to* JIM *and comes up behind him and embraces him around the neck. Then she begins to rub his neck. After a beat or so, she sits next to him on the couch and puts her legs on his lap. During all of this,* JIM *has continued to look at the TV, but responds unconsciously to* EVELYN, *doesn't resist her. She kisses him and he responds, but the TV catches his attention again.* EVELYN *takes* JIM *by the hand and leads him off into the bedroom. A count of fifty,* EVELYN *returns alone. She sits on the couch and stares at the TV.)*

JIM: *(Offstage)* Honey? Honey? My leg's gone to sleep. Isn't that funny?

(EVELYN doesn't get up.)

(Sound of cheap top forty from a bar. JERRY *and* JUDY *are sitting separately—a seat or two between them.* JUDY *checks her watch: She's waiting for someone.)*

VOICEOVER: Where genders meet. *(After a beat,* JERRY *begins to speak—to no one in particular. Trying not to,* JUDY *notices him out of the corner of her eye.* JERRY *sees this and then begins to deliver the speech directly to her.)*

JERRY: Lincoln was elected president in 1860. Kennedy was elected president in 1960. Both men were involved in civil rights for Negroes. Both men were assassinated, on a Friday, in the presence of their wives. Each wife had lost a baby, a male child in fact, while they were living at the White House. Both men had a bullet wound that entered the head from behind. Both men were succeeded by vice-presidents named Johnson who were southern democrats and former senators. Both Johnsons were born one hundred years apart—in 1808 and 1908, respectively. Lincoln was killed in Ford's Theatre. Kennedy was killed while riding in a Lincoln convertible made by the Ford Motor Company. John Wilkes Booth and Lee Harvey Oswald were born in 1839 and 1939, respectively, and had the same number of letters in their names. The first name of Lincoln's private secretary was John—the last name of Kennedy's private secretary was Lincoln.

JUDY: *Will you leave me the fuck alone?*

JERRY: Think about it. Life can be understood. You come in here a lot. You like the bartender?

JUDY: I don't like anyone!! I have responsibilities!!! *(*JUDY *exits.* JERRY *sits for a moment, then squeaks involuntarily and exits.)*

*(*JUDY *enters, yelling.)*

JUDY: Jason! Jennifer! Jason! Jennifer! *(Sees them, exits—the next several lines are done from offstage.)* Get offa her!! Jason!! Right now!! *(Pause)* Don't hit him with that!*(Pause)* Jennifer!! Give me that!! Where did you get that?!*(Pause)* Jason!! Leave her alone!! *Jennifer, come back!!* Jason—don't run off!! *(To some neighbor)* Well, I'm *sorry*, Lady!! Go live in a fuckin' convent if you don't want to listen to *kids!!* *(Back on—to the audience)* You haven't seen a skateboard, have you? Picture of Satan with Mick Jagger's tongue—hanging out? No? Orange wheels— *(Exiting)* I live over there—if you see it. Just leave it in that Blue Pinto—none of the doors lock.*(Pause)* Thanks.

VOICEOVER: The de-coding of behavior provides a key to gender identification.

*(*CATHY *is waiting, looking at her watch.* JUDY *joins her—she's late. They sit for a beat.)*

CATHY: You were so positive!

JUDY: I know.

CATHY: You were so sure.

JUDY: I know.

CATHY: It's incredible!

JUDY: You're telling me. Two Corvettes that much alike! And what the hell did that—that—Cambodian—

CATHY: You said he was from Thailand.

JUDY: Whatever—some skinny oriental guy—anyway, what did he think he was doing parking a car like that on a residential street?

CATHY: He, probably, foolishly, thought it would be safe here.

JUDY: Well, he doesn't know anything—he's just asking questions. What's he doing with a Corvette, anyway?

CATHY: What do we do?

JUDY: Jagger thinks he's got a way into the police computer—if it comes to that.

CATHY: No way!! I'm not encouraging that kid—he's scary enough already.

JUDY: We might be arrested—they know it's two women.

CATHY: They know it's two women! They know it's two women! Oh my god, oh my god, oh my god! How can they know that!?

JUDY: They heard giggling.

CATHY: Giggling! Giggling! Who was giggling? I wasn't giggling. You were giggling!

JUDY: No, I wasn't. I was distraught! I still am!

CATHY: You're distraught! You're distraught! I'm the one who's distraught! Look at my life! It's falling apart!

JUDY: And what do you think mine's doing? Singing a little song?

(A beat)

CATHY: What's his plan? Jagger?

JUDY: Zap the records—it's easy, he says.

CATHY: Good. Good. Tell him we'll pay him in cash.

(JUDY *exits, leaving* CATHY. CATHY *starts to exit, addresses the audience.*)

CATHY: *(To the audience)* Lately, I've been having trouble breathing. Several times a day, I forget how. I'll notice that I'm running out of breath because I haven't exhaled. So I exhale, and then I'm fine until a few hours later and I realize that I'm out of breath again. So I inhale or exhale, whichever is appropriate.

(JERRY *enters.* CATHY *crosses to join him—they are in his house.*)

VOICEOVER: They are concerned with interior decoration.

JERRY: So I'm tearing out that entire wall. Open this all up.

CATHY: Uh-huh.

JERRY: Then I buy good furniture. *(Squeaks)*

CATHY: Uh-huh.

JERRY: I might take out that wall, too.

CATHY: Don't want to take out too many walls.

JERRY: Well, then, no more—just those two. *(Squeaks)*

CATHY: Uh-huh.

JERRY: How's the therapy?

CATHY: What therapy?

JERRY: Right. Right. That's the best kind. In my opinion. *(Emits a high-pitched rhythmic laugh)*

CATHY: *(Starts to leave)* Well, I should—

JERRY: Yes. *(Pause)* Did you enjoy the magazine?

CATHY: It was...interesting. *(Returning the magazine to him)*

JERRY: *(Giving it back to her)* Keep it.

CATHY: I'm having a hard time reading, lately. Everything seems to be some kind of message.

JERRY: Message?! Yes. Did you see my ad? Wait— *(Finds it, shows it to her)* Read it.

CATHY: *(Reads)* "Top-Risk Action Group for hire by individuals, organizations, and governments. Rescue a speciality. No Reds as sponsors. Call The Watcher, (719) 555-9564. Before noon or after midnight. *(Pause)* But you're not a group.

JERRY: I can be.

CATHY: I have to go. Thanks for the dinner.

JERRY: Next time I'll get the hot mustard sauce instead of the sweet and sour. And more fries.

CATHY: Thanks.

JERRY: And a hot apple pie for you. If you want it.

CATHY: Thanks.

JERRY: I wouldn't want to get it if you didn't want it.

CATHY: Thanks.

JERRY: *(Squeaks)* Bye.

CATHY: Bye.

(She exits. JERRY *bangs his head against something, exits.)*

(In another space, CATHY *re-enters, reads from the magazine.)*

CATHY: The young Basque terrorist walked
Out of the apartment house
On Calle Reina Cristina Street
Heading toward his car.
He froze in mid-stride,
Slapped a hand to the side of his head,
As if he had just remembered something very important,
And fell to the asphalt, dead.

The bullet that killed him
Was fired by a friend,
A fellow terrorist from another faction,
Hiding in the lobby of the apartment building
They shared.

These pictures show the aftermath:
Tan car, right center, is faced against traffic
As colleagues of the sniper confirm the kill,
Next photo, accomplices drag body to car.
Middle photo, dark sedan picks up accomplices.
Bottom right photo, tan car carries body to common disposal site. *(Pause)*
This is very well-written. Art is everywhere.

(CATHY *exits.* JUDY *enters and sings.)*

JUDY: *(Singing)* O crocodile night,
You've always been there
In the thin air
Or on the dune.
O crocodile night,
You're always waiting,
Tonight you're mating
With the moon. *(Pause)*
The song of the hamper,
The song of the screen,

The song of the dishes,
The song of the green,
The song of the streetlights,
The song of the park,
The song of the lawnchair,
The song of the dark. *(To her offstage children, at the top of her lungs) Now for Chrissake go to sleep! (She exits.)*

VOICEOVER: Why they sing is under investigation.

(JERRY is sleeping—suddenly he is surrounded by ALIENS. They lift him up, carry him away—he wakes up during this.)

JERRY: *Aaaaaaaaaaeeeeeeeeeeeee!*

(ALIENS exit with JERRY.)

VOICEOVER: This is a good place for an intermission.

END OF ACT ONE

ACT TWO

(To signal the end of the intermission, JIM *enters and begins talking to the audience. He is in possession of all of his faculties. After a few beats of the speech,* CATHY *enters, drawn by this vision of* JIM, *and listens.)*

JIM: Jack's a smart guy, smarter than me in a lot of ways. I'm a carpenter by trade and, before the war, I did my apprenticeship on stick-built, lath-and-plaster houses. One-inch boards laid diagonally on studs with sixteen-inch centers. Hell—pounds of nails. Tens of thousands of nails for one house. Then I got drafted and when I came home, we started putting up roof trusses and making walls of three-quarters or five-eights inch sheet rock. You know there's no rock in sheet rock—it's just plaster pressed between two sheets of heavy paper. That's what's in my home.

CATHY: I dreamed about Dad the way he used to be.

JIM: Jack's getting into modular homes which you buy pre-fab in two to four sections which you haul to the site and put together. Now these have one-eighth inch paneling made of wood products that have been fused into a solid sheet and melded with a surface of plastic photo-reproduction of your favorite wood-grain. These houses go up very fast, of course, and sometimes come with the curtains already on the windows. People laugh, but why today would you want to build a house that would last a hundred years? Think of the changes in the last hundred years. Can you imagine the next hundred? What will be here—right where I'm standing? All the nails in the world won't keep those walls from cracking when the bulldozer comes. So Jack is right. I mean that. *(*JIM *exits.* EVELYN *enters.)*

EVELYN: I figured it out. We're going to get in the car. And we're going to travel west.

CATHY: What good will that do?

EVELYN: It's worked for our families for 200 years. We started in New Jersey and Massachusetts. We've managed a state about every two generations.

CATHY: But we're already in the west.

EVELYN: There's more to go.

CATHY: I don't understand how this will help.

EVELYN: I don't believe in medical science. They're making it up as they go along. They laugh at us when we leave the room.

CATHY: Will Dad go?

EVELYN: When I put him in the car. I'll just pack him up. As soon as we start to drive, his brain will start to clear. Memories will come flooding in. Vocabulary, too. Words of songs he's forgotten. Jokes. Anecdotes. Our life together—it's all floating around in the air. We just have to gather, gather it in. I'm gonna keep driving until he's back together. It may take as far as San Diego, but I'm not stopping until every piece is there again.

CATHY: What about Eric?

EVELYN: We'll put a message on the answering machine.

CATHY: We don't have an answering machine.

EVELYN: We'll *get one!!*

(They exit.)

(ERIC crosses to a pay phone, puts in a dime, dials, gets the ANSWERING MACHINE MESSAGE.) *[The following voices are on the answering machine.]*

CATHY's VOICE: Hello. Eric? This is Mom. We've taken a little trip.

EVELYN's VOICE: For your Grandpa—to make him better.

JIM's VOICE: Huh? What is this thing?

CATHY's VOICE: Please come home anyway—a neighbor will let you in. Please.

VOICE OF TELEPHONE OPERATOR: Please deposit fifty cents for an additional minute—please— *(ERIC can't get his money fast enough—he gets a dial tone—he beats the phone with the receiver, hangs it up, exits.)*

(EVELYN and CATHY are in the car, traveling. JIM is lying down in the back seat.)

EVELYN: Do you have any idea where we are?

CATHY: Where else? The car.

EVELYN: Jim?

CATHY: Mom, we've been traveling in circles—I don't know where the hell we are.

(EVELYN looks in the back seat.)

EVELYN: Jim—?

CATHY: On the plains somewhere. Mom? What is it?

EVELYN: We'd better go back.

CATHY: Is he all right?

EVELYN: Please. It didn't work.

(JIM *sits up, looks out window.*)

JIM: There's that old man again. That spindly-legged old guy running against the side of the car.

EVELYN: What?

JIM: Been running alongside me all my life. Look at him go.

EVELYN: *(To* CATHY*)* He's talking!

CATHY: What're you talking about, Dad?

JIM: That old guy—that long-legged old man. Boy, can he run.

EVELYN: It's working.

CATHY: What old man?

JIM: Look.

CATHY: Oh, him.

EVELYN: Where? Where?

CATHY: Rows of something, Mom. It's rows of corn or something out the window. See?

JIM: Running, running, running. Oh, it's a strange place—this... where are we?

(EVELYN *and* CATHY *look quickly at each other, panicked—decide to lie.*)

EVELYN: Ohio.

CATHY: *(Overlapping* EVELYN*)* Iowa.

EVELYN: Idaho.

CATHY: *(Overlapping* EVELYN*)* Ohio.

JIM: Oh. IdahoIowaOhio. OhioIowa. Idaho— *(Heavy hillbilly)* Hey, hey, HEY! Your boy pissed in the snow outside my cabin. It's frozen there! *(Another hillbilly voice)* It'll thaw next spring—what's your worry? *(First hillbilly voice)* I recognize my daughter's handwriting! *(Another memory comes)*
Uh—uh—uh— This is the forest Primeval, the murmuring pines and hemlock, bearded in moss and in garments green, stand like Druids of eld with beards that rest on their—their— *(Trying not to let his memory loss stop him—he sings)* Sometimes I wonder why I spend these lonely hours, dreaming of a song, a melody...haunts my...memory....*(Speaks)* Stop the car. *(Gets out of car.)* Left—loose. Right—tight. Left loose. Right tight. Crying so loud—must be a boy. No, it's a little girl—it's a little, little girl— (EVELYN

*gets out of the car—*JIM *grabs her and takes her to him, as if to dance.)*
Evelyn—we're making love in the graveyard and scaring the hell out of
those kids. They think our sounds are coming from the dead lying below us.
(Scared, breaks from her) My tongue's stuck on the clothesline! Trying to lick
the ice—Mama, Mama, help! *(Really reverting)* First bath outside in sun.
Fireflies in jar.
Night-night. *(Climbs back in the car)*
Warm pee.
Bosom.
Mmmmm. Mmmmm. Mmmmmm.
Shhhhhhh. *(He lies back down.)*

EVELYN: *(After a long beat)* Jim?

CATHY: What happened?

EVELYN: *(Gets back in the car, upset)* He was dreaming. I guess. Let's go home.

(CATHY *breathes a sigh of relief.* EVELYN *glares at her.)*

CATHY: I'm sorry—I'm just so worried about Eric.

EVELYN: *(Pretending to forget with a vengeance who her grandson is)* Who?

CATHY: Mom!

EVELYN: Sorry.

CATHY: Which way?

EVELYN: I don't know!

CATHY: Tell me which way!

EVELYN: For Chrissakes! You're a grown up!! *Pick one!!*

CATHY: We'll go this way.

EVELYN: What are you *doing?* It's that way!!

(ALIEN *played by the* JUDY *actor is reading a copy of the* "National Enquirer"
*—she notices the picture of an alien on the front of it, looks at it closely, then puts it
into a large Zip-loc bag and seals it. Other* ALIENS *enter rolling* JERRY *in on a
dolly—he wakes up and opens his mouth to scream, but can't make a sound.)*

ALIEN: *(Putting her face very close to* JERRY's *face and talking very deliberately)*
What—can—we—do—about—your—fear?

(JERRY *can't answer—he just stares at them, screaming silently. They massage his
jaws and shut his mouth for him. They all begin to pet him roughly to comfort him,
like inept children stroking a dog. They proceed with an examination—it should
satirize the examination of field scientists on "National Geographic" of an animal
in the wild. They put incomprehensible stickers on him, measure him, take blood,
etc.,—all with the air of completely dispassionate scientists. One* ALIEN *finds a pair*

of clip-on sunglasses in JERRY's *pocket, holds them up for other* ALIENS *to see, and they all laugh rhythmically. An* ALIEN *produces* Playboy *magazine, opens it to the centerfold, and moves it in front of* JERRY, *trying to arouse him. Another* ALIEN *unzips* JERRY's *fly, looks inside, and waits for an erection. After a beat,* ALIEN *takes out a Dustbuster and inserts it into* JERRY's *pants through his fly and turns it on briefly.* JERRY *reacts as the semen is sucked from him. This finishes the exam. An* ALIEN *tags* JERRY *on his ear, zaps him unconscious, and they lay him down gently and exit.)*

(EVELYN *and* CATHY *are looking at snapshots of their trip west.)*

EVELYN: Here we are at the Blasted Pine. *(Pause)* Here's that rock that looks like a—

CATHY: —baked potato.

EVELYN: Yes. *(Pause)* Here we are at Glen Canyon.

CATHY: Full of water.

EVELYN: They filled it in. *(She passes through several pictures quickly.)* That's the rest of Utah. He wouldn't let me stop the car, so these are all blurry.

CATHY: He seemed to be in such a hurry.

EVELYN: No, he still knows he hates—

CATHY: —the Mormons. Yeah.

EVELYN: Here's—

CATHY: —Reno.

EVELYN: *(Correcting her)* Las Vegas. *(Pause)* Here's—

CATHY: Death Valley.

EVELYN: *(Correcting her)* Barstow. *(Pause)* Here's San Bernadino. *(Pause)* Here we are at...at the zoo.

CATHY: Where?

EVELYN: San Diego.

CATHY: Who's this guy with the wet drawers, walking out of the picture? He's looking off to the right, like he doesn't notice...he looks so...old...he's lost, completely lost. *(She exits.)*

EVELYN: Here's the other Blasted Pine. *(Pause)* Here's the Pacific Ocean. *(Pause)* Here's a shell on the beach. *(Pause)* Here's a piece of a shell. *(Pause)* Here's a sliver of driftwood. *(Pause)* Here's....*(She exits with the snapshots.)*

VOICEOVER: They seem to enjoy what is called dreaming—

(During the VOICEOVER, CATHY *joins* JUDY *outside—they are smoking dope.)*

VOICEOVER: —and spend one-third of their lives in this comatose state, allowing their minds to make stories of whatever stimuli are left over from the day or the life. Significance is then divined from these neural and electronic collages and the process is deemed therapeutic.

JUDY: I found this in Jason's drawer.

CATHY: What? No—all of a sudden I feel so weird smoking this now.

JUDY: I grounded him for life.

CATHY: That's a long time when you're his age. This *is* good.

JUDY: Imagine what it does to the brain of a twelve year old?

CATHY: So, anyway, you were Eve? Man.

JUDY: I can't control my subconscious, alright? Would you rather hear the Spider Dream?

CATHY: No!

JUDY: Okay. I was naked in the Garden and I was looking at all the leaves and stuff and, suddenly, it really began to grow right before my eyes—you know, like that speeded-up photography on nature programs of the opening of a flower or whatever? But this was closing up—you know—the leaves out of control, covering up the sky.

CATHY: Like kudzu.

JUDY: Yeah. Like some paradisical kudzu—some mojo kudzu—

CATHY: —of Eternity.

JUDY: No, not Eternity—don't say that.

CATHY: Okeedokee.

JUDY: And the fruit got real big and started hanging lower and lower on the trees. Ever seen a cow that needs to be milked and the farmer's on vacation or something? Mooo. Moooo. Ridiculous, man. I mean, moooooooo. I'm a cow.

CATHY: You're not a cow.

JUDY: I don't want to be a cow.

CATHY: You don't have to be a cow.

JUDY: What is this? Some feminist accusatory bullshit? I know I don't have to be a cow.

CATHY: Listen—are you listening? What was I talking about? I mean, it's not belief. It's feeling. You feel things. And maybe they are assholes. But it's love. How can love be bad? I mean, love is good.

JUDY: Love is very good.

CATHY: Yes, we love and that's good.

JUDY: But we're fucked.

CATHY: Oh, yeah. Go on, I am listening.

JUDY: At that very moment—

CATHY: What moment?

JUDY: In this Garden. Keep up.

CATHY: The Snake.

JUDY: No. No Snake. The Snake was in the next grove, helping Adam—

CATHY: Helping Adam name things.

JUDY: At that very moment—

CATHY: Like the Blue-Footed Booby.

JUDY: I hear this something—sound. Sssssssss.

CATHY: It is a snake!

JUDY: No snake. Get off of this snake thing!

CATHY: Then what was it?

JUDY: Pressure.

CATHY: God.

JUDY: No. The Tree. The Major Tree. The whole place.

CATHY: What? This is the Knowledge?

JUDY: Yeah. It was all about to bust—*open!* So I just sort of jumped—like Superman? And it worked! So—whoosh—I flew up through the limbs, through the Mojo Pardisical Kudzu, and—whoosh—broke through all the Green stuff. *(Pause)* And I was *free!* And the light poured in—

CATHY: And then you woke up.

JUDY: What?

CATHY: You woke up. You were dreaming all this.

JUDY: Oh yeah. I woke up—I woke up.

CATHY: Alone.

JUDY: No—he was there. The guy—you know.

CATHY: You lucky.

JUDY: I'd been flying. I had felt so free. And I looked down and what did I have in my hand? The Fruit of the Tree—still sticky, the little bishop, its one eye staring blankly at me. *(Long pause)* I finally told him I loved him—love him. You know, just sitting there—not in the throes of passion or anything.

CATHY: Not again.

JUDY: Different guy—they don't know each other.

CATHY: What did this one say?

JUDY: "We don't have time for abstractions." And then he said, "Be here now."

CATHY: So that was it.

JUDY: Oh no, I'm seeing him next Sunday. I love him. Really. Everything's gonna be fine.

CATHY: Wake up, Jude.

JUDY: Well, at least I'm trying. You're not even *trying*. At least I'm trying to be *alive*.

(JUDY *exits.* EVELYN *enters.*)

EVELYN: I'm leaving for the ah—

CATHY: Oh, Mom! Judy just left—I— Should I go?

EVELYN: No, it's my day. Thursday. Thursday is my day.

CATHY: I took him the—

EVELYN: Good. Did he ah—?

CATHY: Yeah. Well, a little. His eyes seemed to...a little.

EVELYN: Oh, well, then he must've known—

CATHY: Oh, he knew. He— Sure.

EVELYN: Well, I've got some new— *(Holds up one of those plastic bags from a mall store)*

CATHY: Great.

EVELYN: So— *(She exits.)*

CATHY: Tell him— *(She waves instead.)*

CATHY: *(To herself)* Get straight. Get straight. Wake *up!*

(JERRY *wakes up.* CATHY *doesn't notice and exits.*)

JERRY: Hmmmmmmmm. *(Stretches)* Oh my God, I'm outside!!! Oh my God, I'm lying *in my driveway!* (Looks around to see if the neighbors see him—checks *his watch.)* Oh my God, I've got to get to work! Oh my God, my fly is open! Oh my God, I hope I'm an alcoholic! *(He exits.)*

(CATHY *is on the phone.)*

CATHY: Finally.
Yes. May I speak to Eric, please.
Well, then, let me speak to his—his father.
Yes, "Michael." *(Waits)* Hello, Mike?
Where's Eric—is he there or over at Todd's?
You *what?????*
Well, *he's not!!* He's *not* here!!!! When did he leave? *A week ago!!! A week ago!!!* We've been gone for a week and a half!!!!
You put him on the *plane* and *never called me?????* OhmyGod ohmyGod ohmyGod ohmyGod. *Didn't* you *worry* when you didn't *hear from him???*
I know he doesn't call *a lot!!* Well, ever—alright—*but why didn't you call me to see if he arrived!!!!*
Hello?? Hello!!
This is *who????*
Nice to *meet me??? Where is my son!!!!*
What do *mean* "He can take care of himself!!" How do *you* know? You're only 18 yourself!!! *Go practice your fucking oboe!!!*
Mike? *Mike!!* What are you doing!!! Our *son* is lost somewhere between New York and Colorado and you put your *child girlfriend* on the *phone????*
"*Only* the Midwest?" What do you think the Midwest is—Rhode Island? *Look at a map, you imbecile!!! It's huge!!!*
No, I will *not* calm down. *You will* call the airline and check the passenger list and find out if he had to change planes. And if he did, *where*—and *pray* he didn't land at *O'Hare*—that's in Chicago, by the way.
I'll wait up for your report!! *(Hangs up)* Mom? Mom! Mooooooooooommmmmmmmmmm!!!!! *(She crosses, looking for* EVELYN, *runs into* JERRY.)

JERRY: I'm looking for my sunglasses.

CATHY: *(Turning and crossing away from him)* Mooommmmmm!

JERRY: Are you looking for your mother now? (CATHY *exits.*) And sometimes therapy just makes things worse. I know. I understand. *(He speaks to the audience.)* I talk to her so much better when she's not here. *(He exits.)*

(JIM *and* EVELYN *are looking at menus.)*

JIM: I'm gonna get the country chicken. I know that's boring, 'cause I always get it.

EVELYN: Wait—how did we get here? Oh my god—something...

JIM: No—sometimes I get the liver and onions. That's good. Their liver and onions is good.

EVELYN: Jim—where's the desk? Where's the...nurse? I was holding a straw for you, I—

JIM: They have *some* good things here.

EVELYN: You're so much better all of a sudden.

JIM: You know you're at Big Boy. The table is sticky.

EVELYN: *(Feeling the table)* It is! It is! Oh, it *is!!*

JIM: Look at those plants.

EVELYN: Are they—?

JIM: Real. They're real. Those are real plants.

EVELYN: It's beautiful in here. The Big Boy is beautiful.

JIM: How do they water all these plants? They probably stand on the booths. *(Beat)* I'm gonna get the salad bar.

EVELYN: Me, too.

JIM: *(About the plants)* Maybe that *is* the salad bar. (EVELYN *is staring across from them at something, doesn't respond.)* Do you think? Baby?

EVELYN: Look at that couple over there.

JIM: What.

EVELYN: Over there.

JIM: She looks sort of like you.

EVELYN: No, *him*. He reminds me of you—kind of.

JIM: Am I that skinny?

EVELYN: He's not skinny.

JIM: He's skinny.

EVELYN: And she looks like—

JIM: Oh no, you're much prettier than that, Baby.

EVELYN: Don't look!

JIM: Did she see us? It doesn't matter. She's probably thinking the same thing we are.

EVELYN: Oh my God— Don't look.

JIM: Damn! I'm missing something good. What's wrong?

EVELYN: I don't know.

JIM: What's *he* doing?

EVELYN: He's just sitting there, staring.

JIM: Are they having a fight?

EVELYN: No. She's holding a straw for him—ohmyGod.

JIM: What?

EVELYN: Wait. *(She moves her hand up very slowly and moves it back and forth, watching the woman while she does it, as if she is checking her reflection in a mirror.)*

JIM: What are you doing, Evelyn?

EVELYN: Shhhhh. *(She moves her body back and forth, watching the woman, then does one quick hand movement, turns away, thinks, looks back at woman—stops, stares, bewildered and afraid.)*

JIM: I can't take you anywhere.

EVELYN: *(Grabbing* JIM's *hand)* Let's get out of here.

JIM: I don't care. I'm looking. *(Looks at woman, looks away)* She's crying and looking at us. What's wrong?

EVELYN: She's remembering—she's remembering—

JIM: *What?*

EVELYN: She's remembering *now.* Oh *God,* let's get *out* of here!

JIM: Evelyn, Baby— *(*EVELYN *drags* JIM *by the hand.)*

EVELYN: Come on—while we've still got some *time!!!*

(She exits, pulling him—he laughs, following her, still not understanding.)

(Female ALIEN *enters and gives this report in a smooth documentary style. It is juxtaposed with the actions of* JERRY, *who is fantasizing about* CATHY.*)*

ALIEN: Hello. This segment of our presentation is about masochism.

(During the following speech, JERRY *sits and imagines* CATHY. *He begins to become aroused. His* FANTASY CATHY *swoops in and kisses him passionately—she swoops away and he still can feel her there. He continues to imagine love-making, laughter, and himself being witty. The fantasy is broken, when the real* CATHY *enters after the masochism speech is over. Then* JERRY *returns to his state of nervousness and fear with her.)*

ALIEN: Masochism is a rather disorganized but, nevertheless, growing religion with many followers of both genders. It seems to be a form of worship of the Mating Process by celibate non-participants and centers on, usually, the idealization of the Worship-Object. The ceremonies are held in private and usually include solitary fertility rites. Prayer is also solitary and silent and can be observed several times a day, depending on the devotion of the Masochistic supplicant. *(FANTASY CATHY enters.) (Pause)* The Object is called up through telepathy, conversations and encounters are constructed by the supplicant, and the mating act is imagined silently. The experienced Masochist can pray at any time, anywhere. Once the Worship-Object has been selected and a true masochistic state has been achieved, the Masochist eschews contact with the real Object— *(FANTASY CATHY exits.)* —communicating only when necessary, and then through broken sentences or a high-pitched rhythmic laughter. This action is designed to repel the real Object, thereby protecting the contemplative life of the now securely celibate Masochist.

(The ALIEN presenter has exited and the real CATHY enters, sees JERRY.)

CATHY: Hello.

(JERRY emits a high-pitched, rhythmic laugh.)

CATHY: *(Starting to exit)* See you.

JERRY: Excuse—

CATHY: *(Not seeing him)* Huh?

JERRY: I've avoiding you—been— Me—sorry.

CATHY: I just came to talk.

JERRY: Thank—thank you. A lot on mind—my mind. Things...happen...to...me. *(He exits laughing with his high-pitched, nervous laugh.)*

CATHY: Me, too. You're not the only one things happen to! You know?! I'd like to be weird! I'd love to have permission to be weird! *(She exits.)*

VOICEOVER: They wash their clothes in public places.

(JERRY and EVELYN are in a laundromat—they've never met, but JERRY begins talking.)

JERRY: Black eggs, warm rocks, gelatinous material falling from the sky—I mean, were these people all crazy? Think of the toads! Great storms of toads, falling in deluges, piling up on the roads. Fish! In Singapore, it rained fish. And Ed Mootz of Cincinnati and his peach tree destroyed by red glop that fell from some strange-looking cloud—there's a picture of him standing by his dead tree in a book I have at home. Angel hair and star jelly—scientists always laugh at these—but people have picked this stuff up. I'm not kidding! Not to mention the weird metal shit that falls from the sky and the ice—brains some old lady or destroys her television. And you hand 'em the goddam thing and they put it in one of those giant baggies and take it away. And that's the last you ever hear of it! *(Long beat as EVELYN looks at him)*

EVELYN: People—people on game shows buying vowels because they don't know the most commonest phrase. I mean—ignorance.

JERRY: *(After a beat)* Baron Rodemire de Tarazone of France was assassinated by Claude Volbonne—twenty-one years earlier, Baron Rodemire de Tarazone's father had been assassinated and by a man named Claude Volbonne. But it was a different Claude Volbonne and they were not related!!!

EVELYN: And that second dryer is *shot!*

JERRY: I know—I lost a quarter in it last week.

EVELYN: They say they're working on these things. They say, "We're working on it!" "Lady!" But are they? I mean, where are the results?! And for that matter, where are they? Huh? When was the last time you actually saw someone in charge? I mean, in the flesh?

JERRY: On television.

EVELYN: Exactly! On television.

JERRY: On television.

EVELYN: When was the last time you saw the person who owns this laundromat? I mean, *who is in charge? Who is running this place? Huh?!*

JERRY: *(Grabbing* EVELYN*)* That's what I want to know!

EVELYN: That's what I want to know, too!

JERRY: I really want to know that.

EVELYN: So do I.

JERRY: *(Letting go of her)* Excuse me.

EVELYN: *(Quickly folding a piece of her laundry)* I usually do this at home.

JERRY: Not me. I do it in public all the time. I think it's job stress.

EVELYN: My dryer's broken.

JERRY: *(About the incompetency of the world)* Of course. Is someone working on it?

EVELYN: My husband's boss. I mean, his ex-boss, came over and tried, but...

JERRY: An *ex*-boss, of course. Power just...leaks.

EVELYN: *(Thinking about* JIM *and everything)* How can a country that sent a man to the moon—

JERRY: Maybe they didn't. Maybe he didn't go.

EVELYN: You mean he didn't go?

JERRY: Maybe.

EVELYN: But we saw it.

JERRY: Where?

EVELYN: *(She gets it.)* On television! *(Pause)* How did I used to know things? I mean, when we first came here, it was just a bunch of houses built on concrete slabs. The contractor's wife named all the streets. My husband helped build it. And now you're telling me it was all a dream?

JERRY: No—no, we're awake! I know that.

EVELYN: I can't sleep.

JERRY: *(Coming to her, very tender)* You need to sleep. You should sleep.

EVELYN: I'm afraid to close my eyes. Change happens so fast. *(JERRY and EVELYN sit silently next to each other watching the clothes turn in the dryer.)*

VOICEOVER: Change happens.

(Sound of country music—EVELYN arises from her chair in the laundromat, leaving her laundry. She crosses and exits with purpose. JERRY picks up her laundry and tries to pursue her.)

JERRY: Wait. Wait!! Wait!! Come back!! *(To audience)* Why do people always say that? Like—someone steals your car and you yell, "Hey, come back here!" like they're going to put on the brakes, back-up and give you back your car. I mean, if they wanted to come back, they would.

(EVELYN has re-entered and is lying on the floor of a shower in her panties. She is curled into a tight knot. Sound of a shower dripping. She's asleep. Upstage is a bed with a large lump in it and a chair with a pile of clothes by it.)

EVELYN: *(A drip from the shower hits her.)* What? *(Half wakes up, shivers, reaches for something like someone who's thrown off the covers, finds a shirt, puts it on, sits up, looks up at the shower.)* I'm in a shower.

VOICEOVER: She is in a shower.

(EVELYN stands, burps, waits, burps, crosses to a chair, sits. She finds a man's boots and puts them on. She finds cigarettes and lights up.)

EVELYN: These aren't my boots.

VOICEOVER: Motel. Mo—tel. When a traveler is tired, a motel is used.

(EVELYN crosses to curtain, shuffling in the boots, parts the curtain, reads a neon sign.)

EVELYN: Ang-La. Ang-La. Ang-La. Angri— Shangri—

VOICEOVER: She doesn't know where she is.

EVELYN: Shangri-La. Oh.

(A large mound of blankets sits up and speaks.)

JACK: Baby? Where are ya?

EVELYN: Who is that?

JACK: *(The mound lays back down.)* Jack. Jack. Hey, I'm a little queasy—okay, baby?

(EVELYN starts to gather her stuff, frantically.)

EVELYN: What am I doing? What am I doing? Oh my God. That's it—I'm alone. *(She looks off in space for a beat while her aloneness hits her, then exits in JACK's shirt and boots.)*

JACK: Evelyn? Evelyn? It wasn't charity. *(Beat. No answer.)* I knew it. Damn.

(CATHY is sitting in the house, surrounded by maps—the TV is on. JERRY enters with EVELYN's laundry—he puts it down beside CATHY. CATHY looks at him and he exits. After a beat, CATHY hears someone else entering the house from the opposite direction.)

CATHY: Mom?

EVELYN: *(Offstage)* Yeah?

CATHY: Where you been?

EVELYN: *(Still offstage)* Oh—out with some friends. I ran into some people I knew at the—the—they asked about your dad, so I—I...

VOICEOVER: Never force anything.

CATHY: Anybody I know? *(EVELYN enters, her coat on and wearing JACK's boots, carrying a grocery bag.)*

EVELYN: No. Heard anything from Eric?

CATHY: No.

EVELYN: *(Sits on the couch)* Did Mike check on the planes?

CATHY: Yeah. He never got on. He cashed in the ticket. He's a missing person, Mom. *(Rattling the maps)* Look at this! Look at this! This is America. How did it get to be so enormous?

EVELYN: *(Simple statement of fact)* We took it from the Indians.

CATHY: That's not Eric's fault! I mean, what are we supposed to do with all this land?! Didn't anybody think about that?!! I mean, didn't anybody think back then that people could get *lost?!!* Didn't anybody think about the *Goddam future?!*

EVELYN: What's an A P B?

CATHY: I tried to get one. He's not a criminal. I'm gonna go to bed—I'm gonna sleep with this telephone.

EVELYN: Stranger things have happened.

CATHY: What's in the bag?

EVELYN: Clothes.

CATHY: Should I leave the TV on?

EVELYN: Uh-huh.

CATHY: Nice boots.

EVELYN: Thanks.

(CATHY *exits with the telephone.* EVELYN *lies down on the couch, her head on the grocery bag, and stares at the TV. After a beat,* CATHY *re-enters and looks at her mother with curiosity.* EVELYN *doesn't notice her. Unable to figure out what it is exactly that bothers her about* EVELYN, CATHY *quietly exits again.* EVELYN *flicks through the channels with the remote and finds* The Tonight Show *theme.*)

EVELYN: Heeeeeere's Johnny.

(ERIC *is asleep in a mall at night. Suddenly, a Muzak version of* "Raindrops Keep Falling on My Head" *comes over the PA.*)

VOICE ON PA: Hey, Haircut.

ERIC: *(Waking up with a start)* Where—where—where?!!

VOICE ON PA: Up here. The eye.

ERIC: *(To the source of the* VOICE*)* Listen—they told me this was a DEAD mall. They specifically said this was a *dead* mall.

VOICE ON PA: "They?"

ERIC: Nobody.

VOICE ON PA: *(Knowing that* ERIC *is witholding names)* Yeah. Right.

ERIC: I'm outta here. *(Starts to go.)*

VOICE ON PA: Says who?

ERIC: I didn't touch nothin'. I didn't do nothin".

VOICE ON PA: Yeah yeah. Listen, Wonder Bread. Get out of here—alright. But you tell the other "Nobodies" to stay away from here, too. And to stop sleeping in the Goodwill Box.

(ERIC *tries to get himself to leave—the reality of being outside alone hits him.*)

ERIC: *(To the source of the* VOICE*)* Well, boy, I'm goin'. I'm outta here. *Dude.* I'm hittin' the road. I'm hittin' the fuckin' road, man. I am *out o' here. (He begins to cry.)* Mr. Eye? I'm lost. *(Static on PA.* ERIC *exits.)*

(CATHY *is standing, feeding* JIM *in the cafeteria of a nursing home. He is standing, doing a kind of frenetic bounce, like someone whose shoes are stuck to the floor would do to get free. He is staring at a door that sunlight is leaking through. He's lost a great deal of weight—we can see this because his pants are much too big for him. The shirt he's wearing isn't his own—the sleeves are a little too short. And his hair has been slicked back—the effort of a nurse's aid to make the patient look tidy.)*

VOICEOVER: We used to be nomads.

CATHY: *(About the spoon she's holding up to his face)* Here, Dad. Over here. Over here, Dad. Look, Dad. Please. Please, Dad. Eat. Eat something. Dad— *(He takes a bite and goes back to looking at the door and dancing.)* Good! Want some more? Here's some more. Dad? Dad? Dad? Daddy? *(She holds the spoon out for a couple more beats, then lowers it to the plate.)* They'll put you on an IV, Dad. In your arm. *(She takes his arm and tries to show him.)* They'll put an IV in your arm. Here. If you don't eat. Do you hear me? So you gotta eat— (JIM *is staring at the door.)* What's out there? It's just an old alley. It's just an old dirty alley, filled with garbage cans. And falling down fences. And oil spots. And junk. Stay here and eat. Please. (JIM *crosses to the door in a kind of scooting walk.)* No, Dad! Stay away from the door!

(JERRY *enters.)*

JERRY: Don't worry. You have to hold something down and then pull—he won't be able to figure it out. *(About the tray)* Is he done? Well, I gotta take it anyway. *(Takes tray—shouts to* JIM*)* Jim! There's nothing out there! What do you want to go out there for? Here's your daughter to feed you!

CATHY: *(To* JERRY*)* I didn't know you worked here.

JERRY: I told you I'm a nurse.

CATHY: *(To* JERRY*)* Why are you so calm?

JERRY: Am I? Don't worry about the door. He'll get tired of trying. Then we'll put him to bed. *(He exits with tray.)*

CATHY: *(Afterthought, to* JERRY*)* Wait! My father's a mechanical genius! He can figure out how anything works. You don't understand! Hey!

(CATHY *gives up, looks at* JIM. *He's trying the door with no success. She sits and watches him as he continues to try the latch. The lights change to night, and* JIM *slides slowly down the door, exhausted, still holding on to the door handle.)*

VOICEOVER: Light change. Night.

(JERRY *re-enters.)*

JERRY: My shift's done. I thought I'd help put him to bed. *(Crosses to* JIM *and helps him up, removing his hand from the door handle)* Jim? Hey, you're my buddy. *(Getting him up)* That's a boy. *(Straightening out his trousers)* What you want to go out there for anyway? That big, bad world—whew, listen to the news. *(Winking at* CATHY*)* It's better in here. *(Presenting* JIM*)* Say goodnight to your daughter. *(*JIM *looks over* CATHY*'s head—he doesn't seem to see her.)* He says "Good night." *(*JERRY *exits with him.* CATHY *crosses to the door that* JIM *was struggling with. She opens it with ease and exits.)*

*(*CATHY *sits in the chair in* JERRY*'s house.* JERRY *is there and they are listening to Mozart.)*

JERRY: This music came with the house. But I would've bought some, anyway. It's nice to have you here.

CATHY: I've been here lots of times.

JERRY: You never sat down.

CATHY: Oh yeah. *(Beat)* How can you work there?

JERRY: I like to help people. I like to comfort people.

CATHY: I could use...that.

JERRY: Well, the world is round. And we're all on it together. Take off your blouse.

*(*CATHY *unbuttons and takes off her blouse.* JERRY *crosses to her, amazed.)*

JERRY: You're so.... How can you live in the world with this skin? Look at this beautiful skin.

CATHY: I'm cold. I'm cold. *(*JERRY *embraces her.)* This is beautiful music.

JERRY: It's Mozart.

CATHY: He understood, didn't he? He knew.

JERRY: Yes, he died of poison. Someone was poisoning him. And he knew it.

CATHY: No, no—that's not what I meant. You don't understand— *(She starts putting on her blouse again.)*

JERRY: But I thought you finally understood. I thought that's why you were here.

CATHY: No, no—it was something about—about just trying to be alive. *(She is exiting.)*

JERRY: But John F. Kennedy, Marilyn Monroe—someone murdered them, too. *(*CATHY *has gone.* JERRY *stops, looks at the audience.)*

JERRY: *(Lost, wanting an answer)* It's not funny, is it? *(To himself, exiting)* Think about it. Think about it. *(He exits.)*

VOICEOVER: Death and flying.

(CATHY *enters carrying two milkshakes to go.* EVELYN *enters.*)

EVELYN: Oh, honey...

CATHY: What?

EVELYN: He's dead.

(CATHY *just stands there, not moving for a long beat.*)

CATHY: But...I have the milkshakes.

EVELYN: I have to call people.

(EVELYN *exits.* CATHY *crosses to the right, then to the left, then to the right, then she stops.* JIM *enters and talks to her, but she can't see or hear him.*)

JIM: I just had the most incredible dream. Honey? I dreamed I was flying, surrounded by light. But it was so real. I could feel this hot... wind on my neck. The tops of trees were just whizzing past below me. And, I'm not kidding, the sound of wings! I reached back to rub myself. And that's when I saw the nest and the open mouths. (*He grabs onto something that seems solid at his sides and then bends his head up and back to see what is above him. He realizes that something is clutching him. He looks at the audience.*) Oh. I get it. Beyond the light. Angel meat. Noooo.

VOICEOVER: We hear the sound of sirens.

CATHY: Wait a minute.

VOICEOVER: We hear the sound of sirens.

CATHY: *Not yet.*

(CATHY *and* EVELYN *are looking at a plate of Jello with fruit salad suspended in it.*)

EVELYN: Good. Eat that. We don't have any more room in the refrigerator.

CATHY: I was just looking at it. Wondering how Judy's mom got it to...

EVELYN: Yeah. It's all even—the cherries and the grapes didn't go to the....I don't know what to do next. We used to be nomads, you know.

CATHY: Women did all the work.

EVELYN: But it kept your mind off everything. Your husband says it's time to leave and you leave. The baby you lost, whatever, you have to leave it. Someone is always making you do something. You don't have to find a reason to go on.

CATHY: What's that? (*Sound of far-off arguing*) Judy and her mother.

EVELYN: This whole street—it's practically all women now. I thought my father knew everything when I was a girl. And then the president.

CATHY: I thought you knew everything when I was little, Mom.

EVELYN: Oh, let's not lie—after everything we've seen. *(She exits.)*

CATHY: *(Sensing something)* Somebody there? *(No answer)* Somebody there? *(ERIC enters.)*

ERIC: Whatsup, Mom.

CATHY: Oh my God!

(CATHY stands—afraid to touch him—a long beat.)

CATHY: Are you all right? *(ERIC nods.)* Grandpa's dead, Eric. And you weren't even here.

ERIC: I know.

CATHY: How did you get here?

ERIC: I called Kim for money.

CATHY: Kim?

ERIC: Kim. You know—Dad's...girlfriend.

CATHY: You didn't talk to your dad?

ERIC: I thought he'd be mad. *(Pause)* You look mad, too.

CATHY: You don't care about anybody but yourself!!

(EVELYN enters.)

EVELYN: Oh—

ERIC: Hi, Grandma.

CATHY: So Kim knew where you were and didn't call me?!!!

ERIC: Only for twelve hours or so. Mom, give her a break—she's pregnant and she's only eighteen, and—

CATHY: Oh, big deal—that's how old I was when I had you, and you turned out al— *(CATHY stops, unable to say "alright".)*

ERIC: It fuckin' pisses me off!! This fuckin' life!!!

EVELYN: Eric, for crying out loud!!

ERIC: *Gramma, get off my fuckin' back!!!*

CATHY: *Eric, how can you talk to your—* Wait— Wait— Come here. Both of you. I'm having a moment.

VOICEOVER: Oh— She finally has a Moment.

EVELYN: What?

ERIC: What, Mom?

CATHY: I'm having a moment of...peace.

ERIC: Where?

EVELYN: I want that.

CATHY: Listen.

EVELYN: I hear the traffic on the interstate.

ERIC: I hear a TV.

CATHY: Listen.

EVELYN: I can't hear anything.

CATHY: Something— It's going. It's gone. Nevermind.

ERIC: What was it?

CATHY: I don't know. I just had this feeling that everything—

EVELYN: Will be all right? How can it?

ERIC: No shit.

CATHY: No, that everything *is* all right.

ERIC: Well, that's fucked, I can tell you that.

EVELYN: Goes double for me. (ERIC *and* EVELYN *exit into the house.*)

CATHY: *(After a long beat)* Dad? *(She seems to see him.)* Daddy? *(She listens for him, decides she's missed him somehow, goes inside the house, carrying* ERIC'S *bag.)*

VOICEOVER: We hear the sound of sirens. *(No objection—*ALIEN *makes siren sound.)*

(CATHY *and* EVELYN *stand on a hill overlooking Formican. We hear the sound of sirens. They speak in a very detached way.)*

CATHY: Look! It's Elvis Presley flying overhead.

EVELYN: Yeah. He's really burning.

CATHY: Uh-oh.

EVELYN: He'll catch those shake shingles—they'll go like— *(Snaps her fingers)* —that.

CATHY: They should've used fake ones like Denny's.

EVELYN: Is that the Pizza Hut that just went up?

CATHY: No, Mom, that's the somethingorother church.

EVELYN: Too near the mall. Big mistake.

CATHY: *(Just noticing)* The dumpster at Roy Rogers! Look, it's caught the roof!

EVELYN: There goes the Flea Market! Those booths go up fast.

CATHY: The wind is carrying it. Look! All the recliners are smoldering.

EVELYN: It's getting very close— They won't be able to keep it out. They won't be able to keep it out. Look at the sparks—

CATHY: Down the air conditioning vents.

EVELYN: Only a matter of time.

CATHY: Flaming gas running into the redwood flower boxes.

EVELYN: It's surrounded.

CATHY: It's glowing from the inside. It went up so fast.

EVELYN: The mall is burning.

CATHY: The mall is burning.

(JUDY *enters, carrying a small paper bag. She takes round ice cream sandwiches out and gives one to* EVELYN *and* CATHY.)

JUDY: Have a Dilly Bar.

EVELYN: *(Sudden realization—the Dairy Queen has burned.)* Not the Soft Serve?

JUDY: Yes, it just blew up. Jagger helped it along. I wonder where he got the money for the gas. (JUDY *and* CATHY *give each other a sidelong glance, then turn back to watch the fire.)*

JUDY: *(To* CATHY*)* I was hoping you could get past your pain into Despair and/or Terror.

CATHY: You're a fine one to talk.

JUDY: Despair and Terror are intolerable.

CATHY: Yes, they lead to action. Pain is gentle. Pain is the River of Life, and you can ride it to the Sea.

JUDY: You are very introspective And somewhat articulate. You are On to Yourself. *(Pause)* You'd better eat your Dilly Bar.

CATHY: Alright. Thank you.

JUDY: Is that all you've got to say? Alright. Thank you?

CATHY: Where are the kids?

JUDY: *(Points down at the site of the fire)* Disneyland.

(JUDY *gives them each sunglasses to wear.)*

JUDY: For the glare. *(They put the sunglasses on and become* ALIENS.*)*

ALL: *(In relief)* Ahhhhh.

EVELYN/ALIEN: That's better.
(Sings) Just a song at twilight,
When the lights are low.
(CATHY/ALIEN & JUDY/ALIEN *join singing.*)
And the flick'ring shadows,
Softly come and go.
(ERIC/ALIEN *joins the group—he is also wearing sunglasses—he joins in the singing. After a beat, the* ACTOR/ALIEN *who played several parts, most recently* JACK, *enters and joins in the singing.*)
Though the heart be weary,
Sad the day and long.
Still to us at twilight,
Comes love's old song,
Comes love's old sweet song.

(CATHY/ALIEN *talks to audience—as she does,* ERIC/ALIEN *shows the kitchen chair from the beginning of the play and sets it near her. He waits while she talks.*)

CATHY/ALIEN: There were so many Formicans long ago. Fifteen erts ago I lived with a small group. Their culture was complex, yet strangely intangible, and the artifacts are a constant source of...wonder. *(About the chair)* I used to know what this was for. Several of these survived. *(She and the* ERIC/ALIEN *look quizzically at the chair, then at the audience.)*

CATHY/ALIEN & JUDY/ALIEN *sing—the song* JUDY *sang as a lullabye at the end of Act One. After a few lines of the song,* JERRY *enters and spreads newspapers on the floor. He lies down on them, takes out a pistol, checks to see if it's loaded and puts the barrel into his mouth—he pauses. The* ALIENS *try to soothe him with the lullabye, even though he can't see them.)*

JUDY/ALIEN: *(Sings)*
O dinosaur light,
How death becomes you,
And oozes from you,
Red as Mars.
O dinosaur light,
The sky is turning,
Each night you're burning,
With the stars.

The dream of the screendoor,
The dream of the stoop,
The dream of the clothesline,
The dream of the hoop,
The dream of the dirt road,
The dream of the bird,

The dream of the big tree,
The dream of the word.

O Crocodile night,
You've always been there,
In the thin air,
Or on the dune.
O Crocodile night,
You're always waiting,
Tonight you're mating
With the moon.

Goodnight,
Goodnight,
Goodnight,
Silence—

Goodnight.

(JUDY/ALIEN & CATHY/ALIEN *exit, tiptoeing to be quiet.* JERRY *has fallen asleep with the pistol in his mouth. He snores contentedly.*)

VOICEOVER: Goodnight.

END OF PLAY

THE UNDOING
William Mastrosimone

THE UNDOING
© Copyright 1983 by William Mastrosimone

All other rights to this play are represented by George Lane, William Morris Agency Inc, 1350 Sixth Ave, NY NY 10019, 212 903-1155.

To George Lane
and to the memory of Susan Kingsley, Flossy, and Donna.

ABOUT THE AUTHOR

William Mastrosimone is also the author of THE WOOLGATHERER, EXTREMITIES, A TANTALIZING, SHIVAREE, CAT'S-PAW, TAMER OF HORSES, and SUNSHINE. He resides in Enumclaw, Washington.

THE UNDOING was first produced by Actors Theatre of Louisville on 16 March 1984, with the following cast:

LORRAINE TEMPESTA ....Debra Monk
LORR .... Tania Myren
BERK ....Clarence Felder
MRS. CORVO ....Lynn Cohen
MRS. MOSCA .... Elizabeth Moore

Director ....Jon Jory
Set Design .... Paul Owen
Lighting Design .... Jeff Hill
Costume Design .... Marcia Dixcy
Sound Design ....James M. Bay

CHARACTERS

Lorraine Tempesta
Lorraine, *her daughter, called "Lorr"*
Berk, *a man, with a severe limp and black leather patch over his left eye*
Mrs. Corvo *and* Mrs. Mosca, *neighborhood crones*

TIME: *Now*

SETTING: The back room of a poultry shop.

If there are walls, they are streaked with steam and years of grime. The windows have turned gray. Feathers are stuck to everything.

A half-wall, chest high, divides upstage and downstage. On the upstage side stand a defeatherer (a cylindrical machine of stainless steel), a butcher block, and a table for wrapping chickens, equipped with a roll of waxed butcher's paper.

Downstage, 'the killing room', with four fifty-gallon drums. Stage right, two of the drums act as blood collectors, where the chickens are slaughtered. Stage left, two of the drums over-brim with steam rising constantly from the boiling water. A gas burner is underneath; its flame reflects on other surfaces.

There are three doors: the first, the back door, leads to an alleyway and Lorraine's house; the second leads upstairs to Berk's room; the third leads to 'the front', where the customers wait.

Suspended from the ceiling is a car windshield, broken and webbed with that unmistakable dent of a head. Behind the glass, police flashers greet the audience as they enter.

NOTES FROM THE PLAYWRIGHT

In the ATL premiere, director Jon Jory had the actors mime the slaughter of chickens. A routine was established, to keep the action consistent throughout the run: mime grabbing a chicken from an empty cage, by feet or wings, wrap its feet with a heavy twine, hang it in one of the blood collectors, take a real knife, and cut the throat. The sound of flapping wings would follow, beating on the metal drum. When sufficient time passed to allow the blood to pump out by action of the beating heart, the dead bird would be soaked in the boiling water to sterilize it and soften the feathers. Then the bird would be thrown in the defeatherer, butchered on the block, if the customer so desired, or left whole. Metal baskets were used to transport imaginary chickens from defeatherer to butcher block to wrapping table (also to keep track of where the chickens were). To avoid wrapping nothing, director Jory had the actor wrap a bean bag. This convention serves the play more strongly than using real chickens, or pretending to use real chickens. What is important is not the chicken, but the effect of butchering, upon the behavior of the characters.

ACT ONE

(Darkness. In the dark we hear a siren blare. It rises to a frightful pitch, and as it fades, lights rise on LORRAINE, *back to audience, standing over a barrel, cutting a chicken's throat, hanging it upside down in the barrel, its frantic wings beating for a time against the metal. She dips an already lifeless chicken in a steaming drum of boiling water and, with an adept motion, flings it into the defeatherer. A cigarette dangles from the side of her mouth. Her hair is stringy. Her underarms and chest are sweat-stained. A bit of blood is smeared on one cheek. Her apron is splashed with blood, liver, and gizzard. She is unaware of her appearance. It no longer matters. Even at nine-thirty a.m. she moves with the false sobriety of an alcoholic. She takes a drink of a pint of hard liquor hidden in some convenient place. She wipes the steam off her face with her backhand and unknowingly smudges her forehead. She winces at the sporadic customer bell. She opens a cage and grabs a reluctant chicken.)*

LORRAINE: What'd ya think — you'd live forever? *(The customer bell rings. She goes to the swinging door, opens it slightly, and says to customers:)* You want me to kill it or you want a pet? *(She goes back to work.)* Sonofagoddambitchinbastards. *(She goes into the killing room, slaughters the chicken, and its wings beat against the metal drum. She listens, puts a cigarette in her mouth, can't find a match. The phone rings. She answers.)* Leo's. *(Grabbing a pencil on the end of a long string and not being able to find the pad, which is in her apron pocket, she writes on a paper bag.)* Name. Spell it. How many? Parts or whole? *(Pause)* Cut up or whole? Take your time. I'll send out for a sandwich. You sure? I mean once I cut it up I can't put it back together again, right or wrong? Four o'clock. *(She hangs up, finds a book of matches, but sees no matches inside, so looks around. Finds a pint of liquor instead. Takes a drink.)*

(Enter LORR. *She sees her mother drinking.)*

LORRAINE: You know Saturdays are busy! *(She puts on a fresh, crisp white apron — a startling contrast to* LORRAINE'S *clothes.)* Where you been?

LORR: The shore.

LORRAINE: With that old creep? *(Pause)* Can't you call?

LORR: I did. Nobody answered.

LORRAINE: If you can't be here to open, don't come at all.

LORR: You got Bo.

LORRAINE: I fired him.

LORR: When?

LORRAINE: Wednesday.

LORR: You worked *alone* three days?

LORRAINE: I got a big order. Twenty-five birds. Tell other customers it'll be a long wait.

LORR: So what happened between you and Bo?

(Customer bell rings.)

LORRAINE: Get out front. Bring the chicken.

(Exit LORR. LORRAINE looks for the half pint. She finds a man's shirt somewhere. She looks at it and rips it to pieces and throws it away. She finds the half pint and drinks. Enter LORR.)

LORR: Ma, Jesus Christ, don't drink from the bottle.

LORRAINE: I can't find the cups.

LORR: Right in front of you.

(LORRAINE grabs a cup. There's something in it. She dumps it on the floor and pours the last of the liquor in it.)

LORRAINE: Take some money out the register and go get me eight half pints JD.

LORR: It's cheaper to get two quarts.

LORRAINE: I want half pints!

LORR: All right.

LORRAINE: I don't need you to run my life!

LORR: All right.

LORRAINE: Or anybody else!

(LORR sees a burnt spot on the wall, touches the carbon.)

LORR: What happened here?

LORRAINE: I tried to set the place on fire. It didn't take.

LORR: And then how would you make a living? Answer me that.

LORRAINE: Anybody comes to apply for the job, get name and number on this pad. Did you hear me?

LORR: Yeah.

LORRAINE: If we don't get anybody, you might have to work alone Tuesday, Wednesday, Thursday. When people call, don't get yourself backed up. Give yourself enough time.

LORR: What's Tuesday?

LORRAINE: You open up.

LORR: Ma, that's the week after next.

LORRAINE: That's this Tuesday.

LORR: Ma, that's not what you said.

LORRAINE: I know what I said.

LORR: The minute you said it, I marked it on the calendar.

LORRAINE: I don't care what you marked.

LORR: Look. Here.

LORRAINE: You be here Tuesday morning.

LORR: I made plans.

LORRAINE: Unmake them.

LORR: We were going away.

LORRAINE: How old's he?

LORR: Forget it.

LORRAINE: How old?

LORR: Forty-one.

LORRAINE: That what he told you?

LORR: Let's not get into it now?

LORRAINE: I see him when he drops you off. If he's not fifty...

LORR: I don't sleep with anybody who works here.

(A siren passes by. LORRAINE listens to it approach and fade. LORR watches her. Pause.)

LORRAINE: You be here.

LORR: Why don't we close next week?

LORRAINE: Close? — They're turning the phone off Thursday if I don't pay this bill.

LORR: Just for one day.

LORRAINE: No.

LORR: Just for the anniversary.

LORRAINE: No.

LORR: Can't you go to the hospital the week after next? *(Pause.* LORRAINE *can't believe she heard it.* LORR *can't believe she said it.* LORRAINE *dials the phone, reading a number scrawled on the wall among many others.)* It's only a routine thing, right?

LORRAINE: Is it? — *(To phone)* Doctor please. Lorraine Tempesta.

LORR: They can do that anytime.

LORRAINE: Doctor?

LORR: Ma?

LORRAINE: Cancel me for Tuesday.

LORR: I'll work.

LORRAINE: I got employee problems.

LORR: Ma, I said I'll work.

LORRAINE: I can't close.

LORR: Ma, I'm talking to you.

LORRAINE: What do you mean why?

LORR: Ma?

LORRAINE: I close, people go somewheres else. You should understand that. We're both in the meat market business, right or wrong?

LORR: Ma.

LORRAINE: I'll reschedule when I get somebody.

LORR: You got somebody.

LORRAINE: Right. *(Hangs up)*

LORR: I said I'll work.

LORRAINE: Go.

LORR: Call back the doctor.

LORRAINE: Have a good time.

LORR: Where's that number?

LORRAINE: Get out front.

LORR: Ma, I can't be here on the anniversary. You can't either.

(Customer bell rings.)

LORRAINE: Bring the man that chicken.

LORR: That's why you scheduled it that way.

LORRAINE: It's just another day to me.

LORR: You know everybody's going to come in and say, "What is it, a year now? — God bless you." — Let's close, Ma. Who needs that? *(Pause)* You should go away, too.

(The phone rings. Exit LORR. LORRAINE *picks up the phone.)*

LORRAINE: Leo's. — We don't sell turkeys. Well we don't sell them anymore. Because of the turkey plague. You didn't hear about it? — Yeah, well, there's some kind of terrible virus goin' around in turkeys now. — You want a chicken? — What's the name? How many? Whole or butchered. Five o'clock. Right.

(Enter LORR. *She puts an order slip on a board.)*

LORR: Two fryers butchered. No feet. — Some guy Povio says he called for twenty-five chickens.

LORRAINE: Tell him to wait.

LORR: He says if it's not done, forget it.

LORRAINE: He just called two hours ago! — When's he want 'em? Yesterday? Do a chicken. I'll straighten this bastard out.

(Exit LORRAINE. LORR *grabs a chicken. Enter* BERK *through back screen door. He uses a cane — really uses it, not merely carries it.)*

BERK: The boss in?

LORR: Yeah. Ma! Some guy's here about the job.

(Phone rings.)

BERK: No. I'm not.

LORR: *(Answering phone)* Leo's Poultry. Fryer or roaster? Whole or butchered? Four-thirty. Name. Yes. Bye.

BERK: Excuse me.

(Enter LORRAINE, *not looking at* BERK.*)*

LORR: Here's another order.

LORRAINE: Put it on the spike.

LORR: Right.

LORRAINE: Get up front — and write more clear!

LORR: That's your writing.

(Exit LORR. LORRAINE *slaughters a chicken.)*

BERK: Excuse me. *(She looks up from barrel.)* Do you work here?

LORRAINE: No, I just do this to get out of the house.

BERK: I don't know what to say.

LORRAINE: What?

BERK: Look — I'm sorry.

(Enter LORR.*)*

LORR: Povio just walked out, Ma.

LORRAINE: So what should I do? Fold up the business? Screw 'em.

(Phone rings.)

LORR: *(Answering phone)* Leo's Poultry. Fryer or roaster? Whole or butchered? At noon?

LORRAINE: Tell 'em five o'clock.

LORR: That'll be one — they need by noon.

LORRAINE: Can't.

LORR: We can.

LORRAINE: Can't. Tell 'em.

LORR: We can't have it at noon. — Said that's too late.

LORRAINE: Hang up.

LORR: I'm sorry.

LORRAINE: Give me that phone — Look, you want a quick chicken — go to the supermarket. You can get one there in two seconds. And it's been dead for three months. But if you want a fresh one, we have to kill it, pluck it, clean it, butcher it — and believe it or not you're not our only customer — now you want a chicken at five or not? *(Pause)* Name. Right. *(Hangs up)* Get up front. *(Exit* LORR*)* You kill before?

BERK: Kill?

LORRAINE: Chickens.

BERK: No, listen...

LORRAINE: You go to school?

BERK: What do you mean?

LORRAINE: School, like first grade?

BERK: Yeah.

LORRAINE: They teach you to read?

BERK: Yeah.

LORRAINE: Paper said "experience only" — right or wrong?

BERK: I'd like to talk.

LORRAINE: What talk? — I got people three-deep out there. I need somebody quick. I don't have time to train you. *(She searches herself for a cigarette, finds one that's crooked.* BERK *hands her matches, but they won't strike because of her wet hands.* BERK *lights it for her.)* Thanks. — Can't use you. *(The phone rings. While* LORRAINE *turns to answer the phone, stops, sees* BERK *still standing there, looking at her, obviously upset. Beat. He turns and exits. She answers the phone.)* Leo's. She's working. *(*LORR *enters.)*

LORR: That for me, Ma?

LORRAINE: Yeah, this is her mother. What am I supposed to say to the man who's boffing my daughter?

LORR: Ma! Give me that phone.

LORRAINE: So what's the problem, Pudgy? Can't get somebody your age?

LORR: Give me the phone!

LORRAINE: This is a business phone — so if you want a chicken, I'd be glad to kill a pudgy one for you —

LORR: Don't you! —

LORRAINE: But if you want Lorr, call her on her free time.

LORR: Don't hang that up! *(*LORRAINE *hangs up the phone.)* You work on the anniversary!

*(*LORR *runs out. The screen door bangs closed. The phone rings.* LORRAINE *doesn't answer. The customer bell rings.* LORRAINE *ignores it. She takes a drink, sees* BERK *standing at the door.)*

LORRAINE: I told you experience only.

(Phone rings. LORRAINE *goes to answer it, but buckles with pain.)*

BERK: You all right?

LORRAINE: No.

BERK: Want me to get it?

LORRAINE: Yes.

BERK: What do I say?

LORRAINE: Leo's.

BERK: *(Answering phone)* Leo's — ah — chicken shop. — What? — Wait a minute. — It's Spanish.

LORRAINE: Leo's. — Qué quiéres? No tengo carne de vaca. Solamente de gallino. Si. Lo quiéres o nó? Su madre. *(Hangs up. Customer bell rings.)*

BERK: Can I do anything?

LORRAINE: No. *(Customer bell rings.)* Yes.

BERK: What?

LORRAINE: Go out front and tell them we're closed. Please.

BERK: Closed?

LORRAINE: Tell 'em all to go.

BERK: All right.

(Exit BERK. LORRAINE shuts off defeatherer. Takes another drink. Enter BERK. He sees her drinking.)

BERK: They went.

LORRAINE: I never did that before.

BERK: What, close up?

LORRAINE: Leo'd kill me.

BERK: Your husband?

LORRAINE: You knew him?

BERK: No.

LORRAINE: He was killed.

BERK: Yeah.

LORRAINE: Drunk driver. Ran a STOP sign.

BERK: Yeah.

LORRAINE: So you need work bad, eh?

BERK: Jesus Christ.

LORRAINE: What?

BERK: I'm going nuts.

LORRAINE: It don't pay to train somebody, because while they're learning, they're not working, right or wrong?

BERK: I thought maybe we could talk.

LORRAINE: Got no time for some sob story. *(Phone rings.)* Leo's. No, I'm not scared of some goddamn D&C. I got nobody to work. Look, Doc. I can't talk now, the building's on fire. *(Pause)* You got a family?

BERK: No.

LORRAINE: How you gonna work with a cane?

BERK: Work?

LORRAINE: Didn't you come for the job in the paper?

BERK: Jesus Christ. Jesus Christ. — Yeah.

LORRAINE: We get busy, you gotta *move*.

BERK: I can move. I don't need this thing.

LORRAINE: Then why do you carry it.

BERK: Habit.

LORRAINE: Half pay till you learn.

BERK: Good.

LORRAINE: And if you don't catch on, I have to let you go because I'm all alone here now and I need somebody bad, today.

BERK: I can do it.

LORRAINE: We open at six. *(Pause)* A.M. *(Pause)* On the dot.

BERK: Good.

LORRAINE: What's your name?

BERK: Berk. Yeager.

LORRAINE: I don't go in for late bullshit. *(Pause)* Half pay. *(Pause)* Seventy-five.

BERK: All right.

LORRAINE: No lunch.

BERK: No problem.

LORRAINE: Half-hour supper.

BERK: All right.

LORRAINE: Close by eight. You got any problems with that, tell me now.

BERK: None.

LORRAINE: We'll see.

BERK: I appreciate it if you can pay me under the table.

LORRAINE: I got to have you on the books for insurance.

BERK: I understand. — Teach me.

LORRAINE: Grab a chicken.

BERK: How?

LORRAINE: By the wings.

BERK: It bite?

LORRAINE: They don't call 'em chicken for nothin'.

BERK: Show me.

LORRAINE: By the wings, see?

BERK: Will they break?

LORRAINE: What's it matter? — No.

BERK: Just grab it?

LORRAINE: Grab the legs.

BERK: Good.

LORRAINE: Tie it up, like this.

BERK: Just wrap the string?

LORRAINE: Put it on the scale.

BERK: All right.

LORRAINE: They ask for a five-pound chicken, you get a seven pounder and shout up front, it's a little over.

BERK: How come?

LORRAINE: Feathers and guts weight about a pound and a half.

BERK: Over.

LORRAINE: Never under.

BERK: Got it.

LORRAINE: Make 'em pay.

BERK: When I grab it, how can I tell how much it weighs?

LORRAINE: I'll teach you.

BERK: Good.

LORRAINE: Later.

BERK: Good.

LORRAINE: This is the Killing Room. Hang it on the drum. Cut the throat here, across, quick, one slit.

BERK: Jesus.

LORRAINE: Wings flap, heart pumps, all the blood shoots out. You going to be sick?

BERK: No.

LORRAINE: Tell me now.

BERK: No.

LORRAINE: Maybe this ain't for you.

BERK: I can do it.

LORRAINE: There's no big deal. Be kind to the birds. Keep the knives sharp. Don't let your mind wander or you'll lose a finger. What'd you do before?

BERK: Ironwork.

LORRAINE: Good money, right or wrong?

BERK: Not bad.

LORRAINE: That eye's not going to be a problem, is it?

BERK: No.

LORRAINE: Leg?

BERK: No.

LORRAINE: Just don't use it as an excuse to fuck the dog around here.

BERK: I won't.

LORRAINE: I expect you to keep up with me.

BERK: I can do anything any other man could do.

LORRAINE: Yeah?

BERK: That's right.

LORRAINE: Married?

BERK: Was.

LORRAINE: Separated?

BERK: No.

LORRAINE: The other?

BERK: Yeah.

LORRAINE: Kids?

BERK: No.

LORRAINE: That's good.

BERK: She didn't want any.

LORRAINE: You?

BERK: Yeah. Jesus.

LORRAINE: What?

BERK: Wings on the drum.

LORRAINE: You'll get used to it.

BERK: I hope.

LORRAINE: A human being can get used to anything.

BERK: Think so?

LORRAINE: You got a girl?

BERK: No.

LORRAINE: How come?

BERK: Just don't.

LORRAINE: Don't go out?

BERK: No more.

LORRAINE: Why not?

BERK: Just don't.

LORRAINE: You're not weird, are you?

BERK: No.

LORRAINE: Where do you live?

BERK: YMCA. I took it temporary. Place I had was sold. I'd like to find a place in the neighborhood.

LORRAINE: If I hear anything, I'll let you know.

BERK: I appreciate it.

LORRAINE: How'd you lose that eye?

(Pause)

BERK: Accident.

(Pause)

LORRAINE: How far'd you fall?

(Pause)

BERK: Fall?

LORRAINE: Your accident. Didn't you say you fell?

(Pause)

BERK: Oh. One story.

LORRAINE: Lucky.

BERK: That's what they told me.

LORRAINE: Disability?

BERK: Can't live on it.

LORRAINE: So you need a few extra bucks.

BERK: I need work. Can't sit around. Go nuts.

LORRAINE: You won't quit on me, will you?

BERK: No.

LORRAINE: They won't take you back?

BERK: I'm spooked.

LORRAINE: What's that?

BERK: Can't walk the beams.

LORRAINE: Oh.

BERK: Favor the limp.

LORRAINE: Oh.

BERK: Once you fall, you keep seeing it. The more careful you are, the more it wants to happen.

LORRAINE: You didn't work after that?

BERK: D&J Junkyard.

LORRAINE: What happened?

BERK: Fired.

LORRAINE: Least you honest.

BERK: I didn't see how you cut the throat.

LORRAINE: Poco a poco.

BERK: What's that.

LORRAINE: Little by little. — You're not ready.

BERK: I am.

LORRAINE: You're too eager. See this part of the chicken? It's called the pope's nose. Leo used to call me pope's nose.

BERK: How come?

LORRAINE: It's useless. *(Pause)* What's the matter?

BERK: What now?

LORRAINE: Dip it in the water, let it soak, then into the defeatherer.

BERK: All right.

LORRAINE: Here's the switch.

BERK: All right.

LORRAINE: If you're sentimental about your hands, don't grab the chicken till the machine's off.

BERK: Got it.

LORRAINE: That's all I can teach you for now. Learn by watching. To butcher takes some time. You're not ready now. This business is crazy. You could stand around for half a day, nobody walks in the door. Then in two seconds, the whole world wants a chicken. For now you kill, defeather, and work out front.

BERK: I'd rather not work with people. I'd rather work back here.

LORRAINE: You have to do it all, it's the job.

BERK: I'll do it.

LORRAINE: Don't like people?

BERK: Not much.

LORRAINE: People are dogs, dogs, worse than dogs. — Don't take no crap up front. Some of these uppity assholes come in here, see us dirty, think they can talk like we're paupers. That's the public, right or wrong? You don't get friendly with nobody. You don't smile and don't say good morning. They walk in, you say what do you need? That's all, because they're always looking for something for free, right or wrong? If the bill comes to three dollars and two cents, that's what you take. Not three. Not two cents next time. Today, no breaks. So why'd you get fired?

BERK: I had a problem.

LORRAINE: What kind?

BERK: Drink.

LORRAINE: Still?

BERK: No.
LORRAINE: How'd you stop?
BERK: Just did.
LORRAINE: Just like that?
BERK: Yeah.
LORRAINE: Ever get a relapse?
BERK: No.
LORRAINE: Never?
BERK: No.
LORRAINE: I drink.
BERK: I know.
LORRAINE: How?
BERK: I can see.
LORRAINE: See what?
BERK: I don't know.
LORRAINE: Smell it?
BERK: No.
LORRAINE: What?
BERK: I can just tell.
LORRAINE: One day you just said no more.
BERK: Stopped.
LORRAINE: All by yourself, one, two, three.
BERK: That's right.
LORRAINE: Can I tell you something?
BERK: Sure.
LORRAINE: Don't take it personal.
BERK: I won't.
LORRAINE: You're full of shit.
BERK: Yeah?
LORRAINE: Nobody just stops.
BERK: I did.

LORRAINE: How can I stop?

BERK: You got to want to.

LORRAINE: You can't stop if you like it, right or wrong?

BERK: I guess you're right.

LORRAINE: You're goddamn right I'm right. Swig?

BERK: No thanks.

LORRAINE: You want it.

BERK: No I don't.

LORRAINE: Bullshit.

BERK: I don't; neither do you.

LORRAINE: Don't give me that AA bullshit. Take this away and I got no skin. I can't answer the phone. But when I got it, nothing can touch me. Nothing. *(Pause)* Don't go quitting on me after I give you what I know.

BERK: I want to work, here, for you.

LORRAINE: We'll see. — We'll see. When the air sweats, ninety-seven degrees, a pesky little fly circles you all day, and the steam in here rises, 101, 102, 103, at noon, and the chicken dung crawls around in your nostrils and you taste it in your food and your clothes stink and no hot bath can get the smell of blood off. So hot, chickens don't mind when you kill 'em. *(She opens her dress a little to cool herself. He looks, averts his eyes.)* Excuse me. It's hot. (BERK *sees an old fan, plugs it in.)* Don't work.

BERK: What's wrong?

LORRAINE: I plug it in and the blades don't turn.

(BERK *fidgets with the wire, plugs it in. It works.)*

BERK: Need a new wire.

LORRAINE: You handy like that?

BERK: It's simple.

LORRAINE: Leo was good like that, too.

(There's a knock on the door, the handle jiggles.)

BERK: Who is it?

(More knocks. LORRAINE *peeks through a hole in the shade.)*

LORRAINE: The F.B.I. — go out and clean the truck.

BERK: Then what?

LORRAINE: Put the empty cages on the truck — tie 'em up good — and I'll tell you where to pick up the chickens.

BERK: I don't have a license.

LORRAINE: You'll get one. It's part of the job.

(*Exit* BERK. LORRAINE *takes a long drink. Enter* MRS. CORVO *and* MRS. MOSCA, *all dressed in black.*)

CORVO: We saw the CLOSED sign up and got scared something happened.

MOSCA: Santa Madone. (*Abbreviated form of Madonna, pronounced "Mud-on"*) You sick?

LORRAINE: I'm sick of it all.

CORVO: Went by the bakery, smelled fresh bread, got you a stick, fifty-nine cents, don't worry about it.

(*As is their custom, the women get two folding chairs, sit, pour coffee.*)

MOSCA: So how's Lorr?

LORRAINE: Good.

CORVO: She in the house?

LORRAINE: She took the day off.

MOSCA: I thought I saw her running up the street. What can I see with these cataracks?

CORVO: So how are you, Lorraine?

LORRAINE: Cellini the mortician came in for a chicken, told me I look great.

MOSCA: He buried my Vinnie! — What a job he did on the face.

CORVO: And what a job he did on your Leo.

MOSCA: Oh, he's a regular Michaelangelo that Cellini.

CORVO: That was artwork!

MOSCA: My Vinnie's face was all there, but Leo's after the crash, Madone, that was a hard one!

LORRAINE: If you want the eggs, take 'em.

CORVO: God bless her!

MOSCA: We started another novena for you at Our Lady of Sorrows.

LORRAINE: Don't waste your time.

CORVO: So where's Bo?

LORRAINE: Fired.

CORVO: What'd he do?

LORRAINE: Came in late.

CORVO: How could he? He lived upstairs.

LORRAINE: He was out all night.

MOSCA: You're better off.

LORRAINE: Am I? Doing the work of three people?

MOSCA: He talked.

LORRAINE: What talk?

MOSCA: What's it matter now? He's gone.

LORRAINE: About what?

CORVO: You know how men talk after a few drinks at the bar.

LORRAINE: What?

MOSCA: I don't like to get between two people.

LORRAINE: There was nothing.

MOSCA: I don't repeat ugly talk.

CORVO: That he had to screw you to keep his job.

LORRAINE: Sonofagoddamnbitchinbastard.

CORVO: But I said to myself, even if it's true — which I know it ain't — Lorraine's a young woman, she needs a little sausage in the diet, eh?

LORRAINE: Get the eggs. I want to lock up.

MOSCA: Thank you, honey. You know we appreciate it.

CORVO: Especially me with so many ailments.

(They rifle the cages for eggs.)

MOSCA: You? — What about me? — I got cataracks and sugar.

CORVO: I got one breast and migraines.

MOSCA: What's that, bad? That supposed to be bad? I died once.

CORVO: She didn't die.

MOSCA: Ask Doctor Cantaluppo.

CORVO: He said you fainted, from your sugar.

MOSCA: I died, I was dead, they called Cellini, ordered the coffin.

CORVO: Don't believe this, Lorraine.

MOSCA: Father Albert was giving me Last Rites and Cantaluppo was pounding on my chest. I had one foot in Heaven and then I came back.

CORVO: Senza vergogna! *(Literally, "without shame" or shameless)* How'd you get to Heaven?

MOSCA: If you're not with a man for seven years, you become a virgin again. And virgins go to heaven.

CORVO: Dio bello! *(Literally, "beautiful God")* — Double yolk.

LORRAINE: I have to get out of this hole.

CORVO: Do it. Do it.

MOSCA: Leo could hardly do it, and he was an animal.

CORVO: You're still a young woman. Sell it, sell it.

LORRAINE: How can I sell it? He left me so many bills. If I sell it, I won't have anything left over. When the bills are paid, then I sell it.

MOSCA: And do what?

(Pause)

LORRAINE: This is all I know.

CORVO: For you, life's half over now.

MOSCA: The crow starts to take a walk around your eyes.

CORVO: Every year, something else goes.

MOSCA: Whose cane?

CORVO: Doctor give you a cane?

LORRAINE: Leave it alone. It belongs to the new man.

MOSCA: You didn't say nothing.

LORRAINE: He just started.

CORVO: What happened to his eye?

LORRAINE: Accident.

CORVO: Where.

LORRAINE: Don't know.

MOSCA: Who is he? Where's he from?

LORRAINE: Don't know.

MOSCA: Is he married?

LORRAINE: Don't know.

MOSCA: What's his name?

LORRAINE: Talk, pick, this, that, bitch, moan! — What's the dirt this week? — From my mouth to your ear, to your mouth, clothesline to clothesline, porch to porch, once around the block, and back to me! Every day I get eviscerated, wrapped in waxed paper, sealed, weighed, priced, sold, and eaten by a hundred little mouths up and down the street! Chewed and chewed over spotless kitchen tables! What else do you want? See me in a widow's dress. Go back to church and blow the candle out. *(Pause)*

MOSCA: Wanna play a number? (LORRAINE *waves them away. They exit. She goes to the door to bring them back, but they're gone. The phone rings. She fights herself not to answer. She takes a drink.)*

LORRAINE: Berk!

BERK: *(Offstage)* Yeah?

LORRAINE: Inside.

BERK: *(Entering)* Yeah?

LORRAINE: I don't need you.

BERK: What?

LORRAINE: You're fired.

BERK: I do something wrong?

LORRAINE: I need sex.

BERK: What's that?

LORRAINE: You don't want to work here. It don't get better.

BERK: You don't know who I am.

LORRAINE: Another cripple who can't do anything else. Who else would do this work?

BERK: Look at me. You know who I am?

LORRAINE: I know you. I attract freaks. I go through one every two or three weeks. In three days I'd have you drinking again. Get out. *(He starts to hang up his apron.)* How? How? How'd you get off the juice and not lose your fuckin' mind?

BERK: You got to want to come up again.

LORRAINE: Want to? Suppose you don't want to? Answer me that. How do you want to if you don't want to? No answer for that, right or wrong, one-eye?

BERK: You didn't hit bottom yet.

LORRAINE: What bottom? There's no bottom. It goes and it goes and it goes and you keep falling and nothing stops you, nothing, and I fall when I lay in my bed and think I'm dying and I don't care. I don't care until I think of Mosca and Corvo running to see the cops come and force my door and carry my corpse out under the sheet, and they come in and look to see how I lived and they talk, all their talk. So don't talk this life-is-beautiful bullshit until you tell me how to care if you don't care.

BERK: I don't know.

LORRAINE: You're goddamn right you don't know, because it can't happen. Hit the bricks, Mister. Go on. Go on. Wait. I'll write a check.

BERK: Don't worry about it.

LORRAINE: How many hours you work?

BERK: Five minutes.

LORRAINE: I'll pay you for two hours.

BERK: Forget it.

LORRAINE: You stay right here, Mister, and you take this check. *(She dashes off the check so quickly that we know it can't be legible. She hands it to* BERK. *He rips it up and drops the pieces in the barrel.)* Who says there's a bottom?

BERK: I say.

LORRAINE: You been there?

BERK: Yeah.

LORRAINE: How do you know you hit bottom?

BERK: You feel like you got to die to get better. You been there?

LORRAINE: I live there. *(Pause)* Grab a bird.

BERK: What?

LORRAINE: You want to work here or not?

BERK: Sure.

LORRAINE: Don't go. Please, don't go. What's the matter?

BERK: I don't like that noise.

LORRAINE: The first one's hard.

BERK: Does it get easier?

LORRAINE: After a while it's like driving a car.

BERK: What do you mean?

LORRAINE: You don't even think about it.

BERK: Oh.

LORRAINE: Tie it.

BERK: All right.

LORRAINE: Hang it in the barrel.

BERK: All right.

LORRAINE: Knife.

BERK: Which one?

LORRAINE: Enie meanie minie mo.

BERK: All right.

LORRAINE: Finger under beak.

BERK: You do it.

LORRAINE: You.

BERK: Finger where?

LORRAINE: Like this.

BERK: What for?

LORRAINE: Pops the vein.

BERK: I feel it.

LORRAINE: One cut.

BERK: How?

LORRAINE: Deep and across.

BERK: Show me.

LORRAINE: Do it. *(He does so. The chicken flaps wings.)* There's no big deal.

BERK: Yeah.

LORRAINE: Grab a bird.

BERK: Which?

LORRAINE: That.

BERK: Good?

LORRAINE: Finger under beak.

BERK: Here?

LORRAINE: Feel the vein?

BERK: Yeah.

LORRAINE: How do you cut?

BERK: Deep to the bone and across.

LORRAINE: Do it.

BERK: Good?

LORRAINE: Perfect.

BERK: You're right. It gets easier.

LORRAINE: Don't be so serious.

BERK: Am I?

LORRAINE: Your forehead's all wrinkled.

BERK: Is it?

LORRAINE: You'll never get through the day.

BERK: You're right.

LORRAINE: Pace yourself.

BERK: I'm ready.

LORRAINE: You still in love with her?

BERK: Who?

LORRAINE: Your wife.

BERK: No.

LORRAINE: Don't bullshit me, alright?

BERK: I'm not.

LORRAINE: I just asked a civil goddamn-legitimate question.

BERK: I'm in the hospital for seven months. I'm in leg and arm casts, on the ends of wires, tubes up my nose, eyes all bandaged up. I hear somebody come in the room. I try and say, who's there? But my jaw's all wired up. Then this sheriff sticks papers between my fingers and explains divorce procedure, leaves. Next time I see her I'm in court. They wheel me in. I look at her. She can't look back because she was glad. Not that I was a cripple. But that it proved her right...all the nights she was home watching my supper get cold while I was with the guys after work. Ironworkers get like family up there. Me and Loretta never had that. *(Pause)* But no, I don't still love her.

LORRAINE: Before Leo died, we didn't talk for over a year.

BERK: How come?

LORRAINE: He was a selfish lying heartless sonofagoddamnbitchinbastard. But I was Pazz *(From "Pazzo", crazy, pronounced "Pots")* for him.

BERK: What's that?

LORRAINE: Pazz, pazz. — Don't you speak English?

BERK: I thought I did.

LORRAINE: Pazz is when you know you shouldn't do something but you do it anyway because you can't help it. *(Pause)* How can you live on seventy-five a week?

BERK: I don't need much, anymore.

LORRAINE: I'll make it one twenty-five, and double it when you learn.

BERK: Don't worry about it.

LORRAINE: I don't want to lose you.

BERK: You won't.

LORRAINE: I got a room upstairs.

BERK: To rent?

LORRAINE: Furnished.

BERK: Yeah?

LORRAINE: The guy before had it.

BERK: What happened to him?

LORRAINE: He quit on me.

BERK: What's it go for?

LORRAINE: It's yours. Watch out around here. Walls are thin. You sneeze and the lady down the street says God-bless.

BERK: How much?

LORRAINE: Don't worry about it.

BERK: No, how much?

LORRAINE: Don't worry about it.

BERK: Bed?

LORRAINE: Rollaway.

BERK: Stove.

LORRAINE: You got to hook it up.

BERK: Fridge?

LORRAINE: Small.

BERK: Perfect.

LORRAINE: I can give you linens and things.

BERK: I appreciate it.

LORRAINE: Sure.

BERK: How much?

LORRAINE: Don't worry about it.

BERK: Thanks.

LORRAINE: You can take the fan up there.

BERK: Don't need it.

LORRAINE: It's an oven up there. — Coffee?

BERK: Thanks.

(She pours two cups. LORRAINE pours liquor in hers, starts to put the cap on, pauses, pours some liquor in his coffee, puts the bottle away.)

LORRAINE: Feel the vein?

BERK: Yeah.

LORRAINE: Do it. *(Pause)* What's the matter?

BERK: It hangs there so still?

LORRAINE: It knows it's time.

BERK: Think so?

LORRAINE: Make it clean. The way the priest wipes the chalice clean after he eats the wafer and drinks the wine. One, two, three. Clean.

BERK: I see.

LORRAINE: What would make me want to come up?

BERK: To feel again.

LORRAINE: Feel what?

BERK: A hand. A mouth. A dog's head. A baby. Hear Sinatra. Or rain on the roof. Laugh. Taste good food. Feel.

LORRAINE: If I felt again, they'd have to tie me down and gag me.

(She sips her coffee. He sips his, pause, spits it out on the floor.)

BERK: What's this?

LORRAINE: JD.

(Pause)

BERK: Why'd you do this?

LORRAINE: So I could watch.

BERK: Watch what?

LORRAINE: You.

BERK: Do what.

LORRAINE: To see if you still want it.

BERK: I don't.

LORRAINE: Bullshit.

BERK: I don't.

LORRAINE: You sneak it, right or wrong?

BERK: Not a drop.

LORRAINE: You're a liar.

BERK: You don't believe me because you're too weak to quit.

LORRAINE: You can't just chuck the juice! You drank until you landed in the hospital and they took it away from you.

BERK: The guys brought me stuff. I poured it down the sink.

LORRAINE: Take a drink and show me you don't need another one. *(He takes the cup and puts it to his lips. They share a long hard look.)* Prove it to me!

BERK: Nobody can prove nothin' to you. *(He dumps it out.)*

LORRAINE: You phony! You sneak it.

BERK: Think what you want.

LORRAINE: You're a sneak. Show me! Show me! *(She offers the bottle.)*

BERK: No thanks.

LORRAINE: Nobody just chucks the juice!

BERK: You're so dead inside, you want everybody else around you to be dead.

LORRAINE: If you was me you'd drown yourself in it.

BERK: I was worse than you. Much worse.

LORRAINE: Nothin's worse than me! I drink not to feel! Not to see! Not to hear!

(A siren passes. She takes a deep drink from the bottle.)

BERK: And a dog has to eat its own vomit.

(As if the liquor has turned to vomit in her mouth, she spits it out.)

LORRAINE: A siren goes by and I have to live it all again. Two, three, four times a day. Three, four, five times a night. *(Addressing the siren)* How many times can I live it again! *(The siren kindly goes away. Pause.)* I'm in bed. Waiting for Leo to come home. I hear a knock. Mosca and Corvo. 'Come quick.' 'What's amatter?' 'Leo.' They pull me and Lorr down the street. Sirens and flashers, red and blue, red and blue, spinning faster than my head. Cop cars and fire engine headlights aimed at two car wrecks stuck together. Cops with crowbars tearing at the doors. Firemen with chain saws. Paramedics on the hood of the car that ran the STOP sign, pull the man out the windshield. He's dead. They stretch him out and wire his chest and electrify his heart and give him life again. And in the other car, a screaming man with a broken steering wheel in his chest and blood on his face, calls my name.... 'Lorraine'...'Lorraine'...and it's Leo's voice. And I see him. And he sees me. And I laugh. That's right. A laugh as big as a car wreck. It just pukes out of me, all the years and all the talk and all the cups of coffee and the fights and the making-up and the nights he flicked his headlights in the alley and I'd climb out my window when I was fifteen and he was thirty-one and we'd skinnydip in the quarry and he'd throw a blanket on the roof of his '57 Chevy and turn up the radio and he'd laugh and love me and bite me and adore me and destroy me with his pleasure till the birds sang and hold me like he wanted to break me in half...and I laugh. Out in the street. And he was nothing to me. Just another chicken in the barrel flapping around. Nothing. I laugh and the cops stop. The firemen, the paramedics stop. All the neighbors with their hungry eyes and garbage mouths stop. Police dogs stop. The air, the world, the moon, stop. *(She drinks. He takes the bottle.)* Give me that. *(He tosses it in the killing room. It shatters.)* You one-eye cripple! *(She finds another bottle. They contend for it. He wins.)*

LORRAINE: Get out!

(He grabs her arm, takes the bottle, tosses it away. She breaks, he holds her.)

LORRAINE: Make me feel again....*(He lifts her. The lights fade and the phone rings.)* Up there....Up, up, up there....Make me pazz again...up.

END OF ACT ONE

ACT TWO

(The sound of a baseball game on a small TV. Lights up. BERK *works adeptly. The room is cleaner, tidier. He stops working when the TV announcer becomes excited. A home run is scored.* BERK *whoops and claps.)*

BERK: Yeah!

(A moment later, enter LORRAINE, *in a robe.)*

LORRAINE: Who hollered?

BERK: Damn kids in the alley. Stay in bed.

LORRAINE: Can't sleep.

BERK: Why not?

LORRAINE: Noise!

BERK: Where?

LORRAINE: Wings against the drum.

BERK: You can hear that up there?

LORRAINE: Car horns. People hollering. Church bells. A dog barked. Another dog barked back. All the dogs in the neighborhood barked.

BERK: Somebody got married up the street.

LORRAINE: Car horns wouldn't stop.

BERK: Wedding party went by.

LORRAINE: What's today?

BERK: Saturday.

LORRAINE: What happened to Friday?

BERK: You slept through it.

LORRAINE: All day?

BERK: You never woke up once.

LORRAINE: What died in here? Smells.

BERK: You got your senses back again.

LORRAINE: You have to keep that defeatherer on?

BERK: It's cheaper.

LORRAINE: You don't pay the electric here.

BERK: It costs more to turn it off and on than to keep it on.

LORRAINE: Turn it off.

BERK: All right.

LORRAINE: Run it when you need it. *(He turns it off.)* No wonder I can't sleep.

BERK: Why don't you sleep in the house?

LORRAINE: Phone rings, bell rings, defeatherer rattles.

BERK: It's quieter in the house.

LORRAINE: I can't stand that house. It creaks like somebody walking around.

BERK: I'll make you some eggs.

LORRAINE: I can't.

BERK: Force yourself.

LORRAINE: No.

BERK: You should have something in your stomach.

LORRAINE: Hey. You want me to send you a telegram? Forget it. We need chickens.

BERK: I was going for a bunch when you got up.

LORRAINE: Why didn't you wake me up?

BERK: You needed sleep.

LORRAINE: I told you never to let the chickens get down that low.

BERK: We had a rush.

LORRAINE: And suppose you get another one?

(Bell rings.)

BERK: It's slowing down now.

(Bell rings.)

LORRAINE: You got somebody out there?

BERK: They're waiting for this chicken.

(Bell rings.)

LORRAINE: Then take it to 'em.

BERK: What can I do?

LORRAINE: Go to Mexico. *(Bell rings.)* Take care of that. Hide that goddamn bell!

(BERK touches her. She throws his arm away. Exit BERK up front. LORRAINE goes to a hiding place, finds an unopened half-pint of liquor. She looks at it, lays a water glass next to it. Enter BERK.)

BERK: Where'd you get that?

LORRAINE: It's from before.

BERK: You have more bottles hidden around here?

LORRAINE: No.

BERK: You sure?

LORRAINE: Mind your business.

BERK: You have more?

LORRAINE: I don't know.

BERK: Do you?

LORRAINE: Leave me alone.

BERK: Lorraine! — Don't break that seal on that bottle! It's poison. And you don't need poison. You're off it now — what is it? — seven days. Four more days and all the alcohol's out of your bloodstream. You're coming back to life.

LORRAINE: I can taste it through the glass. I love the color. I love the smell. I crave the taste.

BERK: I crave your color, smell, and taste. Let's go upstairs, make love.

LORRAINE: Make love? You don't make love. Leo made love. You jerk off in my body. *(BERK grabs her by the collar explosively.)* Oh, the freak gets mad! The freak's got a temper!

(A siren goes by. Pause. BERK lets her go.)

LORRAINE: Why do you take all this from me?

BERK: 'Cause I'm pazz.

LORRAINE: Where'd you come from, Mister? Out of the sky? You beautiful son of a one-eyed bitch.

(Pause. The phone rings. BERK answers it.)

BERK: Leo's. Just a second. — Lorraine in today? *(She shakes her head no.)* Where is she? — She's out of town on business. Who should I tell her called? Mrs. Riciardelli? Extra feet? I'll see what I can do. How many pounds? Whole or butchered? You got it. *(He hangs up.)* I'll do this order and go pick up the chickens.

LORRAINE: Don't go. Call and tell 'em to deliver.

BERK: Why waste twenty-five bucks?

LORRAINE: So what?

BERK: We're not busy.

LORRAINE: Don't leave me alone here. *(She hands him the bottle.)* Don't leave me. *(Pause)* I can't be alone for a second.

BERK: Where am I going?

LORRAINE: If you do. Tell me. Tell me something: Does a blind eye cry?

BERK: How do I know?

LORRAINE: No....*(Pause)*....Last night I touched your face in the dark. It was wet. *(Pause)* From crying. I asked you why. You pretended to sleep. You got a secret, right or wrong?

BERK: Wrong.

LORRAINE: You talk and cry in your sleep, you know. I listen half the night, but I can't understand.

BERK: Bad dreams.

LORRAINE: About what?

BERK: This and that.

LORRAINE: Yeah? I'm gonna keep on listening to this and that and one night you'll slip and I'll know your secret. *(Pause)* You dream of her?

BERK: No.

LORRAINE: Know something? I don't care. And know what else? I don't care. And guess what? I don't care. Not only that — I don't care. *(Pause)* So tell me!

BERK: I don't know where to start, I don't know how to say it.

LORRAINE: About her?

BERK: Will you forget her?

LORRAINE: I lose everything from buttons to daughters to husbands, so don't tell me forget nothing. I don't want to lose you.

BERK: You won't lose me.

LORRAINE: What things?

BERK: So many things.

LORRAINE: So what's the first thing?

BERK: Someday you'll know.

LORRAINE: Someday? Can't you see I'm dying here?

BERK: Lorraine —

LORRAINE: This! This! This is the very shit that ruins every man and woman on the face of the Earth! Somebody holds out for someday!

BERK: I think about you and your kid.

LORRAINE: What about?

BERK: The accident.

LORRAINE: What about it?

BERK: You stuck here.

LORRAINE: Yeah.

BERK: All because of some mindless drunken sonofabitch.

LORRAINE: Yeah.

BERK: You ever think about him?

LORRAINE: Why?

BERK: Just wondered.

LORRAINE: Yeah, I do.

BERK: Ever think what he goes through?

LORRAINE: Yeah.

BERK: You think he suffers? *(Pause)*

LORRAINE: No.

BERK: I think he suffers the second he opens his eyes in the morning. I think he can't tie his shoe laces and not get stomach sick when he thinks he put a man under, ruined a family. I think he can't get in his car without killing Leo again. He can't ever be happy because he took your happiness away.

LORRAINE: I think he blames the shots and beers.

BERK: Once upon a time I wrecked my father's car. I was a kid. Sat behind the wheel and played like I was a racecar driver. Released the emergency brake, put it in neutral. It rolled down the driveway, cracked into a parked car. I ran away. Out in the woods. All night. I starved. Mosquitoes ate me alive. I saw monsters in the dark. But nothing was bad as what I thought my father'd do to me. He had a temper. Bad temper. So I figured I'd spend my whole life in the woods. I curled up and fell asleep in a tree. Woke up the next morning, my father was standing there, looking up. And then he said the most unbelievable thing. He said — you all right? *(Pause)* Then he took me home.

(Pause)

LORRAINE: That's the stupidest story I ever heard.

BERK: You know, Lorraine, sometimes, sometimes you're ignorant.

LORRAINE: I'd of whipped your ass.

BERK: Read the paper.

LORRAINE: I can't, I'm ignorant.

BERK: Look at the pictures.

LORRAINE: Tell me another story?

BERK: Get lost.

LORRAINE: Tell me a stupid story.

BERK: Once upon a time there was a pain in the ass. Her name was Lorraine. The end.

LORRAINE: I got a story.

BERK: If you get time, don't tell me.

LORRAINE: Once upon a time pain in the ass had a dream that One-eye split — just hung up his apron and split — and she came down he was gone, no note, no nothin', and left everything so clean. The end.

BERK: Once upon a time there was a chicken woman so full of shit it's unbelievable. The end.

LORRAINE: Oh yeah? — Well once upon a time she never had nothin' as good as One-eye in her life —

BERK: —which is bullshit because what she had with Leo nothin' else could ever touch. The end.

LORRAINE: That's not the end — One-eye made her feel fifteen again because when he touched her like the way he touched her she wanted to give him her eyes and she knew that when you give somebody your eyes, they go. The end.

BERK: Once upon a time, One-eye took her upstairs —

LORRAINE: Yeah? — And she went first and waited on his bed —

BERK: And he came up the stairs —

LORRAINE: Slow —

BERK: Slow —

LORRAINE: And that made her excited because he came up the steps slow and she knew it was him because of his limp —

BERK: So slow that he stopped halfway up the stairs and had a sandwich and beer —

LORRAINE: Not that slow because he wanted her —

BERK: Who wouldn't?

LORRAINE: And he didn't forget to put up the OUT TO LUNCH sign —

BERK: And she gave up the bottle —

LORRAINE: But kept it near her —

BERK: No she didn't —

LORRAINE: Yes she did —

BERK: No, because he dumped it out —

LORRAINE: No because she just wanted to have it around to see if she could really do it by herself —

BERK: And this was total alcoholic bullshit —

(*The bell rings.* BERK *exits to front.* LORRAINE *breaks the bottle's seal, unscrews the cap, smells the liquor, pours it into a water glass, smells it, hides it. Enter* BERK. *He begins to exit into the coop but sees the bottle opened.*)

BERK: Goddamit.

LORRAINE: I couldn't help it.

BERK: Why?

LORRAINE: I'm weak.

BERK: Why? Why?

LORRAINE: I just am.

BERK: You piss me off.

LORRAINE: Berk —

BERK: You like to be weak.

LORRAINE: You're pazz, you know?

BERK: You think this's funny?

LORRAINE: Sweetheart —

BERK: Want me to go get a few more pints?

LORRAINE: No.

BERK: To hold you off for a few hours?

LORRAINE: Berk.

BERK: How about a fifth? Or quart?

LORRAINE: No.

BERK: How about a case? This is funny? *(LORRAINE laughs and reveals the glass.)* You drank some.

LORRAINE: Not a drop.

BERK: Pour it back in the bottle.

LORRAINE: Watch. *(With trembling hands, she pours the liquor back in the bottle. It fills up.)* You're proud of me, right or wrong?

BERK: You're a pain in my ass, right or wrong?

(They laugh. There's a knock on the door.)

LORRAINE: If it's Mosca and Corvo, make them go away.

BERK: It's your daughter.

LORRAINE: Don't open it.

BERK: She's going around the front.

LORRAINE: I can't face her like I am now.

BERK: Upstairs.

LORRAINE: Don't go.

BERK: I'm here.

LORRAINE: Please.

BERK: Up.

(Exit LORRAINE. BERK enters the Killing Room, where he throws the chicken in the defeatherer. Enter LORR from the front.)

LORR: Ma?

(BERK comes out of the haze, sees LORR. They stare at each other for a moment. He turns off the defeatherer.)

BERK: How ya doin'?

LORR: Where's Lorraine?

BERK: Out.

LORR: When's she due back?

BERK: Don't know.

LORR: You work here?

BERK: Yeah.

LORR: Since when?

BERK: Week.

LORR: Where'd she go?
BERK: Delivery.
LORR: For what?
BERK: Chickens.
LORR: Yeah?
BERK: And feed.
LORR: Yeah?
BERK: I'll tell her you came by.
LORR: How's she carry all them sacks and cages?
BERK: What's that?
LORR: On her back?
BERK: What do you mean?
LORR: Truck's here. *(Pause)*
BERK: She's asleep.
LORR: Why couldn't you tell me that? *(*BERK *is silent.)* She tell you to say that?
BERK: Yeah.
LORR: I have to see her.
BERK: Can you come back?
LORR: I'm her daughter.
BERK: I know.
LORR: How do you know?
BERK: I can see.
LORR: She drunk?
BERK: No.
LORR: Why's she asleep in the afternoon?
BERK: Can't sleep at night.
LORR: No?
BERK: She'd appreciate a few more hours.
LORR: She's supposed to go to the hospital Monday.
BERK: She doesn't know about it.
LORR: I'll make her go.
BERK: I don't think she'll go.

LORR: Tell her I was by.

BERK: Sure.

LORR: I'll open up at six Monday.

BERK: Sure.

LORR: I guess we'll be working together.

BERK: Looking forward.

LORR: What do you know how to do so far?

BERK: Everything.

LORR: Kill?

BERK: Yeah.

LORR: Butcher?

BERK: Yeah.

LORR: Work the front?

BERK: Yeah.

LORR: You learned all that in a week?

BERK: That's right.

LORR: What's your name?

BERK: Berk.

LORR: Lorr.

BERK: Lorr?

LORR: Lorraine. My father gave me that so my mother wouldn't answer when he called me.

BERK: Who do you take after?

LORR: My father.

BERK: I don't think so.

LORR: I have a few things from my mother.

BERK: More than a few.

LORR: She has to be at the hospital eight o'clock.

BERK: She won't go, I'm telling you.

LORR: She's got to be there. I just want to peek in her room.

BERK: You open the door, she'll wake up.

LORR: I just want to see she's all right.

BERK: Believe me.
LORR: I just want to hear her breathe through the door, or move in the sheets.
BERK: Least little thing wakes her up.
LORR: So what?
BERK: You ever come off the stuff?
LORR: No.
BERK: If you did, you wouldn't go in there.
LORR: She off the stuff?
BERK: Cold turkey.
LORR: How long for?
BERK: Week.
LORR: She tell you to say that too?
BERK: No.
LORR: How is she?
BERK: No skin.
LORR: Huh?
BERK: Too fragile, can't say too much to her.
LORR: I know all about it.
BERK: Do her a favor then: Let her sleep a few more hours.
LORR: I saw it all before.
BERK: She tried to stop before?
LORR: Many times.
BERK: And what happened?
LORR: She drank again.
BERK: How come?
LORR: She's got a thing in her.
BERK: What thing?
LORR: To wreck herself.
BERK: What for?
LORR: She's got a lot to pay for.
BERK: Like what?
LORR: You know about my father?

BERK: Yeah.

LORR: She tell you about the accident?

BERK: Yeah.

LORR: What'd she tell you?

BERK: Drunk driver...didn't know he was drunk...lost in the neighborhood...ran a STOP sign....

LORR: Ask her the rest of the story.

BERK: I know the rest.

LORR: Don't believe one thing she tells you about Leo.

BERK: Why not?

LORR: He was the best. The best.

BERK: Yeah?

LORR: She didn't deserve him. He only stayed with her because of me. The day I turned fourteen Leo towed an old Chevy on the lawn. For a year he stripped that car down and built it back up from nothin'. Everyday with sandpaper. And when I was fifteen he said, You like fresh air, Baby? And I said, yeah, and he hacksawed the roof off and put on a convertible top. And when I was sixteen he said, What color, Baby? And I said, Red! And that year he made that car the most kickass candyapple red you ever saw. And he souped it up: four on the floor, V-8 fuel-injected engine, mirrors, mags and double-chrome exhaust, plush bucket seats, C.B., and dolby ghetto blasters front and back. And he took me out and taught me to shift and people used to stop and take pictures of my car and ask him how much he wanted and he said, you ain't got enough, and he put a sign out front: CAR NOT FOR SALE. And when I turned seventeen, he gave me the keys and a map of the U.S.A. with five one-hundred dollar bills stuck in it, and he traced the roads I should take with Magic marker, coast to coast, and he said, Get lost, Kid. And Lorraine said, Over my dead body! And Leo said, Any way you want it. And two days before me and my girlfriend are leaving, he takes the car out one night, to get away from her, and some shitfaced hotdog who's got no use for STOP signs takes Leo away from me. *(Pause)* The best.

BERK: I'm sorry. I am.

LORR: See you Monday.

BERK: Sure.

LORR: Tell her I was by.

BERK: Sure.

LORR: What time do you get in?

BERK: Six.

LORR: If I'm late, wait outside.

BERK: I live upstairs.

LORR: That right? She don't waste no time, does she?

BERK: What do you mean?

LORR: Sonofabitchinbastard.

(Pause. Enter MOSCA *and* CORVO. *They embrace her.)*

MOSCA: Faccia bella! C'mer and let me kiss that face!

CORVO: Your bones show! Don't you eat?

MOSCA: She's in love's what I heard.

LORR: Who said?

MOSCA: Who was it?

CORVO: I can't remember.

MOSCA: Somebody.

CORVO: What's he, an older man?

MOSCA: What's your mother think of him?

LORR: I don't care what she thinks.

CORVO: You care, of course you care.

(Exit LORR.*)*

BERK: Lorraine doesn't want anybody back here.

CORVO: We're Mrs. Corvo and Mrs. Mosca.

MOSCA: The back door's been locked all week.

BERK: Lorraine wants it locked.

MOSCA: Not for us.

BERK: For everybody.

CORVO: Lorraine lets us take the eggs.

BERK: She stopped that.

MOSCA: How come?

BERK: We sell the eggs now. This is a business.

CORVO: Don't get so huffy, young man! You don't know who we are! One word from us, you'll be collecting unemployment!

MOSCA: Don't talk to help. — We seen your kind come and go. — Where's the boss? She back there?

BERK: No. Out.

CORVO: She's not out.

MOSCA: We've been taking the eggs for seventeen years!

CORVO: You go tell her Mrs. Mosca and Mrs. Corvo want to see her.

BERK: That's no more. Have a good day.

CORVO: We're on our husbands' pensions. You don't know how a little egg here and there helps out!

BERK: Have a bad day then.

CORVO: What'd you say your name was?

BERK: I didn't.

MOSCA: I understand. You're just doing your job. So don't feel bad about the eggs. I ate yesterday.

CORVO: It's a shame about your eye. But whattaya gonna do?

MOSCA: Too bad a nice-looking boy like you has to go around with a limp and one eye. If I had an extra eye, I'd give it to you.

BERK: That's nice of you.

MOSCA: Anytime. But you don't want one of these eyes. Cataracks. I only see you when you talk.

CORVO: We know all about your accident.

BERK: From who?

CORVO: Lorraine.

BERK: What'd she say?

CORVO: What was it?

MOSCA: I can't remember too good.

CORVO: Car accident, eh?

BERK: She said *car?*

CORVO: Like Leo, but, hey, let's face it, Leo got mangled.

MOSCA: You know about Leo?

BERK: Yeah.

MOSCA: But what a funeral. The roast pork was out of this world.

CORVO: You couldn't get a space in the parking lot.

MOSCA: I never got that recipe.

CORVO: Everybody loved Leo; and who wasn't there, the cops, the firemen, the mayor....

MOSCA: To this day, we don't know who made the roast pork...

CORVO: It was like they had a sale; you couldn't get near the coffin...

MOSCA: It was like the pork came out of the sky, from God...

CORVO: Who's crying, who's fainting, who's grabbin who....Cellini and Rocco the pizza man telling dirty jokes in the back...

MOSCA: Micks, polocks, hunkies, black people...

(Enter LORR.)

LORR: She's not in the house. Where is she?

BERK: Upstairs.

LORR: You, too, eh?

BERK: What?

LORR: You're screwin' her, right or wrong? *(Pause)* Look, all it means to me is another 1040 slip to fill out in January. I got slips for Nick, Sam, Larry, Bo, — and some I forgot.

(She begins to go upstairs. BERK stands in her way.)

BERK: Nobody's going to take her sleep away.

MOSCA: He won't let us take the eggs, Lorr.

LORR: Why?

CORVO: Leo let us take the eggs.

MOSCA: Seventeen years we been coming here.

BERK: Both of you, out.

LORR: Stay here! — Move it!

BERK: Lorr, I can't let you.

LORR: Let me?

MOSCA: Who's who here?

LORR: You're fired.

BERK: Lorraine hired me.

(Enter LORRAINE. Long pause.)

LORR: You don't even let the sheets get cold.

LORRAINE: You're talking personal in front of the whole neighborhood.

LORR: Nobody thinks much of you anyway.

LORRAINE: Lorr, this time's different.

LORR: I've seen too many strangers come and go up and down those stairs...

LORRAINE: He works like three men.

LORR: You need three men to replace the one you lost.

CORVO: Lorr, be nice.

LORRAINE: This one's different.

LORR: In the dark, they're all the same to you. You shut your eyes and make them all be Leo. I want him gone.

LORRAINE: Lorr, how can you ask that? (BERK *takes his apron off, hangs it up.*) What are you doing?

BERK: Take your daughter back home.

LORRAINE: Stay here!

BERK: I'm sorry I came here.

LORR: I want him out, now.

LORRAINE: You can't ask that! It's not fair!

LORR: Don't tell me about fair. I picked you up when I found you on the floor. I put you to bed. Slept outside your door. Woke you up. Sponge-bathed you. Dressed you. Fed you. Made your bed. Did your laundry. Ironed, shopped, cleaned, cooked, mopped up your stinking vomit, holding back my own, and with the smell still in my nostrils, you made me go and stand at the liquor store counter and ask for six half-pints of JD. I was your mother when I needed a mother myself.

MOSCA: Your mother needs you now.

LORR: I have no mother. She died with my father in that car crash...when he called her...when she looked at him in the face and laughed!

LORRAINE: It wasn't a laugh!

LORR: I heard it — all the neighbors, cops, firemen, — and Leo! — heard you laugh!

LORRAINE: You don't know all the years and the turning and the waiting in that bed when that unforgiving motherless bastard comes home after whorin' around and gets in my bed with the scent of another woman and I'm pretending to sleep and I want him so bad to just touch me with his hand, his foot, and wake me up and want me again and hold me again. — He made me feel like nothin', nothin'! And he's screaming in the car wreck with blood in his mouth — Lorraine! — Lorraine! — And I laugh because I don't have to wait for him to come home no more!

LORR: That's what killed him! Not a drunk driver — you! — you killed Leo!

BERK: No she didn't! *(Pause)* I did.

MOSCA: Dio bello!

(LORRAINE *makes an eerie laughing cry — like she made when she saw Leo in the car wreck.*)

BERK: I twisted in my hospital bed till the I.V. tubes pulled out. Nurses saved me every time. I lay there seven months...jaw wired...couldn't talk...or see...or move...alone with myself and the sound of the man in that wreck....I read his obituary..."Survived by his wife Lorraine Tempesta and their daughter."...They had to strap me down. I kept pulling the tubes out to stop that voice of the man in the wreck screaming....They kept saving me. They told me I was lucky. Another quarter inch and I'd be an asparagus. I bumped wheelchairs with the terminal ill, double amputees who only had a cup of soup and maybe a chair in the sun to hope for. I was only a quarter inch from being one of the slobbering morons who talked twenty-four hours to the air, to memories, and I knew I had to save myself from that....I knew I had to forgive myself to stop the sound of that voice of the man in the wreck...or dive out my window...somebody already thought of that...it was barred...but that wasn't enough to stop the voice..."Survived by his wife Lorraine Tempesta and their daughter"....I called from my hospital room....I hung up when I heard your voice say, "Leo's"....I wanted to say something to you....But what could I say? I thought I should get the chair...but the judge fined me five hundred dollars...took away my license for a year...for murder — murder! — They didn't punish me, so I punished myself....So I came here. I saw you in your bloody apron, gizzard in your hair, liver stains on your fingers, bloodshot eyes....You thought I came for a job....The scream of the man in the car wreck stopped....Stopped....That's what the sign said.... STOP....I wanted to give back something....I gave you my life....I didn't have anything else to give.

(The phone rings several times, calling them back to routine. After a long pause, LORRAINE answers it, fighting the tremor in her voice.)

LORRAINE: Lorraine's....No, it used to be Leo's....What can I do for you? Name. Half hour.

(She hangs up, goes to a coop, grabs a chicken, takes it into the killing room. Fighting her trembling hands she almost kills the bird. She goes to BERK, hands him the knife. He makes the kill. The wings beat frantically against the drum. The phone rings. She answers it, throwing the defeatherer switch on the way.)

LORRAINE: Lorraine's....No, you got the right number....What can I do for you? How many? Name. We're busy as hell, but I'll put you first. Come right over. Right. *(Pause. To LORR:)* I need your help. *(LORR puts on an apron. To CORVO and MOSCA)* No eggs today.

MOSCA: Hens must be nervous.

LORRAINE: Try tomorrow.

MOSCA: You never had no luck, Lorraine.

CORVO: What luck? If it rained soup, you'd catch the bone. (MOSCA *and* CORVO *begin to exit.*)

LORRAINE: Wait till the neighbors hear this one.

MOSCA: Hear what? You hear anything?

CORVO: Niente.

MOSCA: Me, too.

(*Exit* MOSCA *and* CORVO.)

LORRAINE: Could you pick up a load of chickens?

BERK: I'll go.

LORR: No, I will.

BERK: Sure?

LORR: Yeah.

LORRAINE: Thanks.

LORR: Yeah.

LORRAINE: And count 'em — and watch that bastard — he small talks to make you lose count. (*Exit* LORR *with the truck keys. Phone rings.*) Lorraine's. What do you need? One chicken? You heard about our sale? — Buy one at the regular price, get another one for the same price. Yeah. Whole or butchered. What's the name on that? One hour.

(*She hangs up the phone, turns, locks eyes with* BERK. *Pause. She turns away. He moves toward the door. She grabs his apron off the hook and rolls it in a ball and throws it at him. He holds it a moment, puts it on, and grabs a bird. He hangs it in the barrel and cuts its throat. The wings flap against the drum. Lights fade to darkness.*)

END OF PLAY

CHRONOLOGY OF NEW PLAYS PRESENTED AT ACTORS THEATRE OF LOUISVILLE

1966-67

David Rayfeil — NATHAN WEINSTEIN'S DAUGHTER

1967-68

Frank Gagliano — THE NIGHT OF THE DUNCE

1968-69

Bland Simpson — THE CRESTA RUN

1971-72

Jon Jory, Lonnie Burstein, Jerry Blatt — TRICKS *(musical)*

1972-73

Daniel Stein — KENTUCKY!
Jon Jory, Lonnie Burstein, Jerry Blatt — IN FASHION! *(musical)*

1973-74

Jon Jory, Anne Croswell, Jerry Blatt — CHIPS 'N' ALE *(musical)*

1976-77
(1st Festival of New American Plays)

D.L. Coburn — THE GIN GAME
John Orlock — INDULGENCES IN THE LOUISVILLE HAREM

1977-78

Marsha Norman — GETTING OUT
Enid Rudd — DOES ANYBODY HERE DO THE PEABODY?
Jon Jory and Jerry Blatt, from Shakespeare — ANDRONICUS
Daniel Stein — AN INDEPENDENT WOMAN
Frederick Bailey — THE BRIDGEHEAD
Douglas Gower — DADDIES
Assorted anonymous authors — THE LOUISVILLE ZOO

One-Acts

Marsha Norman   THIRD AND OAK: THE LAUNDROMAT and POOL HALL

1978-79

Full-Lengths

Beth Henley	CRIMES OF THE HEART
Marsha Norman	CIRCUS VALENTINE
Jim Wann and Jon Jory	GOLD DUST
Olwen Wymark	FIND ME
Peter Ekstrom	MATRIMONIUM *(musical)*
Charles Jurrist	THE HOME FIRES

One-Acts

James McLure	LONE STAR
James McLure	PVT. WARS

Mini-Plays

Marsha Norman	MERRY CHRISTMAS
Tom Eyen	INDEPENDENCE DAY
Megan Terry	FIREWORKS
Preston Jones	JUNETEENTH
John Guare	IN FIREWORKS LIE SECRET CODES
Oliver Hailey	I CAN'T FIND IT ANYWHERE
Lanford Wilson	BAR PLAY
Douglas Turner Ward	REDEEMER
Ray Aranha	NEW YEAR'S
Israel Horovitz	THE GREAT LABOR DAY CLASSIC
Darryl Alladice	PETER AND KAREN
Jim Beaver	SPADES
Sallie Bingham	IN THE YURT
Edward Clinton	TEN YEARS LATER
Stuart Hample	PAINT THE ICEBERG
Lee Johnson	JOYFUL NOISE
Jon Klein	CHANGING OF THE GUARD
Wendy McLaughlin	WATERMELON BOATS
Charles Peters	WINE AT NINE O'CLOCK MUSIC
Paula Vogel	APPLE BROWN BETTY

1979-80

Full-Lengths

Michael Kassin	TODAY A LITTLE EXTRA
John Pielmeier	AGNES OF GOD
Kent Broadhurst	THEY'RE COMING TO MAKE IT BRIGHTER

New American Plays Presented

Adele Edling Shank	SUNSET/SUNRISE
David Blomquist	WEEKENDS LIKE OTHER PEOPLE
Peter Ekstrom	DOCTORS AND DISEASES *(musical)*

One-Acts

Ray Aranha	REMINGTON
Shirley Lauro	POWER PLAYS: THE COAL DIAMOND and NOTHING IMMEDIATE

Mini-Plays

Carol Bolt	STAR QUALITY
Alexander Buzo	VICKI MADISON CLOCKS OUT
John Byrne	HOORAY FOR HOLLYWOOD
Brian Clark	SWITCHING
Gordon Dryland	SIDE OF THE ROAD
Brian Friel	AMERICAN WELCOME
Athol Fugard	THE DRUMMER
Stewart Parker	TALL GIRLS HAVE EVERYTHING
Wole Soyinka	THE GOLDEN ACCORD
Keith Dewhurst	SAN SALVADOR
Bruce Serlen	THE SIT-UP SET-UP
H.A. Blanning	THE EX-MISS CARROLL COUNTY
Alan Gross	MORNING CALL
Crispin Larangeira	OPENINGS
Claudia Johnson	PROPINQUITY
Sallie Bingham	THE ACT
Terri Wagener	GRADUATION DAY NIGHT AT CRIDER'S DEW DROP INN
Rebecca Jernigan	EARRINGS
Allan Knee	RUSHING
Lloyd Gold	SELECTIVE SERVICE
Jon Jory	CAMPING
Ara Watson	THE DUCK POND
Jon Klein	AN IMPERFECT WORLD
Renice McGarrity	IN CHARGE
John Pielmeier	CHAPTER TWELVE THE FROG
Gus Kaikonnen	WHAT ARE FRIENDS FOR?
Andy Wolk	ALIVE IN THE EIGHTIES
Lee Johnson and L. Susan Rowland	FIRE ESCAPE

1980-81

Full-Lengths

Paul D'Andrea	A FULL-LENGTH PORTRAIT OF AMERICA
Ken Jenkins	SWOP

Wendy Kesselman	MY SISTER IN THIS HOUSE
Martin Epstein	AUTOBIOGRAPHY OF A PEARL DIVER
William Mastrosimone	EXTREMITIES

One-Acts

Mary Gallagher	CHOCOLATE CAKE
Alan Gross	MORNING CALL
Stuart Hample	THE MOST TRUSTED MAN IN AMERICA
Ken Jenkins	CHUG
Nick Kazan	JUST HORRIBLE
Vaughn McBride	LET'S US
Terri Wagener	SEMI-PRECIOUS THINGS
Ara Watson	FINAL PLACEMENT
David Kranes	FUTURE TENSE: PARK CITY: MIDNIGHT and AFTER COMMENCEMENT

Mini-Plays

Jane Martin	TWIRLER
Jon Jory	QUADRANGLE
Judy Romberger	THE WAITING ROOM
Stuart Hample	THE ASSHOLE MURDER CASE
L. Susan Rowland	CLASS EXAMINATION TIME
Rebecca Jernigan and Lee Johnson	THE YOUNG NUNNE'S SONGE
Craig Volk	AND IF YOU GO CHASING RABBITS
Bob Manning	CAR TALK
Jon Jory	PICKUPS
Jon Jory	BLONDES
Jon Jory	EXAMS
Jane Martin	THE BOY WHO ATE THE MOON
Jeffrey Sweet	PRIVATE SHOWING
Paula Cizmar	CUPCAKES
William Tyler	TRUE SUBSTANCE
Jon Jory	CAMPING
Daniel Meltzer	INTERMISSION
Vaughn McBride	REFLECTIONS, ROUND AND ROUND
Robert Schenkkan	LUNCH BREAK
Burton Cohen	THE PICKLE

1981-82

Full-Lengths

Thomas Murphy	THE INFORMER
Terrence Shank	THE GRAPES OF WRATH
Lee Blessing	OLDTIMERS GAME
Company-developed	THE ARABIAN NIGHTS

New American Plays Presented

Jane Martin — TALKING WITH
Conrad Bishop and Elizabeth Fuller — FULL HOOKUP

One-Acts

Kent Broadhurst — THE EYE OF THE BEHOLDER
Mark Stein — THE GROVES OF ACADEME
Vaughn McBride — THE NEW GIRL
Michael Neville — A PALE LION
John Olive — CLARA'S PLAY
Patrick Tovatt — GUN FOR THE ROSES
Ara Watson — IN BETWEEN TIME
Wendy Kesselman — MERRY-GO-ROUND
Richard Whelan — WASH, RINSE, SPIN, DRY
Ara Watson — A DIFFERENT MOON
Trish Johnson — BUTTERFLY, MARGUERITE, NORMA...AND IRMA JEAN
Larry Atlas — THE SUBJECT ANIMAL
Robert Schenkkan — THE SURVIVALIST
Dare Clubb and Isabell Monk — SLOW DRAG, MAMA
Peter Ekstrom — THE GIFT OF THE MAGI (*musical*)
Jane Martin — THE BOY WHO ATE THE MOON

Mini-Plays

Judy Romberger — THE SAINT OF THE DAY
Jane Martin — CLEAR GLASS MARBLES
Jane Martin — FIFTEEN MINUTES
Jane Martin — HANDLER
Jane Martin — MARKS
Jane Martin — RODEO
Jane Martin — SCRAPS
Jane Martin — CUL-DE-SAC
Jane Martin — LAMPS
Ken Jenkins — CEMETERY MAN
Ken Jenkins — RUPERT'S BIRTHDAY
Terry Wagener — DAMN EVERYTHING BUT THE CIRCUS
John Pielmeier — GOOBER'S DESCENT
Ken Jenkins — CHECK-OUT STICK-UP
James Nicholson — LOVE AND PEACE, MARY JO
D.L. Crutcher — CHERIE, AMOUR
Daniel Jenkins — LITTLE PEOPLE
Fred Sanders — SUNBURN
D.L. Crutcher — TEACH ME
Jon Huffman — STUDY BREAK

Julie Beckett Crutcher	TYPE CASTING
Michael Wright	DROPPING
Murphy Guyer	THE INTERROGATION
Willie Reale	FAST WOMEN
Jon Jory	LAGUNA DI MARANO
Claudia Johnson	THE DAY JEAN-PAUL SARTRE DIED
Julie Beckett Crutcher	WHAT HAPPENS AFTER
Glen Merzer	CO-OPTED
Fred Sanders	ON THE WAY TO ALCATRAZ

1982-83

Full-Lengths

Timothy Mason	IN A NORTHERN LANDSCAPE
Adele Edling Shank	SAND CASTLES
James McLure	THANKSGIVING
Gary Leon Hill	FOOD FROM TRASH
Murphy Guyer	EDEN COURT
Kathleen Tolan	A WEEKEND NEAR MADISON
Barbara Field	NEUTRAL COUNTRIES
John Pielmeier	COURAGE

One-Acts

Jane Martin	COUP
Jane Martin	CLUCKS
Lee Blessing	NICE PEOPLE DANCING TO GOOD COUNTRY MUSIC
David Epstein	MINE
Trish Johnson	THE ART OF SELF-DEFENSE
Stephen Feinberg	THE HAPPY WORKER
Vaughn McBride	GOOD OLD BOY
William Mastrosimone	A TANTALIZING
Jeffrey Sweet	THE VALUE OF NAMES
Barbara Schneider	FLIGHT LINES
William Borden	I WANT TO BE AN INDIAN
Wendy Kesselman	I LOVE YOU, I LOVE YOU NOT
Ray Fry	THE CAMEO
Lezley Havard	IN THE BAG
Patrick Tovatt	BARTOK AS DOG
Dave Higgins	PARTNERS

Mini-Plays

Corey Beth Madden	MODERN GARDEN APARTMENTS
Lezley Havard	TERMINATION POINT
Tim Powers	THE KINGDOM OF FISH

New American Plays Presented   401

Dave Higgins   JUST LIKE DIZZY DEAN
Gean Murphree   STATELINE CASINO/HIGHWAY
David Jean Fowler   GTT (GONE TO TEXAS)
Robert Spera   TRACKS
Becky Mayo   MOVING IN
Corine Jacker   RITES OF PASSAGE
Fred Sanders   BACKTRACKING
Becky Mayo   BABIES
Daniel Crutcher   STRAIGHT POKER
Jon Jory   STOPWATCH
Andy Backer
          IN THE GARDEN OF TIME BEHIND THE PALACE OF GOLD
Dennis Reardon   SUBTERRANEAN HOMESICK BLUES AGAIN
Karl Haas   TOTAL ECLIPSE
William Tyler   LABORS
Corey Beth Madden   BAD GUYS
Corey Beth Madden   TOES
Jon Huffman   THE STICK-UP
Jon Jory   CERVELLES AU BEURRE NOIR
Jane Martin   FRENCH FRIES
Carol K. Mack   HI-TECH
Andy Backer   CASTING

                              1983-84

                            Full-Lengths

Kent Broadhurst   LEMONS
Horton Foote   COURTSHIP
Emily Mann   EXECUTION OF JUSTICE
Ken Jenkins   007 CROSSFIRE
William Mastrosimone   THE UNDOING
P.J. Barry   THE OCTETTE BRIDGE CLUB
John Patrick Shanley   DANNY AND THE DEEP BLUE SEA
Lee Blessing   INDEPENDENCE

                             One-Acts

Romulus Linney   THE DEATH OF KING PHILIP
Sallie Bingham   COUVADE
John Pielmeier   A GOTHIC TALE
Michael David Quinn   BUSINESSMAN'S LUNCH
Ellen Byron   GRACELAND
Patrick Tovatt   HUSBANDRY
Corey Beth Madden   COASTAL WATERS
Kenneth Pressman   THE GIRL IN GREEN STOCKINGS
Daniel Meltzer   WHAT COMES AFTER OHIO?

Julie Beckett Crutcher	APPROACHING LAVENDAR
Susan Sandler	THE RENOVATION
Andrew J. Bondor	WELL LEARNED
Fred Sanders	CREATIVE PLEAS
Max Apple	TROTSKY'S BAR MITZVAH
Roy Blount, Jr.	FIVE IVES GET NAMED
David Bradley	SWEET SIXTEEN
Lee Eisenberg	CUFFS
Richard Ford	AMERICAN TROPICAL
Jane Martin	SHASTA RUE
John Pielmeier	CHEEK TO CHEEK
Paul Rudnick	ARTS AND LEISURE

Mini-Plays

Jim Luigs	NO. 2 PENCILS
Corey Beth Madden	ANDANTE CON MOTO
Becky Mayo	IDLING
Tim Powers	NEVERLAND
Nancy Beverly	STRAWBERRY ROLL-UPS
Robert Spera	SACRIFICES
Julie Beckett Crutcher	HOME FOR THE HOLIDAYS
Jon Jory	HEADS
Jason Milligan	SHOES
Corey Beth Madden	POSITIVITY CONCENTRATION CAMP
Barbara White	TAILS
Nancy Beverly	FLIPPIN' THE DIAL
Becky Mayo	L IS FOR...LEARNING
Jim Luigs and Mark Lord	GOING FOR THE GOLD
John Patrick Shanley	WELCOME TO THE MOON
Mark Evans Lord	WOMEN WHO SMOKE
Jon Jory	A LEAVING BEHIND

1984-85

Full-Lengths

Heather McDonald	AVAILABLE LIGHT
Larry Larson, Levi Lee, Rebecca Wackler	TENT MEETING
James McLure	THE VERY LAST LOVER OF THE RIVER CANE
Lee Blessing	WAR OF THE ROSES
Ellen McLaughlin	DAYS AND NIGHTS WITHIN
J.F. O'Keefe	RIDE THE DARK HORSE
Frank Manley	TWO MASTERS

New American Plays Presented

One-Acts

Jane Martin	SUMMER
Murphy Guyer	THE AMERICAN CENTURY
Gary Leon Hill	THE BLACK BRANCH
Roy Blount, Jr.	THAT DOG ISN'T FIFTEEN
Charles Leipart	MY EARLY YEARS
Cindy Lou Johnson	THE PERSON I ONCE WAS
Patrick Tovatt	I'M USING MY BODY FOR A ROADMAP
Romulus Linney	LOVE SUICIDE AT SCHOFIELD BARRACKS
Douglas Soderberg	THE ROOT OF CHAOS
Christopher Davis	PRIVATE TERRITORY
Wendell Berry	THE COOL OF THE DAY
Bruce Bonafede	ADVICE TO THE PLAYERS

Mini-Plays

Cornelia Evans	SUNDAY LAUNDRY
Romulus Linney	YANCEY
Becky Mayo	NEVER TRY TO TEACH A PIG TO SING
John Pielmeier	VAS DIFFERENCE
Leif Rustebakke	BLACK DICE BLUES
Steve Decker	BACKWASH
Nancy Beverly	BOB'S LOUNGE
Murphy Guyer	LOYALTIES
John Patrick Shanley	BAD NEWS ON A CRACKED PLATE
Andy Backer	BREAD
Nancy Beverly	ATTACK OF THE MORAL FUZZIES
Lee Blessing	REPRODUCTION
Mary Gallagher	PERFECT
Craig Johnson	STATE OF THE ART
Romulus Linney	JESSE
Jim Luigs	CRYPTUS AND CINEREA
William Tyler	STATEMENTS OF PURPOSE
Ara Watson	JUST A LITTLE HICCUP ON THE ROAD
John Williams	LOOKING GOOD

1985-86

Full-Lengths

Mary Gallagher	HOW TO SAY GOODBYE
John Steppling	THE SHAPER
Conrad Bishop and Elizabeth Fuller	SMITTY'S NEWS
Jonathan Bolt	TO CULEBRA
Constance Congdon	NO MERCY
Claudia Reilly	ASTRONAUTS
Larry Larson and Levi Lee	SOME THINGS YOU NEED

	TO KNOW BEFORE THE WORLD ENDS: A FINAL EVENING WITH THE ILLUMINATI

One-Acts

Ellen McLaughlin	A NARROW BED
Grace McKeaney	CHICKS
Kevin Kling	21A
Stephen Metcalfe	MEGS
Larry Larson, Levi Lee, Rebecca Wackler	ISLE OF DOGS
Randy Noojin	BOAZ
Raima Evan	GOODNIGHT FIREFLY RAVINE
Grace McKeaney	HOW IT HANGS
Martin Epstein	HOW GERTRUDE STORMED THE PHILOSOPHER'S CLUB
John Olive	KILLERS *(workshop)*
Neal Bell	VOICES IN THE HEAD *(workshop)*

Mini-Plays

Rebecca Wackler	WILD STREAK
Becky Mayo	IDLING
Melia Bensussen	STYLE
Lee Blessing	COLD WATER
Mark Nash	OUT OF ORDER
Shirley Lauro	SUNDAY GO TO MEETIN'
Michael Dixon and Valerie Smith	BLIND ALLEYS
Jonathan Bolt	LOVE AND THE INTERNATIONAL CHEF
Nancy Beverly	DATELINE: THANOS' LAMPLIGHTER
Eva Patton	THE 270TH DAY
Jim Luigs	GRACES BEFORE THE MIRROR

1986-87

Full-Lengths

Jonathan Bolt	GLIMMERGLASS
Kendrew Lascelles	WATER HOLE
Grace McKeaney	DEADFALL
Jon Klein	T BONE N WEASEL
Julie Beckett Crutcher and Vaughn McBride	DIGGING IN
Mayo Simon	ELAINE'S DAUGHTER
Frederick Bailey	GRINGO PLANET

New American Plays Presented

One-Acts

Deborah Pryor	THE LOVE TALKER
Howard Korder	FUN
Andy Foster	CHEMICAL REACTIONS

Mini-Plays

David Garcia	DOWNSTAIRS AT DOCTORS
Nancy Gage	ROCK HUDSON AND OTHER CONFUSING TOPICS
Michael Dixon and Valerie Smith	THE SHACK ATTACK
Nancy Beverly	REVOLVING ACCOUNT AT GOODWILL
Jeffrey Sweet	COVER
David Howard	DO YOU LOVE ME?
Sarah Tucker	FROM OUR MAILBAG
Adam LeFevre	AMERICANSAINT
Michael Dixon and Valerie Smith	CLEAN
Nancy Gage	CRICKETS
Richard Dresser	THE ROAD TO RUIN
David Howard	DREAMLOVER
Deborah Pryor	RATTLESNAKE TRAP
Jeffrey Sweet	COUCH
Mark O'Donnell	MARRIED BLISS
Reid Davis	THE LAST SUPPER

1987-88

Full-Lengths

Jimmy Breslin	THE QUEEN OF THE LEAKY ROOF CIRCUIT
Barbara Damashek	WHEREABOUTS UNKNOWN
Kevin Kling	LLOYD'S PRAYER
Richard Dresser	ALONE AT THE BEACH
Judith Fein	CHANNELS
Murphy Guyer	THE METAPHOR
Marsha Norman	SARAH AND ABRAHAM (workshop)

Mini-Plays

Laurence Klavan	SEEING SOMEONE
Marcia Dixcy	PYRAMID EFFECT
Debra Mitchell	THE HOUR OF LAMPS
Jeffrey Hatcher	DOWNTOWN
Matthew Greenberg	KNIFE CUTS PAPER
Lisa Diamond	MONEY FOR NOTHING
Wendee Pratt	KRUPS DON'T LAST FOREVER
Michael Dixon and Valerie Smith	APRES OPERA
Michael Dixon and Valerie Smith	$E=MC2$
Howard Korder	WONDERFUL PARTY

Bob Krakower	4 A.M. (OPEN ALL NIGHT)
Kathleen Chopin	DOUBLE TAKE
David Howard	ELECTRIC ROSES
Marcia Dixcy	EATING OUT
Richard Dresser	VICTIMS OF SLOTH
Jule Selbo	THE WEDDING
Wayne Pyle	BURNT TOAST
Denise Dillard	THE SCHOOL OF HARD KNOCKS

1988-89

Full-Lengths

Jonathan Bolt	THE WHORE AND THE H'EMPRESS
William F. Buckley, Jr.	STAINED GLASS
Steven Dietz	GOD'S COUNTRY
Constance Congdon	TALES OF THE LOST FORMICANS
Charlene Redick	AUTUMN ELEGY
Arthur Kopit	BONE-THE-FISH
Harry Crews	BLOOD ISSUE
Richard Strand	THE BUG

Mini-Plays

Julie Beckett Crutcher	THE SON
Bob Krakower	THE BEST MAN
Nancy Klementowski	ON THE AIR
Jonathan Bolt	A PARTY FOR ALICE
Deborah Mitchell	FAINT LIGHTS
Judith Fein	SCRUTINY